金融经济论丛
金雪军文集

第四卷 行为金融与金融科技

金雪军 编著

ZHEJIANG UNIVERSITY PRESS
浙江大学出版社
·杭州·

卷首语

这卷收集的是一部分关于行为金融与金融科技研究的论文。

传统的货币银行学在反映货币金融一般规律与基本原理的同时,有几个明显的局限性:一是缺乏需求的维度,只从金融机构提供金融产品的角度,而缺乏对需求方特别是企业融资需求的讨论;二是缺乏人在金融市场中的特殊性的维度,只从商品经济中把人作为理性人,标准化的维度,而缺乏对人在金融市场和商品市场中具有差异性的讨论;三是缺乏对技术在金融发展中作用的维度,比较静态地看待金融产品、金融机构与金融市场,而缺乏对技术影响金融运行的讨论;四是缺乏对制度变动作用的维度,基本看不到制度变动的因素与作用。针对第一个局限性,我的研究主要围绕中小企业融资创新展开,针对第四个局限性,我的研究主要围绕金融改革展开,针对第二个和第三个局限性,主要围绕行为金融和金融科技展开,这也是本集的主要内容。

对于金融科技的研究,是从我对中小企业融资创新研究的发展而来,中小企业融资难是一个在金融理论与实践中的突出难题,也有人把它称为世界性难题。浙江是中小企业大省,是民营经济大省,如何解决中小企业融资难是推动经济健康快速发展的迫切要求,因此也就成为我的研究的重要方面。在中小企业融资创新方面,通过理论与实践研究,我主持出版了系列研究著作,包括《桥隧模式:架通信贷市场与资本市场的创新型贷款担保运作模式》《从桥隧模式到路衢模式——解决中小企业融资难问题的新探索》《融资平台浙江模式创新——合政府与市场之力解决中小企业融资难》《打破不动产的束缚——破解中小企业融资难的金融仓储模式探索》《股权投资与经济转型升级——以浙江省为例》《纾解中小企业融资困境策略研究》等;作为团队总负责人承担了国家自然科学基金应急管理招标项目"纾解中小企业融资困境策略研究",项目成果后也作为专著出版;提出了"桥隧模式""路衢模式"等,关于中小企业融资创新的新模式的研究成果也得到了党和国家领导人的充分肯定,研究成果也获得了教育部的优秀成果奖。在中小企业融资创新的研究过程中,我也深深感到作为中小企业融资难的基本原因是信息不对称,因此解决融资难的问题也需要围绕如何解决信息不对称问题展开,而解决这一问题,既要靠金融体制改革,也需要技术创新。我们所处的时代是信息技术不断突破,或者可以说是以信息技术革命为主线的科技发展时代,信息技术革命在经济上的一个重要成果就是 90 年代电子商务和网络金融的发展,浙江省又处在信息技术发展与应用的前沿,由此,从事中小企业融资创新的研究,通过网络金融与互联网金融的研究进入金融科技与数字金融的研究,就成为必然。作为信息技术与金融相结合的金融科技的发展,大致经过了网络金融—互联网金融—金融科技—数字金融的发展阶段,上世纪末本世纪初,我和浙大计算机学院、管理学院的教授合作,申报成立电子服务的研究平台与相关学科,我是其中"网络金融"研究方向的负责人,开始把信息技术与金融的结合作为研究的重要方面,并结合加以研究。2014 年我牵头申报了在此领域的全国第一个博士点;与计算机学院、管理学院、法学院、数学学院相关学科的专家一起共建了该领域全国最早的跨学科交叉性的研究平台,至今浙江大学已形成了该领域从本科到博士后的完整的人才培养体系。

行为金融的研究源于我对人们在商品市场与金融市场上理念与行为差异性的认识,从进一步的分析发现,金融既要符合商品经济的一般规律又有其自身独特的运行规律,作为一个和传统货币银行学与证券投资研究有联系又有区别的领域,也有一个研究方法的选择问题。2000 年,浙大研究生院进行研究生教学改革研究项目的申报,我牵头申报了"经济学案例库和案例实验室建设"的项目,最初的想法,是把案例教学能纳入经济学的教学之中,拓宽经济学的案例教学,丰富经济学的实验教学,为此,我牵头组织了数十位专家学者编写出版了一套"经济学教学案例系列丛书",也开始用实验经济学的方法进行教学,并指导博士生开始把实验经济学用于金融领域的研究,案例教学与实验金融也就成为我在行为金融中研究的特点之一。2008 年,申报获批了国家留学基金国际合作项目,去德国克劳斯塔尔工业大学从事与实验经济学与行为经济学相关的进修访学与合作研究。

大致概括起来,我在金融科技与行为金融领域的研究主要体现在以下几个方面:一是大数据金融的研究,通过数据挖掘的方法探讨了货币政策与商品价格的变动关系,研究了社交网络对股票价格波动的影响。二是社交金融的研究,在大数据方法的基础上,我们重点研究了社交网络对投资者行为的影响,通过这一研究,把行为金融与大数据金融结合起来。围绕这一研究,我牵头申报获批了国家自然科学基金项目"基于投资者关注度与社交学习解释股市过度波动"。三是实验金融与神经金融的研究,运用实验经济学的方法研究股票价格的波动,在行为金融与实验金融的研究过程中,进一步发现神经网络对人的行为包括证券投资者行为所产生的影响。四是数智化金融运行体系的研究,结合浙江省"十四五"金融发展规划的研究,提出构建数智化区域金融运行体系,从金融大脑、金融综合服务平台、链式金融、金融技术生态、数字支付与数字货币、监管沙盒与监管制度等多要素集合的角度提出了这一构想。

在本集出版之际,我要感谢浙江大学和浙江大学研究生院、经济学院在我40年中从事金融经济教学科研工作包括金融科技与行为金融方面的教学研究工作的关心支持与帮助,无论是我牵头从事互联网金融博士点的申报与建设、经济与金融案例库与案例实验室的建设等,还是在我和相关学科专家共建金融科技和数字金融平台的设立与发展;感谢在互联网金融博士点申报与建设过程中提供指导与帮助的国内外、校内外各位专家;感谢在行为金融和金融科技研究上给予我各种帮助指导的专家学者;感谢德国克劳斯塔尔工业大学海克·申克-马茨(Heike Y. Schenk-Mathes)教授;感谢我的合作研究者。

CONTENTS

目　录

The Effect of Knowledge Economy on the Management and Labor Relations[①]

Abstract   With the emergence of the knowledge economy and its penetration into every aspect of society, many industrial functions have been changing, including management and labor relations. In this paper, the author first presents a systematic view of management and labor relations under the knowledge economy, and then based on it, elaborates on effects of the knowledge economy on them, using the case of HP as a demonstration. In the end, the conclusion is made that a new dynamic equilibration will develop, depending upon the dynamic power contrast of the above two subjects under dynamic changing circumstances of knowledge economy.

Key words   knowledge economy; management and labor relations

1   Introduction

To begin a discussion on management and labor relations requires an in-depth inquiry into the many factors that affect the relationship. At a first glance, this field may appear to be relatively transparent, although there are numerous factors affecting the relationship. Therefore, unlike some other cases, management and labor relations have no generally accepted theory or model to

①   Originally published in *Journal of Zhejiang University-Science A (Applied Physics & Engineering)* (Vol. 1, 2001) by Jin Xuejun and Yu Jinjin.

base the study, because study in this area can be approached in several different ways.

Generally speaking, there are two extreme situations in the management and labor relationship: complete opposition and complete cooperation. And the common situation between them is the clash of interests and power conflict between management and labor. The kind of management and labor relationship is decided by the outcome of negotiations, one of the key factors deciding management and labor relations(Fossum, 1995). The more powerful labor is in the negotiation, the more benefits it will gain for itself: the more interests of labor accord (conflict) with those of management, the more the situation inclines to cooperation (opposition), vice versa. Enough seious conflict of interests and power will doubtlessly bring about labor movement against management (Mills, 1994).

In recent years, with the emergence of knowledge economy and its penetration into every part of the society at every level, not only the interests and negotiation power of labor and those of the management but also other factors affecting industrial relations have been changing greatly day by day. This requires the old system view to be expanded. As labor-management relations become more divergent, any model of the process needs to be expanded in order to reflect the new environment in which interactions take place. A more realistic model of industrial relations should recognize the active role played by management in shaping industrial relations as opposed to the traditional view, which sees management as"reactionist", responding to union pressures. The new model should also recognize the different levels of decision making that occur within business, and their independent effects on industrial relations outcomes.

The author has created a new systematic view within which the effect of the knowledge economy can be more easily seen. The structure of this view allows the numerous factors at work within this relationship to be clearly identified. The factors have been divided into both micro and macro classifications in order to show their origin. And the role of the government can be put into the macro classifications. So different from the famous John

Dunlop model, the subsystem of this system focuses on management and labor (Fig. 1).

Fig. 1   Simplified system view of management and labor relations under knowledge economy

Knowledge, innovation and creativity are keys to success with the globalization of the knowledge economy in the new millennium. The winners in today's knowledge-based economy will be companies that consistently leverage and increase their intellectual capital (knowledge of an organization's workforce, documented processes, methodologies, patents, guidelines, and software). These forms of intellectual capital are often loosely defined and fragmented across the organization, making it difficult to locate the needed knowledge and expertise, identify organizational knowledge gaps, and maintain vital competencies and know-how as employees leave the organization. In this environment, knowledge exerts an important influence on the management and labor relations by affecting the micro and macro factors that underlay the labor-management relations system and the interests and the negotiation power of management and labor. The effects of knowledge economy on the labor-management relations can be listed as follows.

(1) The first effect is that the new information technology has been facilitating changes in organizational structures, business process, even the nature, way and location of work. This has resulted in less management by command and supervision and in more emphasis on cooperation, information sharing and communication and in a more participant approach to managing employees. Flatter organizations, virtual enterprises, virtual offices and

reengineering of process are the cases in point.

（2）The second effect is the increased transparency of the labor-management relations system because of the law under new circumstances. In the field of employment relations one can expect an increase in the scope and coverage of the legal rights of employees, and a continued redefinition of durable and uniform working relationships between labor and management. With the accumulation of knowledge and progress of society, labor relations laws actually impact the management and union behavior more than before. The U. S. is at the high end of the transparency trend, as revealed by its laws, such as the Fair Labor Standards Act, the National Labor Relations Act, the Occupational Safety and Health Act, the Labor Management Relations Act, etc. , which impact both management and labor. However, it is quite different in China, where companies in business tend to engage lawyers. They will have to get a better feel for the institutions on the ground and the power, for example, of labor unions, which will not be reflected in the codes.

（3）The third effect is that all businesses are becoming more dependent on one key factor of production: the super-skilled employee (Zhao, 1999). The role of key individuals has been greatly enhanced by the growth of large knowledge-based enterprises that service global market through extensive use of modern distribution and communication channels. In this environment, an incremental level of skill can be efficiently levered so as to have a major economic impact on a company's profitability. Due to this, the employees have stronger negotiation power with employers and can gain higher salary, more benefits and better working conditions.

（4）The fourth effect is that labor unions are changing their roles. Workers have always felt a need to gain power through collectivization in order to negotiate their rights (Fossum, 1995). This helps to equalize the relationship between themselves and their managers. It is uncertain how the role of the labor union will be affected by the knowledge economy. As the labor force in general becomes more skilled, the power of the labor union may increase, but may also decrease, because the employees will even have power to negotiate on there own. During the cold war, political considerations sometimes dominated or influenced union activities, attitudes and their role (Sival, 1998). Now, unions are gradually focusing more on the working conditions and interests of their members. And at the same time, the influence of unions is decreasing. In the U. S. , trade unions now represent no more than 10% percent of workers working in private firms. Members and non-members who are covered by collective bargaining are about the same percentage. In Canada, the range is from 25% to 30% of private sector workers. It is declining, but at much slower rate than that in the U. S.

(5) The fifth effect is that cooperation, trust and loyalty are highly regarded in corporation culture, especially in knowledge-based enterprises, i. e. virtual enterprises. Accordingly, good labor relations appear to involve a wider mixture of human characteristics and open communications that build mutual respect and loyalty, as summarized below (Siva, 1998).

①Attitude: A cooperative, friendly attitude is evidence that the employer is interested in his employees and their success. It shows that to the employee the employer is a person he can get along with. He's more apt to ask questions before he acts on his own if the boss's attitude encourages it.

②Expectations: Letting employees know what they are expected to do, and not to do, is very important to them, especially when jobs are to be done in a certain way or at a certain time. In some cases, it may be helpful to explain "why" the specifics of what is to be done are important. It is better to over communicate expectations than to assume the employee knows.

③Supervision: Supervision needs to be tailored to the employee. During the early stages of the relations, it is advisable to visit the employee and get his opinion how much supervision he wants or needs, as he is able to assume more responsibility, direct supervision can be reduced.

④Recognition: When the employee has done a good job, let him know. Expressing gratitude or giving sincere praise may be as important as greater pay.

(6) The sixth effect is on the wage pattern. Evaluation of performance becomes more and more difficult because brain-based work is mostly intangible

and unquantifiable. There is no precise standard or systems that can quantitatively evaluate work performance, which has become a factor causing inharmonious relations between management and labor. A rating of the employee's performance on a regular basis is a good communication tool. A rating form listing the factors from which an employee is being evaluated let him know how he is being evaluated. The rating factors might include timeliness, avoiding waste, safety, job skill, care of equipment, willingness, honesty, pride, high quality, efficiency, reliability, or other factors pertinent to his job. Probably no more than three ratings are needed, e. g. excellent, good and fair. The rating should be done on a regular basis, such as quarterly or semiannually and review with the employee. The review with the employee should be candid and stress his performance rather than his personal characteristics.

(7) The seventh effect is the inducement of the mutual benefits for knowledgeable management and knowledgeable labor. In new knowledge economy, more and more employees work for the managers and expect to realize self-improvement at the same time. On one hand, the significance of knowledge to employees is not only more power in negotiations with management, but also active cooperation with the management. The employess can enjoy trust, freedom of creation, feeling of satisfaction and success, acknowledgement by others, etc. And the self-development and self-advancement of the educated labor can be achieved in coordination with management. On the other hand, promising businesses can create and cultivate. So, there is a tendency that the benefits of management and labor will merge to a certain degree.

(8) The eighth effect is that more and more companies conduct knowledge management(KM) program and set up information systems (IS) as the essential tool. According to Knowledge Management Research Report by KPMG Consulting Co. , one of the world's famous consulting companies, we know that the rate of sample companies conducting KM program increased from 43% in 1998 to 67% in 2000. And the table below shows us the percentage of the IS set up inside the investigated companies, showing that

KM technologies have been widely implemented.

Table 1 Survey of IS inside companies by KPMG Consultants, 2000 *

Kinds of IS	Perentage (1998)	Percentage (2000)
Internet	90%	93%
Intranet	66%	78%
Document management system	63%	61%
Groupware	49%	43%
Decision Support	38%	49%
Data warehousing/mining	36%	63%
Extranet	16%	38%
Artificial intelligence	—	22%

* http://www. kpmg. com/#

2 Case study

Hewlett-Packard Corporation(HP) is a large, successful company with over $ 31 billion revenues in early 1995. The fast annual revenue growth of approximately 30% from such a large base have astounded observers. The company competes in markets, including computers and peripheral equipment, test and measurement devices, electronic components, and medical devices. It has 110,000 employees and over 400 branches around the world (Thomas, 1996). As representative of the IT industry, HP's success lies in its harmonious industrial relationships based on RHR (road of human resource), which is made up of the ideas and strategies as follows: trust and freedom, respect, acknowledgement and participation, insurance and individual problem settlement, profit and responsibility share, mutual communication and help between management and labor, target-oriented management, and decentralized organizational structure (Lu, 2000). HP is a good example of how knowledge economy affects the industrial relations inside the company.

2.1 HP has relaxed, open corporation culture

All employees, including the CEO, call each other by first names directly, and work in open cubicles. Many employees are technically oriented engineers who enjoy learning and sharing their knowledge. The company is perceived as being benevolent to its employees, and its fast growth has obviated the need for major layoffs. All employees participate in a profit-sharing program.

2.2 HP is known for its decentralized organizational structure and mode of operations

This means, that in HP, business units that perform well have a very high degree of autonomy. There is little organized sharing of information, resources, or employees across units. HP managers feel that the strong business-specific focus brought by decentralization is a key factor in the company's recent success. It is common, however, for employees to move from one business unit to another; this mobility makes possible some degree of informal knowledge transfer within HP.

2.3 HP creates a web of inclusion in enterprises

As for a human-centered relationship between management and labor, the web of inclusion plays a role as running base of a successful enterprise, which differs a lot from the obsolete management-labor relations. There is no hierarchy, no boundary, no limits of self-improvement and no obstacle to information in the web of inclusion, so labor can easily contact management and take part in the decision making in their enterprise. The employees share the profit and responsibility of the company and they devote themselves to their work. They can truly own the enterprise and themselves. In fact the development and utilization of IT contribute greatly to the establishment of the web of inclusion (Thomas, 1996).

3 Conclusions

As Prof. Peter Drucker predicted, the knowledge-based economy will be the future economy for mankind. Knowledge, as creation and valuable wealth of mankind, is also influencing ourselves: our thoughts, our lives, our society, and our political and economic systems. Nowadays, kowledge economy has already been affecting many industry functions, even though this phenomenon only appears in its beginning stages. Industries have already adapted and increased levels different of knowledge and stayed competitive. Although it is obvious that the knowledge economy will have far reaching effects on the relationship between management and labor, it is not scientific to draw conclusion on what kind of management-labor relation will be like in the future. More cooperation or increased opposition? We know that all the factors affecting management-labor relations, affecting labor's and management's interests, demands, power distribution in society, and negotiation power inside or outside the companies, etc. , which are changing in the new circumstances. Knowledge economy will result in new dynamic equilibrium between management and labor. While some effects are already visible, the full impact of the changing knowledge economy on management and labor relations is still developing.

References

Allen R E, Timothy J K, 1988. Contemporary labor relations [M]. 2nd edition. New York: Addison-Wesley Publishing Co. : 16-17.

Fossum J A, 1995. Labor relations: Development, structure, process[M]. 6th edition. Chicago: Irwin: 2-3＋269.

KPMG Consulting Corp, 2000. Executive summary to the knowledge managemnet research report 2000 [R/OL]. [2000-06-30]. http://www. kpmg. Interact. nl.

Lu F, 2000. Successful case of human resources[EB/OL]. [2000-06-30]. http://www. thinkreal. com. cn/case-study/hp. htm.

Mills D Q, 1994. Labor-management relations[M]. 5th edition. New York: McGraw-Hill, Inc. ;118-120.

Silva S R de, 1998. Elements of a sound industrial relations system[EB/OL]. [1999-06-30]. http://www. ilo. org/public/english/di-alogue/actemp/papers/ 1998/srseleme. htm.

Thomas H D，1996. Knowledge management case study：Knowledge management at Hewlett-Packard early 1996[EB/OL]. [1999-06-30]. http://www. bus. utexas. edu/kman/ hpcase. htm.

Zhao J，1999. Knowledge management：The source of competitive capacity of enterprise[EB/OL]. [1999-06-30]. http：//www. chi-nakm. com/mpapers/1999-03-23-1. htm.

Empirical Study on Mutual Fund
Objective Classification[①]

Abstract　Mutual funds are usually classified based on their objectives. If the activities of mutual funds are consistent with their stated objectives, investors may look at the latter as signals of their risks and incomes. This work analyzes mutual fund objective classification in China by statistical methods of distance analysis and discriminant analysis; and examines whether the stated investment objectives of mutual funds adequately represent their attributes to investors. That is, if mutual funds adhere to their stated objectives, attributes must be heterogeneous between investment objective groups and homogeneous within them. Our conclusion is to some degree, the group of optimized exponential funds is heterogeneous to other groups. As a whole, there exist no significant differences between different objective groups; 50% of mutual funds are not consistent with their objective groups.

Key words　Mutual funds classification; Distance analysis; Discriminant analysis

①　Originally published in *Journal of Zhejiang University-Science A* (*Applied Physics & Engineenry*) (Volume 5, 2014) by Jin Xuejun and Yang Xiaolan, thanks to National Social Sciences Program (No. O2BJY131) and Zhejiang Provincial S&T Program (No. 021110168).

1 Introduction

Financial theory and practices suggest that mutual funds can use information advantage and subdivide financial markets according to the preferences of investors. They are the reasons for the emergence and tremendous development of the mutual fund industry in recent decades. Mutual funds investors have different risk preferences resulting from different levels of income, resources of income and psychological characters. Consequently, they will choose mutual funds to suit their needs. It was reported by Sharpe (1966) that mutual funds select a risk class and then invite investors with similar risk preferences to invest. He stresses that a fund must remain in the same risky class so that investors may arrange portfolio holdings.

Generally, mutual funds should show their characters of "selecting risk class" or "subdividing markets" to investors by their investment objectives. Investment objectives are stated in mutual fund's prospectus to explain their investment style, strategy, and philosophy, which is distilled into fund objective categories such as growth, income, balanced, etc. Investors can make decisions on the basis of the fund's objectives that implicitly assumes activities of mutual funds consistent with their stated objectives. However, if the stated objectives are not the actual objectives the funds pursue, conclusions drawn by investors and researchers based on the stated objectives will be misleading (Kim et al., 2000). For instance, if income-oriented funds have attributes of growth-oriented funds or vice versa, the stated objectives may seriously misinform investors and lead them to wrong investment decisions. For these reasons, regulations in the mutual fund industry require mutual funds to adhere to their stated investment objectives. [1]

---

[1] The USA Securities and Exchange Commission (SEC) requires that mutual funds disclose risk to potential investors through the prospectus. These investment objectives must be adhered to and may only be changed with approval of the shareholders by a majority vote. Similar regulation has also been made in China by the Chinese Securities Regulatory Commission (CSRC).

In China, the mutual fund industry has been burgeoning in recent years. Currently, in the securities market there are more than 40 closed-end mutual funds with different objective categories including aggressive growth, moderate growth, balanced, optimized exponential, and so on. It is meaningful to ask whether those investment objectives can properly convey information to investors. That is, if we classify mutual funds on the basis of their stated objectives or, whether it is homogeneous within investment objective groups and heterogeneous between them. This paper will argue such questions using data in the Chinese securities market by statistical methods of distance analysis and discriminant analysis.

There has been some recent research in this area. diBartolomeo and Witkowski (1997) focused on the question of whether funds are misclassified, if the misclassification is random, and if misclassification is a hindrance to investors. They regress a fund's returns against the returns of the various objective indices and then classify the fund as belonging to the objective group whose index provides the best fit. They found that the current classification system is indeed insufficient in classifying funds and that about 40% of funds are misclassified. Brown and Goetzmann (1997) investigated whether fund classifications are useful in providing benchmarks for evaluating historical fund performance and in explaining differences in future returns among funds. They also found that the current classification system is inefficient in answering such questions. Kim et al. (2000) classified funds based on their attributes (characteristics, investment style, and risk/return measures). They concluded that the stated objectives of more than half the funds differed from their attributes-based objectives, and over one third of the funds were severely misclassified.

In this paper, our methodology consists of analyzing mutual funds based on their actual attributes and measuring the separation between different groups of funds in multidimensional space by Mahalanobis distance. And this idea is original from Kim et al. (2000). Our conclusion is that to some degree, the group of optimized exponential funds is heterogeneous to other groups. As a whole, there are no significant differences between different objective groups; and 50% of mutual funds are not consistent with their objective groups.

The paper is organized as follows: Section II describes the mutual fund sample, Section III describes the method of distance analysis and discriminant analysis, Section IV describes the analysis process and results, and Section V provides discussion and conclusion.

2　Mutual fund data

In this research, we chose 22 samples of closed-end mutual funds, which were all founded before 2000. Mutual fund data were collected from their annual financial reports in 2000. Some data were obtained from websites such as www. p5w. net and www. homeway. com. cn.

Our research begins with analyzing the actual attributes of funds in different groups. Firstly, we needed a market benchmark. However in the Chinese market there are two stock exchanges, which have their respective indexes: Shanghai's index and Shenzhen's index. So we calculated the growth rate of incorporated index by the average growth rate of these two indexes as follows:

$$INDEX = \ln \frac{\dfrac{INDEXH_{t+1}}{INDEXH_t} + \dfrac{INDEXS_{t+1}}{INDEXS_t}}{2} \tag{1}$$

$INDEX$: logarithm growth rate of incorporated index;

$INDEXH_t, INDEXH_{t+1}$: Shanghai's index of period t and $t+1$;

$INDEXS_t, INDEXS_{t+1}$: Shenzhen's index of period t and $t+1$.

Then, we regarded the 28 days national debt repurchase interest rate of the Shanghai exchange as risk-free rate and got its logarithm.

And then, in order to describe the actual activities of funds, we use the following characteristic variables of fund: (1) percent stock; (2) concentricity of stock; (3) average return for month; (4) standard deviation; (5) beta; (6) R-square.

Percent stock is the percentage of the fund's holdings held as stock, which represents the structure of its asset allocation. Concentricity is calculated as the ratio of the first ten stocks in a fund's portfolio to its amount of stock asset. Concentricity shows whether the investment style of the fund is relatively more concentrated or more dispersed. Standard deviation is a measure of the total risk of a fund. Beta is a measure of the systematic risk for a fund. The R-square measures fund diversification. ①

3   Research method

The main objective of this study is to examine whether funds with the same stated objectives are similar and whether funds with diverse objectives are indeed different. We assume that if mutual funds adhere to their stated objectives, attributes must be heterogeneous between investment objective groups and homogeneous within them. Our methods are designed to test this assumption. Distance analysis is used to measure the difference of diverse groups. Furthermore, discriminant analysis determines whether one fund should be classified into its stated objective group on the basis of its actual characters.

3.1 Distance analysis

We classify the mutual fund samples into groups on the basis of their stated objectives. Then, each group can be regarded as a population with dimensions of $n \times m$(that means each group includes n mutual funds and each fund can be characterized by m variables). If funds with the same stated objectives have similar attributes, and these attributes differ from the funds in other objective groups, funds will be clustered by their stated objectives, and will be distinct from the clusters of other fund objectives. The separation between these clusters in multidimensional space is measured by Mahalanobis distance.

---

①   The R-squared measures the explanatory power of the market index relative to the fund behavior. If the market index used had a small number of members, a high R-squared would not necessarily indicate a diversified portfolio. We use R-square here to measures fund diversification, because Shanghai's index and Shenzhen's index both have large number of members.

There are two populations: mutual fund groups G_1 and G_2. Each group has n mutual funds; each mutual fund was described by m characteristic variables. Our null hypothesis H_0 was that these two groups have identical average values. If the null hypothesis H_0 was rejected, that means G_1, G_2 are really diverse. If H_0 cannot be rejected, that suggests the difference between average values of G_1 and G_2 was not significant.

We assume mutual fund group G_i, $G_i \sim N(\mu^{(i)}, \sum_i)(i=1,2)$, vector of average values $\mu = (\mu_1, \mu_2, \cdots, \mu_m)'$, covariance matrix $\sum = (\sigma_{ij})_{m \times m}$ and mutual fund sample $X = (x_1, x_2, \cdots, x_m)'$. For the purpose of testing $H_0: \mu^{(1)} = \mu^{(2)}$, we calculate the Mahalanobis distance $d^2(1,2)$ between these groups:

$$d^2(1,2) = (\overline{X}^{(1)} - \overline{X}^{(2)})' S^{-1} (\overline{X}^{(1)} - \overline{X}^{(2)}), \tag{2}$$

Where, S was covariance matrix of incorporated samples.

Further, F-statistics is calculated as follows:

$$F = \frac{(n_1 + n_2 - m - 1) n_1 n_2}{m(n_1 + n_2)(n_1 + n_2 - 2)} d^2(1,2) \tag{3}$$

In Eq. (3), n_1 and n_2 are the number of funds in the two groups. Under the null hypothesis that funds in two groups have the same average values, F was characterized by F distribution with numerator's degree of freedom m and denominator's degree of freedom $(n_1 + n_2 - m - 1)$. Further, we can calculate the p-value. If p-value was less than the given significant level α, the null hypothesis H_0 was rejected. That is, these two fund groups are significantly different from each other. While, if p-value is greater than α, H_0 cannot be rejected. That means although these two groups have diverse investment objectives, they do not show significantly different attributes in operation. Each of them does not have its own particular investment style and relative risk and income.

3.2　Discriminant analysis

Discriminant analysis is used to determine into which group a fund should be classified on the basis of their attributes. Our principle is that we classify a fund into the group closest to it. This approach is concerned with separating several groups, based on measurements of multiple attributes (discriminating variables) for the members in the groups. Discriminant analysis is based on maximizing the Mahalanobis distance, which is a measure of separation between two groups.

We have fund $X = (x_1, x_2, \cdots, x_m)'$. The Mahalanobis distance between X and an objective group G_i can be defined as:

$$d^2(X, G_i) = (X - \mu)' \sum^{-1} (X - \mu) \tag{4}$$

As to fund X, we set the following discriminant function:

If $\qquad d^2(X, G_1) < d^2(X, G_2), X \in G_1$ (5)

If $\qquad d^2(X, G_1) \geqslant d^2(X, G_2), X \in G_2$ (6)

That is, we classify a fund into a group which is closest to it.

4   Empirical research results

The 22 mutual funds are classified into 6 groups on the basis of their investment objective: moderate growth, assets restructuring, optimized exponential[①], balanced, middle and small enterprise growth, aggressive growth. [②] We measure the degree of diversity between each other. Each fund is described by 6 variables including percent stock, concentricity of stock, and average return for month, standard deviation, beta and R-square. Distance analysis and discrimiant analysis are implemented by software SAS.

4.1   Results of distance analysis

Table 1 shows the Mahalanobis distances between stated objective groups in multidimensional space. F-statistics and p-value are listed in Table 2 and Table 3. The above results suggest that if α is given as 0.05, no couples of

---

① Optimized exponential fund in China is similar to index fund in US and other countries. Optimized exponential fund put 30% of its portfolio in positive investment. And this is the difference between optimized exponential and index fund holding totally passive investment style.

② In our country, managers of funds frequently state inconsistent investment objectives. In this paper we mainly investigate the prospectus of funds and partly refer to Quanjing website (2002).

funds can pass the significance test (each p is greater than 0.05). That means the stated objective groups are not distinct from each other. When α is given as 0.1, optimized exponential and moderate growth, optimized exponential and balanced, optimized exponential and aggressive growth, balanced and assets restructuring, balanced and middle and small enterprise growth pass the test. Hence, those couples are diverse at significance level 0.1. As we can see, in those 6 groups, optimized exponential fund group is distinct from other groups more significantly. However, moderate growth, aggressive growth and middle and small enterprise growth are very close, which suggests similarity in investment characters.

Table 1   Squared distance to group

From group	Moderate growth	Assets restructuring	optimized exponential	Balanced	Middle and small enterprise growth	Aggressive growth
Moderate growth	0	10.66441	10.98309	5.14556	8.22608	2.39935
Assets restructuring	10.66441	0	14.08073	18.68796	6.93418	4.03729
Optimized exponential	10.98309	14.08073	0	22.12258	7.89869	11.78212
Balanced	5.14556	18.68796	22.12258	0	19.79169	6.86633
Middle and small enterprise growth	8.22608	6.93418	7.89869	19.79169	0	5.40004
Aggressive growth	2.39935	4.03729	11.78212	6.86633	5.40004	0

Table 2   *F*-Statistics, NDF=6, DDF=11 for squared distance to group

From group	Moderate growth	Assets restructuring	optimized exponential	Balanced	Middle and small enterprise growth	Aggressive growth
Moderate growth	0	1. 83294	3. 02035	1. 17919	1. 41386	0. 74980
Assets restructuring	1. 83294	0	2. 15122	2. 56960	0. 79454	0. 66087
Optimized exponential	3. 02035	2. 15122	0	4. 34551	1. 20674	3. 00008
Balanced	1. 17919	2. 56960	4. 34551	0	2. 72136	1. 47519
Middle and small enterprise growth	1. 41386	0. 79454	1. 20674	2. 72136	0	0. 88394
Aggressive growth	0. 74980	0. 66087	3. 00008	1. 47519	0. 88394	0

Table 3   Prob>Mahalanobis distance for squared distance to group

From group	Moderate growth	Assets restructuring	optimized exponential	Balanced	Middle and small enterprise growth	Aggressive growth
Moderate growth	1. 0000	0. 1817	0. 0536	0. 3837	0. 2924	0. 6224
Assets restructuring	0. 1817	1. 0000	0. 1284	0. 0832	0. 5932	0. 6829
Optimized exponential	0. 0536	0. 1284	1. 0000	0. 0172	0. 3716	0. 0546
Balanced	0. 3837	0. 0832	0. 0172	1. 0000	0. 0715	0. 2725
Middle and small enterprise growth	0. 2924	0. 5932	0. 3716	0. 0715	1. 0000	0. 5375
Aggressive growth	0. 6224	0. 6829	0. 0546	0. 2725	0. 5375	1. 0000

4.2   Results of discriminant analysis

Through discriminant analysis we can classify funds based on their actual attributes. While, the categories of objective groups are based on their stated objectives. Comparing the results of discriminant analysis with the objective groups, we can conclude which fund is heterogeneous within its own group and should be classified into another group on the basis of its attributes. Error Count Estimates for group shown in Table 4 suggests the percentage of misclassified funds in one group. The higher error count suggests the greater mutual distinction within an objective group. However, the lower error count suggests funds from this group are more homogeneous in attributes.

Our results showed only 11 funds could be classified into their stated groups through discriminant analysis. And the others were misclassified. Among those groups, optimized exponential group had the lowest error count, while balanced had the highest. Reclassification results can be seen in the appendix.

Table 4   Error count estimates for group

From group	Moderate growth	Assets restructuring	Optimized exponential	Balanced	Middle and small enterprise growth	Aggressive growth
Rate	0.5000	0.5000	0.2500	0.6667	0.5000	0.6000

5   Conclusions

This work examines whether the stated investment objectives of mutual funds adequately represent their attributes to investors. This is extremely important if an investor attempts to compare risks and returns to choose investment within an investment objective group.

Results from this study revealed that different fund groups were not really distinct from each other on the whole. Therefore, stated investment objectives of mutual funds fail to completely capture attributes. In addition, we conclude that the optimized exponential fund group showed some investment characters in some degree is different from funds in other groups.

Although regulations in the mutual fund industry require mutual funds to adhere to their stated investment objectives, some departures may still occur. Najand and Prather(1999)concluded that this phenomenon might be explained by the intense competition in the mutual fund industry, imperfect monitoring by the SEC and investors, and portfolio manager compensation contracting. The above argument may be also applicable in China. While in our stock market, fund managers, investors and even supervisors have not attached importance to fund's objective. There are no specific guidelines as to how to declare fund objectives and how to manage portfolios exactly in pursuance of the declared objectives. From our point of view, objective groups may play a relatively important role in the development of the whole mutual fund market.

References

Brown S J, Goetzmann W N, 1997. Mutual fund styles [J]. Journal of Financial Economics, 43(3): 373-399.

diBartolomeo D, Witkowski E, 1997. Mutual fund misclassification: Evidence based on style analysis[J]. Financial Analysts Journal, 53(5): 32-43.

Kim M, Shukla R, Tomas M, 2000. Mutual fund objective misclassification [J]. Journal of Economics and Business, 52:209-203.

Najand M, Prather L J, 1999. The risk level discriminatory power of mutual fund investment objectives: additional evidence [J]. Journal of Financial Markets, 2:307-328.

Sharpe W F, 1966. Mutual fund performance[J]. Journal of Business, 39: 119-138.

Appendix:Discrimnant results

Fund name	Objective classifications (from group)	Discrimnant results(into group)
An Shun	Moderate growth	Moderate growth
Tong Sheng	Moderate growth	Moderate growth
Tong Yi	Moderate growth	Moderate growth
Xing hua*	Moderate growth	Assets restructuring
Jin xin*	Moderate growth	optimized exponential
Jing Hong*	Moderate growth	Middle and small enterprise growth
Yu Yuan	Assets restructuring	Assets restructuring
Yu Yuang*	Assets restructuring	Aggressive growth
Xing He	optimized exponential	optimized exponential
Pu Feng	optimized exponential	optimized exponential
Tian Yuan*	optimized exponential	Assets restructuring
Jing Fu	optimized exponential	optimized exponential
Jin Tai	Balanced	Balanced
Tai He*	Balanced	optimized exponential
Han Xing*	Balanced	Middle and small enterprise growth
Jing Bo	Middle and small enterprise growth	Middle and small enterprise growth
Jing Yang*	Middle and small enterprise growth	Aggressive growth
Han Sheng	Aggressive growth	Aggressive growth
An Xin*	Aggressive growth	Assets restructuring
Pu Hui*	Aggressive growth	Balanced
Kai Yuan*	Aggressive growth	Assets restructuring
Yu Long	Aggressive growth	Aggressive growth

"Objective classifications" are initial categories that funds declare to investors. "Discrimnant results" are obtained from reclassification according to fund's performance. Funds with marks are misclassified. That is, they cannot be classified into their stated groups through discriminant analysis.

Losing by Learning? A Study of Social Trading Platform[①]

Abstract   This paper is the first to use a unique dataset extracted from a popular social trading platform in China to investigate whether social learning on average encourages riskier trading and hurts stock portfolio returns. We observe an increasing trading frequency and a preference for high-volatility stocks for signal followers on average in the network over time. Furthermore, we find out that leading trades performs relatively better than lagging ones, indicating social learning in a social trading network is not positively associated with portfolio performance. Taken together, our empirical results are in support of Han et al. (2018).

Key words   Social trading; Portfolio management; Risk-taking behavior

1   Introduction

Whether social interaction has a positive or negative influence on security investment performance has been under heated debates. To the best of our knowledge, this is the first empirical investigation about the impact of social learning on trading outcomes from the perspective of signal followers within a social trading network. Such a study greatly contributes to our understanding of the role played by social learning in influencing individual investors' portfolio choice and trading behavior. Our empirical evidence is in support of

①   Originally published in *Finance Research Letters* (vol. 28, 2018) by Jin Xuejun, Zhu Yu and Huang Ying.

the theoretical model advanced by Han et al. (2018), where they predict that investor interaction within a community propagates risky trading strategies and lowers returns of participants. On one hand, their model implies that active traders are more likely to earn short-term high returns and initiate a conversation (conversation senders). On the other hand, conversation receivers' propensity to attend to and be converted by the senders is increasing and convex in senders' return. Overtime, due to biases in the social transmission of behaviors, active trading strategies and over-optimism become prevalent throughout the population and investors earning lower returns on average.

Our contributions are twofold. First, since individual investors' level of transaction data and their social connections are hard to come by, direct empirical investigations on social interactions and their trading behavior are scant. We attempt to fill the gap by tapping into a popular social trading platform in China①with both recorded transaction history and social links of its users. The detailed and time-stamped transaction level data and the "copy trading" mechanism enable us to directly test if learning by copying others' strategies would help to enhance investment performance. Consistent with the self-enhancing transmission bias hypothesis, we find strong evidence to suggest an increased trading frequency and preference for high-volatility stocks in the social trading network, which indicates a propagation of active trading strategies throughout the online community. Furthermore, in addition to an overall negative excess return, we document that for signal followers, their lagging trades——trades that are more likely to be made under the influence of signal providers perform much worse than their leading trades——trades that are more likely to be made independently.

Second, we also contribute to the emerging literature on trading choice on social trading platforms. An increasing number of research papers have documented that social media like Facebook or microblogs can influence investors' financial decisions (Siikanen et al., 2018; Zhang et al., 2017). However, research on social trading platforms is still scant and tends to focus

---

① Details are provided in Section 2.1.

on signal providers, such as their portfolio performance (Doering et al., 2015; Oehler et al., 2016) and behavioral biases (Heimer, 2016; Wohlgemuth et al., 2016; Glaser & Risius, 2016). Due to the unavailability of data, the trading behavior and profitability of signal followers have yet to be examined. Our sample encompasses transaction records of both signal providers and signal followers, thereby allowing us to compare the trading risks and returns of these two types of investors and evaluate if signal followers can really benefit from copying signal providers in social trading networks. To the best of our knowledge, this study is the first empirical investigation on individual investors' trading regarding their social learning outcomes from the perspective of signal followers.

The reminder of the paper is organized as follows. Section 2 describes the data and develops relevant hypotheses. Section 3 presents the empirical results and Section 4 concludes.

2 Data and hypotheses

2.1 Data

We code a special web crawling algorithm to browse and download data from China's largest social trading platform——xueqiu. com. ①Our sample includes all transactions by signal providers and signal followers as well as their connections within the network. The sample period spans from July 2016, when the signal follower/provider roles were initially introduced, to September 2017. Xueqiu, like other typical online social trading platforms works as follows. Some users register as "signal providers". They create either real or virtual portfolios, publish their trading strategies and portfolio performance, which are regarded as signals and hence attract followers in the network. The platform rule is such that every historical trade made by signal providers must be freely accessible to every user of the network. The other

① The literal translation of "Xueqiu" is "snowball".

group of users, known as "signal followers", are given the opportunity to copy signal providers' stock holdings by subscribing to or "following" their interested users. Usually signals published by subscribed users are automatically executed into signal followers' brokerage accounts by the social trading platform proportionally ① (Doering et al., 2015).

Fig. 1 intends to illustrate a few important functions of the Xueqiu platform. Panel 1 of Fig. 1 shows that one ② can browse the daily updated ranking (in the recent 1 year, 6 months or 3 months) of signal providers and add to his "watchlist" any signal provider that he is interested in. By doing so, a signal follower will receive signal alerts whenever his/her "followed" signal provider makes a new trade. Upon receiving a signal alert, one can check the portfolio detail page to see the signal provider's historical performance (Panel 2), transaction records and current holdings (Panel 3). Whenever the signal follower decides to "copy"③the signal, he can easily click on the "place order" button and it prompts up a buy confirmation page (Panel 4). One can decide on the order type or inputs any amount to buy and the system will calculate the proportion automatically.

Fig. 1 shows how a signal follower copies a signal provider's portfolio on Xueqiu App. Panel 1 presents the rankings of all signal providers in the recent 3 months, 6 months and 1 year. A signal follower could add any signal provider into his "watchlist". By doing so, signal followers will receive signal alerts whenever the signal providers he follows make a new trade. Panel 2 displays a signal provider's historical performance, while Panel 3 shows his historical transactions and portfolio holdings. Panel 4 shows a stock buy

---

① For example, if a signal provider has a portfolio of stocks A and B, with weights of 40% and 60%, respectively, then a subscription of \$1,000 would result in a holding of \$400 and \$600 invested in A and B, respectively.

② Anyone, including the non-registered Xueqiu users, can see the ranking. But only the registered signal followers with a brokerage account can use the "copy trading" feature.

③ By default, the system calculates the weights on the basis of replicating a signal provider's whole portfolio. However, a signal follower can manually change the stocks to buy and their weights. For example, he could choose to buy only the stock that was just bought by the signal provider.

1. Ranking

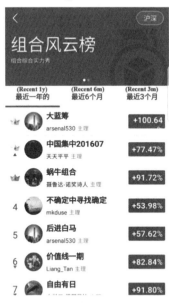

Panel 1

2. Performance

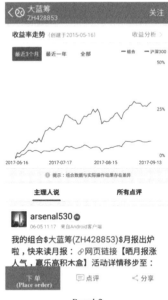

Panel 2

3. Transactions & Holdings

Panel 3

4. Buy Confimation

Panel 4

Fig. 1 An illustration of the process of how a signal follower copies a signal provider's portfolio on Xueqiu App

confirmation page. A signal follower can input any amount he wants to buy when placing the order and the system will calculate the proportion automatically.

On Xueqiu, a signal provider can create as many as 20 "virtual" portfolios and demonstrate them without any cost. Signal followers, however, can only open one account on the platform and trade with "real money". Additionally, slightly different from other social trading platforms, where all signals published by the subscribed users are automatically executed into the follower's account, signal followers on Xueqiu are required to manually decide if they wish to follow a signal. Moreover, a signal follower on Xueqiu can trade without directly copying others, resulting in a portfolio holding of stocks from both signal-following and self-trading.

The data cleaning process goes like this. We start by selecting signal providers who only trade A-shares, then we eliminate signal providers and signal followers who exist for less than 60 days, and we remove non-user-initiated trades, such as dividend distributions. After filtering, our final sample consistsed of 161,972 signal provider virtual portfolios and 9,505 signal follower real portfolios. In Fig. 2 we present the visualization of the entire Xueqiu network, with each color representing a community detected by the Louvain algorithm, and the size of each node representing the number of followers. A larger node indicates one has more followers in the network.

Our study focuses on transactions made by signal followers, because they trade with real money on Xueqiu and we intend to fill the void on the research from their perspective. In addition, we only include "buy" trades due to the following two considerations. First, buying trades better reflect an investor's active choice and more importantly better represent one's attitude towards the riskiness of stocks. Especially, certain sell transactions are likely to be primarily determined by liquidity needs. Second, shorting or marginal trading is not allowed on Xueqiu for signal followers.

Table 1 presents the summary statistics of portfolios created by signal providers and signal followers. It shows that both signal providers and the portfolios they create outnumber those of signal followers and their portfolios,

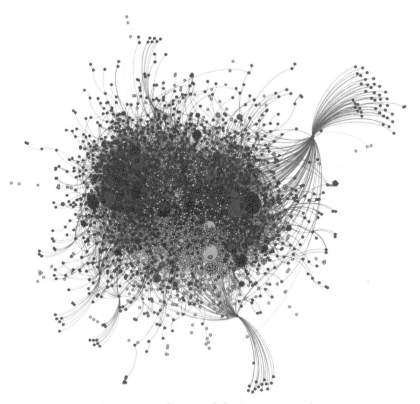

Fig. 2 Visualization of the Xueqiu network

Fig. 2 presents the visualization of the Xueqiu network. The size of each node is associated with the number of followers. A larger node indicates more followers. The colors represent different communities within the network detected by the Louvain algorithm. This figure was generated using the network software Gephi.

probably because being a signal provider is costless and one can create up to 20 virtual portfolios. On average, signal followers earn a higher return. It should be noted that although generally signal followers and signal providers yield positive returns, they perform much worse than the market, which increased by 13% during the same sample period. ① We can see that signal providers trade more actively, trading 2. 3 times on average in a week, while a typical signal follower trades 1. 2 times in a week.

---

① This finding is not totally unexpected, since most of the Xueqiu users are individual investors, and as Barber et al. (2008) document, individual investors generally underperform the market.

Table 1　Summary statistics of main variables of interest

Panel A: Return

User type	Portfolio	User	Min	25% percentile	Mean	Median	75% percentile	Max	Std. Dev.
Signal provider	161,972	89,231	−62.1	−23.2	2.4	−0.5	22.1	127.1	35.1
Signal follower	9,505	9,505	−62.2	−12.6	5.6	1.8	19.9	126.7	30.6

Panel B: Trading frequency

User type	Min	25% percentile	Mean	Median	75% percentile	Max	Std. Dev.
Signal provider	0	0.3	2.3	0.7	1.5	45	11.8
Signal follower	0	0.4	1.2	0.8	1.7	8	1.3

Table 1 reports summary statistics of return and trading frequency for signal providers and signal followers on Xueqiu. On one hand, since a signal provider is allowed to create up to 20 virtual portfolios, the portfolio number for signal providers is greater than the user number. On the other hand, since a signal follower is only allowed to open one account with real money, the portfolio number and the user number are the same for signal followers. The portfolio return is calculated as each portfolio's current net value in excess of one. Trading frequency is defined as the average number of trades in a week. Because a signal follower can receive multiple signals at a time, we set a rebalancing weight threshold of 25%. For example, a signal of increasing the weight of a stock from 10% to 12% is not considered, while an increase of a stock from 5% to 31% is considered. We have tried different thresholds from 0% to 50% and the main results remain the same.

2.2　Hypotheses

According to Han et al. (2018), traders who adopt a riskier style (e. g. trading more frequently) have a higher possibility to yield a short-term high return, therefore more likely to be observed by more conservative traders (e. g. , trading less frequently). These conservative traders gradually convert into active traders, which eventually help the propagation of riskier trading styles. Therefore, we postulate our first hypothesis as follows.

*H*1: *The trading risk of social trading networks increases over time.*

However, shifting to a more active trading style which may differ a lot from an individual investor's previous trading style, and an increased trading frequency are usually associated with lower performance (Barber et al. ,

2008). In line with this reasoning, we propose our second hypothesis as follows.

H2: *Following "signals" or copy trading decreases individual investors' performance.*

3 Empirical results

Our first hypothesis implies a propagation of risky trading styles in the social trading network. We adopt two alternative risk measures when testing the first hypothesis. First, in accordance with Han et al. (2018), we use trading frequency as a proxy for risk. The weekly average trading frequency of the Xueqiu online community is computed and plotted for the sample period in Fig. 3. The few large drops in the trading frequency occur during the weeks of major public holidays, such as the National Day, the Spring Festival and the Labor Day, when the market is closed. In general, we can see an upward trend in trading frequency over time for the Xueqiu platform.

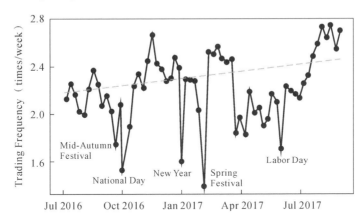

Fig. 3 Trading risk measured as trading frequency of signal followers

Fig. 3 presents the weekly average trading frequency of the online community plotted against time. Trading frequency, as a proxy of trading risk, is defined as the total number of buy transactions made in a week divided by the number of users. The gray dashed line represents the OLS regression of the data.

Second, since portfolio risks rise with the purchase of high-volatility stocks, we calculate the percentage of high-volatility stocks in the total trading volume. Specifically, we classify stocks into quintiles according to their idiosyncratic volatility. ① In Fig. 4 we plot such risk measurement which is calculated as the percentage of trades that fall into the top one volatility quintile each week. For example, a reading of 0. 2 implies that in a particular week, 20% of the trades are concentrated on stocks with the highest volatility. It can be seen that at the beginning only 20% of trades target high-volatility stocks, the proportion jumps to almost 60% at the end of the sample period. Again, a visible upward trend is observed and it corroborates our projection in the first hypothesis about the increasing trading risk for social trading networks.

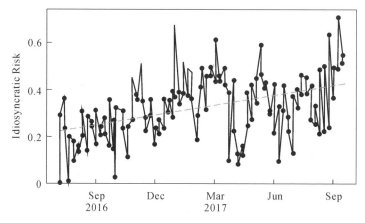

Fig. 4　Trading risk of signal followers measured as idiosyncratic volatility

Fig. 4 shows trading risks measured as the idiosyncratic volatility of purchased stocks. We first group stocks into deciles according to their idiosyncratic volatility, and then calculate, for each week, the percentage of trades that fall into the top one volatility quintile.

To test the second hypothesis, we classify trades into three different groups according to whether it is made before or after a signal. Fig. 5 illustrates our classifications. We classify a trade as a "leading trade" if it is made on the same stock sometime within four weeks before receiving a signal, and a "lagging trade" if it is made on the same stock sometime within four weeks after the signal. Trades made outside these time windows/ranges are classified as "others" for benchmarking. We expect that lagging trades are

---

①　Idiosyncratic volatility is calculated as the residual from a regression of daily stock returns on the market index returns (Campbell et al. , 2001).

more likely to be made by following particular signals, whereas leading trades are more likely to be made independently. If our projection in the second hypothesis is true, we would observe worse performance for lagging trades (copy trading). The inference of connections between two investors according to their trading time and the target stock is nothing new. In setting up an empirical investor network using all trades on the Istanbul Stock Exchange (ISE) in 2005, Ozsoylev et al. (2014) define that any two investors are connected if they trade the same stock in the same direction within 30 min on the ISE. Even though there is no guarantee that lagging (leading) trades are purely made due to social learning (independent reasoning), we believe that our classification to distinguish between pre- and post-signal trading serves as a meaningful endeavor to explore the potential impacts of social learning on the trading behavior of individual investors.

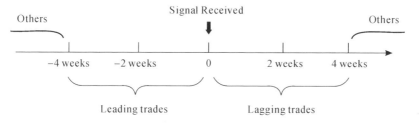

Fig. 5 Classification of trades made by signal followers

Fig. 5 illustrates the classification of trades into three categories: leading trades, lagging trades and others. A "leading trade" is a buy trade made on the same stock sometime within four weeks before receiving a signal, while a "lagging trade" is a buy trade made on the same stock sometime within four weeks after the signal.

Since a signal follower can receive multiple signals at a time, we only consider "strong" signals by setting a rebalancing weight threshold of 25%. ① We have tried different thresholds for the rebalancing weight from 0% to 50% and the main findings remain the same. We further classify these leading and lagging trades into four subgroups: $2 \sim 4$ week leading trades, $0 \sim 2$ week leading trades, $0 \sim 2$ week lagging trades, and $2 \sim 4$ week lagging trades, respectively. We have also tried other time windows, and the results still

---

① For example, a signal of increasing the weight of a stock from 10% to 12% will not be considered, while an increase from 5% to 31% will be included.

hold. In the final dataset, about 3% of the trades are classified as leading trades and 3.6% as lagging trades, with all the rest as benchmarks. It should be noted that as we lower the threshold of the rebalancing weight for signals, the percentage of leading and lagging trades increase accordingly at the expense of the precision of classifications for the two kinds of trades.

Next, we proceed to track the buy-and-hold return of each type of trades up to 90 days. We report the relevant results in Fig. 6 and Table 2. For each panel of Fig. 6, the left-hand-side plot tracks the average daily return in excess of the market return from day 0 to day 90, and the right-hand-side plot shows the corresponding cumulative net value. Dashed lines represent performances of four types of leading or lagging trades, while solid lines represent "others" or benchmark trades.

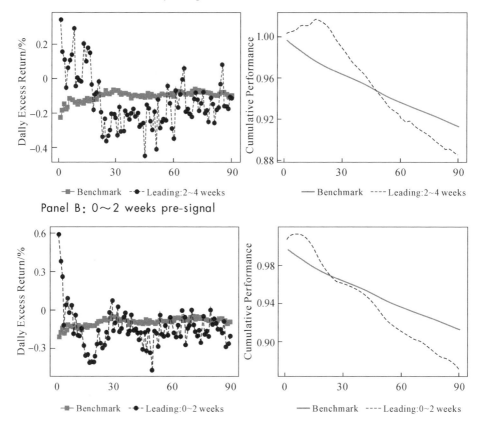

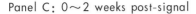

Panel C: 0~2 weeks post-signal

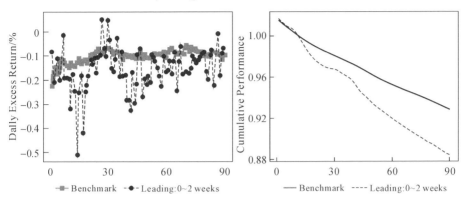

Panel D: 2~4 weeks post-signal

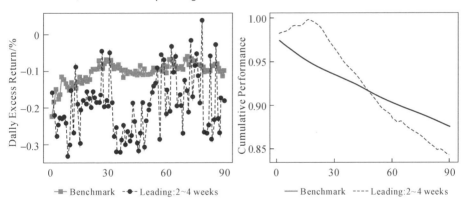

Fig. 6　Cumulative performance of different types of trade by signal followers

Panels of Fig. 6 present the buy-and-hold returns of each type of trades up to 90 days. In each panel, the left-hand-side plot tracks the average daily return in excess of the market return from day 0 to day 90, and the right-hand-side plot shows the corresponding cumulative net value. Dashed lines represent performances of four types of leading or lagging trades, while solid lines represent "others" or benchmark trades.

Table 2 Cumulative return of different trade types

Trade type		N(%)	Average daily excess return (%)	30-day cumulative performance (%)	60-day cumulative performance (%)	90-day cumulative performance (%)
Leading or lagging trades	2~4 weeks pre-signal	2,815 (1.4%)	−0.14	−1.1	−7.9	−3.9
	0~2 weeks pre-signal	2,919 (1.5%)	−0.13	−3.9	−8.8	−11.5
	0~2 weeks post-signal	3,881 (2.0%)	−0.15	−4.9	−9.6	−12.9
	2~4 weeks post-signal	3,019 (1.6%)	−0.16	−5.8	−11.8	−13.0
Others (Benchmark)		180,180 (93.4%)	−0.09	−3.6	−6.4	−8.7

Table 2 reports the performance of different trade types. As in Fig. 6, the average daily excess return is defined as the return in excess of the market return, and the cumulative performance is defined as the buy-and-hold cumulative return.

We find that the timing of a trade is associated with its ensuing performance and leading trades generally perform better than lagging trades. For example, leading trades (Panels A and B of Fig. 6) beat the benchmark, at least for the initial two weeks, while lagging trades (Panels C and D of Fig. 6) systematically perform below the benchmark. According to Table 2, we find that individual investors on average yield negative excess returns, with worse performance for post-signal trading or copy trading. For less correlated trades, especially those with longer time lag post-signal, the performance is even worse. The results lend support to our H2 that following signals may not enhance performance.

However, one should be cautious in claiming that signals are of no value. Signal followers suffer poor performance on average may simply because they fail to duplicate the valuable signals in time. It could be that a signal follower needs some "evaluation time" (learning and deciding on the credibility of the signal) before he actually makes a trade. We encourage future research to ascertain how different in individual investors (such as personal traits and learning abilities) contribute to their diverse performance.

4   Conclusions

In this study we tap into a new data source——social trading platform——to empirically investigate two hypotheses implied in Han et al. (2018). Using two different trading risk measures (trading frequency and stock's idiosyncratic volatility), we show that the online social trading network witnesses increasingly risky trading styles and higher volatilities over time. By further dividing trades into "leading" and "lagging" groups according to whether they are made before or after a signal, we find that lagging trades tend to perform much worse than the leading ones, indicating social learning from others in the network may harm portfolio performance. Taken together, our results offer direct empirical support of Han et al. (2018). The results obtained in a social trading network environment are of high relevance for regulators who have a strong focus on the oversight of consumer protection and sound financial service industry regulation.

References

Barber B M, Lee Y T, Liu Y J, et al, 2009. Just how much do individual investors lose by trading? [J]. Review of Financial Studies, 22(2):609-632.

Campbell J Y, Lettau M, Xu M Y, 2001. Have individual stocks become more volatile? An empirical exploration of idiosyncratic risk[J]. Journal of Finance, 56(1):1-43.

Doering P, Neumann S, Paul S, 2015. A primer on social trading networks - institutional aspects and empirical evidence [J]. Social Science Electronic Publishing:1-29.

Glaser F, Risius M, 2018. Effects of transparency: Analyzing social biases on trader performance in social trading[J]. Journal of Information Technology, 33 (1):19-30.

Han B, Hirshleifer D A, 2022. Social transmission bias and investor behavior

［J］. Journal of Financial and Quantitative Analysis，57(1)：390-412.

Heimer R Z，2016. Peer pressure：Social interaction and the disposition effect ［J］. Social Science Electronic Publishing，29(11)：3177-3209.

Oehler A，Horn M，Wendt S，2016. Benefits from social trading? Empirical evidence for certificates on wikifolios［J］. International Review of Financial Analysis，46(Jul.)：202-210.

Ozsoylev H N，Johan W，Deniz Y M，et al，2015. Investor networks in the stock market［J］. Review of Financial Studies，5：1323-1366.

Siikanen M，Baltakys K，Kanniainen J，et al，2018. Facebook drives behavior of passive households in stock markets［J］. Finance Research Letters，27：1-11.

Wohlgemuth V，Berger E S C，Wenzel M，2016. More than just financial performance：Trusting investors in social trading［J］. Journal of Business Research，69(11)：4970-4974.

Zhang Y，An Y，Feng X，et al，2017. Celebrities and ordinaries in social networks：Who knows more information? ［J］. Finance Research Letters，20：153-161.

Performance Evaluation and Herd Behavior in a Laboratory Financial Market[①]

Abstract   We consider the effect of performance evaluation on the herd behavior of fund managers in a laboratory financial market. Subjects acting as fund managers receive imperfect private information concerning the fundamental value of a stock, which they then trade in sequence with a market maker. When prices are flexible, subjects regard their private information and herd less frequently than when the price is constant. When price is constant, subjects evaluated by relative performance tend to "go with the flow" to reduce any price deviation from their peers, but when the price is flexible, herd behavior almost disappears under relative performance evaluation as the increasing trading costs squeeze the net profit of follow-up imitators. Overall, the likelihood of rational decisions under relative performance evaluation is higher than under absolute performance evaluation.

Key words   Herd behavior; Relative performance evaluation; Fund managers

1   Introduction

Extensive empirical evidence suggests that herding is quite common among fund managers. Using data on US pension funds, Lakonishok et al. (1992)

---

①   Originally published in *Journal of Behavioral and Experimental Economics* (vol. 75,2018) by Yang Xiaolan, Gao Mei, Wu Yun and Jin Xuejun.

find that fund managers tend to hold similar asset portfolios to avoid replacement in the fierce competition with their peers. Likewise, Wermers (1999) suggests that, from 1975 to 1994, the level of herding was higher among growth-oriented mutual funds than among income funds. Moreover, Brown et al. (2014) indicate that the herd behavior of career-concerned fund managers could be induced by analyst recommendation revisions, especially under a consensus analyst downgrade, and this could destabilize stock prices. Lastly, Kremer and Nautz (2013) employ two alternative herding measures on the German stock market, namely, the measures of Lakonishok et al. (1992) and Sias (2004), and reveal the presence of herding in low-frequency financial institution transaction data.

The method by which fund managers' performance is evaluated has a major influence on traders' behavior and asset price formation (Kleinlercher et al., 2014; Holmen et al., 2014). For example, the optimal contracts derived under agency problems typically employ relative performance evaluation (Mookherjee, 1984). Maug and Naik (1995) claim that fund managers with relative performance contracts have a motivation to "go with the flow" to avoid falling behind their peers, instead of maximizing expected return. Eichberger et al. (1999) show that under relative performance contracts, there is an equilibrium in which all fund managers follow the goals of fund owners. Besides, there is an alternative equilibrium where fund managers mutually deviate from the desires of fund owners. However, equilibrium herding models of this type set asset prices as constant and do not analyze more realistic situations in which traders' decisions to buy and sell affect prices.

In contrast to the above models under the fixed price hypothesis, Avery and Zemsky (1998) take account of the price mechanism in their asset prices and informational cascades[①] model. Overall, they conclude that an

---

① Bikhchandni et al. (1992) present a basic model which assumes that individuals decide whether to accept or reject certain behaviors one by one, after observing previous decisions and receiving imperfect private information. They find that an information cascade occurs when it is optimal for individuals to follow the decision ahead of them without regard to their own information.

informational cascade is impossible when new information is fully reflected in prices. Cipriani and Guarino (2005) test the predictions of Avery and Zemsky (1998) in a laboratory financial market by comparing herd behavior between markets with a flexible price mechanism (where a market maker updates asset prices according to trade history) and markets with a fixed price mechanism (where asset prices are constant). Their results reveal that the frequency of herding under a flexible price mechanism is lower than the one under a fixed price mechanism, but unlike the predictions of the theoretical models, the flexible price does not completely prevent herding.

In the setup of Cipriani and Guarino (2005), traders' payoffs depend on their absolute gains. Conversely, in real-world markets, fund managers are frequently paid by relative performance (Maug & Naik, 1995; Chevalier & Ellison, 1997; Huddart, 1999; Eichberger et al., 1999; Palomino et al., 2005). Since herding may decrease the payoff of fund managers when prices are flexible, it is interesting to examine the effect of relative performance evaluation on herd behavior in markets with flexible prices. Research to date has made little progress in responding to this question. Some of the literature on the effect of tournament contracts in financial markets addresses a similar issue. For example, Yin and Zhang (2013) examine whether tournament compensation structures incentivize financial analysts. They find that interim losers are unlikely to herd since herding cannot help them improve their relative ranking. James and Isaac (2000) show that tournament contracts have a destructive effect on an asset market, generating misleading prices. Berlemann and Vopel (2012) find that under strong tournament incentives, traders may profit from early herding.

In this paper, we investigate the impact of incentives and price mechanisms on herd behavior in an experimental asset market. Subjects receive private information on the fundamental value of an asset, which they then trade sequentially with a market maker. Drawing on the experimental structure proposed by Cipriani and Guarino (2005), we adopt a 2×2 design with four treatments comprising two performance evaluation mechanisms and two price mechanisms. We then compare subjects' herd behavior across the four treatments: (1) a fixed price and absolute performance evaluation (treatment Fixed-A); (2) a fixed price and relative performance evaluation (treatment Fixed-R); (3) a flexible price and absolute performance evaluation (treatment Flexible-A); and (4) a flexible price and relative performance evaluation (treatment Flexible-R).

Our main contribution is to introduce both relative performance evaluation and flexible price mechanisms into herd behavior experiments. Our experimental results suggest that relative performance evaluation plays a significant role in increasing the proportions of rational decisions, whereby there is no herding when price is flexible, but herding persists when price is fixed. These findings may motivate more behavioral research on the role of incentives in financial markets and may also have policy implications regarding the regulation of fund management companies.

The remainder of the paper is as follows. Section 2 presents the experimental design. Section 3 describes the theoretical predictions. Section 4 details the results of our experiment. Section 5 concludes and discusses our findings.

2　Experimental design

We designed our experiment to observe herd behavior under two different performance evaluation mechanisms and two alternative pricing mechanisms. The experimental analysis is based on the information cascade model in Bikhchandni et al. (1992) and the experimental structure in Cipriani and Guarino (2005). [1] Using a 2×2 design, we vary both the performance evaluation mechanism and the price mechanism independently.

We programmed the experiment using z-Tree (Fischbacher, 2007), with all sessions conducted at Zhejiang University in September 2013, March 2014, November 2015, and March 2017. Overall, we recruited 150 subjects from

---

[1] Cipriani and Guarino (2005) allowed subjects not to trade, while we merely asked subjects to either buy or sell. Moreover, we introduced relative performance evaluation into their basic experimental design.

several different majors. As shown in Table 1, there were four treatments over some 25 sessions. The average payment was approximately 30 Yuan including a show-up fee of 5 Yuan.

Table 1　Experiment design

Treatment	Price mechanism	Incentive mechanism	Number of sessions
Fixed-A	Fixed	Absolute performance evaluation	6
Fixed-R	Fixed	Relative performance evaluation	6
Flexible-A	Flexible	Absolute performance evaluation	7
Flexible-R	Flexible	Relative performance evaluation	6

The trading market in each session consisted of six participants acting as fund managers with the computer acting as the market maker. The procedure was as follows.

(1) Each session commenced with a public reading of the instructions, followed by 10 trading periods.

(2) At the beginning of each period, the computer assigned a random number between one and six to each subject without replacement. Then subjects were asked to trade one after another, following the assigned order from one to six.

(3) Before deciding whether to sell or buy a stock at a given price proposed by the market maker in each trading period, each trader received a private signal on the value of the stock. Subjects also observed the history of past trades.

(4) At the end of the trading period, we randomly chose one of the 10 periods to determine the real payoff for the subjects.

(5) At the end of the sessions, we introduced the Holt and Laury (2002) risk preference task to measure individual risk aversion. We used the crossover point, where the subject switched from the safe option to the risky option, to infer the degree of risk aversion.

2.1　Private signal and stock value

We endowed every trader with 100 tokens of cash and one unit of stock at the beginning of each trading period. The fundamental stock value V is a variable randomly distributed on $\{0,100\}$ with the same probability of 50%. Subjects traded with the market maker in an exogenously decided sequential order in each period. Every trader, indexed by t, was required to either buy or sell the stock at time t, and his/her action space was $s = \{\text{buy, sell}\}$. The trader's action at time t is denoted by $D_t \in S$, and the history of trades until time t-1 is denoted by H_t.

Before making a decision, the trader would receive a private signal X about the stock value V. However, X was not perfectly accurate information about the real value of the stock. The signal was presented to subjects in the manner of a game used by Anderson and Holt (1997), in which subjects could observe draws of colored balls from one of two cups and could form an opinion about which of the two cups was being used. More specifically, there were two identical cups, a red cup containing 70 red and 30 blue balls and a blue cup containing 30 red and 70 blue balls. Before each trading period, the computer randomly chose one cup from these two identical cups with the same probability of 50%. If the red cup containing 70 red and 30 blue balls was selected, the real value of the stock was 100. If the blue cup containing 30 red and 70 blue balls was selected, the real value of the stock was 0. Without knowing the real color of the selected cup, each subject could draw a ball from the selected cup in a prespecified sequence to get the private signal X, and then they needed to decide whether to buy or sell the stock. Draws included replacement.

To elaborate, imagine a trader drawing a red (blue) ball, which means that the signal X is equal to 100 (0). We can illustrate the relationship between the signal X and the stock value V using the following conditional probability function:

$$\rho = (V=100 \mid X=100) = P(V=0 \mid X=0) = P(\text{red cup} \mid \text{red ball})$$
$$= P(\text{blue cup} \mid \text{bule ball}) = 0.7 \qquad (1)$$

where ρ is the accuracy of signal X

Therefore, the accuracy of the private signal ρ is 70%. The first trader had no history information but for the private signal X. The second trader could then make a decision based on two observations: The first decision made by the first trader and the second draw, known only to him/her. In the same manner, the third person would observe two decisions by the previous two traders and one draw.

2.2 Pricing mechanism

After receiving the private signal, traders should make a binary choice about whether to sell or buy the stock at the current price which was proposed by the market maker. For trader t, without consideration of the private signal, the expected value of the stock was $E(V \mid H_t)$, where H_t was the trading history of the former traders.

There were two different pricing mechanisms in our design, namely a fixed price and a flexible price corresponding to the treatment Fixed-A and Fixed-R and the treatment Flexible-A and Flexible-R, respectively. For treatment Fixed-A and Fixed-R, the trading price was fixed and equaled the stock's unconditional expected value:

$$P = E(V) = 0 \times 50\% + 100 \times 50\% = 50 \tag{2}$$

For treatment Flexible-A and Flexible-R, the trading price was updated in a Bayesian way based on the previous order flow:

$$P_t = E(V \mid H_t) \tag{3}$$

At time t, we used n to denote the number of previous buy orders and m to denote the number of previous sell orders. A trader could observe all previous trades (the value of n and m) until time $t-1$, and we then inferred that there were n traders who must have received positive signals, while m traders must have received negative signals.

Based on Bayes' rules, we estimated the conditional probability function of the asset value as follows:

$$
\begin{aligned}
& P(V = 100 \mid n, m) \\
&= \frac{P(n, m \mid V = 100) \times P(V = 100)}{(P(n, m \mid V = 100) \times P(V = 100) + P(n, m \mid V = 0) \times P(V = 0)} \\
&= \frac{1}{1 + \rho^{m-n}(1-\rho)^{n-m}}.
\end{aligned} \tag{4}
$$

where ρ was the accuracy of signal X. Therefore, the expected value of asset was:

$$E(V \mid H_t) = P(V = 100 \mid n, m) \times 100 + P(V = 0 \mid n, m) \times 0$$
$$= 100 / (1 + \rho^{m-n} \times (1-\rho)^{n-m}) \tag{5}$$

For any trading sequence, we defined the excess demand, denoted by z at time t, as the number of buy orders (n) minus the number of sell orders (m) until time $t-1$. Therefore, the expected value of the asset was:

$$E(V \mid H_t) = 100 / (1 + \rho^{-z} \times (1-\rho)^z) \tag{6}$$

Substituting $\rho = 70\%$ into the above equation, we generated the price according to the different excess demand at time t, $P_t = E(V \mid H_t) = 100 / (1 + 3/7)^z)$. As shown in Fig. 1, at point $z = 0$, where the number of buy orders equaled that of the sell orders, the stock price equaled 50 tokens. As more subjects chose to buy, the excess demand increased, and the computer reset the price to a higher level. Conversely, as more subjects sold, the excess demand decreased, and the price became lower.

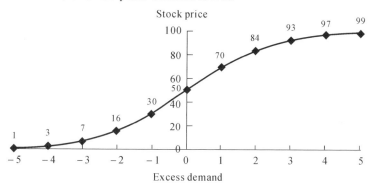

Fig. 1　Excess demand and stock price under flexible price mechanism

In the treatments with a fixed price mechanism, subjects were informed that the trading price set by the market maker was always 50 tokens. In the treatments with a flexible price mechanism, subjects knew that the market maker set the trading price according to the trading orders, such that, if more traders decided to sell (buy), the trading price would decrease (increase). They had no information about the precise relationship between excess demand and stock price, as described in Fig. 1.

2.3 Payment

Participants received a 5-token payment for showing up on time, with the remaining payment (U) based on their performance in the experiment. We endowed each trader with 100 tokens as initial investable cash (K). And one of the 10 periods was randomly chosen to determine the real payoff for the subjects. The exchange rate with real earnings is that 1 token equaled 1 Yuan.

We adopted absolute performance evaluation in treatments Fixed-A and Flexible-A, where traders were paid a fixed percentage of the stock return in each trade. We set this fixed percentage as $r=0.2$. Therefore, the traders' payoff function U was:

$$U(V,D_t,P_t) = \begin{cases} (K+V-P_t) \times r, & \text{if } D_t = \text{buy} \\ (K+P_t-V) \times r, & \text{if } D_t = \text{sell} \end{cases} \tag{7}$$

We adopted relative performance evaluation in treatments Fixed-R and Flexible-R, where the payment of traders depended on their performance rank among all six traders in the same session. We defined the benchmark as the return earned by the median trader for all six traders in one period, and ranking was according to subjects' returns in this period. If one trader's stock return was not lower than the benchmark, he/she was a winner, and got 35 tokens. Conversely, if his/her stock return was lower than the benchmark, this trader was a loser, and would only get 5 tokens. We denoted the return of trader t as :

$$R_t(V,D_t,P_t) = \begin{cases} k+v-p_t, & \text{if } D_t = \text{buy} \\ k+p_t-v, & \text{if } D_t = \text{sell} \end{cases} \tag{8}$$

The trader payoff function U was:

$$U(R_0,R_t) = \begin{cases} 35, & \text{if } R_t \geq R_0 \\ 5, & \text{if } R_t < R_0 \end{cases} \tag{9}$$

In the fund management industry, fund managers care about their performance relative to that of their peers. For example, a hedge fund typically pays its investment manager a fixed annual management fee and a performance fee. Some performance fees include a "hurdle", so that the fee is only paid on the fund's performance in excess of a benchmark rate (e. g., either the interest rate or the growth rate of the market index). A hurdle is intended to ensure that a manager is only rewarded if the fund generates returns in excess of the returns that the investor would have received if they had invested their money elsewhere.

In our relative performance treatments, the payments of fund managers also include two parts, namely a 5-token fixed payment and a performance-based bonus. The bonus is only paid if their profits exceed a certain benchmark, which is the median profit of all the subjects. This design is close to the performance fees including a "hurdle" in the real world.

3 The theoretical predictions

According to the design of our four treatments, we obtain theoretical predictions about herd behavior for each treatment. Following Cipriani and Guarino (2005), we introduce the concept of a potential information cascade, which refers to a situation in which the excess demand is at least 2, or is not higher than -2, and the subject receives a private signal against the excess demand. In our paper, we define herding as being when a trader chooses to follow the majority's choice against his/her private signal when a potential information cascade arises.

Information cascades and herding are considered significantly different in the literature (Smith & Sørensen, 2000; Çelen & Kariv, 2004). An informational cascade occurs when a sequence of individuals makes a decision without regard to their private information, whereas herding behavior occurs when a sequence of individuals follows the behavior of the majority, but not by necessarily ignoring their private information. In our study, owing to the setup of the private signal space, herding can be either rational (as in an information cascade) or irrational.

To understand better the judgment of a potential information cascade, we consider the example in Table 2.

Table 2 An example of a potential information cascade

Trader	1	2	3	4
Historical trades	Buy	Sell	Buy	Buy
Inferred ball color	●	○	●	●

Note: ● *means the color of the ball is red* ; ○ *means the color of the ball is blue.*

As per the example, at time 5, the history of trades is $H_5 = \{buy, buy, buy\}$. Suppose that trader 5 receives a signal that the color of the ball that is drawn from the cup chosen by the computer in his/her turn is blue, informing him/her that the value of the stock is 0 token. From the history of trades, trader 5 can infer that the excess demand is 2. So according to Fig. 1, the expected value of the stock by Bayes' rule is approximately 84, and even after he/she updates the Bayesian probability using his/her own private signal, the expected value of the stock is 70 tokens. If the fixed price is 50 tokens, trader 5 will never consider a private signal and buy, which leads to a cascade. Similarly, when the excess demand is either less than or equal to -2, there is also a potential opportunity to form an information cascade.

3.1 When price is fixed and there is absolute performance evaluation

In most of the earlier herding models[1], the trading price is fixed and equals the asset's unconditional expected value, i. e. , formula (2). As in the example in Table 2, to maximize the expected value of payoff, it is obvious that the trader should ignore his/her private signal and buy once the excess demand is either higher than or equal to 2, and similarly ignore his/her private signal and sell once the excess demand is either less than or equal to -2. This brings about herd behavior.

It is important to note that herd behavior is a boundedly rational decision, given the limited available information. However, once the information cascade starts, private signals are ignored and cannot be publicly reflected by trading behaviors (Shachat &. Srinivasan, 2011). The rationality of

---

[1] See Banerjee (1992), Bikhchandani et al. (1992) and Welch (1992) for theoretical models of herd behavior with fixed prices.

individuals then results in the inefficiency of public actions.

Prediction 1 (***Bikhchandani et al., 1992***): *When price is fixed and there is absolute performance evaluation, herding will occur once the absolute value of excess demand is either higher than or equal to 2.*

3.2 When price is fixed and there is relative performance evaluation

Under relative performance evaluation, the compensation of traders depends on their performance rank among all six traders. When price is fixed, according to formula (8), the stock return is either $K+V-P$ for buyers or $K+P-V$ for sellers.

As above, the return of the median trader, that is the relative performance evaluation benchmark, always equals the return of the majority. Following the majority and discarding the opposite private information, herding could then reduce deviations from the benchmark and yield a better rank, which appears to be a rational choice under limited information. As Park and Sabourian (2011) demonstrate, herd behavior can be the result of subjects' rational decisions after observing others' actions.

Prediction 2: *When price is fixed and there is relative performance evaluation, herding (i. e., following the majority and ignoring the opposing private signal) is always a rational decision.*

3.3 When price is flexible and there is absolute performance evaluation

In earlier herding studies, price remains fixed over trades, which is inconsistent with reality. Based on Avery and Zemsky(1998), we construct a flexible price mechanism, under which the trading price is updated in a Bayesian way based on the previous order flow, as per formula (3). Therefore, the trading price is the same as the expected fundamental stock value, which means there is no difference in buying or selling, depending on the historical trades.

In general, the history of trades does not give traders additional information on the asset value beyond that already contained in the asset price.

Therefore, a rational agent should act according to his/her private signal, irrespective of whether his/her decision is consistent with the majority's choice.

Prediction 3 (Avery & Zemsky, 1998; Cipriani & Guarino, 2005): When price is flexible and there is absolute performance evaluation, rational traders will trade according to their private signal.

3. 4 When price is flexible and there is relative performance evaluation

In the flexible price mechanism, the trading price is equal to the expected value of the asset in formula (3) and (6). It is obvious that, when more traders choose to buy, the excess demand increases, and the price is reset by the computer to a higher level, which means that trader t who wants to follow most people's choices has to buy the stock at a higher price. Similarly, when more subjects sell, the excess demand decreases, and the price becomes lower, which means that trader t who wants to follow most people's choices has to sell the stock at a lower price. Furthermore, the more that traders choose to herd, the higher the cost of herding, as the trading cost increases with excess demand.

When there is relative performance evaluation, if a trader expects higher yields than the performance benchmark, he/she not only needs to evaluate the real value of the stock but also needs to consider the cost of herding. If the trader chooses directly to follow the choice of the majority, even if his/her judgment on the real value of the stock is correct, the herding cost will be so high that the trader will not be rewarded, as his/her return will be below the benchmark. In this case, the rational choice is to rely on a private signal to update the Bayesian probability and combine the private signal and historical information to make decisions, rather than blindly follow the majority's choice.

Prediction 4: When price is flexible and there is relative performance evaluation, rational traders will consider both their private signal and the high herding cost to defeat the benchmark.

According to our analyses of the four theoretical predictions, we know that, in a fixed price mechanism, relative performance evaluation makes herding a rational choice, while in absolute performance evaluation, herding still depends on the size of the excess demand. As a flexible price raises the cost of herding and squeezes the net profit of follow-up imitators, we believe that the proportion of herding will be lower for a flexible price mechanism than for a fixed price mechanism. When the price is flexible and there is relative performance evaluation, traders should consider the private signal and herding cost in comparing the benchmark, so we predict that the proportion of herding will be lower than when the price is flexible and there is absolute performance evaluation.

Prediction 5: *The order of herding frequency in the four treatments should be*: *Fixed-R>Fixed-A>Flexible-A>Flexible-R.*

We now test the above five predictions using our experimental data.

4　Experimental results

4.1　Analysis of herding

We collect the experimental data from 25 sessions, comprising 1,500 trades in total. In these, there are 211 relevant periods of a potential information cascade, in which there are 127 periods of herding.

Panel 1 in Table 3 details the experimental results for our four treatments. Among the treatments, herding frequency is highest in treatment Fixed-R, which comprises a fixed price and relative performance evaluation. Here, there are 73 periods in which the excess demand is either at least 2 or at most -2, and traders receive an opposing private signal. In these periods, 82.19% of subjects decide to neglect their private information and follow what other subjects have done. The lowest herding frequency occurs in the Flexible-R treatment, which refers to a flexible price and relative performance evaluation, where only 30.95% of subjects decide to trade against their own signal. The frequency of herding for Fixed-A and Flexible-A is 64.29% and

45. 00%, respectively. Our results thus provide evidence for *prediction* 5 concerning the order of herding frequency across the four treatments.

Table 3 Information cascade and herd-like behavior

Treatment	Fixed-A	Panel 1		Flexible-R	Panel 2	
		Fixed-R	Flexible-A		Fixed	Flexible
Trading against the signal	64. 29%	82. 19%	45. 00%	30. 95%	52. 00%	12. 00%
Trading following the signal	35. 71%	17. 81%	55. 00%	69. 05%	22. 00%	46. 00%
Relevant periods	56	73	40	42	58	66

Note: Relevant periods are when the excess demand is at least 2 (at most -2) and subjects receive a negative (positive) signal. Panel 1 consists of the results of our experiment, and Panel 2 reproduces the results of Cipriani and Guarino (2005) whose subjects had a third option not to trade evaluated by absolute performance.

To compare the proportion of herding under the fixed price mechanism (Fixed-A and Fixed-R treatments) with the flexible price mechanism (Flexible-A and Flexible-R treatments), we perform a Mann-Whitney test, and the null is rejected at the 1. 00% significance level. This shows that herding frequency significantly decreases when price is flexible. The results are also in line with the results of Cipriani and Guarino (2005), as shown in Panel 2 in Table 3, which reveals that, with the price updating mechanism, subjects regard their private information and herd less frequently than when the price is held constant.

When prices are fixed, our results show that the proportion of herding under relative evaluation (Fixed-R treatment, 82. 19%) is significantly higher than that is under absolute evaluation (Fixed-A treatment, 64. 29%), which is in line with *predictions* 1 and 2 indicating that relative evaluation leads to more significant herding (Mann-Whitney test, $p = 0.0214$). When prices are flexible, the proportions of herding under absolute evaluation are insignificantly higher than that is under relative evaluation (Flexible-R treatment, 30. 95%; Flexible-A treatment, : 45. 00%; Mann-Whitney test, $p = 0.1925$).

Fig. 2 and Fig. 3 depict the average proportions of herding in each period by treatment. In later periods, the herding percentages of treatments Fixed-A and Fixed-R remain stable at a higher level, and the herding percentage of Fixed-R is always significantly higher than that of Fixed-A. The herding percentage of treatment Flexible-A exhibits relative volatility in early periods, which decreases gradually in later periods. In contrast, the herding percentage of Flexible-R remains lower than that of Flexible-A in most periods. These results are consistent with *prediction* 5 and demonstrate the effect of social learning, such that subjects learn through the observation of rewards, adjusting their strategies and converging to the rational choices.

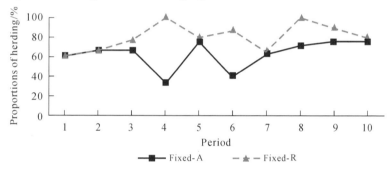

Fig. 2   Proportion of herding in different periods for treatments Fixed-A and Fixed-R

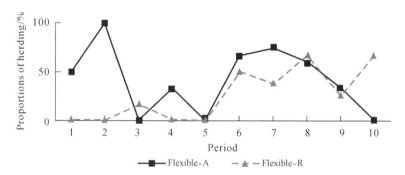

Fig. 3   Proportion of herding in different periods for treatments Flexible-A and Flexible-R

We also find that relative evaluation induces "anti-herd behavior" under a flexible price mechanism, i. e. , subjects trade against both the market history and their private signals to buy at a low price or sell at a high price, a strategy that may yield a higher return. This is also a kind of irrational behavior, hindering the market from aggregating private information correctly. This behavior is in line with some related findings that losing sports teams are more likely to take more risky decisions and that financial analysts who are interim losers in competition are more likely to increase the boldness of their forecasts (Yin & Zhang, 2013).

4.2 Analysis of rational behavior

There is an important assumption applied in deducing our models, which is that subjects are rational traders, making full use of any available information and acting in a Bayesian way. During our experiments, a rational subject would join the majority (herd) under a fixed price, and follow his/her own signal (not herd) under a flexible price when potential information cascades existed. However, subjects are not always as rational as we expect. Those findings are in line with previous studies in the literature that reveal that deviations from rationality always exist in decisions of subjects (Weizsäcker, 2010; Bao et al., 2017).

Table 4 shows that relative performance evaluation makes subjects more rational in both the fixed- and flexible-price treatments. Using the Mann-Whitney test, the proportions of rational decisions under a fixed price and a flexible price under relative performance evaluation are both significantly higher than under absolute performance evaluation ($p = 0.0214$ and $p = 0.0287$). Nevertheless, irrational decisions still exist in each treatment, given the bounded rationality of subjects.

Table 4　Proportions of rational and irrational decisions for the different treatments

Treatment	Fixed-A	Fixed-R	Flexible-A	Flexible-R
Rational decisions	64.29%	82.19%	45.00%	69.05%
Irrational decisions	35.71%	17.81%	55.00%	30.95%

We also investigated how the rational decisions are distributed among the subjects. ① Overall, 21.42% percent of subjects who never make rational

---

①　The figures for the distribution of rational decisions among subjects can be found in *Appendix II*.

decisions are highly irrational, and 29. 76% percent of subjects who always make rational decisions are highly rational. The proportion of highly rational subjects under relative performance evaluation is higher than that is under absolute performance evaluation (17. 86% vs. 11. 90%), which is consistent with the results of Table 4.

4. 3　Correlation between herding and the excess demand

An excess demand is the number of buy orders (n) minus the number of sell orders (m) until time t-1, which reflects the judgments made by predecessors. Fig. 4 illustrates the relationship between herding frequency and the excess demand. It reveals that the frequency of herding increases with the absolute value of the excess demand, which is consistent with our theoretical predictions. However, it is obvious that the relationship between the frequency of herding and the excess demand in the fixed and flexible price treatments differs, as Fig. 4 depicts. The proportion of herding in the fixed price mechanism is always at a high level, while in the flexible price mechanism, the proportion of herding is low when the absolute value of the excess demand is small and becomes higher as the absolute value of excess demand increases. This implies that, under the fixed price mechanism, most subjects herd once the absolute value of the excess demand is at least 2, which is consistent with *predictions* 1 and 2. However, under the flexible price mechanism, additional factors, such as the cost of herding and private signals other than the excess demand, will influence the herding behavior of subjects, as per the analyses of *predictions* 3 and 4.

4. 4　Empirical analysis

We employ two logit models to examine the effect of incentives on herd behavior under the fixed and flexible price mechanisms. The dependent variable is *herd*, which is a dummy variable, and which equals one if herding occurs when there is a potential information cascade, and otherwise zero. We set a dummy variable *Relative-Evaluation*, to equal one for relative performance evaluation and otherwise zero; and a *Risk-Attitude*, to represent

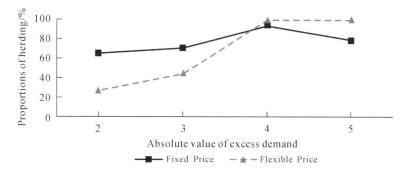

Fig. 4   Proportion of herding for different absolute values of excess demand

the absolute value of the excess demand and subjects' risk attitude, as measured by the numbers of safe options chosen in the lottery choice test. We also include *period* as a variable to control for any possible learning effect.

To compare the effect of evaluation methods under different price mechanisms, we run the same regression separately for two fixed price treatments (Fixed-A treatment and Fixed-R treatment) and two flexible price treatments (Flexible-A treatment and Flexible-R treatment). Table 5 provides the results of the logit models.

Table 5   Regression results for herd behavior

	Fixed price (Treatments Fixed-A and Fixed-R)	Flexible price (Treatments Flexible-A and Flexible-R)
Relative-Evaluation	0. 95 * * (2. 24)	−1. 14 * * (−1. 97)
$\|z\|$	0. 36 (1. 74)	1. 55 * * * (3. 23)
Risk-Attitude	−0. 10 (−0. 79)	0. 15 (1. 07)
Period	0. 09 (1. 24)	0. 09 (0. 90)
C(intercept)	−0. 52 (−0. 51)	−4. 94 * * * (−3. 26)
Pseudo R^2	0. 0761	0. 1944
P-value	0. 0247	0. 0003
Observation	129	82

Notes: Significance level: * * * 1 percent; * * 5 percent; * 10 percent; *t* values in parentheses.

According to the regression results, *Relative-Evaluation* in the fixed price treatments is significant at the 5% level and its coefficient is positive, while in the flexible price treatments, it is also significant at the 5% level, but its coefficient is negative. It is also obvious that, in fixed price treatments, relative performance evaluation significantly improves the frequency of herding, while in flexible price treatments, the effect of the relative performance evaluation reverses. This is in line with *predictions* 2 and 4. This means that when the price is fixed, herding appears to be a rational choice under limited information, as the benchmark of relative performance evaluation always equals the return of the majority, whereas under a flexible price mechanism, traders need to consider both the private signal and the cost of herding, which partly prevents herding.

The estimated coefficient of the variable $|z|$ is significant at the 1% level and positive in the flexible price treatments. That is, the larger the absolute value of the excess demand, the greater the probability of herding in a subsequent transaction. However, in the fixed price treatments, the coefficient for $|z|$ is not significant. These results are consistent with what we find in Fig. 4, namely that the relationship between $|z|$ and herding differs between the fixed and flexible price treatments. One possible explanation for this is that, when there is an information cascade in the fixed price treatments, the subjects' rational choice is herding, irrespective of the size of $|z|$. Therefore, it is reasonable that the coefficient for $|z|$ is not significant in the regression. While prices can float up and down based on the previous trading decisions in flexible price treatments, and even though traders' judgment based on historical trades may be correct, their herding costs have increased following the majority's choice. So, to obtain a higher payoff with greater certainty, subjects in the flexible price treatments may focus more on the value of $|z|$ than those in the fixed price treatment, which results in a statistically significant estimated coefficient.

The coefficient of *Risk-Attitude* is not significant in either model, which implies that the subjects' risk attitudes have no influence on their probability of herding. A possible reason for this is that, the price mechanism in our experimental design is simple but intuitive. There is a clear heuristic solution in the fixed-price treatments, where as long as the absolute value of the excess demand is no less than 2, subjects can clearly judge that it is better to follow the majority's behavior. And, in the flexible-price treatments, rational subjects prefer to trade according to their own signal. Therefore, there may be no direct link between herd behavior and subject risk attitude. [1]

According to the above analysis, we find highly consistent evidence in support of our predictions. Though not every subject in the Fixed-A treatment herds once the absolute value of the excess demand is at least 2, most subjects' behavior is consistent with *Prediction* 1. *Prediction* 2 also works because 82. 19% of subjects decide to herd when the price is fixed, and there is relative performance evaluation. More than half of the subjects trade following their private signal in treatment Flexible-A, which is consistent with *Prediction* 3. In the flexible price treatments, compared with the absolute performance evaluation, the frequency of herding is significantly reduced under relative performance evaluation due to the increasing trading costs, which is in line with *prediction* 4. *Finally, prediction* 5, which concerns the order of herding frequency across the four treatments, is definitely true according to the experimental data in Table 3.

5   Conclusions

In this paper, we examine whether the incentives under two different price mechanisms affect traders' herd behavior. We design four treatments with relative/absolute performance evaluation under flexible/fixed price mechanisms. Following the basic models in Avery and Zemsky (1998), Bikhchandni et al. , and Cipriani and Guarino (2005), we propose several

---

[1]   We have also tested the relationship between *risk attitude* and herding frequency at the individual level. Subjects are clarified as risk averse if the number of safe choices is more than four, non-averse (risk neutral and risk seeking) if the number of safe choices either equals or is less than four. We ran a Mann-Whitney test and the result showed that there was no significant difference in herding frequency between the two groups with different level of risk attitude ($z=0.053$, $p=0.9575$).

predictions about herd behavior, given these four alternative treatments. The experimental results strongly support our predictions about herd behavior, as derived from the theoretic models.

Overall, our experimental results reveal that relative performance evaluation outperforms absolute performance evaluation in encouraging the rational behavior of fund managers. Relative evaluation significantly improves the probability of herding when trading prices remain fixed, which is, in line with previous theoretical research (Eichberger et al., 1999). However, a relative performance mechanism in flexible price can effectively suppress the generation of herd behavior. According to the analysis of rational behavior, relative performance evaluation brings higher proportions of rational decisions than does absolute performance evaluation. In addition, there are individual differences of rationality among subjects. More subjects behave rationally under relative performance evaluation than under absolute performance evaluation.

Our paper sheds light on the effect of payment schemes on fund managers' trading behavior and could provide some evidence for incentive structure design of fund companies. Relative performance evaluation is a common method used in the fund industry, where fund managers' performance would be compared with other similar funds managed within the institution (for purposes of monitoring internal controls), with performance data for peer group funds, and with relevant indices. However, there are heated debates over whether the relative performance should be given weight in the compensation schemes for fund managers, as their concerns about relative performance would affects the risk-taking behavior and asset allocation. Our results support the idea that a payment scheme with relative performance evaluation could play a positive role in increasing the rational decisions of fund managers. Besides, from our experimental setting, we can infer that the relative evaluation method could encourage fund managers to devote more effort to searching and analyzing information to gain an excess return beyond the benchmark, for private signals are not exogenous but are collected and analyzed by fund managers themselves in real markets. Fund managers can then improve the accuracy of these signals with diligence and effort to beat the benchmark.

Appendix A

Instruction

In this experiment, you will act as a fund manager to trade in the stock market. The show-up fee is 5 tokens. Your payoff will depend on your decisions in the experiment. Please be careful and make good decisions. The payoff will be paid to you privately in cash at the end of the experiment. Please note that the exchange rate is as follows: 1 token＝1 Yuan.

The experiment will consist of 10 trading periods following 3 practice periods in which you can become familiar with the trading rules. The payoff is only calculated in the formal 10 periods.

The trading market in each session consists of six participants acting as traders and a computer acting as the market maker. At the beginning of each period, 100 tokens of cash are given to you. In each period, we will assign each of you an order which is randomly determined by the computer, and then all of you will be asked to make a trading decision in order. Your trading decision is a binary choice: to buy a unit of stock from the market maker or to sell a unit of stock to the market maker. The real value of the stock is equally likely to be either 0 or 100 tokens.

Before making your decision, you can see the trading decisions of previous traders in your session. The trading price of the stock will be displayed on the computer screen. You also receive a private signal regarding the real value of the stock. However, the accuracy of this signal is only 70%.

To elaborate, imagine that there are two identical cups, a red cup containing 70 red balls and 30 blue balls and a blue cup containing 30 red balls and 70 blue balls. Before each trading period, the computer will randomly choose one cup from these two identical cups with the same probability of 50%. If the red cup containing 70 red and 30 blue balls is selected, the real value of the stock is 100. If the blue cup containing 30 red and 70 blue balls is selected, the real value of the stock is 0. Without knowing the real color of selected cup, you draw a ball from the selected cup with replacement in order and then decide whether to buy or sell the stock.

At the end of each period, after all six participants have traded once, the real value of the stock is revealed and your stock return in this period will display on the computer screen. If you choose to buy the stock, your return is 100 tokens plus the real value of the stock and subtract the trading price of the stock; if you choose to sell the stock, your return is 100 tokens plus the trading price of the stock and subtract the real value of the stock.

The above trading task will repeat for 10 periods. In each period, your trading order, your private signal, and the real value of the stock will be determined randomly. In other words, all the periods are independent to each other.

The trading price of the stock and the payoff calculation method are described as follows.

(1) For fixed price and absolute performance treatment

The trading price of the stock is constantly 50 tokens for all the traders in all the periods.

After the tenth period, only one period is randomly chosen out of the total 10 trading periods, and you are paid a fixed percentage of the return in the selected period. We set this fixed percentage at $r = 0.2$. For example, in the selected period, if you decide to sell the stock and the real value of the stock is 100 tokens, your stock return is 50 tokens ($100 + 50 - 100 = 50$), and your final payoff is 10 tokens ($50 \times 0.2 = 10$).

(2) For fixed price and relative performance treatment

The trading price of the stock is constantly 50 tokens for all the traders in all the periods.

After the tenth period, only one period is randomly chosen out of the total 10 periods, and your payment depends on your performance ranking. The ranking is computed according to your stock returns in the selected period. We define a benchmark as the stock return earned by the median trader of all six traders. For example, in the selected period, if you decide to sell the stock and the real value of the stock is 100 tokens, your stock return is 50 tokens (100+50−100=50). If your stock return (50 tokens) is not lower than the benchmark, your final payoff will be 35 tokens. Conversely, if your return (50 tokens) is lower than the benchmark, you may only receive 5 tokens.

(3) For flexible price and absolute performance treatment

The trading price of the stock is updated based on the previous order flow. When the number of buying orders equals that of selling orders, the price of the stock equals 50 tokens. As more subjects choose to buy, the price is reset by the computer to a higher level. As more subjects sell, the price becomes adversely lower.

After the tenth period, only one period is randomly chosen out of the total 10 periods, and you are paid a fixed percentage of the return in the selected period. We set this fixed percentage at $r=0.2$. For example, in the selected period, if you decide to sell the stock at the current trading price which is 70, and the real value of the stock is 100 tokens, your stock return is 70 tokens (100+70−100=70), and your final payoff is 14 tokens (70×0.2=14).

(4) For flexible price and relative performance treatment

The trading price of the stock is updated based on the previous order flow. When the number of buying orders equals that of selling orders, the price of the stock equals 50 tokens. As more subjects choose to buy, the price is reset by the computer to a higher level. As more subjects sell, the price becomes adversely lower.

After the tenth period, only one period is randomly chosen out of the total 10 periods, and your payment depends on your performance ranking. The ranking is computed according to your stock returns in the selected period. We define a benchmark as the stock return earned by the median trader of all six traders. For example, in the selected period, if you decide to sell the stock at the current trading price which is 70 and the real value of the stock is 100 tokens, your stock return is 70 tokens (100+70−100=70). If your stock return (70 tokens) is not lower than the benchmark, your final payoff will be 35 tokens. Conversely, if your return (70 tokens) is lower than the benchmark, you may only receive 5 tokens.

After the above 10-period trading task，there is a lottery task that you should complete. You will see a table with 10 decisions in 10 separate rows，and each row contains a pair of choices between Option A and Option B. Choose Option A or Option B，for each of the 10 rows. One of the rows is then selected at random，and the Option (A or B) that you choose in that row will be used to determine your earnings. You will not know in advance which one will be selected，so please think about each one carefully. After one of the decisions has been randomly selected，the computer will generate another random number that corresponds to the throw of a 10-sided die. The number is equally likely to be 1，2，3，…，10. This random number determines your earnings for the Option (A or B) that you previously selected for the decision being used.

Table 6 The lottery task

Decision	Option A	Option B	My choice (circle A or B)	
1	10% chance of 2.0, 90% chance of 1.6	10% chance of 3.85, 90% chance of 0.10	A	B
2	20% chance of 2.0, 80% chance of 1.6	20% chance of 3.85, 80% chance of 0.10	A	B
3	30% chance of 2.0, 70% chance of 1.6	30% chance of 3.85, 70% chance of 0.10	A	B
4	40% chance of 2.0, 60% chance of 1.6	40% chance of 3.85, 60% chance of 0.10	A	B
5	50% chance of 2.0, 50% chance of 1.6	50% chance of 3.85, 50% chance of 0.10	A	B
6	60% chance of 2.0, 40% chance of 1.6	60% chance of 3.85, 40% chance of 0.10	A	B
7	70% chance of 2.0, 30% chance of 1.6	70% chance of 3.85, 30% chance of 0.10	A	B
8	80% chance of 2.0, 20% chance of 1.6	80% chance of 3.85, 20% chance of 0.10	A	B
9	90% chance of 2.0, 10% chance of 1.6	90% chance of 3.85, 10% chance of 0.10	A	B
10	100% chance of 2.0, 0% chance of 1.6	100% chance of 3.85, 0% chance of 0.10	A	B

For example, the computer randomly selects the row shown above. If you choose Option A in the row, you will have a 1 in 10 chance of earning 2.00 tokens and a 9 in 10 chance of earning 1.60 tokens. Similarly, Option B offers a 1 in 10 chance of earning 3.85 tokens and a 9 in 10 chance of earning 0.10 tokens.

At the end of the experiment, your payoffs in trading task and lottery task will display on your computer screen. You will be paid in cash.

Appendix Ⅱ

Appendix Fig. 1. The distribution of rational decisions among subjects

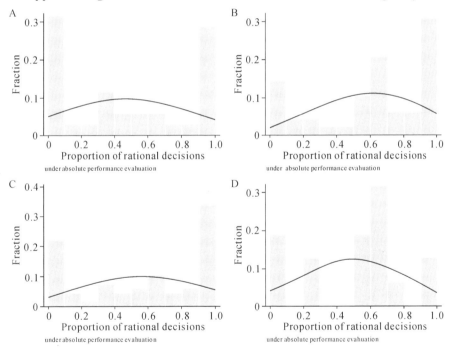

Notes: This is a set of four histograms showing the fraction distribution of the proportion of rational decisions among subjects under two different performance evaluation mechanisms and two alternative pricing mechanisms: (a) Under absolute performance evaluation; (b) Under relative performance evaluation; (c) Under fixed price mechanism; (d) Under flexible price mechanism.

References

Anderson L R,Holt C A, 1997. Information cascades in the laboratory[J]. American Economic Review, 87(5): 847-862.

Avery C, Zemsky P, 1998. Multidimensional uncertainty and herd behavior in financial markets[J]. American Economic Review, 88(4): 724-748.

Banerjee A V, 1992. A simple model of herd behavior[J]. The Quarterly Journal of Economics, 107(3):797-817.

Berlemann M, VoPel H, 2012. Tournament incentives and asset price bubbles: Evidence from a field experiment[J]. Economics Letters, 115(2): 232-235.

Bikhchandani S, Welch H I, 1992. A theory of fads, fashion, custom, and cultural change as informational cascades[J]. Journal of Political Economy, 100(5):992-1026.

Chevalier J A, Ellison G, 1996. Risk taking by mutual funds as a response to incentives[J]. Journal of Political Economy, 105(6): 1167-1200.

Cipriani M, Guarino A, 2005. Herd behavior in a laboratory financial market [J]. American Economic Review, 95(5): 1427-1443.

Elen B, Kariv S, 2004. Distinguishing informational cascades from herd behavior in the laboratory[J]. American Economic Review, 94(3): 484-498.

Eichberger J, Grant S, King S P, 1999. On relative performance contracts and fund manager's incentives[J]. European Economic Review, 43(1):135-161.

Fischbacher U, 2007. Z-tree: Zurich toolbox for ready-made economic experiments[J]. Experimental Economics, 10(2):171-178.

Gumbel A, 2005. Herding in delegated portfolio management: When is comparative performance information desirable? [J]. European Economic Review, 49(3): 599-626.

Holmen M, Kirchler M, Kleinlercher D, 2014. Do option-like incentives induce overvaluation? Evidence from experimental asset markets[J] Journal of Economic Dynamics and Control, 40: 179-194.

Holt C A, Laury S K, 2002. Risk aversion and incentive effects[J]. American

Economic Review, 92(5): 1644-1655.

Huddart S J, 1994. Reputation and performance fee effects on portfolio choice by investment advisers[J]. Journal of Financial Markets, 2(3): 227-271.

James D, Isaac R M, 2000. Asset markets: How they are affected by tournament incentives for individuals[J]. The American Economic Review, 90 (4): 995-1004.

Kleinlercher D, Huber J, Kirchler M, 2014. The impact of different incentive schemes on asset prices[J]. European Economic Review, 68:137-150.

Kremer S, Nautz D, 2013. Short-term herding of institutional traders: New evidence from the German stock market[J]. European Financial Management, 19(4):730-746.

Lakonishok J, Shleifer A, Vishny R W, 1992. The impact of institutional trading on stock prices[J]. Journal of Financial Economics, 32(1): 23-43.

Maug E, Naik N, 2011. Herding and delegated portfolio management: The impact of relative performance evaluation on asset allocation[J]. Quarterly Journal of Finance, 1(2):265-292.

Mookherjee D, 1984. Optimal incentive schemes with many agents[J]. Review of Economic Studies, 51(3): 433-446.

Palomino F, 2005. Relative performance objectives in financial markets[J]. Journal of Financial Intermediation, 14(3):351-375.

Park A, Sabourian H, 2011. Herding and contrarian behavior in financial markets[J]. Econometrica, 79(4): 973-1026.

Shachat J, Srinivasan A, 2013. Informational price cascades and non-aggregation of asymmetric information in experimental asset markets[J]. SSRN Working Papers:1813383.

Sias R W, 2004. Institutional herding[J]. The Review of Financial Studies, 17(1): 165-206.

Smith L, Sørensen P, 2000. Pathological outcomes of observational learning [J]. Economics Papers, 68(2): 371-398.

Wei K D, Brown N C, Wermers R R, 2014. Analyst recommendations, mutual fund herding, and overreaction in stock prices[J]. Management Science, 60(1): 1-20.

Weizsäcker G，2010. Do we follow others when we should? A simple test of rational expectations[J]. American Economic Review，100(5)：2340-2360.

Welch I，1992. Sequential sales, learning, and cascades[J]. The Journal of Finance，47(2)：695-732.

Wermers R，1999. Mutual fund herding and the impact on stock prices[J]. Journal of Finance，54(2)：581-622.

Yin H，Zhang H，2013. Tournaments of financial analysts[J]. Review of Accounting Studies，19(2)：573-605.

Economic Policy Uncertainty and Stock Price Crash Risk[①]

Abstract   This paper studies the impact of economic policy uncertainty on stock price crash risk using data from China. We develop a new index to measure Chinese economic policy uncertainty and find that economic policy uncertainty has a remarkable positive effect on stock price crash risk. However, the effect reverses later. The results also indicate that the positive effect of economic policy uncertainty on stock price crash risk is more prominent for state-owned enterprises. Moreover, this effect is more prominent for firms with higher information asymmetry and firms with greater disagreement among investors, indicating that economic policy uncertainty affects crash risk through two mechanisms: managers' concealment of bad news and investors' heterogeneous beliefs.

Key words   Economic policy uncertainty; Chinese stock market; Crash risk

1   Introduction

Recently, the impact of economic policy uncertainty on stock markets has attracted a great deal of attention from academics, investors and policy makers. Economic policy uncertainty refers to the uncertainty about

---

①   Originally published in *Accounting & Finance* (vol. 58, 2019) by Jin Xuejun, Chen Ziqin and Yang Xiaolan.

macroeconomic policies including fiscal, regulatory and monetary policies (Baker et al., 2016). Many studies have examined the impact of economic policy uncertainty on stock markets. Theoretical models suggest that stock prices will fall at the announcement of a policy change, and policy uncertainty commands a risk premium that increases in weaker economic conditions (Pástor & Veronesi, 2012, 2013). Empirical analyses also show that policy uncertainty makes stocks more volatile and more correlated (Pástor & Veronesi, 2013), and economic policy uncertainty commands an equity premium (Brogaard & Detzel, 2015; Li, 2017). The most recent research finds that policy risk is systematically priced in equity returns across 49 countries (Lam et al., 2018). These studies focus on the impact of economic policy uncertainty on stock prices or volatility, but few studies consider the impact of economic policy uncertainty on the distribution of returns.

This paper investigates the relationship between economic policy uncertainty and stock price crash risk. Stock price crash risk is an important characteristic of the distribution of returns, and the factors affecting stock price crash risk have been extensively studied. Many firm-level characteristics and managerial incentives have been identified, including financial reporting opacity (Jin & Myers, 2006; Hutton et al., 2009), the maintenance of reputation (Ball, 2009), corporate tax avoidance (Kim et al., 2011a), equity incentives (Kim et al., 2011b), excess management perks (Xu et al., 2014), corporate social responsibility (CSR) (Kim et al., 2014), accounting conservatism (Kim & Zhang, 2016), and investor protection (Zhang et al., 2017). In addition to these firm's internal factors, some firm's external factors have also been discussed, such as analyst coverage and analyst optimism (Xu et al., 2013), religion (Callen & Fang, 2015), social trust (Li et al., 2017) and media sentiment (Zhu et al., 2017). However, most of these studies focus on firm-level factors, whereas few studies take a macro perspective.

There are two main explanations for the causes of stock price crashes. One is that managers have incentives to withhold bad news in the case of asymmetric information, and the stock price crashes once the accumulated bad news comes out (Jin & Myers, 2006). Another is that heterogeneous investor belief could cause stock crash (Habib et al. , 2018). Investors have different beliefs and face short-sales constraints, so negative opinions cannot be expressed instantly and cause the stock price to crash when they finally come out (Hong & Stein, 2003). Economic policy uncertainty may affect stock price crash risk through these two mechanisms. First, managers are more likely to conceal bad news when economic policy uncertainty is higher, because it is harder for investors to get complete information under uncertainty. Second, investors have greater disagreement about stock prices when economic policy uncertainty is higher, and negative opinions are hidden due to short-sales constraints. Through these two mechanisms, higher economic policy uncertainty may lead to higher stock price crash risk as more negative information accumulates and breaks out suddenly.

Prior studies have examined Chinese economic policy uncertainty and its effect on the stock market. Chen et al. (2017) find a negative relation between Chinese economic policy uncertainty and future stock returns. Li (2017) finds that Chinese economic policy uncertainty commands a positive equity premium, and this can be explained by the irrational, risk-seeking behaviour of speculators. Xiong et al. (2018) indicate that changes in economic policy uncertainty have a significant impact on stock market returns in China, and the correlation has large fluctuations.

Stock markets in China and some countries in the Asia-Pacific region are less stable compared to European and American stock markets. The Chinese stock market is dominated by retail investors, and it suffers crashes frequently. Factors that may affect stock crash risk in China have been discussed, such as media sentiment (Zhu et al. , 2017) and political connections (Luo et al. , 2016; Lee & Wang, 2017). Studies regarding stock crashes in other countries in the Asia-Pacific region are also worth learning from. Aman (2013) finds that crash frequency increases with media coverage in Japan. Jang (2017) finds that stocks with a high probability of crashes have a high proportion of retail trading in Korea.

Our study explores the impact of economic policy uncertainty on stock price crash risk using data from China. Chinese data are suitable for our study for several reasons. First, as a developing country, China has explored appropriate ways to boost the economy, and the government makes frequent policy adjustments in this process. Therefore, it is meaningful to study Chinese economic policy uncertainty. Second, as an emerging market, the Chinese stock market suffers crashes more often than the stock markets in developed countries. Third, the Chinese stock market is easily influenced by policies, and it is called a "policy market" for this reason. Therefore, it is of realistic significance to investigate the impact of economic policy uncertainty on stock price crash risk in China.

Previous studies use the Chinese economic policy uncertainty (CEPU) index constructed by Baker et al. (2016) to measure Chinese economic policy uncertainty. However, this measure has some limitations. The index is based on the frequency of articles about policy-related economic uncertainty in the South China Morning Post (SCMP). The sole source may result in bias due to the newspaper's reporting preferences. Furthermore, it is not appropriate to measure Chinese economic policy uncertainty based on an English-language newspaper, with which the Chinese mainland investors are unfamiliar. Because the original CEPU index is not an ideal measure, we construct a new CEPU index based on the frequency of articles related to Chinese economic policy uncertainty published in four Chinese securities newspapers. Our new CEPU index is closely correlated with the original index, but is more suitable to measure Chinese economic policy uncertainty.

In our empirical analysis, we use the two above-mentioned indices to measure Chinese economic policy uncertainty and use the negative coefficient of skewness (NCSKEW), down-to-up volatility (DUVOL) and returns severely below the mean (CRASH) to measure crash risk (Chen et al., 2001; Hutton et al., 2009; Kim et al., 2011a, 2011b). Using a sample of all Chinese A-share listed firms from 2009 to 2017, we find that economic policy uncertainty has a remarkable positive correlation with crash risk, and the impact of economic policy uncertainty on crash risk is more prominent for state-owned enterprises (SOEs). The relationship between economic policy uncertainty and crash risk remains robust after using instrumental variables, including macroeconomic uncertainty variables or replacing the crash risk measure. We also explore the lagged effect of economic policy uncertainty on crash risk. We find that the lagged economic policy uncertainty has negative correlation with crash risk, which is probably due to investors' overreaction. These results indicate that the positive impact of economic policy uncertainty on crash risk is instant and it reverses later.

We further study the mechanisms through which economic policy uncertainty affects stock price crash risk. We find that the impact of economic policy uncertainty on crash risk is stronger for firms with higher information asymmetry and firms with greater disagreement among investors. The results indicate that economic policy uncertainty affects crash risk through two mechanisms: Managers' concealment of bad news and investors' heterogeneous beliefs. When economic policy uncertainty increases, managers of firms with higher information asymmetry will have greater incentives to conceal bad news because it will be harder for their investors to obtain information. At the same time, there will be more disagreement among investors when there is greater uncertainty and more negative opinions might be hidden. These two mechanisms result in higher stock price crash risk when economic policy uncertainty increases.

Our study contributes to the literature in several ways. First, our research links macro-level policy uncertainty with micro-level firms' crash risk, thus expanding the scope of economic policy uncertainty studies and crash risk studies. Second, we construct a new CEPU index, which differs from the CEPU index constructed by Baker et al. (2016) in the selection of articles and the source newspaper. Third, our empirical results indicate that the new CEPU index outperforms the original CEPU in explaining stock crash risk. Fourth, we examine the mechanisms through which economic policy uncertainty affects crash risk, thus providing additional evidence to explain stock price crashes.

The reminder of the paper is organised as follows. Section 2 develops the hypotheses for the empirical tests. Section 3 introduces the sample, variables and empirical methodology. Section 4 presents the empirical results. Section 5 presents the robustness tests. Section 6 concludes.

2 Hypothesis development

Theoretical models indicate that stock prices will fall when policy changes, and the price decline will be large if the policy uncertainty is large (Pástor & Veronesi, 2012). In theory, risk-averse investors demand a higher expected return for holding stocks during periods of high political uncertainty, and stock prices should drop to reflect this higher required rate of return when political uncertainty increases (Pástor & Veronesi, 2013). Empirical studies also prove that economic policy uncertainty is an important risk factor (Brogaard & Detzel, 2015), and higher economic policy uncertainty leads to significant increases in market volatility (Liu & Zhang, 2015). Chen et al. (2017) suggest that high uncertainty amplifies behavioural biases and generates speculative mis-pricing under short-sales constraint. Therefore, we propose our first hypothesis as follows:

H1: *Firms face higher stock price crash risk when economic policy uncertainty increases.*

Although previous studies have explored whether the impact of policy uncertainty on asset prices is more prominent for SOEs than non-SOEs, they have not reached a consensus. Some argue that SOEs are more sensitive to political uncertainty, as they belong to the current authority and thus are more easily affected by policy changes (Liu et al., 2017). Zhu et al. (2017) also indicate that the stock price crash risk of SOEs is more sensitive to media reports. However, others argue that it is easier for SOEs to obtain policy information than non-SOEs, so they can prepare earlier and perform better when the policy uncertainty increases. We prefer the former opinion, holding the view that SOEs' stock prices are more easily affected by economic policy uncertainty, thus proposing the following hypothesis:

H2: *The impact of economic policy uncertainty on crash risk is more prominent for SOEs.*

Previous studies explain why stock prices crash from two main perspectives. The first is managers' concealment of bad news in the case of information asymmetry. Lack of full transparency concerning firm performance enables managers to absorb losses due to temporary bad performance to protect their jobs (Jin & Myers, 2006). The negative information accumulates and suddenly comes out, leading to a stock price crash. The second is investors' heterogeneous beliefs. Previous studies propose that investors have different beliefs and negative information is not instantly revealed due to short-sales constraints. When the hidden negative information finally breaks out, it causes the stock price to crash (Hong & Stein, 2003).

Economic policy uncertainty may affect stock price crash risk through these two mechanisms. First, managers are more likely to conceal bad news when economic policy uncertainty is higher, and firms with higher information asymmetry are more prone to stock crashes because their managers are more likely to hide bad news. Therefore, we propose the following hypothesis:

H3: *The impact of economic policy uncertainty on crash risk is more prominent for firms with higher information asymmetry.*

Second, investors have greater disagreement about stock prices when economic policy uncertainty is higher, and negative opinions are hidden due to short-sales constraints. Stocks with greater disagreement among investors are more likely to crash when economic policy uncertainty is higher. Hence, we propose the following hypothesis:

H4: *The impact of economic policy uncertainty on crash risk is more prominent for firms with greater disagreement among investors.*

3 Data and methodology

3.1 Data

Because the Chinese stock market experienced a disaster in 2008, which was partially due to the global financial crisis, we investigate the impact of economic policy uncertainty on stock price crash risk after 2008. The sample includes all Chinese A-share listed firms in the 2009—2017, and we collect data from various sources. To measure Chinese economic policy uncertainty, we obtain the CEPU index constructed by Baker et al. (2016) (from http:// www. policyuncertainty. com/china_monthly), and access the China National Knowledge Infrastructure (CNKI) newspaper database to construct a new CEPU index based on the frequency of articles related to Chinese economic policy uncertainty published in the four major securities newspapers. We obtain data on stock returns, firm-level control variables, and macroeconomic variables from the China Securities Market and Accounting Research (CSMAR) database, and obtain the institutional shareholding ratio from the Wind database.

For the sample, we exclude: (i) Financial services firms, (ii) firms with fewer than 30 trading days of stock returns in a quarter, (iii) firms listed for less than a year, and (iv) firm-quarter observations with missing information. Our sample includes 72,240 firm-quarter observations from 2,670 firms. We also winsorise the continuous variables at the 1 and 99 percent levels to eliminate the effect of outliers.

3.2　Measuring economic policy uncertainty

We measure Chinese economic policy uncertainty in two ways.

3.2.1　CEPU1 index

Our first measure of Chinese economic policy uncertainty is the CEPU index constructed by Baker et al. (2016), which we call the CEPU1 index. Baker et al. (2016) developed economic policy uncertainty (EPU) indices for 12 major economies, and the EPU index for the United States is based on the frequency of articles related to economic policy uncertainty in 10 leading US newspapers. The Chinese index (CEPU1) is widely used in studies related to Chinese economic policy uncertainty (Wang et al., 2014; Chen et al., 2017; Li, 2017).

The CEPU1 index is constructed by a scaled frequency count of articles about policy-related economic uncertainty in the SCMP. First, SCMP articles about economic uncertainty pertaining to China are identified by flagging all articles that contain at least one term from the set of terms related to economic uncertainty in China: {China, Chinese}, {economy, economic} and {uncertain, uncertainty}. Second, a subset of articles that also discuss policy matters is identified. For this purpose, an article must satisfy the following text filter: {policy OR spending OR budget OR political OR interest rates OR reform} and {government OR Beijing OR authorities} OR tax OR regulation OR regulatory OR central bank OR People's Bank of China OR PBOC OR deficit OR WTO. Third, these requirements are applied in an automated search of every SCMP article published since 1995, which yields a monthly frequency count of SCMP articles about policy-related economic uncertainty. Fourth, the monthly frequency count is divided by the number of all SCMP articles in the same month, and the resulting series is normalised to a mean value of 100 from January 1995 to December 2011. We collect the CEPU1 index from http://www.policyuncertainty.com/china_monthly.

3.2.2 CEPU2 index

Although the CEPU1 index is widely used, the source newspaper of this index is just one English-language newspaper, the SCMP, which most investors in Chinese mainland A-share markets never read. Given the limitations of this index, we construct a new CEPU index, and name it the CEPU2 index, based on the frequency of articles related to Chinese economic policy uncertainty in four Chinese major securities newspapers: *China Securities Journal*, *Shanghai Securities News*, *Securities Times and Securities Daily*. These four major securities newspapers are the most authoritative and influential securities newspapers in China. They are the first to report the securities market information and government policies and thus are important sources of market information for investors.

We identify articles related to Chinese economic policy uncertainty as follows: articles that contain {央行 (central bank) OR 证监会 (China's Securities Regulatory Commission) OR 财政 (fiscal) OR 监管 (regulation) OR 税收 (tax) OR 出口 (export) OR 进口 (import)} and {政策 (policy)} and {不确定 (uncertainty) OR 不明确 (ambiguity) OR 多变 (changeable) OR 风险 (risk)}. Economic policies include monetary, fiscal, regulatory and trade policies. Our selection of words covers these different categories. Moreover, because Chinese and English use different expressions, we select several words that express uncertainty, which is different from the method of Baker et al. (2016). After filtering these articles, we manually exclude articles not related to Chinese economic policy uncertainty.

We count the number of articles related to economic policy uncertainty published from January 2009 to December 2017. We scale the raw counts by the total number of articles in the same newspaper and month, and average them across the four securities newspapers by month. Then we normalise the series to a mean of 100 from January 2009 to December 2017. To compare the two CEPU indices, we adjust the CEPU1 index to a mean of 100 for the same period.

Fig. 1 presents the variation in Chinese economic policy uncertainty from January 2009 to December 2017 measured by CEPU1 and CEPU2. Both indices show an upward trend from 2009 to 2017. At some points, both indices reach high spots, but CEPU1 is more volatile than CEPU2, especially in the two most recent years. Considering the actual economic policy situation in China, the gap may not be as large as presented by CEPU1. We believe that the stable, increasing trend pictured by CEPU2 is closer to China's reality. Furthermore, the correlation coefficient between the two measures is 0.48, which means that the two measures are consistent to some extent. In summary, both measures can represent Chinese economic policy uncertainty, but the CEPU2 index is closer to the actual situation.

3.3 Measuring firm-specific crash risk

In our main analyses, we use two firm-specific crash risk measures: the negative coefficient of skewness ($NCSKEW$) and down-to-up volatility ($DUVOL$) (Chen et al., 2001; Hutton et al., 2009; Kim et al., 2011a, b). Because our regression is estimated by quarter rather than by year, we use daily returns not weekly returns to increase the number of observations.

First, in every quarter, we obtain the residual return from the expanded market regression model (1):

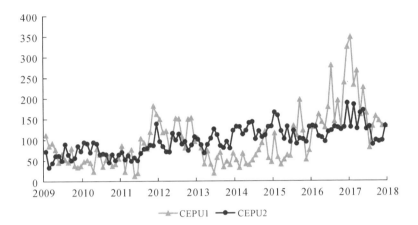

Fig. 1　Time series of *CEPU*1 and *CEPU*2. This figure displays the monthly change of Chinese economic policy uncertainty measured by *CEPU*1 and *CEPU*2 from January 2009 to December 2017.

$$R_{i,t} = \alpha_i + \beta_1 R_{m,t-2} + \beta_2 R_{m,t-1} + \beta_3 R_{m,t} + \beta_4 R_{m,t+1} + \beta_5 R_{m,t+2} + \varepsilon_{i,t} \qquad (1)$$

where $R_{i,t}$ is the return of stock i on day t, and $R_{m,t}$ is the weighted average return on the A-share circulated market value. To adjust the effect of desynchronised trading, we add the lagged terms and advanced terms to Model (1). Then we calculate the firm-specific daily returns $W_{i,t}$:

$$W_{i,t} = \ln(1 + \varepsilon_{i,t}) \qquad (2)$$

where $\varepsilon_{i,t}$ is the residual return in model (1).

The first crash risk measure, $NCSKEW_{i,T}$ is calculated by the following equation:

$$NCSKEW_{i,T} = -[n(n-1)^{3/2} \sum W_{i,t}^3] / [(n-1)(n-2)(\sum W_{i,t}^2)^{3/2}] \qquad (3)$$

where n is the number of trading days of firm i in quarter T. $NCSKEW$ represents the left skewness in the distribution of firm-specific returns: the higher the value of $NCSKEW$, the more likely a stock to crash.

The second crash risk measure, $DUVOL_{i,T}$ is calculated as follows:

$$DUVOL_{i,T} = \ln\{[(n_u - 1) \sum_{DOWN} W_{i,t}^2] / [(n_d - 1) \sum_{UP} W_{i,t}^2]\} \qquad (4)$$

We divide the trading days into 'up' days and 'down' days according to whether $W_{i,t}$ is greater than the average firm-specific daily return in quarter T. In Equation 4, n_u is the number of 'up' days, n_d is the number of 'down' days. $DUVOL_{i,T}$ is calculated as the natural logarithm of the ratio of the standard deviation of firm-specific daily returns on 'down' days to the standard deviation of firm-specific daily returns on 'up' days. Firms with higher $DUVOL$ value are more prone to crash.

We use an alternative measure of crash risk, $CRASH_{i,T}$, in our robustness tests. $CRASH_{i,T}$ equals one if a firm experiences at least one crash day during quarter T and zero otherwise. A crash day is a trading day on which the firm-specific daily return falls 3.09 or more standard deviations below the mean firm-specific daily return over quarter T (Hutton et al., 2009).

3.4 Empirical models

We investigate the effect of economic policy uncertainty on stock price crash risk by estimating the following model:

$$CrashRisk_{i,T} = \alpha + \beta \times \ln CEPU_T + \gamma \times ControlVariables_{i,T-1} + \varepsilon_{i,T} \quad (5)$$

where $CrashRisk_{i,T}$ is measured by $NCSKEW_{i,T}$ or $DUVOL_{i,T}$, and $\ln CEPU_T$ is the natural logarithm of the arithmetic average of the $CEPU$ index in the three months of a quarter (Gulen and Ion, 2016). We use $CEPU1$ and $CEPU2$ to calculate $\ln CEPU$, and we obtain $\ln CEPU1$ and $\ln CEPU2$. In Model (5), we use $\ln CEPU_T$ to test the immediate effect of economic policy uncertainty on crash risk. We also include the lagged terms of all control variables in Model (5). All variables are defined in the Appendix.

The control variables are potential factors that have been proposed in the literature to affect crash risk. We include the following variables reflecting firm characteristics: firm size ($SIZE$), which is the natural logarithm of assets, profitability (ROA), leverage (LEV) and market-to-book ratio (MB). We also include the absolute value of abnormal accruals ($ABACC$), which is a proxy for earnings management (Hutton et al., 2009; Kim et al., 2011a, b). We also add the change in turnover ($DTURN$), the standard deviation of firm-specific daily returns ($SIGMA$) and the institutional shareholding ratio ($INSHARE$) as control variables (Chen et al., 2001; Xu et al., 2013). We also control for the firm fixed effects, and quarter and year effects, and cluster standard errors at the firm level.

4 Empirical results

4.1 Summary statistics

Panel A of Table 1 reports the descriptive statistics for the variables used in our main regression models. The two crash risk measures, *NCSKEW* and *DUVOL*, are similar in distribution, but the magnitude of *NCSKEW* is larger than that of *DUVOL*. The mean value of *NCSKEW* is 0. 1087, while the mean value of *DUVOL* is 0. 0147. The standard deviation of *NCSKEW* is also larger than that of *DUVOL*. The mean values of ln*CEPU*1 and ln*CEPU*2 are similar, but the standard deviation of ln*CEPU*1 is larger than that of ln*CEPU*2.

Table 1 Summary statistics

Panel A: Descriptive statistics

Variable	N	Mean	Std. dev.	25th Pctl.	Median	75th Pctl.
NCSKEW	72240	0. 1087	0. 7575	$-0. 3304$	0. 0287	0. 5836
DUVOL	72240	0. 0147	0. 5792	$-0. 3297$	0. 0002	0. 3672
ln*CEPU*1	72240	4. 5040	0. 5516	3. 9982	4. 4314	4. 9644
ln*CEPU*2	72240	4. 6014	0. 2912	4. 4514	4. 6648	4. 8328
$SIZE_{-1}$	72240	21. 9723	1. 2776	21. 0513	21. 8031	22. 7064
ROA_{-1}	72240	0. 0274	0. 0379	0. 0054	0. 0189	0. 0430
LEV_{-1}	72240	0. 4381	0. 2216	0. 2585	0. 4344	0. 6088
MB_{-1}	72240	2. 3181	2. 0847	0. 9593	1. 7139	2. 9256
$ABACC_{-1}$	72240	0. 0746	0. 0727	0. 0239	0. 0527	0. 1001
$DTURN_{-1}$	72240	$-0. 0273$	0. 3546	$-0. 1571$	$-0. 0161$	0. 1129
$SIGMA_{-1}$	72240	0. 0286	0. 0117	0. 0205	0. 0262	0. 0340
$INSHARE_{-1}$	72240	0. 3700	0. 2290	0. 1719	0. 3676	0. 5486

continued

Panel B: Correlation matrix

		1	2	3	4	5	6	7	8	9	10	11	12
1	NCSKEW	1.00											
2	DUVOL	0.85	1.00										
3	lnCEPU1	0.09	0.17	1.00									
4	lnCEPU2	0.35	0.30	0.25	1.00								
5	$SIZE_{-1}$	−0.05	−0.12	0.01	−0.01	1.00							
6	ROA_{-1}	−0.05	−0.06	0.07	0.05	−0.01	1.00						
7	LEV_{-1}	0.00	−0.01	−0.01	0.00	0.45	−0.35	1.00					
8	MB_{-1}	0.13	0.13	0.12	0.01	−0.52	0.21	−0.41	1.00				
9	$ABACC_{-1}$	−0.01	0.00	0.02	0.01	−0.06	0.02	0.08	0.05	1.00			
10	$DTURN_{-1}$	0.02	0.03	0.04	0.06	0.04	−0.02	0.06	−0.02	−0.01	1.00		
11	$SIGMA_{-1}$	0.19	0.19	0.02	−0.07	−0.18	−0.04	−0.04	0.24	0.02	0.19	1.00	
12	$INSHARE_{-1}$	−0.03	−0.06	0.04	0.00	0.41	0.08	0.20	−0.15	−0.05	0.02	−0.12	1.00

Panel A summarises the descriptive statistics of the main variables. Panel A reports the number of observations, means, standard deviations, 25th percentiles, medians and 75th percentiles of the main study variables. Panel B reports the correlation coefficients among the main variables.

Panel B of Table 1 presents the Pearson correlation matrix for the variables used in our main analysis. The two crash risk variables, NCSKEW and DUVOL, are highly correlated, indicating that they are consistent measures of firm-specific crash risk. As for the two measures of lnCEPU, although the correlation coefficient between lnCEPU1 and lnCEPU2 is 0.25, the correlation coefficient between monthly CEPU1 and CEPU2 is 0.48. The correlation weakens because we calculate lnCEPU based on the quarterly average of CEPU and the frequency of lnCEPU is lower than that of CEPU.

Panel B of Table 1 shows that NCSKEW and DUVOL are positively associated with the two lnCEPU measures. The results consistent with H1. Furthermore, lnCEPU2 is more strongly correlated with the two crash risk measures than lnCEPU1. The firm-level variables, NCSKEW and DUVOL, are negatively correlated with SIZE, ROA and INSHARE, and positively correlated with MB, DTURN and SIGMA. These correlation coefficients indicate that firm size, profitability, market-to-book ratio, institutional shareholding ratio and turnover affect firms' crash risk. Therefore, we control these firm-level variables when we investigate the effect of economic policy uncertainty on crash risk.

4.2 Main regression results

Table 2 displays the estimates of the main regression Model (5). Columns (1) — (4) show a significant positive correlation between stock price crash risk and economic policy uncertainty. The two crash risk measures are positively and significantly correlated with lnCEPU1 in Columns (1) and (2), and with lnCEPU2 in Columns (3) and (4). These results indicate that increased economic policy uncertainty is associated with higher crash risk, which support H1.

Table 2　The impact of economic policy uncertainty on crash risk

	(1) NCSKEW	(2) DUVOL	(3) NCSKEW	(4) DUVOL
lnCEPU1	0.2108***	0.2660***		
	(35.37)	(51.16)		
lnCEPU2			1.8363***	1.1574***
			(186.06)	(127.3)
$SIZE_{-1}$	0.0317***	−0.0030	0.0065	−0.0134**
	(4.51)	(−0.5)	(0.98)	(−2.25)
ROA_{-1}	−0.4567***	−0.2835***	−0.3123***	−0.2117***
	(−6.5)	(−4.51)	(−5.28)	(−3.61)
LEV_{-1}	0.0633***	0.0756***	0.0889***	0.0934***
	(3.07)	(4.14)	(4.42)	(5.03)
MB_{-1}	0.0414***	0.0273***	0.0292***	0.0240***
	(12.75)	(11.1)	(12.37)	(10.74)
$ABACC_{-1}$	−0.0302	−0.0637**	−0.0315	−0.0592**
	(−0.81)	(−2.1)	(−0.97)	(−2.03)
$DTURN_{-1}$	0.0885***	0.0744***	0.0254***	0.0436***
	(13.88)	(15.01)	(4.27)	(9.12)
$SIGMA_{-1}$	−5.6309***	−5.5775***	−5.5528***	−6.3827***
	(−26.28)	(−31.35)	(−28.19)	(−36.63)
$INSHARE_{-1}$	−0.0881***	−0.0665***	−0.0830***	−0.0647***
	(−6.26)	(−4.94)	(−6.14)	(−4.9)
Constant	−0.3917***	0.2846**	0.8618***	0.9489***
	(−2.63)	(2.21)	(6.16)	(7.47)

continued

	(1) NCSKEW	(2) DUVOL	(3) NCSKEW	(4) DUVOL
Firm fixed effect	YES	YES	YES	YES
Time effect	YES	YES	YES	YES
Cluster by firm	YES	YES	YES	YES
N	72240	72240	72240	72240
Adj. R^2	0.3608	0.3577	0.4868	0.4305

In this table, we examine the impact of economic policy uncertainty on stock price crash risk. Columns (1) and (2) report the OLS regression estimates using lnCEPU1 as the key independent variable and NCSKEW and DUVOL as the dependent variable, respectively. Columns (3) and (4) report the OLS regression estimates using lnCEPU2 as the key independent variable and NCSKEW and DUVOL as the dependent variable, respectively. Firm fixed effects and time effects are also included. The errors are clustered at the firm level. The t-values are presented in parentheses. ** and *** indicate significance at the 5 and 1 percent levels, respectively.

Columns (1) — (4) in Table 3 also demonstrate that the two crash risk measures are positively associated with LEV, MB and DTURN, and negatively associated with ROA, SIGMA and INSHARE. These results indicate that these control variables affect crash risk, and the positive relationship between crash risk and economic policy uncertainty is still significant after controlling for these variables.

Table 3   The impact of economic policy uncertainty on crash risk for SOEs

	(1) NCSKEW	(2) DUVOL	(3) NCSKEW	(4) DUVOL
lnCEPU1	0.1762***	0.2487***		
	(21.77)	(36.53)		
lnCEPU2			1.8169***	1.1570***
			(132.26)	(97.36)
SOE×lnCEPU1	0.0794***	0.0398***		
	(8.56)	(5.01)		
SOE×lnCEPU2		0.0455***	0.0011	
		(2.57)	(0.07)	
$SIZE_{-1}$	0.0331***	−0.0023	0.0063	−0.0134**
	(4.68)	(−0.37)	(0.96)	(−2.25)

continued

	(1) NCSKEW	(2) DUVOL	(3) NCSKEW	(4) DUVOL
ROA_{-1}	−0.4549***	−0.2827***	−0.3102***	−0.2116***
	(−6.47)	(−4.49)	(−5.24)	(−3.6)
LEV_{-1}	0.0634***	0.0757***	0.0883***	0.0934***
	(3.07)	(4.14)	(4.39)	(5.03)
MB_{-1}	0.0423***	0.0277***	0.0291***	0.0240***
	(12.6)	(11)	(12.36)	(10.74)
$ABACC_{-1}$	−0.0294	−0.0633**	−0.0315	−0.0592**
	(−0.79)	(−2.09)	(−0.98)	(−2.03)
$DTURN_{-1}$	0.0886***	0.0744***	0.0256***	0.0436***
	(13.89)	(15.01)	(4.3)	(9.11)
$SIGMA_{-1}$	−5.5968***	−5.5604***	−5.5531***	−6.3827***
	(−26.08)	(−31.23)	(−28.19)	(−36.63)
$INSHARE_{-1}$	−0.0886***	−0.0668***	−0.0832***	−0.0647***
	(−6.3)	(−4.96)	(−6.16)	(−4.9)
Constant	−0.4243***	0.2683***	0.8682***	0.9490***
	(−2.82)	(2.07)	(6.21)	(7.47)
Firm fixed effect	YES	YES	YES	YES
Time effect	YES	YES	YES	YES
Cluster by firm	YES	YES	YES	YES
N	72240	72240	72240	72240
Adj. R^2	0.3610	0.3576	0.4868	0.4305

In this table, we test whether the impact of economic policy uncertainty on crash risk is more prominent for SOEs. Columns (1) and (2) report the OLS regression estimates using lnCEPU1 and the interaction term of SOE and lnCEPU1 as the key independent variables and NCSKEW and DUVOL as the dependent variable, respectively. Columns (3) and (4) report the OLS regression estimates using lnCEPU2 and the interaction term of SOE and lnCEPU2 as the key independent variables and NCSKEW and DUVOL as the dependent variable, respectively. Firm fixed effects and time effects are also included. The errors are clustered at the firm level. The *t*-values are presented in parentheses. ** and *** indicate significance at the 5 and 1 percent levels, respectively.

4.3 The effect of SOEs

Previous studies have documented that ownership type may influence stock price crash risk. In this subsection, we examine whether the ownership type affects the relationship between crash risk and economic policy uncertainty by estimating Model (6):

$$CrashRisk_{i,T} = \alpha + \beta_1 \ln CEPU_T + \beta_2 SOE_{i,T} \times \ln CEPU_T$$
$$+ \gamma Control Variables_{i,T-1} + \varepsilon_{i,T} \qquad (6)$$

where all variables are the same as those in Model (5) except for SOE. SOE is a dummy variable that equals one if the firm is an SOE, and zero otherwise. In Model (6), we include the interaction term of SOE and lnCEPU to examine whether the effect of economic policy uncertainty on crash risk differs between SOEs and non-SOEs.

In Table 3, Columns (1) and (2) show that the coefficients of $SOE \times$ lnCEPU1 are positive and significant at the 1 percent level, and Column (3) shows that the coefficient of $SOE \times$ lnCEPU2 is positive and significant when the crash risk measure is NCSKEW. Although the coefficient of the interaction term in Column (4) is not significant, it is positive. These results indicate that the impact of economic policy uncertainty on crash risk is stronger for SOEs than non-SOEs. Moreover, Columns (1) − (4) show that the positive relationship between economic policy uncertainty and crash risk remains significant after adding the interaction term. These results support H2: the impact of economic policy uncertainty on crash risk is more prominent for SOEs.

4.4 The two mechanisms

We further study the mechanisms behind the effect of economic policy uncertainty on stock price crash risk. The literature provides two main explanations for the stock price crash risk. The first is that managers hide bad news in the case of information asymmetry, and when the accumulated negative information finally comes out it leads to a stock price crash. We examine this mechanism by adding a variable reflecting the degree of firms' information asymmetry. If economic policy uncertainty affects crash risk through this mechanism, the managers of firms with higher information asymmetry are more likely to conceal bad news when economic policy uncertainty increases, because it is harder for investors to obtain information from firms with higher information asymmetry under an uncertain environment.

We use the variable *ANALYST* to measure the degree of information asymmetry, constructed as follows. First, we rank the number of analysts issuing forecasts and calculate the median number in a quarter. Then, *ANALYST* is constructed as a dummy variable that equals one if the number of analysts issuing forecasts for a firm is larger than the median number in a quarter, and zero otherwise. Analyst coverage is particularly important in terms of providing information to investors, especially in the poor information environment of the Chinese stock market (Xu et al., 2013). Therefore, it is reasonable to measure the degree of information asymmetry by the number of analysts. Firms with fewer analysts have a higher degree of information asymmetry.

We test whether the degree of information asymmetry affects the relationship between economic policy uncertainty and crash risk by estimating Model (7).

$$CrashRisk_{i,T} = \alpha + \beta_1 \ln CEPU_T + \beta_2 ANALYST_{i,T-1} \times \ln CEPU_T$$
$$+ \gamma ControlVariables_{i,T-1} + \varepsilon_{i,T} \tag{7}$$

All variables are the same as those in Model (5), except for *ANALYST*. We use the lagged *ANALYST* to measure the degree of information asymmetry. The regression results of Model (7) are reported in Table 4. Columns (1) — (4) in Table 4 show that the coefficients of *ANALYST* $\times$ ln*CEPU* are negative and significant, and the positive relationship between economic policy uncertainty and crash risk remains significant. These results indicate that the impact of economic policy uncertainty on crash risk is weaker for firms with more analysts. In other words, the impact of economic policy uncertainty on crash risk is more prominent for firms with higher information asymmetry, which supports H3.

Table 4   The impact of economic policy uncertainty on crash risk for firms with higher information asymmetry

	(1) NCSKEW	(2) DUVOL	(3) NCSKEW	(4) DUVOL
ln$CEPU1$	0.2595***	0.2589***		
	(30.19)	(36.79)		
ln$CEPU2$			2.1369***	1.2895***
			(235.81)	(116.74)
$ANALYST_{-1} \times$ ln$CEPU1$	−0.1177***	−0.0687***		
	(−8.52)	(−7)		
$ANALYST_{-1} \times$ ln$CEPU2$			−0.0423***	−0.0233*
			(−3.43)	(−1.66)
$SIZE_{-1}$	0.0731***	0.0336***	0.0377***	0.0186***
	(13.86)	(6.42)	(8)	(3.65)
ROA_{-1}	−0.5406***	−0.3271***	−0.3757***	−0.2491***
	(−7.51)	(−5.31)	(−6.65)	(−4.48)
LEV_{-1}	0.0037	0.0367**	0.0367**	0.0568***
	(0.24)	(2.34)	(2.52)	(3.6)
MB_{-1}	0.0579***	0.0408***	0.0415***	0.0357***
	(28.19)	(22.63)	(25.34)	(21.24)
$ABACC_{-1}$	−0.0490	−0.0733**	−0.0478*	−0.0685**
	(−1.48)	(−2.45)	(−1.73)	(−2.35)
$DTURN_{-1}$	0.0782***	0.0658***	−0.0055	0.0227***
	(12.66)	(13.85)	(−1.06)	(5.13)
$SIGMA_{-1}$	−7.4164***	−7.1616***	−7.8107***	−8.0576***
	(−39.15)	(−43.63)	(−47.1)	(−50.66)
$INSHARE_{-1}$	−0.0383***	−0.0236**	−0.0214**	−0.0159
	(−3.48)	(−2.29)	(−2.22)	(−1.61)
Constant	−1.1631***	−0.4282***	0.5297***	0.4372***
	(−10.4)	(−3.85)	(5.29)	(4.06)
Firm fixed effect	YES	YES	YES	YES
Time effect	YES	YES	YES	YES
Cluster by firm	YES	YES	YES	YES
N	72240	72240	72240	72240
Adj. R^2	0.3643	0.3203	0.5725	0.4436

In this table, we test whether the impact of economic policy uncertainty on crash risk is more prominent for firms with higher information asymmetry. Columns (1) and (2) show the OLS regression estimates using ln$CEPU1$ and $ANALYST \times$ ln$CEPU1$ as the key independent variables and $NCSKEW$ and $DUVOL$ as the dependent variable, respectively. Columns (3) and (4) show the estimates using lnCEPU2 and $ANALYST \times lnCEPU2$ as the key independent variables and using NCSKEW and DUVOL as the dependent variable, respectively. Firm fixed effects and time effects are also included. The errors are clustered at the firm level. The t-values are presented in parentheses. * , * * and * * * indicate significance at the 10, 5 and 1 percent levels, respectively.

The second explanation of crash risk is investors' heterogeneous beliefs. Investors have different beliefs and negative opinions are hidden due to short-sales constraints, and when the hidden negative information finally breaks out it causes a stock crash. If economic policy uncertainty affects crash risk through this mechanism, then there should be greater disagreement among investors when economic policy uncertainty increases. We therefore deduce that the impact of economic policy uncertainty on crash risk is stronger for firms with greater disagreement among investors. We examine this assertion by estimating Model (8).

$$CrashRisk_{i,T} = \alpha + \beta_1 lnCEPU_T + \beta_2 TURN_{i,T-1} \times lnCEPU_T$$
$$+ \gamma ControlVariables_{i,T-1} + \varepsilon_{i,T} \quad (8)$$

Previous studies have pointed out that trading volume contains information about investors' heterogeneous beliefs (Harris & Raviv, 1993; Scheinkman & Xiong, 2003), and turnover has been used to measure the heterogeneity of investor beliefs (Jiao & Yan, 2015). In Model (8), TURN is the average monthly turnover of a quarter, and we use lagged TURN to measure the degree of investors' disagreement. We also add the interaction term of lagged TURN and lnCEPU. The other variables are the same as those in Model (5). Table 5 reports the regression results of Model (8).

Table 5 The impact of economic policy uncertainty on crash risk for firms with greater disagreement among investors

| | (1) | (2) | (3) | (4) |
	NCSKEW	DUVOL	NCSKEW	DUVOL
lnCEPU1	0.0762 * * *	0.1672 * * *		
	(8.62)	(22.79)		
lnCEPU2			1.7832 * * *	1.1123 * * *
			(112.71)	(82.86)
$TURN_{-1} \times lnCEPU1$	0.2058 * * *	0.1510 * * *		
	(18.28)	(17.5)		

continued

	(1) NCSKEW	(2) DUVOL	(3) NCSKEW	(4) DUVOL
$TURN_{-1} \times \ln CEPU2$			0.0516**	0.0425**
			(1.96)	(2.07)
$SIZE_{-1}$	0.0263***	−0.0069	0.0064	−0.0134**
	(3.84)	(−1.15)	(0.96)	(−2.24)
ROA_{-1}	−0.4318***	−0.2641***	−0.3124***	−0.2109***
	(−6.3)	(−4.29)	(−5.28)	(−3.6)
LEV_{-1}	0.0619***	0.0741***	0.0896***	0.0934***
	(3.05)	(4.1)	(4.45)	(5.03)
MB_{-1}	0.0374***	0.0244***	0.0292***	0.0240***
	(12.77)	(10.96)	(12.36)	(10.74)
$ABACC_{-1}$	−0.0301	−0.0635**	−0.0315	−0.0591**
	(−0.82)	(−2.12)	(−0.97)	(−2.02)
$DTURN_{-1}$	0.0808***	0.0688***	0.0254***	0.0436***
	(12.78)	(13.98)	(4.27)	(9.12)
$SIGMA_{-1}$	−5.3650***	−5.3807***	−5.5578***	−6.3825***
	(−25.22)	(−30.33)	(−28.15)	(−36.58)
$INSHARE_{-1}$	−0.0847***	−0.0638***	−0.0836***	−0.0650***
	(−6.08)	(−4.77)	(−6.19)	(−4.92)
Constant	−0.2793*	0.3652***	0.8628***	0.9470***
	(−1.92)	(2.89)	(6.16)	(7.45)
Firm fixed effect	YES	YES	YES	YES
Time effect	YES	YES	YES	YES
Cluster by firm	YES	YES	YES	YES
N	72240	72240	72240	72240
Adj. R^2	0.3647	0.3616	0.4927	0.4432

In this table, we test whether the impact of economic policy uncertainty on crash risk is more prominent for firms with greater disagreement among investors. Columns (1) and (2) report the OLS regression estimates using lnCEPU1 and $TURN \times$ lnCEPU1 as the key independent variables and NCSKEW and DUVOL as the dependent variable, respectively. Columns (3) and (4) report the OLS regression estimates using lnCEPU2 and $TURN \times$ lnCEPU2 as the key independent variables and NCSKEW and DUVOL as the dependent variable, respectively. Firm fixed effects and time effects are also included. The errors are clustered at the firm level. The t-values are presented in parentheses. *, ** and *** indicate significance at the 10, 5 and 1 percent levels, respectively.

Columns (1) − (4) in Table 5 show that the coefficients of $TURN \times$ $\ln CEPU$ are positive and significant, and the positive relationship between economic policy uncertainty and crash risk remains significant. These results indicate that the impact of economic policy uncertainty on crash risk is more prominent for firms with greater disagreement among investors, thus supporting H4.

5 Robustness tests

5.1 Instrumental variable analysis

Economic policy uncertainty and stock price crash risk may be endogenously determined. To address the potential endogeneity problem, we use US economic policy uncertainty lagged by two periods as an instrumental variable for Chinese economic policy uncertainty (Wang et al., 2014). US economic policy uncertainty is closely related to Chinese economic policy uncertainty. Chinese interest rates and exchange rates are quickly affected by changes in US monetary policy. Moreover, US economic policy uncertainty is a suitable instrumental variable because it only affects Chinese firms' crash risk through Chinese economic policy uncertainty.

We estimate Model (5) using the instrumental variable with the 2SLS method. Table 6 presents the results from the instrumental variable method and the results are very similar to those in Table 2. Columns (1) and (4) show the first stage regression results using $\ln CEPU1$ and $\ln CEPU2$ as the dependent variable, respectively. We can see that both $\ln CEPU1$ and $\ln CEPU2$ are significantly correlated with the instrumental variable, and the first stage F-statistics are significant at the 1 percent level. These results indicate that the instrumental variable is appropriate. Columns(2),(3),(5) and(6) show that economic policy uncertainty still has a positive and significant correlation with crash risk when using the instrumental variable. This lends further support to H1.

Table 6   Instrumental variable analysis

	(1) lnCEPU1 1st	(2) NCSKEW 2nd	(3) DUVOL 2nd	(4) lnCEPU2 1st	(5) NCSKEW 2nd	(6) DUVOL 2nd
lnCEPU1		0.4504***	0.3049***			
		(37.68)	(23.01)			
lnCEPU2					3.1496***	2.1324***
					(42.2)	(23.47)
lnUSEPU$_{-2}$	−0.5234***			−0.0748***		
	(−214.17)			(−41.03)		
SIZE$_{-1}$	0.0337***	0.0218***	−0.0046	0.0174***	−0.0178***	−0.0314***
	(10.18)	(3.25)	(−0.77)	(14.43)	(−2.71)	(−5.24)
ROA$_{-1}$	−0.0550*	−0.4222***	−0.2779***	−0.0824***	−0.1873***	−0.1189**
	(−1.84)	(−6.2)	(−4.45)	(−5.46)	(−3.26)	(−2.09)
LEV$_{-1}$	−0.0002	0.0602***	0.0751***	−0.0143***	0.1053***	0.1056***
	(−0.02)	(3.01)	(4.13)	(−4.66)	(5.21)	(5.67)
MB$_{-1}$	0.0268***	0.0335***	0.0260***	0.0096***	0.0154***	0.0138***
	(8.83)	(12.76)	(10.84)	(9.68)	(7.29)	(7.29)
ABACC$_{-1}$	0.0373***	−0.0398	−0.0653**	0.0049	−0.0385	−0.0644**
	(2.74)	(−1.08)	(−2.16)	(0.64)	(−1.2)	(−2.16)
DTURN$_{-1}$	0.0915***	0.0723***	0.0717***	0.0456***	−0.0299***	0.0025
	(24.85)	(11.61)	(14.48)	(24.69)	(−4.35)	(0.41)
SIGMA$_{-1}$	−7.1167***	−4.0931***	−5.3275***	−0.8791***	−4.5293***	−5.6229***
	(−69.95)	(−18.93)	(−27.46)	(−19.19)	(−21.23)	(−28.69)
INSHARE$_{-1}$	−0.0058	−0.0856***	−0.0661***	−0.0033	−0.0778***	−0.0609***
	(−1.05)	(−6)	(−4.9)	(−1.33)	(−5.53)	(−4.48)
Constant	1.8670***	−0.1652	0.3215**	−0.3890***	1.9008***	1.7202***
	(23.47)	(−1.16)	(2.5)	(−12.88)	(12.95)	(12.16)
Firm fixed effect	YES	YES	YES	YES	YES	YES
Time effect	YES	YES	YES	YES	YES	YES
Cluster by firm	YES	YES	YES	YES	YES	YES
N	72240	72240	72240	72240	72240	72240
1st stage F test	3222.70			4005.35		
p-value	0.00			0.00		
Adj. R^2		0.3560	0.3581		0.4567	0.4015

This table presents the results from estimating Model (5) using the 2SLS method. Columns (1) and (4) use the two-period lagged *lnUSEPU* as the instrument in the first stage of the 2SLS, and lnCEPU1 and lnCEPU2, respectively. Columns (2) and (3) present the second stage of the 2SLS, testing the impact of lnCEPU1 on *NCSKEW* and *DUVOL*, respectively. Columns (5) and (6) present the second stage of the 2SLS, testing the impact of lnCEPU2 on *NCSKEW* and *DUVOL*, respectively. Firm fixed effects and time effects are also included. The errors are clustered at the firm level. The first stage F-statistics and p-value are presented. The t-values are in parentheses. *, ** and *** indicate significance at the 10, 5 and 1 percent levels, respectively.

5.2 Controlling for economic uncertainty

A potential concern with our results is that the two *CEPU* indices may capture the effect of general economic uncertainty and not just the effect of policy-related uncertainty. To address this concern, we control for several macroeconomic measures of uncertainty: *GDP growth*, *CPI growth*, and the *Consumer Confidence* Index. The growth in GDP reflects the speed of economic development and the growth in the CPI reflects the change in price level. The *Consumer Confidence* Index reflects consumers' sentiment and expectations of future economic life, and this index is often used to predict economic trends. These three variables measure macroeconomic uncertainty from different angles, so we include them all in our regression model.

Table 7 presents the regression results of Model (5) after adding three economic uncertainty variables. These results are similar to those in Table 3, and the relationship between economic policy uncertainty and crash risk remains positive and significant. Table 7 also shows that *GDP growth* and the *Consumer Confidence* Index are positively correlated and *CPI growth* is negatively correlated with crash risk. These results indicate that economic uncertainty also affects crash risk.

Table 7 Controlling for economic uncertainty

	(1) NCSKEW	(2) DUVOL	(3) NCSKEW	(4) DUVOL
lnCEPU1	0.2416***	0.2957***		
	(36.25)	(51.51)		
lnCEPU2			2.0160***	1.2899***
			(164.3)	(114.24)
SIZE $_{-1}$	0.0292***	−0.0043	0.0057	−0.0147**
	(4.27)	(−0.72)	(0.89)	(−2.54)
ROA $_{-1}$	−0.3816***	−0.2388***	−0.1591***	−0.1186**
	(−5.84)	(−4)	(−3.06)	(−2.2)
LEV $_{-1}$	0.0494**	0.0670***	0.0634***	0.0794***
	(2.52)	(3.83)	(3.46)	(4.59)
MB $_{-1}$	0.0365***	0.0245***	0.0235***	0.0204***
	(13.28)	(11.19)	(11.74)	(10.5)

continued

	(1) NCSKEW	(2) DUVOL	(3) NCSKEW	(4) DUVOL
$ABACC_{-1}$	−0.0107	−0.0522*	0.0067	−0.0393
	(−0.29)	(−1.76)	(0.22)	(−1.4)
$DTURN_{-1}$	0.0265***	0.0453***	−0.0030	0.0366***
	(4.37)	(9.18)	(−0.52)	(7.7)
$SIGMA_{-1}$	0.8059***	−2.2647***	0.4897**	−3.5457***
	(3.71)	(−12.16)	(2.51)	(−19.85)
$INSHARE_{-1}$	−0.0763***	−0.0592***	−0.0650***	−0.0568***
	(−5.17)	(−4.25)	(−4.66)	(−4.24)
$GDP\ growth_{-1}$	3.6780***	2.3980***	14.9258***	10.6059***
	(17.02)	(7.9)	(72.93)	(34.41)
$CPI\ growth_{-1}$	−10.5188***	−7.3215***	−28.3231***	−15.7606***
	(−52.25)	(−30.02)	(−141.68)	(−62.26)
$Consumer\ Confidence_{-1}$	10.5656***	5.0145***	7.2158***	2.8326***
	(113.96)	(62.73)	(80.61)	(34.68)
Constant	−11.2572***	−4.8838***	−7.2694***	−2.5629***
	(−68.21)	(−34.12)	(−45.8)	(−17.89)
Firm fixed effect	YES	YES	YES	YES
Time effect	YES	YES	YES	YES
Cluster by firm	YES	YES	YES	YES
N	72240	72240	72240	72240
Adj. R^2	0.4433	0.3930	0.5645	0.4650

This table reports the results after adding economic uncertainty variables: *GDP growth*, *CPI growth*, and *Consumer Confidence*. Columns (1) and (2) report the OLS regression estimates using lnCEPU1 as an independent variable and *NCSKEW* and *DUVOL* as the dependent variable, respectively. Columns (3) and (4) report estimates using lnCEPU2 as an independent variable and *NCSKEW* and *DUVOL* as the dependent variable, respectively. Firm fixed effects and time effects are also included. The errors are clustered at the firm level. The *t*-values are presented in parentheses. *, ** and *** indicate significance at the 10, 5 and 1 percent levels, respectively.

5.3　An alternative measure of crash risk

We use an alternative crash risk measure, $CRASH_{i,T}$, which equals one if firm i experiences at least one crash day during quarter T and zero otherwise. A crash day is a trading day on which the firm-specific daily return falls 3.09 or more standard deviations below the mean firm-specific daily return over quarter T (Hutton et al., 2009). We use a probit model and the variables are the same as those in Model (5). Columns (1) and (2) in Table 8 present the probit regression results. Column (1) shows that $lnCEPU1$ is negatively associated with $CRASH$, which is surprising because both $NCSKEW$ and $DUVOL$ have positive correlations with $lnCEPU1$. Column (2) shows that $lnCEPU2$ has a significantly positive correlation with $CRASH$. The difference between columns (1) and (2) indicates that our new index $lnCEPU2$ performs better than Baker et al.'s index $lnCEPU1$ in explaining $CRASH$.

Table 8 An alternative measure of crash risk

	(1) CRASH	(2) CRASH	(3) lnCEPU1 1st	(4) CRASH 2nd	(5) lnCEPU2 1st	(6) CRASH 2nd
lnCEPU1	−0.3633***			0.6001***		
	(−35.49)			(45.61)		
lnCEPU2		1.9719***				0.6477***
		(85.4)				(20.84)
$lnUSEPU_{-2}$			−0.5234***		−0.0748***	
			(−214.17)		(−41.03)	
$SIZE_{-1}$	0.1222***	0.1416***	0.0337***	0.0917***	0.0174***	0.1147***
	(24.66)	(25.99)	(10.18)	(19.26)	(14.43)	(23.73)
ROA_{-1}	−2.4544***	−3.5866***	−0.0550*	−3.0120***	−0.0824***	−2.7679***
	(−17.95)	(−24.48)	(−1.84)	(−21.94)	(−5.46)	(−20.2)
LEV_{-1}	−0.2885***	−0.3978***	−0.0002	−0.3538***	−0.0143***	−0.3225***
	(−11.13)	(−14.39)	(−0.02)	(−14.69)	(−4.66)	(−12.96)
MB_{-1}	0.0835***	0.0804***	0.0268***	0.0514***	0.0096***	0.0716***
	(18.06)	(18.37)	(8.83)	(13.74)	(9.68)	(17.65)
$ABACC_{-1}$	0.0583	0.0249	0.0373***	0.0025	0.0049	0.0407
	(1.29)	(0.53)	(2.74)	(0.06)	(0.64)	(0.93)
$DTURN_{-1}$	0.2054***	0.1286***	0.0915***	0.1681***	0.0456***	0.1735***
	(14.93)	(9.13)	(24.85)	(11.91)	(24.69)	(12.56)
$SIGMA_{-1}$	−0.8116**	1.8929***	−7.1167***	0.2942	−0.8791***	0.3078
	(−2.22)	(4.97)	(−69.95)	(0.84)	(−19.19)	(0.84)
$INSHARE_{-1}$	−0.0299	−0.0425*	−0.0058	−0.0712***	−0.0033	−0.0408**
	(−1.43)	(−1.84)	(−1.05)	(−3.47)	(−1.33)	(−1.96)
Constant	−3.1703***	−3.6417***	1.8670***	−2.4114***	−0.3890***	−2.9891***
	(−29.71)	(−31.37)	(23.47)	(−23.81)	(−12.88)	(−29.05)
Cluster by firm	YES	YES	YES	YES	YES	YES
N	72240	72240	72240	72240	72240	72240
1st stage F test			3222.70		4005.35	
p-value			0.00		0.00	
Pseudo R^2	0.0228	0.0688		0.0252		0.0276

This table presents the regression results using CRASH as the crash risk measure. Columns (1) and (2) report the probit regression results using lnCEPU1 and lnCEPU2 as the independent variable, respectively. Columns (3)-(6) report the regression results after adding the instrumental variable, the two-period lagged lnUSEPU. Columns (3) and (5) present the OLS regression results using the instrument as the independent variable and lnCEPU1 and lnCEPU2 as the dependent variable, respectively. Columns (4) and (6) present the probit regression results using CRASH as the dependent variable. Firm fixed effects and time effects are also included. The errors are clustered at the firm level. The first stage F-statistics and p-value are presented. The z-values are presented in parentheses. `*`,`**` and `***` indicate significance at the 10, 5 and 1 percent levels, respectively.

Given that the endogeneity problem may influence the results, we conduct an instrumental variable analysis using US economic policy uncertainty lagged by two periods, as in Section 5. The results are presented in Columns (3) - (6). Columns (3) and (5) show the OLS regression results using lnCEPU1 and lnCEPU2 as the dependent variable, respectively. Column (3) is the same as column (1) in Table 6, and column (5) is the same as column (4) in Table 6. Columns (4) and (6) in Table 8 display the probit regression results using the instrumental method. After controlling for the endogeneity problem, the relationship between economic policy uncertainty and crash risk is positive and significant. This indicates that the results are robust regardless of which crash risk measure we use.

5.4 The lagged effect

Our main regression results show that the simultaneous economic policy uncertainty has positive correlation with stock price crash risk. In order to explore more about their relationship, we study the lagged effect of economic policy uncertainty on crash risk by estimating Model (9).

$$CrashRisk_{i,T}=\alpha+\beta\times lnCEPU_{T-1}+\gamma\times ControlVariables_{i,T-1}+\varepsilon_{i,T} \qquad (9)$$

All variables are the same as those in model (5), except for $lnCEPU_{T-1}$. The regression results of Model (9) are presented in Table 9. Columns (1)- (4) in Table 9 show that both $lnCEPU1_{T-1}$ and $lnCEPU2_{T-1}$ have significantly negative correlation with the two crash risk measures, indicating that the lagged economic policy uncertainty is negatively associated with crash risk. A possible explanation for this reverse is that investors overreact to economic policy uncertainty and the overreaction is revised in the next quarter. These results imply that the impact of economic policy uncertainty on stock price crash risk is instant, and the effect reverses later in an extended period of time.

Table 9   The lagged effect

	(1) NCSKEW	(2) DUVOL	(3) NCSKEW	(4) DUVOL
$lnCEPU1_{-1}$	−0.1860***	−0.1577***		
	(−26.51)	(−25.24)		
$lnCEPU2_{-1}$			−0.9592***	−0.6557***
			(−79.99)	(−61.86)
$SIZE_{-1}$	0.0290***	−0.0019	0.0128 *	−0.0087
	(4.27)	(−0.32)	(1.90)	(−1.43)
ROA_{-1}	−0.4267***	−0.2693***	−0.3718***	−0.2522***
	(−6.40)	(−4.41)	(−6.15)	(−4.20)
LEV_{-1}	0.0545***	0.0690***	0.0777***	0.0860***
	(2.71)	(3.81)	(3.75)	(4.53)
MB_{-1}	0.0386***	0.0275***	0.0351***	0.0281***
	(13.20)	(11.34)	(13.82)	(11.43)
$ABACC_{-1}$	−0.0190	−0.0507*	0.0152	−0.0307
	(−0.52)	(−1.66)	(0.46)	(−1.03)
$DTURN_{-1}$	0.1147***	0.1028***	0.0640***	0.0689***
	(17.86)	(20.38)	(10.36)	(13.99)
$SIGMA_{-1}$	−5.7905***	−6.2455***	−10.9879***	−9.7050***
	(−27.39)	(−35.15)	(−53.16)	(−53.98)
$INSHARE_{-1}$	−0.0919***	−0.0708***	−0.0606***	−0.0514***
	(−6.54)	(−5.24)	(−3.89)	(−3.54)
Constant	1.1476***	1.5472***	2.7889***	2.0985***
	(7.63)	(11.54)	(17.89)	(14.91)
Firm fixed effect	YES	YES	YES	YES
Time effect	YES	YES	YES	YES
Cluster by firm	YES	YES	YES	YES
N	72240	72240	72240	72240
Adj. R^2	0.3679	0.3571	0.4510	0.3987

In this table, we examine the impact of lagged economic policy uncertainty on stock price crash risk. Columns (1) and (2) report the OLS regression estimates using $lnCEPU1_{T-1}$ as the key independent variable and *NCSKEW* and *DUVOL* as the dependent variable, respectively. Columns (3) and (4) report the OLS regression estimates using $lnCEPU2_{T-1}$ as the key independent variable and *NCSKEW* and *DUVOL* as the dependent variable, respectively. Firm fixed effects and time effects are also included. The errors are clustered at the firm level. The *t*-values are presented in parentheses. * and *** indicate significance at the 10 and 1 percent levels, respectively.

6 Conclusions

This paper investigates the impact of economic policy uncertainty on stock price crash risk using Chinese data. The measurement of Chinese economic policy uncertainty is the key to this study. Although the *CEPU* index constructed by Baker et al. (2016) has been widely used, it has some limitations. We develop a new *CEPU* index based on the frequency of articles related to Chinese economic policy uncertainty published in Chinese four securities newspapers. In our empirical study, when we use three different measures of stock crash risk, consistent results are obtained by using our new index. However, the original index developed by Baker et al. yields contradictory results in explaining stock crash risk. Thus, our new *CEPU* index provides an alternative way to measure Chinese economic policy uncertainty, and it can be used in future research related to economic policy uncertainty in China.

Using a sample of Chinese A-share listed firms, we find that economic policy uncertainty is positively and significantly associated with stock price crash risk and the impact of economic policy uncertainty on crash risk is more prominent for SOEs. Then we test the mechanisms behind the effect of economic policy uncertainty on crash risk, finding that the effect is more prominent for firms with higher information asymmetry and firms with greater disagreement among investors. These results imply that economic policy uncertainty affects crash risk through two mechanisms: managers' concealment of bad news and investors' heterogeneous beliefs. Moreover, the positive relationship between economic policy uncertainty and crash risk remains robust after using an instrumental variable, including macroeconomic uncertainty variables or replacing the crash risk measure. Our further study shows that the lagged economic policy uncertainty is negatively associated with stock price crash risk, indicating that the positive impact of economic policy uncertainty on crash risk is simultaneous and it reverses later.

Our findings are consistent with prior studies which state that higher economic policy uncertainty leads to a more volatile stock market. This study broadens the crash risk research field by linking a macro factor to firm-specific crash risk. More importantly, we explore the mechanisms through which economic policy uncertainty affects crash risk. Our findings indicate that economic policy uncertainty is an important factor that is omitted in the literature related to crash risk. The best way to measure economic policy uncertainty is still an important issue that is worth exploring. Recent studies have used text mining or machine learning methods to measure economic policy uncertainty (Azqueta-Gavaldón, 2017; Tobback et al., 2018). This is a new trend, but it is currently difficult for us to use these new methods when investigating information in Chinese language. Because of technical constraints, we leave the exploration of these new frontiers to future studies.

Appendix   Variable definitions

Crash risk variables	
NCSKEW	The negative coefficient of skewness; see Equation 3 for details
DUVOL	The down-to-up volatility; see Equation 4 for details
CRASH	A dummy variable that equals 1 if firm experiences at least one crash day during quarter T and zero otherwise, where a crash day is a trading day in which the firm-specific daily return falls 3.09 or more standard deviations below the mean firm-specific daily returns over quarter T.
Economic policy uncertainty variables	
lnCEPU1	The natural logarithm of the arithmetic average of the CEPU1 index in the three months of a quarter
lnCEPU2	The natural logarithm of the arithmetic average of the CEPU2 index in the three months of a quarter
lnUSEPU	The natural logarithm of the arithmetic average of the US economic policy uncertainty, as constructed by Baker et al. (2016)
Firm-level variables	
SIZE	The natural logarithm of the total assets
ROA	Firm profitability, calculated as income before extraordinary items divided by total assets

continued

Firm-level variables	
LEV	Firm financial leverage, calculated as total liabilities divided by total assets
MB	The market-to-book ratio
ABACC	The absolute value of discretionary accruals, where discretionary accruals are estimated from the modified Jones model
DTURN	The detrended stock trading volume, calculated as the average monthly share turnover for the current quarter minus the average monthly share turnover for the previous quarter, where the monthly share turnover is the monthly trading volume divided by the total number of floating shares on the market that month
SIGMA	The standard deviation of firm-specific daily returns over quarter T
INSHARE	The ratio of institutional shares in tradable shares
Other variables	
SOE	A dummy variable that equals 1 if the firm is a state-owned Enterprise (SOE) and 0 otherwise
ANALYST	A dummy variable that equals 1 if the number of analysts forecasting the firm is larger than the mean number and 0 otherwise
TURN	A dummy variable that equals 1 if the firm belongs to the larger ROE group and 0 otherwise
GDP growth	The growth rate of gross domestic product
CPI growth	The growth rate of the Consumer Price Index
Consumer Confidence	We get the Consumer Confidence Index that is released by the Chinese National Bureau of Statistics, and divide it by 100

References

Aman H, 2013. An analysis of the impact of media coverage on stock price crashes and jumps: Evidence from Japan[J]. Pacific-Basin Finance Journal, 24: 22-38.

Azqueta-Gavaldón A, 2017. Developing news-based economic policy uncertainty index with unsupervised machine learning[J]. Economics Letters, 158(sep.): 47-50.

Baker S R, Bloom N, Davis S J, 2016. Measuring economic policy uncertainty [J]. The Quarterly Journal of Economics, 131: 1593-1636.

Ball R, 2009. Market and political/regulatory on the recent perspectives accounting scandals[J]. Journal of Accounting Research, 47: 277-323.

Brogaard J, Detzel A, 2015. The asset-pricing implications of government economic policy uncertainty[J]. Management Science: Journal of the Institute of Management Sciences, 61: 3-18.

Callen J L, Fang X, 2015. Religion and stock price crash risk[J]. Journal of Financial and Quantitative Analysis, 50: 169-195.

Chen J, Hong H G, Stein J C, 2001. Forecasting crashes: Trading volume, past returns, and conditional skewness in stock prices[J]. Journal of Financial Economics, 61: 345-381.

Chen J, Jiang F, Tong G, 2017. Economic policy uncertainty in China and stock market expected returns[J]. Accounting and Finance, 57(5): 1265-1286.

Gulen H, Ion M, 2016. Policy uncertainty and corporate investment[J]. The Review of Financial Studies, 29: 523-564.

Habib A, Hasan M M, Jiang H, 2018. Stock price crash risk: Review of the empirical literature[J]. Accounting and Finance, 58: 211-251.

Harris M, Raviv A, 1993. Differences of opinion make a horse race[J]. Review of Financial Studies, 6(3): 473-506.

Hong H, Stein J C, 2003. Differences of opinion, short-sales constraints, and market crashes[J]. The Review of Financial Studies, 16: 487-525.

Hutton A P, Marcus A J, Tehranian H, 2009. Opaque financial reports, R2, and crash risk[J]. Journal of Financial Economics, 94: 67-86.

Jang J, 2017. Stock return anomalies and individual investors in the Korean stock market[J]. Pacific-Basin Finance Journal, 46: 141-157.

Jiao J, Yan A, 2015. Convertible securities and heterogeneity of investor beliefs[J]. Journal of Financial Research, 38: 255-282.

Jin L, Myers S C, 2006. R2 around the world: New theory and new tests[J]. Journal of Financial Economics, 79: 257-292.

Kim J B, Li Y, Zhang L, 2010. Corporate tax avoidance and stock price crash risk：Firm-level analysis[J]. Journal of Financial Economics，100（3）：639-662.

Kim J B，Li Y，Zhang L，2011. CFOs versus CEOs：Equity incentives and crashes[J]. Journal of Financial Economics，101（3）：713-730.

Kim J B，Zhang L，2016. Accounting conservatism and stock price crash risk：Firm-level evidence[J]. Contemporary Accounting Research，33：412-441.

Kim Y，Li H，Li S，2014. Corporate social responsibility and stock price crash risk[J]. Journal of Banking and Finance，43：1-13.

Lee W，Wang L，2017. Do political connections affect stock price crash risk? Firm-level evidence from China[J]. Review of Quantitative Finance and Accounting，48：643-676.

Li X，Wang S S，Wang X，2017. Trust and stock price crash risk：Evidence from China[J]. Journal of Banking and Finance，76：74-91.

Li X M，2017. New evidence on economic policy uncertainty and equity premium[J]. Pacific-Basin Finance Journal，46：41-56.

Liu L，Zhang T，2015. Economic policy uncertainty and stock market volatility[J]. Finance Research Letters，15：99-105.

Liu L X，Shu H，Wei K C J，2017. The impacts of political uncertainty on asset prices：Evidence from the Bo scandal in China[J]. Journal of Financial Economics，125（2）：286-310.

Luo J H，Gong M，Lin Y，et al，2016. Political connections and stock price crash risk：Evidence from China[J]. Economics Letters，147：90-92.

Pastor L'，Veronesi P，2012. Uncertainty about government policy and stock prices[J]. The Journal of Finance，67：1219-1264.

Pastor L'，Veronesi P，2013. Political uncertainty and risk premia[J]. Journal of Financial Economics，110：520-545.

Scheinkman J A，Xiong W，2003. Overconfidence and speculative bubbles[J]. Journal of Political Economy，111：1183-1220.

Swee-Sum L，Huiping Z，Weina Z，2018. Does policy instability matter for international equity markets? [J]. International Review of Finance，20（1）：155-196.

Tobback E，Naudts H，Daelemans W，et al，2018. Belgian economic policy uncertainty index: Improvement through text mining [J]. International Journal of Forecasting, 34: 355-365.

Wang Y, Chen C R, Huang Y S, 2014. Economic policy uncertainty and corporate investment: Evidence from China[J]. Pacific-Basin Finance Journal, 26: 227-243.

Xiong X, Bian Y, Shen D, 2018. The time-varying correlation between policy uncertainty and stock returns: Evidence from China[J]. Physica A: Statistical Mechanics and its Applications, 499: 413-419.

Xu N, Jiang X, Chan K C, et al, 2013. Analyst coverage, optimism, and stock price crash risk: Evidence from China[J]. Pacific-Basin Finance Journal, 25: 217-239.

Xu N, Li X, Yuan Q, et al, 2014. Excess perks and stock price crash risk: Evidence from China[J]. Journal of Corporate Finance, 25: 419-434.

Zhang H, Wang M, Jiang J, 2017. Investor protection and stock crash risk [J]. Pacific-Basin Finance Journal, 43: 256-266.

Zhu Y, Wu Z, Zhang H, et al, 2017. Media sentiment, institutional investors and probability of stock price crash: Evidence from Chinese stock markets[J]. Accounting and Finance, 57: 1635-1670.

Stimulating the Dorsolateral Prefrontal Cortex Decreases the Asset Bubble: A tDCS Study[①]

Abstract Many studies have discussed the neural basis of asset bubbles. They found that the dorsolateral prefrontal cortex (DLPFC) played an important role in bubble formation, but whether a causal relationship exists and the mechanism of the effect of the DLPFC on bubbles remains unsettled. Using transcranial direct current stimulation (tDCS), this study modulated the activity of the DLPFC and investigated the causal relationship between the DLPFC and the asset bubbles in the classical learning-to-forecast experiment. 126 subjects were randomly divided into three groups and received different stimulations (left anodal/right cathodal, right anodal/left cathodal, or sham stimulation), respectively. We also conducted a 2-back task before and after stimulation to measure changes in subjects' cognitive abilities and to explore in detail the cognitive mechanism of the effects of DLPFC stimulation on asset bubbles. Based on our results, we found that the bubble of the left anodal/right cathodal stimulation group was significantly smaller than that of the sham stimulation group. In the meantime, subjects performed significantly better in the 2-back task after left anodal/right cathodal stimulation but not right anodal/left cathodal or sham stimulation. The results are in the learning-to-forecast experiment, supporting the cognitive mechanism to some extent.

① Originally Published in *Frontiers in Psychology* (vol. 10, 2019) by Jin Xuejun, Chen Cheng, Zhou Xue and Yang Xiaolan.

Furthermore, we examined different forecasting rules across individuals and discovered that the left anodal/right cathodal stimulation group preferred the adaptive learning rule, while the sham and right anodal/left cathodal stimulation groups adopted a pure trend-following rule that tended to intensify market volatility aggressively.

Key words   asset bubble, cognitive ability, learning-to-forecast, dorsolateral prefrontal cortex, transcranial direct current stimulation.

1 Introduction

The research on asset bubbles can be traced back to the middle of the last century, but there are still many questions to be settled in this field. To date, volumes of studies have indicated that asset bubbles exist in the real financial market. However, the "Efficient Market Hypothesis" (EMH) proposed by Fama (1970) dominated the mainstream literature in the beginning, claiming that the asset price reflected all available information without deflection, which was proven to be contradicted by the real financial market in later empirical studies (Fischer, 1972; Basu, 1977). Such studies have demonstrated through empirical data that the asset price often deviates from its fundamental price by discounting the expected value of future dividends and have defined this phenomenon as the asset bubble. They tried to solve this problem through innovations of economic systems, but none has managed to eliminate bubbles completely (Chancellor, 1999).

With the development of behavioral finance, increasingly more academics have come to the realization that the mechanisms underlying the emergence of bubbles may not be inherent to economic systems but lie in human's bounded-rational trading behavior under certain conditions (Ogawa et al., 2014). Thereafter, many behavioral economists tried to study economic bubble behaviors in a virtual financial market through laboratory experiments, starting with Smith et al. (1988). Many observed large positive bubbles followed by dramatic crashes toward the end of the experiment (Smith et al., 1988; Noussair et al., 2001; Haruvy & Noussair, 2006; Haruvy et al.,

2014; Eckel & Fuüllbrunn, 2015). Among these laboratory experiments regarding asset bubbles, "learning-to-forecast" is a typical one introduced by Marimon et al. (1993). In this type of experiment, subjects participated as professional financial advisers and continuously predicted the price of a pension fund based on its dividend and market interest rate. In addition to the large deviation from the fundamental price frequently observed in other experiments, subjects without rational expectations were found to adopt a trend-following strategy during forecasting (Hommes et al., 2005), which tended to increase the volatility of the asset price and induce an asset bubble.

Some neuroimaging studies have explored the neural basis of economic bubble behaviors and identified the activation of the dorsolateral prefrontal cortex (DLPFC) during bubbles. They found that the DLPFC participated in decision-making during bubbles in a virtual stock exchange and was associated with asset preference that might bias the decision (Ogawa et al., 2014; Ye et al., 2016). Evidence from a field experiment also confirmed the correlation of DLPFC activation with direct access trading in a real stock market. They found that the success of the trading activity, based on a large number of filled transactions, was related to higher activation of the DLPFC (Raggetti et al., 2017). These findings suggested a correlation between DLPFC activity and economic bubble behaviors, but whether a causal relationship exists remains unsettled. Our main contribution is to confirm the neural basis of the DLPFC on asset bubble behaviors using transcranial direct current stimulation (tDCS), one of the brain stimulation techniques.

Moreover, we are interested in the mechanism of the relationship between the DLPFC and bubbles, particularly the cognitive abilities that have been frequently mentioned to affect bubbles by many studies. For example, some researchers who performed learning-to-forecast experiments have pointed out that the observed bubbles in the simplest economic environment may be attributed to subjects' lack of related knowledge or failing to fully understand the experimental market (Bao et al., 2017). In fact, some experimental studies have managed to reduce or even diminish bubbles by illustrating the whole experiment in a simple and understandable way (Teo, 2011; Huber &

Kirchler, 2012; Kirchler et al., 2012; Yamamoto, 2015; Yamamoto et al., 2015). Others found that markets that consisted of subjects with higher cognitive abilities performed better in price efficiency (Bosch-Rosa et al., 2017). Prices in such markets exhibited a more stable pattern and converged closer and more quickly to the rational expectation equilibrium (Zong et al., 2017). Neuroscientific studies have shown that anodal tDCS over the left DLPFC enhances cognitive functioning, especially in working memory (Nitsche et al., 2008; Hoy & Fitzgerald, 2010; Zaehle et al., 2011; Jacobson et al., 2012; Meinzer et al., 2012; Hoy et al., 2013; Dedoncker et al., 2016). Working memory is essentially the capacity to keep information in mind for a short period of time (Kuhnen & Knutson, 2005; Silvanto et al., 2008; Hoy et al., 2013; He et al., 2016; Lerner et al., 2016). Since improvements in working memory have been proven to increase the complexity of thought and action through the ability to manipulate information (Jaušovec & Jaušovec, 2012), it is believed to be the most crucial foundation of cognitive processing, and improvements in working memory can represent a considerable enhancement in cognitive ability. Based on previous literature on asset bubbles, we found that working memory capacity (WMC) is one of the most related factors that influence the asset bubbles in the learning-to-forecast experiment. Intuitively, working memory plays an important role in the prediction of asset price because people need to process the information before forecasting. Indeed, some researchers had provided evidence on the relationship between working memory and prediction. They found that people with higher WMC predicted more accurately (Bröder et al., 2010; Sewell & Lewandowsky, 2012; McDaniel et al., 2014). People with higher WMC tended to maintain and refresh information more actively. They learned from previous data and abstracted systematic regularities to improve their prediction algorithms and hence increased their accuracy of prediction (McDaniel et al., 2014). Furthermore, people with higher WMC predicted more accurately when price movement was approximately non-linear, since they were able to use well-calibrated strategies (Fischer & Holt, 2017). However, lower WMC participants usually adopted simple example-based prediction strategies. In conclusion, previous literature indicated that working memory was important in prediction. Thus, we focused on the influence of WMC in a learning-to-forecast experiment in our paper. Although different studies draw different conclusions on cathodal simulation, most studies have agreed on the positive effects of anodal stimulation on working memory performance measured by either response time or accuracy or both. Therefore, it is reasonable to examine the cognitive mechanism of decreasing bubbles through tDCS over the DLPFC.

Inspired by the above literature regarding neurophysiological traits, asset bubbles and cognitive ability, we compared subjects' economic bubble behavior in a classical learning-to-forecast experiment following left anodal/right cathodal, right anodal/left cathodal and sham stimulation by a tDCS device, in an attempt to identify the neural mechanism of their decisions, which tend to induce asset bubbles. In particular, we also collected their performance measures in a working memory task pre and post stimulation to further explore the role of cognition in this process. Combining these two results, we then discuss the causal relationship between asset bubbles and cognitive abilities.

2 Materials and methods

2.1 Participants and procedure

A total of 126 participants were recruited from Zhejiang University. All of them were asked to complete a self-report questionnaire that included gender, age, major and whether they had participated in a similar experiment before. Each participant was provided with written informed consent. This study was carried out in accordance with the recommendations of the Zhejiang University ethics committee. The protocol was approved by the Zhejiang University ethics committee. None of the subjects are reported any adverse side effects regarding pain on the scalp or headaches after the experiment. The whole experiment was conducted over the course of several stages. In stage 1, all participants were required to perform a 3-min 2-back task before tDCS. Then, they were randomly allocated to receive 20 min of left anodal/right cathodal (42 subjects), right anodal/left cathodal (42 subjects) or sham (42 subjects) tDCS. Then in stage 2, after the stimulation, they were required to complete a 3-min 2-back task again with a different random letter series. In stage 3, every 6 subjects completed a 50-period learning-to-forecast experiment in an experimental market, generally lasting 30—40 min. The whole procedure and schedule were showed in Figure 1. Subjects were asked to take seats randomly. During the session they were separated by partitions, so they could not observe the decisions of other subjects in the same session. The software we used in this experiment was z-Tree (Fischbacher, 2007) which was widely used in experimental researches.

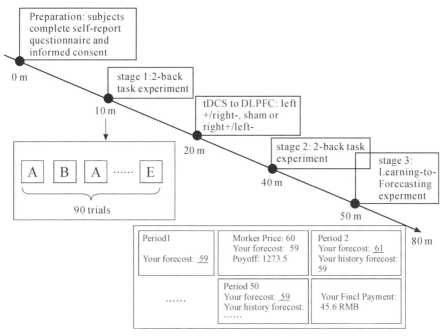

Fig. 1 The procedure and schedule of the whole experiment. The subjects were first asked to perform a 2-back task experiment and then randomly separated into different tDCS groups: left+/right−, sham or right+/left−. After receiving tDCS to the DLPFC, they performed the 2-back task again. Finally, they were asked to perform a 50-period learning-to-forecast experiment.

Our subjects included 73 males and 53 females. Their average age was about 22 and 12. 6% of them were in majors which might be related to the decision tasks of our experiment, e. g. , economics, finance, business, and psychology. 33. 4% of them were undergraduates and others were graduates. The detailed information about the numbers of subjects by treatment, gender, major, and student type was shown in Table 1.

Table 1   Number of subjects

Stimulation type	Male	Female	Related majors*	Other majors	Under-graduate	Graduate
anode	30	12	7	35	15	27
sham	23	19	4	38	12	30
cathode	20	22	5	37	14	28
Total	73	63	16	110	41	85

* Economics, finance, business, and psychology.

2.2   Transcranial direct current stimulation (tDCS)

Transcranial direct current stimulation is a non-invasive form of brain stimulation that has been shown to induce changes in brain activity and subsequent function. tDCS applies a very weak electrical current via two surface electrodes (35 cm2) to the scalp, modulating the activity of neurons and therefore influencing subjects' decision-making process. Anodal stimulation has been shown to depolarize neurons, leading to an increase in brain activity, while cathodal stimulation hyperpolarizes neurons and generally results in a reduction in brain activity. In this study, we used a tDCS device to modulate the subjects' neural activity in the encephalic region. Based on previous studies, the DLPFC plays an important role in cognitive processing and the formation of asset bubbles. Therefore, we set up three simulation groups: (1) left anodal/right cathodal; (2) right anodal/left cathodal; (3)

sham stimulation. ① The anodal stimulation means that the anodal electrode was placed on the left/right DLPFC (F3/F4 site of the EEG system), while the cathode was on the opposite side of DLPFC (F4/F3 site of the EEG system). (Little & Woollacott, 2014; Little et al. , 2014). The EEG system we selected was shown in Fig. 2. Active tDCS was delivered for 20 min at 2 mA with a 30-s ramp up and ramp down of the current. For the sham stimulation, the current was delivered for only 30 s once it reached 2 mA with the identical 30-s ramp up/ramp down at the beginning and the end of the stimulation.

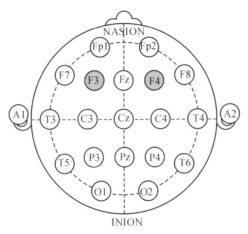

Fig. 2 Electrode placement in dorsolateral prefrontal cortex (DLPFC) stimulations

2.3 Two-back task

We chose an adaptive dual 2-back task to identify the effects of tDCS on working memory (Hoy et al, 2013; Martin et al, 2014). In this task, participants would see a series of random letters presented consecutively on the screen for 3 min. They needed to remember the order of the letters and respond by pressing the SPACE button when the present letter was the same

---

① One-way ANOVA test result showed that there was no significant difference in age for subjects in these three different groups [$F(2,123)=1.68$, $p=0.1915$]. Chi-square test results also showed that there were no significant differences in gender, major and education for subjects in these three groups [Pearson Chi2(2)$=5.14$, $p=0.08$; Pearson Chi2(2)$=1.01$, $p=0.6$; Pearson Chi2(2)$=0.85$, $p=0.65$, respectively].

as the letter presented two trials earlier. The 2-back task as a whole consists of 90 trials containing approximately 25% for the targets. Each letter was presented for 2 s in a trial. All participants were asked to perform a 2-back task before and immediately after the stimulation, and the order of stimulus presentations was exactly the same across different groups.

2.4　Learning-to-forecast experiment

In this phase, we introduced the design of our prime experiment. Our experimental design was mainly based on the classical learning-to-forecast experiment (Hommes et al., 2005). Our experimental parameters were based mainly on the experimental design of Bao et al. (2017) and Zong et al. (2017). The experimental economy was based on a simple asset market with a constant fundamental price. There were six subjects in each market, and each subject played the role of financial adviser in each company. All subjects were told the same information about the asset (dividend=3.3 yuan and risk-free interest rate=5%). Each subject's task was to forecast the asset price in every period, and their experimental rewards only depended on their accuracy of prediction. The whole experiment lasted 50 rounds. In each period, historical prices and their payoffs were displayed to the subjects for reference. Once each of the subjects finished predicting, the realized price based on their predictions would be calculated and made public.

Each period, subjects acted as forecasting advisers and were asked to perform a one-period ahead price predictions. The experimental reward was totally based upon their own prediction errors in every period as follows:

$$Payoff\$\ f_{i,+1} = \max\left\{0, \left[1300 - \frac{1300}{49}(P_{i,t+1}^{3} - P_{t+1})^2\right]\right\} \qquad (1)$$

where $P_{i,t+1}^{e}$ is the prediction of the price at period $t+1$ from subject i in period t and P_{t+1} is the realized market price at period $t+1$.

The subjects' predictions were automatically transformed into excess demand for the asset, yielding the following law of motion:

$$P_{t+1} = 66 + \frac{20}{21}(\overline{P}_{t+1}^{e} - P^f) + \varepsilon_t \qquad (2)$$

where $P^f = 66$ is the fundamental price of the asset, $\overline{P}_{t+1}^{e} = \dfrac{\sum_{i=1}^{6} P_{i,t+1}^{e}}{6}$ is the average prediction price of the six subjects and $\varepsilon \sim N$ (0, 1) is a small independent and identically distributed shock to the price P_{t+1}.

With the above rules of price adjustment rule, the subjects' rewards were maximized if their predictions were all consistent with the fundamental price of 66.

Then, we compared bubbles between different stimulation groups using t-tests. To study bubbles from a different perspective, we also examined whether subjects made biased predictions about future asset prices. We followed Haruvy et al. (2007) and estimated the regression model below:

$$P_t - P_{t-1} = \alpha + \beta(P_t^e - P_{t-1}) \tag{3}$$

This model can be interpreted as follows: if $\alpha = 0$ and $\beta = 1$, then the prediction of price changes is unbiased. Otherwise, the prediction is biased. If $\beta < 1$, subjects overpredicted the price. If $\beta > 1$, subjects underpredicted the price. The absolute value of β measured the degree of prediction bias.

Third, we focused on the cognitive mechanism involved in 2-back task performances. We calculated and compared the accuracy of the 2-back task before and after stimulation to investigate whether tDCS over the DLPFC successfully modulated subjects' cognitive performances. The accuracy was calculated by dividing the number of correct responses made by the subject by the total number of targets, shown as follows:

$$\text{Accuracy} = \frac{Number\ of\ Correct\ Responses}{Number\ of\ Targets} \times 100\% \tag{4}$$

Finally, we investigated the behavioral rules of subjects while predicting asset price. According to Heemeijer et al. (2009), in a learning-to-forecast experiment, subjects mainly adopted two typical rules to forecast asset price: adaptive expectations and trend-following rules. These two classical forecast rules can be shown as follows:

Adaptive expectation rule: $P_t^e = P_{t-1}^e + \varphi(P_{t-1} - P_{t-1}^e)$ $\qquad$ (5)

Trend-following rule: $P_t^e = P_{t-1} + (P_{t-1} - P_{t-2})$ $\qquad$ (6)

The above two forecasting rules can be described as the following linear formula with $\alpha = 1$ and $\beta = 0$ representing the pure trend-following rule and $\alpha + \beta = 1$ representing the adaptive expectation rule.

$$P_t^e = \alpha \times P_{t-1} + \beta \times P_{t-1}^e + \gamma(P_{t-1} - P_{t-2}) \tag{7}$$

The trend-following rule uses an anchor that gives all weight to the last observed price, while the adaptive expectation rule takes the last forecast into consideration as well, revealing a more aggressive attitude of the former and a more cautious attitude of the latter (Bao et al. , 2017).

2.5 Data analysis

All subjects tolerated the tDCS well, and no adverse effects were reported. First, we analyzed the effects of tDCS on bubbles. To compare asset bubbles across different treatments, we quantified the asset bubble following the standard bubble measurement (Porter & Smith 1995; Stockl et al. , 2010) relative absolute deviation (RAD), defined as the relative distance between realized prices and the fundamental price, as shown below:

$$RAD = \frac{|P_t - P^f|}{P^f} \times 100\% \tag{8}$$

where P_t and P^f denote the market price and fundamental price in period t, respectively.

Statistical analysis was performed using Stata statistical software (version 14.0). Statistical description, one-way analysis of variance (one-way ANOVA) and panel regression were used in statistical analysis. [1]

3 Results

3.1 Effect of tDCS on bubbles

There were significant differences in RAD between the left anodal/right cathodal stimulation group and the sham stimulation group ($F(1,698) = 13.47$, $p = 0.0003$, ES = 0.138; shown in Fig. 3). Markets consisted of subjects receiving left anodal/right cathodal stimulation had smaller bubbles than markets consisting of subjects receiving sham stimulation. We also found that bubbles were not significantly reduced after subjects received right anodal/left cathodal stimulation ($F(1,698) = 3.27$, $p = 0.0709$, ES = 0.068). Therefore, we concluded that left anodal/right cathodal tDCS over the DLPFC

---

① All of our data could be find in Supplementary Material Tables 1-4.

significantly reduced market bubbles, whereas right anodal/left cathodal or sham tDCS to the DLPFC had no significant effect on market bubbles.

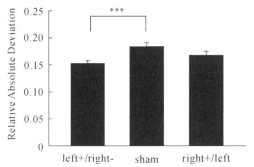

Fig. 3 Relative absolute deviation in different groups. The RAD of the left +/right-the group was significantly smaller than that of the sham group, while there was no significant difference between the right+/left-group and the sham group.
* * * $p<0.001$, Error bars indicated 95% confidence intervals.

There was still an interesting question we wanted to study regarding whether subjects made biased predictions about future market behavior i. e. , whether they consistently over or underpredicted prices. To answer this question, we estimated equation (3).

According to the results of the regression in Table 2, we found that all groups (left anodal/right cathodal, sham, and right anodal/left cathodal) made biased predictions and overestimated the changes in market price ($\beta<1$). In addition, the sham stimulation group ($\beta=0.021$) and right anodal/left cathodal stimulation group ($\beta=0.022$) overestimated the price changes more than the left anodal/right cathodal group ($\beta=0.573$), consistent with larger bubbles in the sham and right anodal/left cathodal stimulation groups. The fact that all groups did not make unbiased predictions explained why asset bubbles generally existed in all groups.

Table 2　Regression on price change

$price_t - price_{t-1}$	(1) left+/right−	(2)sham	(3) right+/left−
$forecast_t - price_{t-1}$	0.573 * * *	0.021 * * *	0.022 * * *
	(0.0703)	(0.0026)	(0.003)
constant	0.184 * * *	0.356 * * *	0.285 * * *
	(0.028)	(0.0466)	(0.045)

Standard errors in parentheses. * * * : $p<0.01$.

3.2 Effects of tDCS on the 2-back task

There was no significant difference in subjects' accuracy of 2-back task (one-way ANOVA: $F_{(2,99)} = 2.89$, $p = 0.0603$, ES = 0.169) before they received stimulation. There was a significant increase in 2-back task accuracy after subjects received left anodal/right cathodal tDCS to the DLPFC (one-way ANOVA: $F_{(1,74)} = 11.13$, $p = 0.0013$, ES = 0.3878; shown in Fig. 4). However, we did not find significant differences in 2-back task accuracy after subjects received right anodal/left cathodal or sham tDCS to the DLPFC (one-way ANOVA: $F_{(1,62)} = 0.32$, $p = 0.5733$, ES = 0.07; $F_{(1,62)} = 1.89$, $p = 0.1745$, ES = 0.17 respectively). The results of our experiment were consistent with previous studies (Hoy et al., 2013; Sellerset al., 2014; Plewnia, 2017; Wang et al., 2018). Therefore, anodal stimulation to the left DLPFC indeed increased subjects' cognitive abilities.

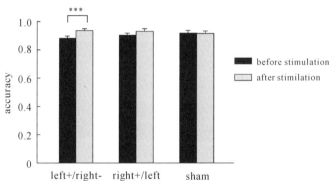

Fig. 4   Accuracy in the 2-back task. Black bars, pre-transcranial direct stimulation (pre-tDCS); gray bars, post-tDCS. The subjects' accuracy in the 2-back task showed a significant increase in the left +/right-group and no significant differences in the right+/left-or sham groups. *** $p < 0.001$, Error bars indicated 95% confidence intervals.

There was no significant difference in subjects' reaction time of the 2-back task (one-way ANOVA: $F_{(2,99)} = 0.50$, $p = 0.6069$, ES = 0.070; shown in Figure 5) before they received stimulation. The decrease in reaction time after receiving left anodal/right cathodal tDCS to the DLPFC was also not significant (one-way ANOVA: $F_{(1,74)} = 2.77$, $p = 0.105$, ES = 0.191). In fact, it was difficult to capture the change of reaction time, since the reaction time was so short (2 s).

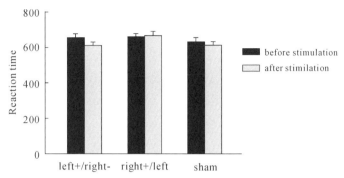

Fig. 5　Reaction time in the 2-back task. Black bars, pre-transcranial direct stimulation (pre-tDCS); gray bars, post-tDCS. The subjects' reaction time in the 2-back task had no significant difference after receiving stimulation. Error bars indicated 95% confidence intervals.

In summary, the results of the 2-back task showed that left anodal/ right cathodal stimulation to DLPFC indeed improved the subjects' cognitive ability.

3.3　Correlation analysis on 2-back task and bubbles

To provide evidence to show that the formation of market bubbles was related to the cognitive ability of subjects, we analyzed the relationship between the average 2-back accuracy of subjects in one market and the bubbles created by their trading. As discussed previously, RAD was used to measure bubbles. Using the aggregate data for the experimental markets, we found that the correlation coefficient between the average 2-back accuracy and RAD was -0.332(Pearson correlation analysis, $p=0.179$).

We tried another way to investigate the relationship between subjects' cognitive abilities and asset bubbles in the markets. Firstly, we ranked all markets by subjects' average accuracy in the 2-back task and divided them into two groups, namely the high cognition group and the low cognition group. Then, we compared bubbles in these two groups. The results showed that the RAD of the high cognition group was significantly smaller than that of the low cognition group (one-way ANOVA, $F(1, 898) = 9.08$, $p = 0.0027$). It indicated that on average, markets with subjects who performed better in the 2-back task created fewer bubbles. Thus, there was a negative relationship between subjects' cognitive abilities and asset bubbles. Combined with our previous results on the effects of tDCS, our findings implied that stimulating the DLPFC decreased the asset bubbles and the main reason could be attributed to the increase of cognitive ability.

3.4 Behavioral rules

In this section, we show the differences in the behavioral rules and discuss the relationship between behavioral rules and asset bubbles. To further examine subjects' behavioral rules for predicting asset price, we estimated equation (7).

$$P_t^e = \alpha \times P_{t-1} + \beta \times P_{t-1}^e + \gamma(P_{t-1} - P_{t-2}) \tag{7}$$

From the regression results in Table 3, we found that the coefficient of the former forecasting price was not significantly different than zero for the sham and right anodal/left cathodal group. The coefficient of the trend (1.138 for sham; 0.748 for right anodal) was large in the sham and right anodal/left cathodal group. In summary, the sham stimulation group was more exposed to pure trend-following behavioral rules, which tended to expand the volatility of market prices and finally caused larger market bubbles (Bao et al., 2017; Bosch-Rosa et al., 2017). Indeed, the bubbles of the sham stimulation group were much larger because they only paid attention to the trend in price without adjusting their expectations. The results of the right anodal/left cathodal group were close to the sham group. The left anodal/right cathodal group took not only the trend but also their last forecasts into account to carefully revise their expectations, which contributed to their better performance in price efficiency. The fact that bubbles in the sham and right anodal/left cathodal stimulation groups were larger than those in the left anodal/right cathodal stimulation group may be partly attributed to the differences between their forecasting rules.

Table 3 Estimated coefficients in the forecasting rules models

$forecast_t$	(1) left$+$/right$-$	(2) sham	(3) right$+$/left$-$
$price_{t-1}$	0.909***	1.061***	1.001***
	(0.061)	(0.052)	(0.046)
$forecast_{t-1}$	0.098***	$-$0.027	$-$0.018
	(0.0214)	(0.022)	(0.022)
$price_{t-1} - price_{t-2}$	0.779***	1.138***	0.748***
	(0.019)	(0.188)	(0.168)
constant	$-$0.572	$-$2.239	1.71
	(0.382)	(3.623)	(2.968)

Standard errors in parentheses. ***: $p < 0.01$.

4 Discussion

In this study, we examined the relationship between the DLPFC and asset bubble formation and discussed the cognitive mechanism behind it. Our studies are good supplements to asset bubble researches. Previous studies have indicated that the DLPFC was activated during stock trading and the market bubble period (Ogawa et al., 2014; Raggetti et al., 2017). However, they did not discuss the causal relationship and transmission mechanism between the DLPFC and asset bubbles. According to the existing literature on asset bubbles, we found that many studies indicated that cognitive ability played an important role in asset trading and that a market consisting of participants with higher cognitive ability would generate fewer asset bubbles (Zong et al., 2017). Therefore, we inferred that cognitive ability might be an important transmission mechanism in reducing asset bubbles. Furthermore, we found that the DLPFC was closely related to cognitive processing (Nitsche et al., 2008; Hoy et al., 2013; Dedoncker et al., 2016). Therefore, we used tDCS to modulate the activity of the DLPFC and compared the asset bubbles and synchronous cognition improvements across different stimulation groups.

Our main concern is the influence of tDCS to the DLPFC on asset bubble formation. This problem has been rarely mentioned in previous studies about asset bubbles, which is our main contribution to asset bubble research. We would like to discuss the neural basis of asset bubbles and enrich the research on asset bubbles in the neuroscience field. In the classical learning-to-forecast experiment, the bubble of the left anodal/right cathodal group is significantly smaller than the bubble of the sham stimulation group. However, the right anodal/left cathodal group and sham group are not significantly different from each other.

We also examined the cognition mechanism of the effect of DLPFC stimulation on asset bubbles. Therefore, we described the changes in cognitive ability pre- and post-stimulation. From the results of the 2-back task, we arrived at the same conclusion as previous studies: anodal tDCS to the left DLPFC improved cognition. Anodal tDCS over the left DLPFC has been reported by many studies to increase subjects' cognitive ability, especially working memory as measured by n-back tasks(Nitsche et al. , 2008; Hoy & Fitzgerald, 2010; Zaehle et al. , 2011). In our experiment, we asked all subjects to complete a 2-back task before and after stimulation. We found that the accuracy of the 2-back task was significantly improved in subjects receiving left anodal/right cathodal stimulation, while sham stimulation and right anodal/left cathodal stimulation had no influence on the accuracy. However, the decrease in reaction time was not significant in any group. It was possibly due to the fact that in our experiment, the reaction time was so short that we were not able to capture the change of it. Overall, these results demonstrated that anodal tDCS to the left DLPFC indeed improved subjects' cognitive ability.

Combining the two results described above, one possible explanation of this phenomenon is that anodal tDCS over the left DLPFC reduced asset bubbles by improving subjects' cognitive ability, to some extent contributing to a causal relationship between asset bubbles and cognitive ability. To examine whether cognitive abilities played a role in reducing asset bubbles, we considered a correlation analysis between the average 2-back accuracy and RAD that we used to measure bubbles. We found a negative correlation between them and the correlation coefficient equaled to -0.332. This result indicated that if one market consisted of subjects with higher average accuracy in the 2-back task, there would be fewer market bubbles. Although there was a smaller bubble in the left anodal/right cathodal group, asset bubbles generally existed in all groups. We explained this phenomenon with the results of the regression from the prediction-biased model. From those results, we noted that all groups overestimated the change in market prices with the sham and right anodal/left cathodal groups making more excessive overestimates than the left anodal/right cathodal group. This finding may explain why asset bubbles formed in all groups and why the bubble of the left anodal/right cathodal was smaller than the others. Our results were consistent with previous studies reporting that both high cognitive ability groups and low cognitive ability groups overestimated the market price, while the high cognitive ability groups made predictions closer to an unbiased estimation (Zong et al., 2017).

We discussed the correlation between 2-back task and learning-to-forecast experiment. Our results showed that the correlation coefficient between the average 2-back accuracy and RAD was -0.332 (Pearson correlation analysis, $p=0.179$). If one market consisted of subjects with higher average accuracy in the 2-back task, there would be fewer market bubbles. However, the p-value showed that the negative relationship between subjects' cognitive abilities and asset bubbles was not significant. We measured asset bubbles using RAD which was a market level data and thus we only had 18 observations in the correlation analysis. That could be a reason why the correlation was not significant. Then we used another way to investigate their relationship. We ranked all markets by subjects' average accuracy in the 2-back task and divided them into two groups. And we found that the RAD of high cognition group was significantly smaller than that of low group. Combined with these results and our previous analysis, we concluded that stimulating the DLPFC decreased the asset bubble and the main reason could be attributed to the increase of cognitive ability.

We also discussed the differences in the behavioral rules of different groups (left anodal/right cathodal, sham and right anodal/left cathodal). These results helped us to understand how the subjects forecasted asset prices and why they produced different magnitudes of asset bubbles. We obtained a similar conclusion as previous studies. Previous studies indicated that a pure trend-following strategy might expand the volatility of the market price and finally induce a larger market bubble (Bao et al. , 2017). Our results showed that the left anodal/right cathodal stimulation group used both adaptive expectation and trend-following rules while predicting prices. However, the sham stimulation group only applied trend-following rules. They failed to consider their former forecast price and only made decisions based on the trend in the market price. The differences in behavioral rules also explained why bubbles in the different groups were significantly different.

Our results could have some implications for financial markets in the real world. According to our results, regulatory authorities of the financial market should make more effort to improve the overall financial literacy of market participants. The higher financial literacy, the less irrational behaviors and the fewer bubbles in the markets. For example, it should be emphasized that the trend-following rule is a short-sighted strategy. Investors should focus on stocks' long-term performances instead of using the trend-following rule frequently. In addition, the left anodal/right cathodal DLPFC stimulation has a positive effect on enhancing cognitive abilities and may be considered in therapeutic applications.

The limitation of our experiment was that the design of the market was relatively simple with only a forecasting task instead of including a trading asset task, which is more complex. In addition, we only considered working memory among the many components of cognitive functioning. These are all feasible extensions for future research to make the results more robust.

In conclusion, we found that left anodal/right cathodal tDCS over the DLPFC decreased the asset bubble, possibly due to the improvement of subjects' cognitive abilities, while sham tDCS or right anodal/left cathodal tDCS had no significant influence.

References

Arndt B, Newell B R, Platzer C, 2010. Cue integration vs. exemplar-based reasoning in multi-attribute decisions from memory: A matter of cue representation[J]. Judgment & Decision Making, 5(5):326-338.

Bao T, Hommes C H, Makarewicz T, 2017. Bubble formation and (in) efficient markets in learning-to-forecast and optimise experiments [J]. Economic Journal, 127: 581-609.

Basu S, 1977. Investment performance of common stocks in relation to their price-earnings ratios: A test of the efficient market hypothesis[J]. Journal of Finance, 32: 663-682.

Bosch-Rosa C, Meissner T, Bosch-Domènech A, 2018. Cognitive bubbles[J]. Experimental Economics, 21(1):132-153.

Chancellor E, 1999. Devil take the hindmost[M]. New York: Farrar Straus Giroux.

Dedoncker J, Brunoni A R, Baeken C, et al, 2016. The effect of the interval-between-sessions on prefrontal transcranial direct current stimulation (tDCS) on cognitive outcomes: A systematic review and meta-analysis[J]. Journal of Neural Transmission, 123: 1159-1172.

Eckel C C, Fuüllbrunn S, 2015. Thar SHE blows? Gender, competition, and bubbles in experimental asset markets[J]. The American Economic Review, 105: 906-920.

Fama E F, 1970. Efficient capital markets: A review of theory and empirical work[J]. The Journal of Finance, 25: 383-417.

Fischer H, Holt D V, 2017. When high working memory capacity is and is not beneficial for predicting nonlinear processes[J]. Memory & Cognition, 45: 404-412.

Fischbacher U, 2007. Z-tree: Zurich toolbox for ready-made economic experiments[J]. Experimental Economics, 10(2): 171-178.

Gianmario R, Ceravolo M G, Lucrezia F, et al, 2017. Neural correlates of direct access trading in a real stock market: An fMRI investigation[J]. Frontiers in Neuroscience, 11:536.

Haruvy E, Lahav Y, Noussair C N, 2007. Traders' expectations in asset markets: Experimental evidence[J]. American Economic Review, 97: 1901-1920.

Haruvy E, Noussair C N, 2006. The effect of short selling on bubbles and crashes in experimental spot asset markets[J]Journal of Finance, 61: 1119-1157.

Haruvy E, Noussair C N, Powell O, 2014. The impact of asset repurchases and issues in an experimental market[J]. Review of Finance, 18(2): 681-713.

He Q, Chen M, Chen C, et al, 2016. Anodal stimulation of the left DLPFC increases IGT scores and decreases delay discounting rate in healthy males[J]. Frontiers in Psychology, 7:1421.

Heemeijer P, Hommes C, Sonnemans J, et al, 2009. Price stability and volatility in markets with positive and negative expectations feedback: An experimental investigation[J]. Journal of Economic Dynamics & Control, 33: 1052-1072.

Homines C, Sonnemans J, Tuinstra J, et al, 2005. Coordination of expectations in asset pricing experiments[J]. Review of Financial Studies, 18(3): 955-980.

Hoy K E, Emonson M R L, Arnold S L, et al, 2013. Testing the limits: Investigating the effect of tDCS dose on working memory enhancement in healthy controls[J]. Neuropsychologia, 51(9): 1777-1784.

Hoy K E, Fitzgerald P B, 2010. Brain stimulation in psychiatry and its effects on cognition[J]. Nature Reviews Neurology, 6: 267-276.

Huber J, Kirchler M, 2012. The impact of instructions and procedure on reducing confusion and bubbles in experimental asset markets [J]. Experimental Economics, 15: 89-105.

Jacobson L, Koslowsky M, Lavidor M, 2012. tDCS polarity effects in motor and cognitive domains: A meta-analytical review [J]. Experimental Brain Research, 216(1): 1-10.

Jaušovec N, Jaušovec K, 2012. Working memory training: improving intelligence—changing brain activity[J]. Brain & Cognition, 79(2): 96-106.

Jensen M C, Black F, Scholes M S, 1972. The capital asset pricing model: Some empirical tests[J]. Social Science Electronic Publishing, 94(8): 4229-4232.

Kirchler M, Huber J, Stockl T, 2012. Thar she bursts: Reducing confusion reduces bubbles[J]. American Economic Review, 102: 865-883.

Kuhnen C M, Knutson B, 2005. The neural basis of financial risk taking[J]. Neuron, 47(5):763-770.

Little C E, Woollacott M, 2015. EEG measures reveal dual-task interference in postural performance in young adults[J]. Experimental Brain Research, 233(1):27-37.

Little D R, Stephan L, Stewart C, 2014. Working memory capacity and fluid abilities: The more difficult the item, the more more is better[J]. Frontiers in Psychology, 5:239.

Marimon R, Spear S, Sunder S, 1993. Expectationally driven market volatility: An experimental study[J]. Journal of Economic Theory, 61:74-103.

Martin D M, Liu R, Alonzo A, et al, 2014. Use of transcranial direct current stimulation (tDCS) to enhance cognitive training: Effect of timing of stimulation[J]. Experimental Brain Research, 232(10): 3345-3351.

Mcdaniel M A, Cahill M J, Robbins M, et al, 2014. Individual differences in learning and transfer: Stable tendencies for learning exemplars versus abstracting rules[J]. Journal of Experimental Psychology General, 143(2): 668-693.

Meinzer M, Antonenko D, Lindenberg R, et al, 2012. Electrical brain stimulation improves cognitive performance by modulating functional connectivity and task-specific activation[J]. The Journal of Neuroscience: The Official Journal of the Society for Neuroscience, 32(5):1859-1866.

Nitsche M A, Cohen L G, Wassermann E M, et al, 2008. Transcranial direct current stimulation: State of the art 2008[J]. Brain Stimulation, 1(3):206-223.

Noussair C, Ruffieux B J M, Robin S, et al, 2001. Price bubbles in laboratory asset markets with constant fundamental values[J]. Experimental Economics, 4(1):87-105.

Ogawa A, Onozaki T, Mizuno T, et al, 2014. Neural basis of economic bubble behavior[J]. Neuroscience, 265: 37-47.

Plewnia C, 2017. Enhancement of processing speed and frustration tolerance with anodal tDCS[J]. Brain Stimulation, 10: 479-480.

Porter D P, Smith V L, 1995. Futures contracting and dividend uncertainty in experimental asset markets[J]. Journal Of Business, 68(4): 509-541.

Sellers K K, Bennett D V, Hlich F, 2015. Frequency-band signatures of visual responses to naturalistic input in ferret primary visual cortex during free viewing[J]. Brain Research, 1598:31-45.

Sewell D K, Lewandowsky S, 2012. Attention and working memory capacity: Insights from blocking, highlighting, and knowledge restructuring [J]. Journal of Experimental Psychology General, 141(3):444-469.

Silvanto J, Muggleton N, Walsh V, 2008. State-dependency in brain stimulation studies of perception and cognition [J]. Trends in Cognitive Sciences, 12(12):447-454.

Smith V L, Suchanek G L, Williams A W, 1988. Bubbles, crashes, and endogenous expectations in experimental spot asset markets [J]. Econometrica, 56(5): 1119-1151.

Stockl T, Huber J, Kirchler M, 2010. Bubble measures in experimental asset markets[J]. Experimental Economics, 13(3):284-298.

Talia N, Li Y, et al, 2016. Communication in neural circuits: Tools, opportunities, and challenges[J]. Cell, 164: 1136-1150.

Teo F, Hoy K E, Daskalakis Z J, et al, 2011. Investigating the role of current strength in tDCS modulation of working memory performance in healthy controls[J]. Frontiers in Psychiatry, 2:45.

Teo M, 2011. The liquidity risk of liquid hedge funds[J]. Journal of Financial Economics, 100: 24-44.

Wang J, Tian J, Hao R, et al, 2018. Transcranial direct current stimulation over the right DLPFC selectively modulates subprocesses in working memory [J]. PeerJ, 6(5655): e4906.

Yamamoto D, Woo C W, Wager T, et al. Influence of dorsolateral prefrontal cortex and ventral striatum on risk avoidance in addiction: A mediation analysis[J]. Drug & Alcohol Dependence, 2015, 149:10-17.

Yamamoto H, 2015. Enhancing engagement behavior using Shikake[J]. Ai & Society, 30(4):519-525.

Ye H, Huang D, Wang S, et al, 2016. Activation of the prefrontal cortex by unilateral transcranial direct current stimulation leads to an asymmetrical effect on risk preference in frames of gain and loss[J]. Brain Research, 1648 (Pt A):325-332.

Zaehle T, Sandmann P, Thorne J D, et al, 2011. Transcranial direct current stimulation of the prefrontal cortex modulates working memory performance: Combined behavioural and electrophysiological evidence [J]. BMC Neuroscience, 12(1):2.

Zong J, Fu J, Bao T, 2017. Cognitive ability of traders and financial bubbles: An experimental study[J]. Journal of World Economy, 40: 167-192.

Predicting the Volatility of the iShares China Large-cap ETF: What Is the Role of the SSE 50 ETF?[①]

Abstract　This study investigates whether the volatility of the Shanghai Stock Exchange (SSE) 50 ETF contains useful information for predicting the volatility of the U. S. -traded iShares China Large-Cap ETF (FXI). We use both in-sample and out-of-sample predictive regressions to empirically show that the realized volatility of the SSE 50 ETF significantly improves the forecasts of the future FXI realized volatility. We also find that the realized volatility of the SSE 50 ETF has predictive power for the future implied volatility of the FXI, which is calculated from the U. S. options market. However, the empirical results show that both the realized volatility and implied volatility of the FXI have limited explanatory ability for the realized volatility of the SSE 50 ETF.

Key words　FXI; SSE 50 ETF; Volatility predictability; Out-of-sample

1　Introduction

Foreign investors' interest in Chinese equity markets has grown rapidly as they seek higher returns from China's "new economy", i. e. , technology, consumer spending and telecom, and international diversification. With the inclusion of

---

①　Originally published in *Pacific-Basin Finance Journal* (vol. 57, 2019) by Zhu Fangfei, Luo Xingguo and Jin Xuejun.

a large number of Chinese A shares into Morgan Stanley Capital International (MSCI) indices since May 2018 and the resulting foreign capital inflow into these stocks, Chinese equities are attracting increased international attention from foreign investors. There is a large body of literature on the returns and volatility predictability of A-shares listed on Chinese mainland's stock exchanges that use different econometric methods and predictors (Goh et al., 2013; Westerlund et al., 2015; Chen et al., 2016; Chen et al., 2017). These existing studies, in particular, demonstrate that U. S. market information can strongly forecast Chinese stock market returns and volatilities. However, apart from the studies on cross-listed stocks, only a few studies focus on foreign-listed Chinese equities. Thus, it is reasonable to ask how the underlying Chinese market affetcs foreign-listed Chinese equities.

In this paper, we examine whether the Chinese domestic market can provide information beyond that embedded in the U. S. market for predicting the volatilities of U. S. -traded Chinese equities. Specifically, we investigate the volatility predictability of the U. S. -traded iShares China Large-Cap exchange-traded fund (FXI), which is an important fund that provides exposure to Chinese stocks. It seeks to track the investment results of the FTSE China 50 index composed of 50 large-capitalization Chinese stocks that trade on the Hong Kong Stock Exchange (HKEX; these underlying stocks are called H shares). As shown in Fig. 1, the FXI, with superb assets under management (USD 5. 73 billion in assets under management) and high daily volumes (average daily volume of USD 38. 1 million), is the largest and most popular China-targeted ETF listed out of Chinese mainland. Therefore, understanding whether the volatility of the FXI is predictable is of great importance to U. S. investors that are interested in Chinese stocks in terms of portfolio diversification and risk management.

We test the lagged realized volatility of the SSE 50 ETF traded in Chinese mainland as a predictor of future FXI realized volatility. The SSE 50 ETF tracks the performance of 50 large-capitalization A-share stocks listed on the SSE. As the SSE 50 ETF provides access to the largest and most liquid Chinese stocks, it is widely regarded as one of the most important equity funds

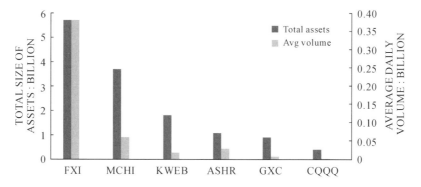

Fig. 1 Top 6 China ETFs listed overseas. Notes: The total assets and average daily volume data are as of December 2018 and obtained from ETFdb. com.

in China. Furthermore, its underlying stocks account for over 25% of the A-share market capitalization (Ahn et al., 2019). Therefore, the volatility of the SSE 50 ETF is likely to reflect the information on systematic risk and investor sentiment in Chinese mainland's stock markets. Moreover, the underlying stocks of the SSE 50 ETF are similar to those of the FXI. Both ETFs track large-capitalization Chinese stocks, half of which belong to the same firms. As shown in Fig. 2, fluctuations in the returns of the FXI are highly correlated with those of the SSE 50 ETF.

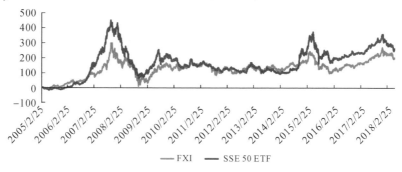

Fig. 2 FXI and SSE 50 ETF returns. Notes: This figure plots fluctuations in FXI and SSE 50 ETF returns.

The FXI is traded on the U. S. stock exchange, while its underlying stocks are those of Chinese firms. Although the underlying stocks of the FXI are required to disclose the same information to all investors, U. S. investors, unlike Chinese domestic investors, may find it difficult to access information on Chinese firms because of information asymmetry (Chan & Kwok, 2005; Chan et al. , 2008). Jia et al. (2017) also notes that Chinese domestic investors are better informed than foreign investors about home assets because of their superior private information. Thus, information on macroeconomic fundamentals such as economic conditions, systematic risk, monetary policy, and correlated industries may flow from Chinese domestic markets to the U. S. markets. This argument parallels the explanation of the home bias hypothesis in the literature, which states that domestic information plays a dominant role in information transmission (Xu & Fung, 2002). Moreover, Menzly and Ozbas (2010) propose a new channel of information flow, in that information diffuses gradually across segmented financial markets with correlated fundamentals. China's capital controls lead to the segmentation of the FXI and SSE 50 ETF markets, while the underlying stocks of the two ETFs are those of Chinese firms with correlated fundamentals. Therefore, information may diffuse gradually amongst investors in the two ETF markets, which allows us to explore the volatility predictability of the two markets.

Furthermore, as the option-implied volatility is widely regarded as a better measure of volatility, we investigate the role of the SSE 50 ETF realized volatility in predicting the implied volatility of the FXI calculated from the U. S. options market. The FXI options market has become the largest options market targeting Chinses stocks available to global investors. More details about FXI options can be seen in Li et al. (2019). Forecasting the implied volatility of FXI options is crucial to an FXI option pricing model and to investors in terms of portfolio management and risk hedging. As the SSE 50 ETF market may have important information pertaining to the underlying ETF of FXI options, the volatility of the SSE 50 ETF may affect the expectations of investors in FXI options market for future price volatilities of the FXI and may therefore predict future FXI implied volatility.

Referring to the literature which argues that the U. S. market generally plays a leading role in the relationship between its own equity markets and those of China, we revisit this issue by examining the predictive power of the realized and implied volatilities of the FXI for the SSE 50 ETF realized volatility. For example, Rapach et al. (2013) illustrates that information on macroeconomic fundamentals relevant to equity markets worldwide diffuses gradually from the U. S. market to overseas markets, and reveals the leading role of lagged U. S. returns in the returns predictability of the Chinese stock market. Luo and Ye (2015) find that the U. S. options market plays a significant role in predicting the volatility of Shanghai silver futures. Goh et al. (2013) and Chen et al. (2016) provide empirical evidence that information on the U. S. economy greatly helped forecast Chinese stock market returns and volatilities after China's admittance to the World Trade Organization. Chen et al. (2017) shows that the U. S. volatility risk (VIX) is effective in forecasting Chinese stock returns. As the U. S. is among China's large trade partners and its equity market is the largest in the world, attracting the most investors, information on macroeconomic fundamentals relevant to equity markets worldwide can diffuse gradually from the U. S. market to China. Thus, with the information on the U. S. market, the realized volatility (RV) of the FXI and the implied volatility (IV) of the FXI options may have predictive power for the SSE 50 ETF volatility.

We use both in-sample and out-of-sample predictive regressions to examine the monthly and daily volatility predictability. We investigate whether the lagged realized volatility of the SSE 50 ETF (hereafter SSE 50 ETF RV) contains forecasting information for future realized volatility of the FXI (hereafter FXI RV) and for the future implied volatility of FXI options (hereafter FXI IV). We also examine the reverse relationship. The evidence from both in-sample and out-of-sample indicates that the SSE 50 ETF RV significantly improves the daily and monthly forecasts of future FXI RV. We also find that the SSE 50 ETF RV has predictive power for future FXI IV calculated from the U. S. options market. However, the reverse results show that both FXI RV and IV have limited explanatory ability for SSE 50 ETF RV. The revealed predictive ability of SSE 50 volatility for FXI RV provides interesting empirical implications for FXI investors with regard to portfolio diversification and risk management. International investors that are interested in Chinese stocks can achieve higher returns and risk hedging by incorporating the information on China's domestic stock markets. Furthermore, we find that information on the Chinese domestic stock market can improve the forecasting performance of the volatility of FXI options, which is useful for options traders in structuring profitable strategies. Besides, our results imply that an option pricing model of the FXI may benefit from incorporating volatility information on the SSE 50 ETF.

Our study contributes to the literature in three ways. First, we reveal a new predictor of monthly and daily FXI volatility: the lagged SSE 50 ETF RV. As the FXI is the largest and most liquid U. S. -traded fund that provides exposure to Chinese stocks, predicting its volatility is of great importance to U. S. traders. To the best of our knowledge, we are the first to provide an additional predictor for predicting FXI volatility. Second, unlike the existing literature that extensively documents the predictive ability of the information on the U. S. market for Chinese stock market returns and volatility (Goh et al., 2013; Chen et al., 2016; Chen et al., 2017), we provide both in-sample and out-of-sample evidence that information on China's domestic market has significant predictive power for the FXI traded in the U. S. market. Further, besides investigating the information contained in the spot market, we also examine the information on IV from the options market to complement the literature. We present evidence that China's SSE 50 ETF RV contains predictive information on FXI IV, implying that the SSE 50 ETF is important to U. S. traders of FXI options.

The remainder of this paper is organized as follows. Section 2 briefly describes the data. Section 3 In-sample analysis, Section 4 Out-of-sample analysis report the in-sample and out-of-sample results, respectively. Section 5 concludes the paper.

2   Data

2.1   Realized volatility

In this paper, we make use of RVs of the SSE 50 ETF and FXI. Following the literature（Paye，2012），we first sum the squared daily returns to represent the monthly variance of the funds' returns and the squared minute returns to represent the daily variance of the funds' returns. Then，we use the natural logarithms of RV. For a specific month，the monthly RV is defined as

$$RV_m = \log\left(\sqrt{\sum_{j=1}^{t} r_{j,m}^2}\right) \tag{1}$$

$$r_{j,m} = 100 \times (\log P_{j,m} - \log P_{j-1,m}), \tag{2}$$

where t is the number of trading days in month m, $r_{j,m}$ is the jth daily return in month m, and $P_{j,m}$ is the closing price for day j in month m.

For a specific day d, the daily RV is defined as

$$RV_d = \log\left(\sqrt{\sum_{i=1}^{h} r_{i,d}^2}\right) \tag{3}$$

$$r_{i,d} = 100 \times (\log P_{i,d} - \log P_{i-1,d}), \tag{4}$$

where h is the number of trading minutes in each day, $r_{i,d}$ is the minute return on day d, and $P_{i,d}$ is the closing price for the ith minute on day d.

To construct the monthly RV，we use the daily prices of the SSE 50 and FXI. The daily price data span March 1，2005 to June 30，2018 and are obtained from the Wind database. We also use 1-min price data of the SSE 50 and FXI for the February 9，2015 to December 30，2016 period to construct the daily RV. These data are for the trading period of each business day, i. e., between 9:30:00 and 16:00:00.

Fig. 3 plots the time series of the monthly FXI RV and SSE 50 ETF RV over the March 2005 to June 2018 sample period. We obtain the following meaningful points. First，the two volatility series follow a similar trend over the sample period. In particular，some large FXI volatilities always occur along with or after the large SSE 50 ETF volatilities. Second，during the 2008 financial crisis（from October 2007 to July 2009），FXI volatilities were much larger than SSE 50 ETF volatilities. The FXI volatility reached its historical peak over the sample period in October 2008 when the U. S. stock market crashed. However，during the November 2014 to October 2015 period when China's stock market crashed，SSE 50 ETF volatilities were larger than those of the FXI.

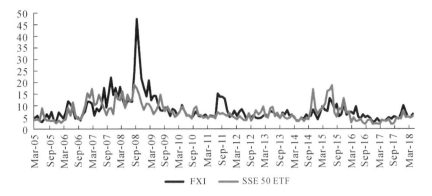

Fig. 3   FXI and SSE 50 ETF RVs. Notes: This figure plots the time series of monthly FXI and SSE 50 ETF RVs over the March 2005 to June 2018 sample period.

2.2   Implied volatility

Previous studies document the option-implied volatility as a better measure of volatility with forward-looking information. As the FXI options market is the largest options market targeting Chinses stocks available to global investors, we also examine the predictive power of SSE 50 ETF RV for FXI IV.

To proxy for the FXI IV, we use the Chicago Board Options Exchange's (C) BOE China ETF Volatility Index (VXFXI), which was published by CBOE in March 2011 and reflects the FXI IV. Due to the data availability[①], the daily VXFXI data covers the April 2011 to June 2018 period. We collect daily VXFXI data from the CBOE website.

Panel A of Table 1 reports the monthly correlation matrix between RV^{FXI}, RV^{50ETF}, and VXFXI at the log level. Due to the availability of VXFXI data, the sample period for monthly correlation analysis spans April 2011 to June 2018. The correlation coefficient between monthly RV^{FXI} and RV^{50ETF} is 0.5886 and statistically significant at the 1% level, between monthly RV^{50ETF} and VXFXI is 0.563, and between monthly RV^{RXI} and VXFXI is 0.82. Panel B of Table 1 shows the daily correlation matrix for the February 9, 2015 to December 30, 2016 period. The correlation coefficient between daily RV^{FXI}

---

① The sample period starts from April 2011 due to the availability of VXFXI data. CBOE first published VXFXI data on March 16, 2011.

and RV^{50ETF} is 0. 43, between daily RV^{50ETF} and VXFXI is 0. 605, and between daily RV^{FXI} and VXFXI is 0. 561. Evidently, the RV^{50ETF} shows relatively strong correlations with RV^{FXI} and VXFXI. As some correlations are larger than 0. 5, we use the variance inflation factor (VIF) to test the multicollinearity of each forecasting model.

Table 1   Correlation matrix at monthly and daily frequencies

	RV^{FXI}	RV^{50ETF}	VXFXI
Panel A: Monthly			
RV^{FXI}	1. 0000		
RV^{50ETF}	0. 589***	1. 0000	
VXFXI	0. 820***	0. 563***	1. 0000
Panel B: Daily			
RV^{FXI}	1. 0000		
RV^{50ETF}	0. 430***	1. 0000	
VXFXI	0. 561***	0. 605***	1. 0000

Notes: Table 1 reports the monthly and daily correlation matrix between, RV^{FXI}, RV^{50ETF} and VXFXI at the log level. ***, **, and * denote coefficient significance levels at 1%, 5%, and 10%, respectively. The sample period of Panel A spans April 2011 to June 2018. Panel B shows the daily correlation matrix for the February 9, 2015 to December 30, 2016 period.

2.3   Holdings of the FXI and SSE 50 ETF

To further investigate the correlation between the FXI and the SSE 50 ETF, we examine the holdings of the two ETFs. The FXI tracks 50 large-capitalization Chinese equities (see Table A1 in the appendix for details) listed on the HKEX. According to its recent released holdings, as of December 2018, while 34 of the 50 stocks are listed both on the SSE (A-shares) and HKEX, the remaining are listed only on the HKEX. Notably, 25 out of the 50 stocks are tracked by both the FXI and the SSE 50 ETF.

Table 2 reports the top 10 FXI and SSE 50 ETF holdings as of December 2018. Among the top 10 FXI holdings, six are financial services stocks, two are energy stocks, and the remaining two are information technology and telecom services stocks. Among the top 10 holdings of the SSE 50 ETF, seven are financial services stocks.

Table 2 Top 10 FXI and SSE 50 ETF holdings

FXI				SSE 50 ETF			
Ticker	Corporation	Industry	Weight (%)	Ticker	Corporation	Industry	Weight (%)
700	TENCENT HOLDINGS LTD	Information Technology	8.99	601,318	PING AN INSURANCE CO OF CH	Financials	14.07
939	CHINA CONSTRUCTION BANK CORP	Financials	8.93	600,519	KWEICHOW MOUTAI CO LTD	Consumer Goods	6.87
1398	INDUSTRIAL AND COMMERCIAL BANK OF CH	Financials	7.28	600,036	CHINA MERCHANTS BANK LTD	Financials	6.02
941	CHINA MOBILE LTD	Telecom Services	6.82	601,166	INDUSTRIAL BANK CO LTD	Financials	4.29
2318	PING AN INSURANCE CO OF CH	Financials	6.23	601,328	BANK OF COMMUNICATIONS LTD	Financials	3.67
3988	BANK OF CHINA LTD H	Financials	4.48	600,016	CHINA MINSHENG BANKING CORP LTD	Financials	3.30
883	CNOOC LTD	Energy	3.93	600,887	INNER MONGOLIA YILI INDUSTRIAL GROUP CO LTD	Consumer Goods	3.20
386	CHINA PETROLEUM AND CHEMICAL CORP	Energy	3.42	601,288	AGRICULTURAL BANK OF CHINA LTD	Financials	3.18
3968	CHINA MERCHANTS BANK LTD H	Financials	2.98	600,030	CITIC SECURITIES COMPANY LTD	Financials	3.03
2628	CHINA LIFE INSURANCE LTD	Financials	2.96	601,668	CHINA STATE CONSTRUCTION ENGINEERING CO LTD	Construction Engineerin	2.79

3 In-sample analysis

3.1 Predicting FXI realized volatility using the SSE 50 ETF realized volatility

In this section, we investigate the predictive power of SSE 50 ETF RV for FXI RV at monthly and daily frequency. We begin with a simple univariate prediction model as the standard benchmark. The benchmark predictive regression is defined as

$$RV_0 : RV_{t+1}^{FXI} = \alpha + \beta RV_t^{FXI} + \varepsilon_{t+1}, t = m, d \tag{5}$$

where RV_t^{FXI} is the FXI RV at time t, RV_m^{FXI} is the FXI RV in month m, and RV_d^{FXI} is the FXI RV on day d. The error term ε_{t+1} is assumed to follow an independent and identically normal distribution.

To examine the predictive information contained in the SSE 50 ETF RV, we include the lagged SSE 50 ETF RV as an additional predictor. The extending predictive regression is defined as

$$RV - RV : RV_{t+1}^{FXI} = \alpha + \beta_1 RV_t^{FXI} + \beta_2 RV_t^{50ETF} + \varepsilon_{t+1}, t = m, d, \tag{6}$$

where RV_m^{50ETF} represents the SSE 50 ETF RV in the month m and RV_d^{50ETF} denotes the SSE 50 ETF RV on day d. $d+1RV_d^{50ETF}$

Table 3 reports the in-sample estimated results for the predictive regressions for FXI RV at monthly and daily frequency. The monthly coefficient of the lagged RV^{FXI} in the RV_0 model is 0.758. When the lagged RV^{50ETF} is added to the benchmark predictive regression (RV_0), the coefficient of the lagged RV^{50ETF} for monthly forecasts is 0.173 and that of the lagged RV^{FXI} declines from 0.758 to 0.632, indicating that the lagged RV^{50ETF} can forecast 17.3% of the future RV^{FXI}. Both coefficients of the lagged RV^{50ETF} and lagged RV^{FXI} at the monthly frequency are statistically significant at the 1% level. The value of adjusted R^2 for monthly forecasts increases from 0.574 to 0.589 after the lagged RV^{50ETF} is added, implying that the lagged RV^{50ETF} can account for an additional 2.7% larger proportion of variations of the FXI RV relative to the benchmark predictive regression (RV_0).

Table 3 In-sample estimated results for predictive regressions of the realized volatility of the FXI

	Monthly estimates: Predicting		Daily estimates: Predicting	
	RV_{m+1}^{FXI}		RV_{d+1}^{FXI}	
	RV_0	$RV-RV$	RV_0	$RV-RV$
RV_t^{FXI}	0.758***	0.632***	0.303***	0.167***
	(13.113)	(9.923)	(4.792)	(3.186)
RV_t^{50ETF}		0.173***		0.316***
		(3.300)		(5.750)
Constant	0.479***	0.409***	0.189***	0.136***
	(4.495)	(3.576)	(6.812)	(4.699)
Adj. R^2	0.574	0.589	0.090	0.174
$R^2(\%)$		2.70		93.78
Mean VIF	1	1.18	1	1.08
Obs.	160	160	444	444

Notes: Table 3 reports the in-sample monthly and daily results of the predictive regressions for FXI RV estimated by OLS along with the Newey-West method. In this table, we report the coefficients of the predictors, Newey-West t-statistics in parentheses, adjusted R^2 statistics, the percentage increase in R^2 of the predictive regressions ($RV-RV$) relative to that of the benchmark model (RV_0), and the mean VIF of each regression. The sample period for the monthly estimation spans March 2005 to June 2018, while that of the daily estimation spans February 9, 2015 to December 30, 2016. ***, **, and * denote coefficient significance levels at 1%, 5%, and 10%, respectively.

The daily results are generally consistent with those of the monthly estimation, suggesting that the coefficient of the RV_t^{50ETF} is positive and significant. Remarkably, our results indicate that the RV_t^{50ETF} improves the forecasts of the RV_{t+1}^{FXI} more at the daily frequency than at the monthly frequency. When the RV_t^{50ETF} is added to the benchmark predictive regression (RV_0), the coefficient of RV_t^{50ETF} for daily forecasts is 0.316 and that of the lagged RV^{FXI} declines from 0.303 to 0.167. The coefficient of RV_t^{50ETF} is economically larger than that of the lagged RV^{FXI}. Moreover, the value of adjusted R^2 for daily forecasts increases from 0.009 to 0.174 after the lagged

RV^{50ETF} is added, implying that the lagged RV^{50ETF} can account for an additional 93. 78% larger proportion of variations of the FXI RV relative to the benchmark predictive regression (RV_0). These results demonstrate that the RV_t^{50ETF} contains more useful information than the lagged RV^{FXI} for predicting daily FXI RV.

Overall, these in-sample estimated results document strong evidence that the SSE 50 ETF in Chinese mainland contains additional information for predicting FXI RV beyond that embedded in the lagged FXI RV at monthly and daily frequencies. According to the literature, the information asymmetry, home bias hypothesis and gradual information diffusion may help explain the predictive power of the SSE 50 ETF. As the SSE 50 ETF is traded only in Chinese mainland and the FXI is not, SSE 50 ETF investors are Chinese domestic investors and FXI investors are foreign investors. Owing to the information asymmetry, foreign investors may find it tough to access information on Chinese firms as compared with Chinese domestic investors and thus have less information than domestic investors with respect to Chinese stocks (Chan & Kwok, 2005; Chan et al. , 2008). Jia et al. (2017) also notes that Chinese domestic investors are better informed than foreign investors about home assets because of their superior private information. Thus, information on macroeconomic fundamentals relevant to Chinese stocks may gradually diffuse from SSE 50 ETF investors in China's domestic market to FXI investors in the U. S. market. The home bias hypothesis in the literature supports this explanation by indicating that domestic information plays a dominant role in information transmission (Xu & Fung, 2002). Moreover, Menzly and Ozbas (2010) provide a closet mechanism of information diffusion, arguing that information diffuses gradually across segmented financial markets with correlated fundamentals due to investor specialization and market segmentation. China's capital controls lead to the segmentation of FXI and SSE 50 ETF markets, while the underlying stocks of the two ETFs are those of Chinese firms with correlated fundamentals. Therefore, information may diffuse gradually among informed and uninformed investors in the markets of the two ETFs.

3.2   Predicting FXI implied volatility using SSE 50 ETF realized volatility

As the option-implied volatility is widely regarded as a better measure of volatility, we further investigate the role of SSE 50 ETF RV in predicting the FXI IV calculated from the U.S. options market. The FXI options market has become the largest options market targeting Chineses stocks available to global investors. Thus, forecasting FXI IV is crucial to an option pricing model of the FXI and to investors in terms of portfolio management and risk hedging. As the SSE 50 ETF market may contain important information pertaining to the underlying ETF of FXI options, the volatility of the SSE 50 ETF may affect the expectations of investors in the FXI options market for future price volatility of the FXI and may therefore predict future FXI IV. To proxy for the FXI IV, we use the CBOE's VXFXI, which reflects the FXI IV.

Consistent with the predictive regressions in Section 3.1, we first build a benchmark predictive regression (IV_0) and then add SSE 50 ETF RV as an additional predictor into the benchmark predictive regression ($IV-RV$). The two predictive regressions are conducted at monthly and daily frequencies respectively. The monthly and daily predictive regressions are defined as

$$IV_0: \quad VXFXI_{t+1} = +VXFXI_t + \varepsilon_{t+1}, t=m,d \tag{7}$$

$$IV-RV: \quad VXFXI_{t+1} = +\beta_1 VXFXI_t + \beta_2 RV_t^{50ETF} + \varepsilon_{t+1} t=m\ d \tag{8}$$

where $VXFXI_t$ is the logarithm of the CBOE's VXFXI at time t, $VXFXI_m$ is the logarithm of the index in month m, $VXFXI_d$ is the logarithm of the index on day d, and RV_m^{50ETF} and RV_d^{50ETF} are defined earlier.

Table 4 reports the estimated results for the predictive regressions for FXI IV at monthly and daily frequencies. The monthly estimated results show that the coefficient of the lagged $VXFXI$ in the IV_0 model is 0.752. After the lagged RV^{50ETF} is added to the benchmark IV_0 model, the coefficient of the lagged $VXFXI$ declines to 0.648 and that of the lagged RV^{50ETF} is 0.0910. These coefficients at the monthly frequency are statistically significant at the 1% level or at the 5% level. The value of adjusted R^2 for monthly forecasts of FXI IV increases from 0.563 to 0.581 after the lagged RV^{50ETF} is added, implying the lagged RV^{50ETF} can account for an additional 3.2% larger proportion of variations of the FXI IV relative to the benchmark predictive regression (IV_0).

Table 4　In-sample estimated results for predictive regressions of the implied volatility of the FXI

	Monthly estimates: Predicting $VXFXI_{m+1}$		Daily estimates: Predicting $VXFXI_{d+1}$	
	IV_0	$IV-RV$	IV_0	$IV-RV$
$VXFXI_t$	0.752***	0.648***	0.962***	0.925***
	(12.154)	(7.645)	(81.808)	(56.369)
RV_t^{50ETF}		0.091**		0.023***
		(2.179)		(3.310)
Constant	0.489***	0.544***	0.023***	0.038***
	(4.031)	(4.591)	(3.264)	(4.123)
Adj. R^2	0.563	0.581	0.924	0.927
R^2(%)		3.20		0.25
Mean VIF	1	1.46	1	1.68
Obs.	87	87	444	444

Notes: Table 4 provides in-sample estimated results for the predictive regressions for FXI IV at monthly and daily frequencies. The numbers in parentheses are Newey-West t-statistics. R^2 is the percentage increase in R^2 of the forecasting model ($IV-RV$) relative to that of the benchmark model (IV_0). The in-sample period for the monthly analysis spans April 2011 to June 2018, and that for the daily analysis spans February 9, 2015 to December 30, 2016. ***, **, and * represent coefficient significance levels at 1%, 5%, and 10%, respectively.

　　The estimated results at the daily frequency for the predictive regressions for FXI IV are similar to those at the monthly frequency. We find that the coefficient of the lagged RV^{50ETF} is 0.023 and remains significant at the 1% level after the lagged $VXFXI$ is controlled. Moreover, the lagged RV^{50ETF} increases the value of adjusted R^2 for daily forecasts of FXI IV from 0.924 to 0.927. In comparison with the results for predicting FXI RV, the coefficient of SSE 50 ETF RV for predicting FXI IV is smaller, indicating that SSE 50 ETF RV has a lower predictive power for FXI IV than it has FXI RV.

　　In sum, SSE 50 ETF RV exhibits significant in-sample predictability of FXI IV at monthly and daily frequencies, suggesting that the information embedded in SSE 50 ETF RV is useful in predicting FXI IV and deserves more attention from investors in FXI options market.

Predicting SSE realized volatility using FXI volatilities

According to the literature, the U. S. market generally plays a leading role in the relationship between its own equity markets and those of other countries (Rapach et al. , 2013) and the information on U. S. variables can strongly forecast Chinese stock market returns and volatilities (Goh et al. , 2013; Chen et al. , 2016; Chen et al. , 2017). We revisit this issue by examining the predictive power of the RVs and IVs of the U. S. -traded FXI for SSE 50 ETF RV.

Consistent with the predictive regressions mentioned above, we first build a benchmark predictive regression (RV_0) and then add FXI RV (FXI IV) as an additional predictor into the benchmark predictive regression ($RV-RV/RV-IV$). The predictive regressions are conducted at monthly and daily frequencies, respectively, and are defined as

$$RV_0: \quad RV_{t+1}^{50ETF} = +RV_t^{50ETF} = \varepsilon_{t+1} t = m\ d, \tag{9}$$

$$RV-RV: \quad RV_{t+1}^{50ETF} = +\beta_1 RV_t^{50ETF} +\beta_2 RV_t^{FXI} +\varepsilon_{t+1} t = m\ d, \tag{10}$$

$$RV-IV: \quad RV_{t+1}^{50ETF} =\alpha+\beta_1 RV_t^{50ETF} +\beta_2 VXFXI_t +\varepsilon_{t+1} t = m\ d \tag{11}$$

where RV_t^{50ETF}, RV_t^{FXI}, and $VXFXI_t$ are defined as before.

Table 5 reports the estimated results for predictive regressions for SSE 50 ETF RV at monthly and daily frequencies. The monthly estimated results show that the coefficients of the lagged RV^{50ETF} in the RV_0 model is 0.758 and significant at the 1% level. When the lagged RV^{FXI} and $VXFXI$ are added to the monthly benchmark RV_0 model respectively, both the coefficients of the lagged RV^{50ETF} slightly decline to 0.683 in the $RV-RV$ model and 0.655 in the $RV-IV$ model. The monthly coefficient of the lagged RV^{FXI} for RV^{50ETF} forecasts is -0.003 and that of the lagged $VXFXI$ is 0.094. Both the coefficients of the lagged RV^{FXI} and $VXFXI$ for RV^{50ETF} forecasts are small and insignificant, suggesting that the predictive power of the lagged RV^{FXI} and $VXFXI$ for RV^{50ETF} at the monthly frequency is quite weak. Moreover, the corresponding values of the adjusted R^2 support this conclusion by showing that both values of adjusted R^2 of the extended regression models ($RV-RV$ and $RV-IV$) are smaller than that of the benchmark RV_0 regression.

Table 5 In-sample estimated results for predictive regressions of the realized volatility of SSE 50 ETF

	Monthly estimates: Predicting RV_{m+1}^{50ETF}			Daily estimates: Predicting RV_{d+1}^{50ETF}		
	RV_0	$RV-RV$	$RV-IV$	RV_0	$RV-RV$	$RV-IV$
RV_t^{50ETF}	0.758***	0.683***	0.655***	0.861***	0.847***	0.796***
	(13.113)	(7.490)	(6.407)	(31.211)	(31.383)	(17.479)
RV_t^{FXI}		−0.003			0.031	
		(−0.031)			(1.150)	
$VXFXI_t$			0.094			0.011
			(0.722)			(0.353)
Constant	0.479***	0.533***	0.388*	0.037***	0.033***	0.123***
	(4.495)	(2.905)	(1.759)	(3.155)	(2.710)	(2.509)
Adj. R^2	0.458	0.452	0.453	0.738	0.738	0.738
R^2(%)		−1.42	−1.09		0.03	0.01
Mean VIF	1	1.12	1.51	1	1.99	2.52
Obs.	87	87	87	444	444	444

Notes: Table 5 reports the in-sample monthly and daily results of the predictive regressions for SSE 50 ETF RV estimated by OLS along with the Newey-West method. In this table, we report the coefficients of the predictors, Newey-West t-statistics in parentheses, adjusted R^2 statistics, the percentage increase in R^2 of the predictive regressions ($RV-RV/RV-IV$) relative to that of the benchmark model (RV_0), and the mean VIF of each regression. The in-sample period for the monthly analysis spans April 2011 to June 2018, and that for the daily analysis spans February 9, 2015 to December 30, 2016. ***, **, and * represent coefficient significance levels at 1%, 5%, and 10%, respectively.

The daily estimated results are consistent with the monthly findings. The coefficient of the lagged RV^{FXI} for RV^{50ETF} forecasts is 0.031 while that of the lagged $VXFXI$ is 0.011. However, the two coefficients are insignificant. The values of the adjusted R^2 of the extended regression models ($RV-RV$ and $RV-IV$) at the daily frequency do not improve significantly relative to that of the benchmark RV_0 model, implying that the FXI RV and IV have limited explanatory ability for SSE 50 ETF RV.

Unlike previous studies, which find that information on U. S. variables can strongly forecast Chinese stock market returns and volatilities, our study indicate that information on FXI and FXI options in the United States contain limited predictive information for Chinese SSE 50 ETF volatility in our sample. The possible reasons may lie in the investor structure and underlying stocks of the two ETFs. The two ETFs are passive index tracking funds that tracks stocks of large-cap Chinese firms. While SSE 50 ETF investors are primarily residents of Chinese mainland, FXI investors are traders in the U. S. market. As noted by Jia et al. (2017), domestic investors are better informed than foreign investor about home assets because of their superior private information. Although the two ETFs track similar underlying stocks, FXI investors are less informed than domestic investors of the SSE 50 ETF, and thus, the information on the FXI and FXI options has limited explanatory ability for the SSE 50 ETF RV.

4　Out-of-sample analysis

Extensive literature (Goyal & Welch, 2008; Kelly & Pruitt, 2013; etc.) show that a predictive model with good in-sample performance does not necessarily dispaly good out-of-sample performance. Therefore, besides in-sample predictions, our study provides out-of-sample results to evaluate the predictive power of variables.

Our in-sample results show that the SSE 50 ETF RV has predictive power for both FXI RV and IV, while the opposite is insignificant. Thus, our out-of-sample analysis focuses on predictive regressions, which use the SSE 50 ETF RV to predict FXI RV and IV.

We first use predictive regressions and the rolling window method to generate out-of-sample forecasts of FXI volatilities. Specifically, we divide the total sample of $T+N$ observations into a training part containing the first T observations and a forecasting part containing the remaining N observations. We use the training part observations to obtain OLS estimates of the parameters of the predictive regressions and conduct the out-of-sample forecasts based on estimated parameters and FXI and SSE volatilities in the forecasting part.

For example, the extending predictive regression of FXI RV is

$$RV_{t+1}^{FXI} = \alpha + \beta_1 RV_t^{FXI} + \beta_2 RV_T^{50ETF} + \varepsilon_{t+1},\tag{12}$$

Therefore, the first out-of-sample forecast of FXI volatility based on SSE 50 ETF volatility is given by

$$\hat{RV}_{T+1}^{FXI} = \hat{\alpha} + \hat{\beta}_{1,T} RV_T^{FXI} + \hat{\beta}_{2,T} RV_T^{50ETF},\tag{13}$$

where $\hat{\alpha}_T, \hat{\beta}_{1T}$, and $\hat{\beta}_{2T}$ are the OLS estimates of α, β_1, and β_2 obtained by regressing $\{RV_t^{FXI}\}_{t=2}^{T}$ on a constant, $\{RV_t^{FXI}\}_{t=1}^{T-1}$ and $\{RV_t^{50ETF}\}_{t=1}^{T-1}$.

For the rolling window estimation, the window size is fixed. Thus, when a new observation is included in the estimation window, the first observation of the old training part should be dropped. For example, the second out-of-sample forecast of the FXI volatility is given by

$$\hat{RV}_{T+2}^{FXI} = \hat{\alpha}_{T+1} + \hat{\beta}_{1,T+} V_{T+}^{FXI} + \hat{\beta}_{T+} V_{T+}^{50ETF},\tag{14}$$

where, $\hat{\alpha}_{T+1}$, $\hat{\beta}_{1,T+1}$ and $\hat{\beta}_{2,T+}$ are the OLS estimates of α, β_1 and β_2 obtained by regressing $\{RV_1^{FXI}\}_{t=3}^{T+1}$ on a constant, $\{RV_t^{FXI}\}_{t=2}^{T}$ and $\{RV_t^{50ETF}\}_{t=2}^{T}$. Hence, we obtain out-of-sample forecasts: $\{\hat{RV}_{T+i}^{FXI}\}_{i=1}^{N}$.

Then, we compute two statistics to evaluate the out-of-sample performance. The first statistic is R_{os}^2 (out-of-sample R^2) (Paye, 2012; Goyal and Welch, 2008), which is given by

$$R_{os}^2 = 1 - \frac{\sum_{t=1}^{N} (RV_{T+t} - \hat{RV}_{T+T})^2}{\sum_{t=1}^{N} (RV_{T+t} - \overline{RV}_{T+t})^2},\tag{15}$$

where is the true value of log RV, $\hat{RV}_{T+t}$ is the out-of-sample forecast, and $\overline{RV}_{T+t}$ is the historical average benchmark, defined as

$$\overline{RV}_{T+t} = \frac{1}{T+t-1} \sum_{s=1}^{T+t-1} RV_s.\tag{16}$$

If $R_{os}^2 > 0$, then the out-of-sample forecast $\hat{RV}_{T+t}$ outperforms the historical average $\overline{RV}_{T+t}$ in terms of mean squared forecasting errors.

The second statistic we use is the CW test's (Clark & West, 2007) mean-squared forecast error (MSFE)-adjusted statistics. The null hypothesis of the CW test is that the MSFE of the historical average benchmark model is less than or equal to that of the predictive regression and the alternative hypothesis is that the MSFE of the historical average benchmark model is greater than that of the predictive regression, i. e. , $H_0: R_{os}^2 \ll$ against $H_A: R_{os}^2 >$. The statistic is given by

$$f_t = (RV_t - \hat{RV}_{t,bench})^2 - (RV_t - \hat{RV}_{t,forecast})^2 + (\hat{RV}_{t,bench} - \hat{RV}_{t,forecast})^2. \quad (17)$$

The MSFE-adjusted statistic is the t-statistic from the regression of f_t on a constant. The out-of-sample forecasting process for FXI IV is similar to that for FXI RV. We conduct the out-of-sample analysis using both monthly and daily frequencies.

Table 6 presents the results of the out-of-sample forecasting performance of SSE 50 ETF RV for FXI RV and IV. Panel A shows the out-of-sample results at the monthly frequency. The out-of-sample period for the monthly forecasts of FXI RV spans March 2005 to June 2018, while that for the monthly forecasts of FXI IV spans April 2011 to June 2018 due to the availability of VXFXI data. Panel B reports the daily out-of-sample results for the February 9, 2015 to December 30, 2016 period. All of the predictive regressions for FXI RV and IV generate positive values for the R_{os}^2 statistic, indicating that the predictive regression forecasts outperform the historical average in terms of mean squared forecasting errors. Moreover, all of the predictive regressions provide significant MSFE-adjusted statistics at the 1% level according to the p-values of the CW test, which suggests statistically significant and economically large improvements in forecasting accuracy. In particular, the extension $RV-RV(IV-RV)$ model with SSE 50 ETF RV as an additional predictor generates a larger R_{os}^2 than the benchmark $RV_0(IV_0)$. Therefore, we conclude that SSE RV shows an additional power for both FXI RV and IV, which is consistent with the in-sample findings in Table 3 and Table 4.

Table 6 Evaluations for out-of-sample forecasting results

Regressions	R_{os}^2	MSFE-adjusted
Panel A: Monthly estimates		
RV_0	55.093	0.1913***
$RV-RV$	57.060	0.2117***
IV_0	56.281	0.0178***
$IV-RV$	57.383	0.0195***
Panel B: Daily estimates		
RV_0	13.904	0.0852***
$RV-RV$	22.871	0.1210***
IV_0	91.494	0.0821***
$IV-RV$	91.982	0.0821***

Notes: Table 6 reports the evaluations for the out-of-sample forecasting results. We provide the values of the out-of-sample R^2 as well as the values of the MSFE-adjusted statistic of the CW test between the predictive model and historical average forecasts. The monthly forecasts are generated using a rolling window with a period of 80 months for the $RV_0/RV-RV$ model and a period of 40 months for the $IV_0/IV-RV$ model. The daily out-of-sample performance is evaluated based on an 80-day rolling window. ***, **, and * denote significance levels of MSFE-adjusted statistics at 1%, 5%, and 10% levels according to the p-values of the CW test.

5　Conclusions

Our study investigates whether the volatility of the SSE 50 ETF contains useful information for predicting the volatility of the U. S.-traded iShares China Large-Cap ETF (FXI). We first examine whether the lagged SSE 50 ETF RV contains forecasting information for future FXI RV. Moreover, as the option-implied volatility is widely regarded as a better measure of volatility, we further investigate the role of the SSE 50 ETF RV in predicting future FXI IV calculated from the U. S. options market. We also revisit the role of the U. S. market in the relationship between its own equity markets and those of China by examining the predictive power of FXI RV and IV for futureSSE 50 ETF RV.

We use both in-sample and out-of-sample predictive regressions to empirically show that the SSE 50 ETF RV significantly improves the forecasts of future FXI RV at monthly and daily frequencies. Furthermore, we find that the SSE 50 ETF RV also has predictive power for future FXI IV. However, the empirical results also show that both the RV and IV of the FXI have limited explanatory ability for the SSE 50 ETF RV.

The revealed predictive ability of SSE 50 ETF volatility for FXI realized volatility provides interesting empirical implications for FXI investors with regard to portfolio diversification and risk management. International investors that are interested in Chinese stocks may achieve higher returns and risk hedging by incorporating the information on China's domestic stock markets. Furthermore, we find that the information on Chinese domestic stock markets can improve the forecasting performance of the volatility of FXI options, which is useful for options traders in constructing strategies. Our results also imply that an option pricing model of the FXI may benefit from incorporating volatility information on the SSE 50 ETF.

Acknowledgments

We are grateful to the guest editors, Mark Liu and Yizhong Wang, for their encouragement. We also acknowledge helpful comments from an anonymous referee, Chloe Chunliu Yang (our CIRF discussant), Xiaoli Yu, Yabei Zhu, Shihua Qin, Jiawei Yu, and participants at the 2018 China International Risk Forum (C) IRF. We gratefully acknowledge the financial support from the National Natural Science Foundation of China (Project No. 71771199 and 71673249) and the Fundamental Research Funds for the Central Universities.

Appendix

Table A1   Holdings of FXI and SSE 50 ETF

FXI holdings	Ticker	SSE 50 ETF holdings	Ticker
AGRICULTURAL BANK OF CHINA LTD	1288	AGRICULTURAL BANK OF CHINA LTD	601288
ANHUI CONCH CEMENT LTD	914	ANHUI CONCH CEMENT LTD	600585

continued

FXI holdings	Ticker	SSE 50 ETF holdings	Ticker
BANK OF CHINA LTD	3988	BANK OF CHINA LTD	601988
BANK OF COMMUNICATIONS LTD	3328	BANK OF COMMUNICATIONS LTD	601328
CHINA COMMUNICATIONS CONSTRUCTIONS	1800	CHINA COMMUNICATIONS CONSTRUCTIONS	601800
CHINA CONSTRUCTION BANK CORP	939	CHINA CONSTRUCTION BANK CORP	601939
CHINA EVERBRIGHT BANK LTD	6818	CHINA EVERBRIGHT BANK LTD	601818
CHINA LIFE INSURANCE LTD	2628	CHINA LIFE INSURANCE LTD	601628
CHINA MERCHANTS BANK LTD	3968	CHINA MERCHANTS BANK LTD	600036
CHINA MINSHENG BANKING CORP LTD	1988	CHINA MINSHENG BANKING CORP LTD	600016
CHINA MOLYBDENUM LTD	3993	CHINA MOLYBDENUM LTD	603993
CHINA PACIFIC INSURANCE (GROUP) LTD	2601	CHINA PACIFIC INSURANCE (GROUP) LTD	601601
CHINA PETROLEUM AND CHEMICAL CORP	386	CHINA PETROLEUM AND CHEMICAL CORP	600028
CHINA RAILWAY CONSTRUCTION CORP LT D	1186	CHINA RAILWAY CONSTRUCTION CORP LT D	601186
CHINA RAILWAY GROUP LTD	390	CHINA RAILWAY GROUP LTD	601390
CHINA SHENHUA ENERGY LTD	1088	CHINA SHENHUA ENERGY LTD	601088
CHINA UNICOM (HONG KONG) OPERATIONS LTD	762	CHINA UNICOM LTD	600050
CITIC SECURITIES COMPANY LTD	6030	CITIC SECURITIES COMPANY LTD	600030
CRRC CORP LTD	1766	CRRC CORP LTD	601766
GUOTAI JUNAN SECURITIES COPORATION	2611	GUOTAI JUNAN SECURITIES COPORATION	601211
HUATAI SECURITIES LTD	6886	HUATAI SECURITIES LTD	601688

continued

FXI holdings	Ticker	SSE 50 ETF holdings	Ticker
INDUSTRIAL AND COMMERCIAL BANK OF CH	1398	INDUSTRIAL AND COMMERCIAL BANK OF CH	601398
NEW CHINA LIFE INSURANCE COMPANY	1336	NEW CHINA LIFE INSURANCE COMPANY	601336
PETROCHINA LTD	857	PETROCHINA LTD	601857
PING AN INSURANCE (GROUP) CO OF CH	2318	PING AN INSURANCE (GROUP) CO OF CH	601318
AIR CHINA LTD	753	360 SECURITY TECHNOLOGY INC	601360
BYD LTD	1211	BANK OF BEIJING CO LTD	601169
CHINA CITIC BANK CORP LTD	998	BANK OF SHANGHAI CO LTD	601229
CHINA EVERGRANDE GROUP	3333	CHINA FORTUNE LAND DEVELOPMENT CO LTD	600340
CHINA GAS HOLDINGS LTD	384	CHINA INTERNATIONAL TRAVEL SERVICE CO LTD	601888
CHINA MOBILE LTD	941	CHINA SHIPBUILDING INDUSTRY CO LTD	601989
CHINA OVERSEAS LAND & INVESTMENT L TD	688	CHINA SOUTHERN AIRLINES COMPANY LTD	600029
CHINA RESOURCES LAND LTD	1109	CHINA STATE CONSTRUCTION ENGINEERING CO LTD	601668
CHINA TELECOM CORP LTD	728	DAQIN RAILWAY CO LTD	601006
CHINA VANKE LTD	2202	FOXCONN INDUSTRIAL INTERNET CO LTD	601138
CITIC LTD	267	GREENLAND HOLDINGS CO LTD	600606
COUNTRY GARDEN HOLDINGS LTD	2007	INDUSTRIAL BANK CO LTD	601166
CNOOC LTD	883	INNER MONGOLIA YILI INDUSTRIAL GROUP CO LTD	600887
FOSUN INTERNATIONAL LTD	656	JIANGSU HENGRUI MEDICINE CO LTD	600276

continued

FXI holdings	Ticker	SSE 50 ETF holdings	Ticker
GEELY AUTOMOBILE HOLDINGS LTD	175	KWEICHOW MOUTAI CO LTD	600519
GF SECURITIES LTD	1776	POLY DEVELOPMENTS AND HOLDINGS GROUP CO LTD	600048
GUANGZHOU AUTOMOBILE GROUP LTD	2238	QINGDAO HAIER CO LTD	600690
HAITONG SECURITIES COMPANY LTD	6837	SAIC MOTOR CORPORATION LIMITED	600104
LONGFOR GROUP HOLDINGS LTD	960	SANAN OPTOELECTRONICS CO LTD	600703
PICC PROPERTY AND CASUALTY LTD	2328	SHANDONG GOLD MINING CO LTD	600547
POSTAL SAVINGS BANK OF CHINA LTD	1658	SHANGHAI FOSUN PHARMACEUTICAL （GROUP） CO LTD	600019
SUNNY OPTICAL TECHNOLOGY LTD	2382	SHANGHAI FOSUN PHARMACEUTICAL （GROUP） CO LTD	600196
TENCENT HOLDINGS LTD	700	SHANGHAI PUDONG DEVELOPMENT BANK CO LTD	600000
THE PEOPLES INSURANCE CO (GROUP)	1339	WANHUA CHEMICAL GROUP CO LTD	600309
XIAOMI CORP	1810	WUXI APPTEC CO LTD	603259

Notes: This table presents the holdings of the two ETFs as of December 2018. The first 25 rows of this table show securities tracked by the two ETFs and the last 25 rows show unique securities tracked by the FXI or the SSE 50 ETF.

References

Ahn K, Bi Y, Sohn S, 2019. Price discovery among SSE 50 Index—based spot, futures, and options markets[J]. Journal of Futures Markets, 39(2): 238-259.

Chan K, Kwok J K H, 2005. Market segmentation and share price premium [J]. Journal of Emerging Market Finance, 4(1): 43-61.

Chan K, Menkveld A J, Yang Z, 2008. Information asymmetry and asset prices: Evidence from the China foreign share discount[J]. The Journal of Finance, 63(1): 159-196.

Chen J, Jiang F, Li H, et al, 2016. Chinese stock market volatility and the role of U. S. economic variables[J]. Pacific-Basin Finance Journal, 39: 70-83.

Chen J, Jiang F, Liu Y, et al, 2017. International volatility risk and Chinese stock return predictability[J]. Journal of International Money and Finance, 70: 183-203.

Clark T E, West K D, 2007. Approximately normal tests for equal predictive accuracy in nested models[J]. Journal of Econometrics, 138(1): 291-311.

Goh J C, Jiang F, Tu J, et al, 2013. Can US economic variables predict the Chinese stock market? [J]. Pacific-Basin Finance Journal, 22: 69-87.

Goyal A, Welch I, 2008. A comprehensive look at the empirical performance of equity premium prediction[J]. The Review of Financial Studies, 21(4): 1455-1508.

Jia C, Wang Y, Xiong W, 2017. Market segmentation and differential reactions of local and foreign investors to analyst recommendations[J]. The Review of Financial Studies, 30(9): 2972-3008.

Kelly B, Pruitt S, 2013. Market expectations in the cross—section of present values[J]. The Journal of Finance, 68(5): 1721-1756.

Li J, Gehricke S A, Zhang J E, 2019. How do US options traders "smirk" on China? Evidence from FXI options[J]. Journal of Futures Markets, 39: 1-21.

Luo X, Ye Z, 2015. Predicting volatility of the Shanghai silver futures market: What is the role of the US options market? [J]. Finance Research Letters, 15: 68-77.

Menzly L, Ozbas O, 2010. Market segmentation and cross—predictability of returns[J]. The Journal of Finance, 65(4): 1555-1580.

Paye B S, 2012. "Déjà vol": Predictive regressions for aggregate stock market volatility using macroeconomic variables[J]. Journal of Financial Economics, 106(3): 527-546.

Rapach D E, Strauss J K, Zhou G, 2013. International stock return predictability: What is the role of the United States? [J]. The Journal of

Finance，68(4)：1633-1662.

Westerlund J，Narayan P K，Zheng X，2015. Testing for stock return predictability in a large Chinese panel[J]. Emerging Markets Review，24：81-100.

Xu X E，Fung H G，2002. Information flows across markets：Evidence from China—backed stocks dual—listed in Hong Kong and New York[J]. Financial review，37(4)：563-588.

Anti-corruption, Political Connections and Corporate Responses: Evidence From Chinese Listed Companies[①]

Abstract　We consider the effects of anti-corruption at the corporate level, using the eight-point frugality code (EPFC) in China as the natural experiment. The EPFC significantly decreases the sales of politically-connected companies, while the firms' profitability remains unchanged in the associated industries. The companies pass through the negative effects of the EPFC shock to the labor market by the layoff and the wage strategies. Furthermore, there exist the regional and the size heterogeneities. State-owned companies, who have the natural political connections, have weaker negative effect than politically-connected private companies. These empirical results are robust.

Key Words: Anti-corruption; EPFC; Political connection

1　Introduction

Since the market-oriented reform in 1979, China has made tremendous achievements in the economic development, despite widespread corruption at almost all kleptocratic levels. Wedeman (2012) calls the coexistence of high-

---

①　Originally published in *Pacific-Basin Finance Journal* (vol. 57, 2019) by Jin Xuejun, Chen Zhenhao and Luo Deming.

speed growth and widespread corruption the "double paradox", which attracts much international attention. Some studies argue that corruption is the main obstacle to economic development (Asiedu & Freeman, 2009; Haselmann et al., Mauro, 1995, 1998; Shleifer & Vishny, 1993). Alternative perspective is that firms seek a certain amount of political capital by establishing political connections with government officials (Faccio, 2006). Political connections contribute to private companies via crisis management (Acemoglu et al., 2013; Faccio et al., 2006), bank loans (Claessens et al., 2008) and investment opportunities (Schoenherr, 2018; Haselmann et al., 2017), thus reducing business costs and improving company performance (Fisman, 2001; Leff, 1964; Li et al., 2008).

The key question is whether and how corruption affects corporate policies and performance. Both central and local governments have very strong power over resource allocation in China. Firms have a strong incentive to build political connections or private relationships (Guanxi) with central and local governments in exchange for large-scale projects, the procurement of contracts, the financial support and government protection (Cai et al., 2011).

We consider the effect of anti-corruption at the corporate level. In December 2012, the Chinese government issued a new anti-corruption policy, the eight-point frugality code (EPFC), with the aim of reducing bureaucracy, extravagance and undesirable work practices among Communist Party of China (CPC) members. With clauses focusing on various forms of corruption and the unauthorized use of government cars, the EPFC plays the significant role in the anti-corruption campaign since 2012. The EPFC and associated clauses definitely challenge the government consumption, as Fig. 3 shows. Through connection with the government, they affect firms' performance and hence corporate policies. Using the EPFC as the natural experiment, we consider how firms respond to the anti-corruption policy. We classify two types of industries: industries not directly associated with vs industries not directly associated with the EPFC. We identify two groups of companies: the treatment group comprising companies with political connections in associated industries, and the control group comprising other firms. We argue that the introduction of the EPFC significantly affects the performance of politically-connected companies in associated industries. The empirical results show that the sales of listed companies with political connections decrease significantly after the introduction of EPFC, whereas profitability does not change remarkably in associated industries. These companies pass through the negative effects of political risk shock on the labor market: They lay off employees or reduce the wage to secure stable profitability.

Furthermore, we find the regional heterogeneity. The decrease in sales revenue caused by EPFC is more serious politically-connected companies in underdeveloped regions than those in developed regions. More importantly, there exists regional heterogeneity in the corporate response to the EPFC shock. Companies take the wage strategy rather than the layoff strategy in underdeveloped regions, whereas companies in developed regions adopt the layoff strategy rather than the wage adjustment under the shock of EPFC. Hence, our evidence supports labor market friction and labor adjustment stickiness in the affected companies.

Corporate size heterogeneity also exists. For large politically-connected companies, the introduction of EPFC does not affect ROA and labor, but significantly decreases the sales revenue, per-capita sales, and labor. For small politically-connected companies, we did not get significant results. The initiation of EPFC does not change the sales, profitability, labor, or wage for small firms.

State-owned companies have natural political connections. Empirical evidence shows that the EPFC has a smaller impact on state-owned companies than politically-connected private companies in associated industries. State-owned companies have the natural political connection, which should be stronger than the political connection in private companies, the effect of EPFC favors state-owned companies. It implies that the EPFC more likely targets the corruption in the private sector.

This paper relates to the literature on the political connection and its impact on the corporate performance and policies. Shleifer and Vishny (1994) theoretically argue that the value of political connection is conditional. Since politicians extract at least some of rents generated by political connections, the corporate value is only enhanced if the marginal benefit outweighs the marginal cost the connections. The empirical literature is huge, and most of them focus on firm value and corporate performance. Faccio (2006) finds that political connections are particularly common in countries with high corruption and add to corporate value. Faccio et al. (2006) show that firms with political connections enjoy higher market valuations and are more likely to get the government bailout. Acemoglu et al. (2013) find that the announcement of Timothy Geithner as Treasury Secretary nominee produces a cumulative abnormal return for financial firms with which he has a prior connection. Recently, some scholars have explored the political connection in China. Wu et al. (2012a) find that private firms with politically connected managers have higher value and obtain more government subsidies than these without connected managers, whereas local state-owned enterprises with connected managers have lower value and employ more surplus labor than those without connected managers. Wang et al. (2018) use China's government officials' corporate site visits as the measure of political connection and examine how political connection affects corporate performance. We contribute to this literature by offering empirical evidence that political connections bring companies higher sales.

This paper also contributes to the literature on corruption. Mauro (1995) uses an assembled data set consisting of subjective indices of bureaucratic honesty and efficiency to provide the negative association between corruption and investment, economic growth. Fisman and Svensson (2007) use a unique data set containing information on the estimated bribe payments of Ugandan firms, and find that both the rate of taxation and bribery are negatively correlated with firm growth. Alternative studies hold the view that the corruption is beneficial to the firm and economic development. Fisman (2001) considers the valuation of rents for a relatively small subsample of Indonesian firms, and finds the corruption plays an important role in many of the world's largest and most important economies. These papers examine the influence of corruptions using the cross-sectional data. We use the EPFC as the natural experiment to explore how the anti-corruption policy affects the sales of politically-connected companies and how affected firm respond to the negative shock in associated industries.

This paper is closely related to the literature that focuses on the China's anti-corruption campaign began in 2012. Qian and Wen (2015) find that since the anti-corruption policy, the conspicuous importation of luxury goods has decreased sharply, whereas the inconspicuous importation of jewelry hasn't be affected. In an event study, Lin et al. (2016) find listed firms' market valuations rise broadly and significantly around the EPFC. Liu et al. (2017) document that the Bo Xilai scandal caused a significant decrease in Chinese stock prices, especially for politically sensitive firms. Pan and Tian (2017) find that the investment of politically-connected firms decline significantly after the ousting of politicians compared with those of non-politically-connected firms. As far as we know, it is unclear how firms respond to the shock of the anti-corruption campaign. The answer to this question is particularly important, and the introduction of EPFC gives us the opportunity to understand the value of political connections and the effects of corruption. Hence, we consider how firms respond to the EPFC shock and explore the firms' risk management mechanisms.

The paper is organized as follows. Section 2 provides the institutional background. Section 3 illustrates our main hypothesis. Section 4 introduces the data and variables, and provides the empirical model. Section 5 presents the main empirical evidences and explanations. Section 6 provides more empirical evidence for robustness, and Section 7 is the conclusion.

2 Institutional background

The corruption is increasingly serious in China. According to a survey by the corruption research organization Transparency International, China scored 39th, 40th, 36th, 37th and 40th of 180 countries or regions in the Corruption Perceptions Index from 2012 to 2017 respectively. Furthermore, the corruption in China has shifted from rampant corruption in the form of bribery and embezzlement of public funds in 1980s and 1990s to more covert forms of corruption that are beyond the jurisdiction of laws and regulations nowadays, such as eating and drinking, spending, travelling and attending grand banquets with public funds, extravagance and waste (Ko & Weng, 2012).

To alleviate the official corruption, Chinese government initiated EPFC on 4 December 2012. At the same time, the central government introduced supporting documents, such as "Six Bans" and "Four Undersirable Work Styles". Local governments followed up quickly, introducing a series of local anti-corruption rules and presenting very detailed requirements about their work styles and daily life for officials at all levels, which were unprecedented. Furthermore, both central and local governments immediately set up investigation teams and inspection groups, who supervise the enforcement of EPFC and discipline government officials involved in corruption.

EPFC and supporting documents, which are very strict and detailed, regulate the life and work styles of government officials, such as eating and drinking using public funds, the private use of public vehicles, extravagance and gifts, for the purpose of fighting against corruption and improving government efficiency. Moreover, the leaders in China promised "zero tolerance to the corruption", which shows their determination to fight against corruption.

The EPFC marks the start of a nationwide anti-corruption campaign. Fig. 1. A shows the daily number of users who search the word anti-corruption (反腐败) using Baidu. It is easy to see that in the following 3 years after the initiation of EPFC Chinese people pay much more attention to anti-corruption than before. Fig. 1. B gives the daily number of users who search for the word EPFC (中央八项规定) using Baidu. After its initiation, EPFC is persistently praised in the media.

Fig. 2 gives the number of punished senior officials after the EPFC enforcement, including the provincial-governor and ministerial cadres. The number of punished senior officials is very small before the EPFC. While after the introduction of the EPFC in 2012, the punished senior officials come to a sharp increase from 5 in 2012 to 76 in 2016.

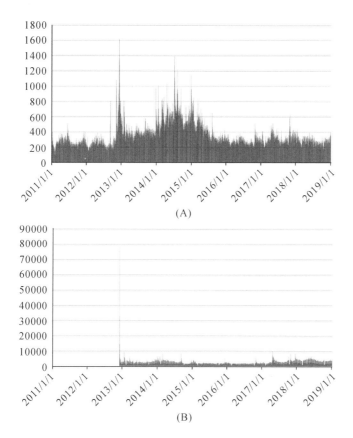

Fig. 1 This figure shows the Baidu Index with the keywords "Anti-corruption" and "EPFC". The Y-axis represents the user attention or media attention based on Baidu search frequency weighted keywords. The X-axis represents the date. Baidu Search is the most popular search engine for Chinese users. Based on this engine, Baidu index can tell users how big a certain keyword search scale in Baidu, the trend of ups and downs over a period of time and the changes of relevant news and public opinion.

The promulgation of EPFC greatly affects the economic environment in China, especially for firms closely related to government. One objective of EPFC is to cut down "Three Public Funds"(TPF), referring to the funds used by government officials to go abroad on business, purchase and operate official vehicles and entertain official guests in China. TPF is used to satisfy government daily needs. However, due to the rapid rise of TPF and the opacity of detailed accounts, some of these funds are diverted for private use. Furthermore, the public is generally confused about the final account of TPF.

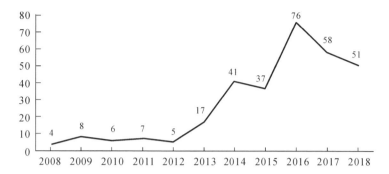

Fig. 2   This figure shows the number of cadres punished after the introduction of EPFC. The Y-axis represents the number of officials which are punished every year. The X-axis represents the year.

TPF contributes important factor that leads to the increasing administrative costs of the Chinese government.

Fig. 3 gives the central government's TPF between 2011 and 2016. We have two bars each year, the left bar is the budget, and the right one is the final account of expenditure. Note that the data is only available from 2011, when the Chinese government began to disclose both the TPF budget and the final account. Fig. 3 gives three pieces of stylized evidence. First, the amount of the central government TPF, both the budget and the final account, decreased significantly since 2012. The budget decreased dramatically from 9.428 billion Yuan in 2011 to 6.316 billion Yuan in 2016. And the final account decreased astonishingly from 9.47 billion yuan in 2011 to 4.711 billion yuan in 2016. In just 5 years, the budget is cut by about one-third, and the final account by nearly half. After the enforcement of EPFC at the end of 2012, the final account is less than the budget in the following years. In 2011 and 2012, the use of TPF was classified as 'no reservations', which means the final account is equal to the budget. However, after 2012, the final account was significantly less than the budget. The differences between the two accounts rose from 42 million yuan in 2013 to 1.605 billion yuan in 2016. After the introduction of the EPFC, the government consciously reduced the TPF expenditure.

Consider the three parts of TPF. Official reception fees and official car spending decreased tremendously after the introduction of EPFC. Specifically,

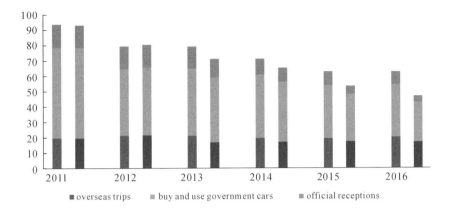

overseas trips ■ buy and use government cars ■ official receptions

Fig. 3　Three public consumptions. This figure shows the actual execution amount and budget amount of the public funds of central administration and public institutions from 2011 to 2016. The bar chart on the left shows the budget accounts of the three public consumptions. The bar chart on the right shows the budget accounts for the three public consumptions. The unit of Y axis is 100 million yuan. The X-axis represents the year.

reception fees decreased from 1. 472 billion yuan in 2011 to 0. 419 billion yuan in 2016, the reduction of reception fees by 71. 5% in 5 years. This big reduction reflects the loss of 'hidden benefits' for government officials, including various banquets, accommodation in luxury hotels, cigarette and alcohol consumption, and gifts, among other expenditures.

Official vehicles expenditure decreased dramatically after the EPFC: It covered half of TPF before the EPFC. After the EPFC, official vehicles expenditure decreased from 5. 915 billion yuan in 2011 to 2. 585 billion yuan in 2016.

The cost of public fund for going abroad and going abroad on business remained stable at approximately 1. 7 billion yuan to 2 billion yuan, although the final account fluctuated every year. The EPFC does not restrict the use of funds. Furthermore, anti-corruption policy does not have a major impact on this project.

TPF has a significant industry focus. The decrease in the TPF expenditure restrains demand in some specific industries, including lodging, catering, liquor, automobile and tobacco industries.

3　Hypothesis development

Chinese government plays an active role in promoting economic development, and government expenditure is an important part of the national economy in China (An et al. , 2016). According to the rent-seeking theory, in the incomplete market, the allocation of resources is often in the hands of the government, which relies on officials to allocate resources (Shleifer & Vishny, 1994). As government officials are responsible for determining the amount of government expenditure, they have the power to allocate the government procurement contracts. This system gives government officials the opportunity to take bribes and rents from companies whom the official has the benefit connection with. Mironov and Zhuravskaya (2016) find that firms which win the government procurement contracts always have a good relationship with the local government. Firms have a strong incentive to pay certain "rents" and build political connections with central and local governments to obtain resources and benefits (Faccio, 2006; Akcigit et al. , 2018).

The EPFC, as an anti-corruption policy, affects sales in the lodging, catering, liquor, automobile and tobacco industries. Before the introduction of EPFC, firms benefit from the political connections by gaining the government procurement contacts with side payment to officials in these industries. EPFC breaks the value of political connections. Firms with political connection suffer from the extra reduction in the government procurement and hence exhibit the decrease in sales. We summarize the above discussion as the following Hypothesis.

3.1　Hypothesis 1

EPFC decreases the sales of politically-connected firms in associated industries.

EPFC a the negative impact on the sales of politically connected firms. This will transmit negatively to the profitability. Whether or not the firms' profitability suffer from EPFC depends on what policies and how quickly firms will take to smooth the EPFC risk. Wang et al. (2014) find that the political uncertainty has the negative effect on the corporate investment. We argue that EPFC has less negative impact on profitability of politically-connected firms if they respond to the negative shock quickly.

Under the EPFC shock, politically-connected firms become very cautious and minimize the foreseeable negative impact by shrinking the business in associated industries, and extending business to unassociated industries, reducing business expenditures, and gaining financial support from local banks. We summarize the above discussion as the following Hypothesis 2.

3.2 Hypothesis 2

EPFC has less impact on the profitability of political connected firms in associated industries.

The EPFC has a negative impact on the sales of political connected firms in associated industries, and as we discuss in Hypothesis 2, may negatively affect the profitability. How do politically-connected firms respond to the negative shock of EPFC policy? The immediately available strategy is to adjust the labor cost, through either the layoff or the wage strategies, when the cost of doing so is quite low. Ku et al. (2018) find that firms primarily respond to tax increases by both the employment and wage adjustment. Cruces et al. (2010) come to similar conclusions through the study of wages and taxes in Norway. Bernal et al. (2017) find that enterprises adjust the wage to ensure profit margin after the risk shock.

In China, even though we have the labor law and the labor contract should be protected by the labor law, the legal enforcement is quite weak (Hu & Schaufeli, 2011). Firms frequently use the notorious strategy of either layoff or wage reduction to smooth the negative shock (Balsvik et al., 2015).

We argue that under the EPFC shock, politically-connected firms take either the layoff or the wage strategies to smooth off the negative effects of EPFC on profitability. We summarize the above discussion as the following Hypothesis 3.

3.3 Hypothesis 3

After the introduction of the EPFC, the politically-connected firms will absorb or weaken the decline in sales by adjusting the employment and the wage in associated industries.

4 Data,variables definitions and empirical model

4.1 Data

We have two data sources. We get the information about the chairman's political background from the China Stock Market and Accounting (CSMAR) database. We manually sort the political connection variable on the quarterly basis according to the tenure and resignation time of the management personnel and link them with the company's quarterly data. We use the controlling shareholders data in CSMAR data to classify firms' ownership into state-owned and private firms.

We get firms' quarterly data from the WIND database, which contains the firms' sales revenue, ROA, total wage, market value, staff number, total assets, and total liability. We exclude listed financial companies, and ST and *ST listed companies. [①] We exclude samples with missing data or these for which total assets, sales, or equities are either zero or negative. We end up with a sample of 948 private listed companies, and 915 state-owned listed companies over 40 quarters from the first quarter of 2008 to the fourth quarter of 2017. We winsorize all of the variables at the 1% and 99% levels.

4.2 Variables

Table 1 gives the definition of variables used in this paper.

---

① ST and *ST shares: "Shanghai and Shenzhen stock exchange announced in April 22, 1998, according to a 1998 on the implementation of stock listing rules, to finances or other abnormal condition of the listed company stock trading for Special processing, in English is a special treatment (abbreviation is ST), and the stock is referred to as ST or *ST shares.

Table 1   Variable definition

Variable name	Variable definition
Lnsales	Sales, the logarithm of sales
Labor	Employment, the logarithm of employment
Persales	Per capita sales=ln(sales/labor)
Wage	Wage, the logarithm of the firm's total salary
Perwage	Per capita wage=ln(wage/labor)
Pol	Political connection dummy. If the firm has political connections, Pol=1; otherwise, Pol=0
Post	EPAR time dummy. After EPFC introduction, Post=1; otherwise, Post =0
Size	Firm size=ln(market value)
Debt	Asset-liability ratio=total liabilities/total asset
Intensity	Capital-intensity=fixed assets property/sales
Baidu	Baidu Index from Baidu search engine
Soe	State-owned dummy. If the firm is a state-owned company, Soe = 1; otherwise, Soe=0

4.2.1   Key dependent variables

Sales. We use the listed company's prime operating revenue as the measure of sales.

Profitability. Following the literature, we use ROA (Return on Assets) to measure a company's profitability.

Labor. The labor refers to its number of employees, and we take the natural logarithm.

Per-capita sales. Per-capita sales is defined as Sales divided by Labor.

Wage. We use the 'Cash paid to and on behalf of employees' in the cash flow statement to measure the total wage of a listed company.

4.2.2   Core independent variables

Political connection (Pol). Political connection is the core independent variable in our paper. Thus, how we measure the political connections of listed companies is critical. Many papers on political connections (Fisman, 2001; Yu et al., 2012, Wu et al., 2012a, Wu et al., 2012b) take the political background of senior executives as the proxy variable for companies' political connections.

Fan et al. (2007) consider the general manager's political connection. Whereas in the Chinese market system, the chairman is the legal representative of a company. The chairman is the highest authority in the company and is responsible for overall operations. Most chairmen are also the highest paid employees in the company (Wu et al., 2012b). Therefore, for private companies, we follow Wu et al., 2012a, Wu et al., 2012b and Yu et al. (2012) and define the political connections using the chairman's political background. If the chairman of the board has ever served in a government department or as a deputy of the National People's Congress, this company has political connection. Hence we introduce the dummy for political connections, denoted as Pol, such that Pol equals one if the firm is politically-connected, and zero otherwise.

State-owned companies have natural political connections. They are quite easier to access the government controlling resource. For example, Allen et al. (2005) argue that the state-owned firms gain biased financial support from state-owned banking system, even though the driving force of economic development comes from the private sector. We differentiate the natural political connections endowed with the state-owned companies with private firms' political connections. For this purpose, we use the ownership structure as the proxy, where the company has the natural political connection if it is state-owned, otherwise it has no natural political connections. Hence, we introduce the dummy variable 'Soe', where Soe equals one when the company is state-owned and has the natural political connection. As the state-owned firms have natural political connections, we use private company observations in our main regression, and both the state-owned and private companies in the robust test.

Post. Post is a time dummy variable. After EPFC introduction, Post equal one, and zero otherwise.

Indus. Indus is a dummy variable which equals one if the firm belongs to associated industries, including accommodation, catering, liquor, automobile manufacturing and tobacco, and zero otherwise.

4.2.3 Control variables

We control for the following corporate characteristics.

Size. We define firm size as the logarithm of the market capitalization of the listed company.

Debt. The asset-liability ratio, denoted as Debt, is calculated by the ratio of total liabilities to total assets.

Intensity. Capital intensity, denoted as Intensity, is the ratio of fixed assets to sales revenue.

4.3 Summary statistics

Table 2 gives the summary statistics. Table 2A gives the summary statistics for politically-connected firms. The left side is these before the introduction of the EPFC. The average value of the logarithm of sales is 19.54, with a maximum value of 24.58 and a minimum value of 12.07. The right side of Table 2A is those after the introduction of the EPFC. The average value of the sales is 19.99, with a maximum value of 24.75 and a minimum value of 14.44.

Table 2   Summary statistics

A: Firms with political connection

Variable	Before EPFC					After EPFC				
	N	Mean	Sd	Min	Max	N	mean	Sd	Min	Max
lnsales	5502	19.54	1.290	12.07	24.58	8688	19.99	1.360	14.44	24.75
industry	5510	0.040	0.190	0	1	8689	0.0600	0.240	0	1
labor	5510	7.320	1.220	2.400	11.29	8689	7.660	1.130	2.640	11.73
persale	5502	12.96	1.170	6.900	19.90	8688	13.09	1.060	8.220	18.77
lnwage	5498	16.90	1.200	10.97	21.53	8675	17.60	1.180	11.42	23.47
perwage	5498	9.580	0.800	2.920	17.26	8675	9.940	0.540	6.590	13.41
Size	5377	22.09	0.860	19.74	25.67	8255	22.62	0.870	20.41	25.79
Debt	5510	0.410	0.310	0.0500	11.31	8689	0.410	0.230	0.0100	10.08
Intensity	5502	1.600	34.13	0	2307	8688	1.030	2.550	0	137.6

B：Firms without political connection

Variable	Before EPFC					After EPFC				
	N	Mean	Sd	Min	Max	N	mean	Sd	Min	Max
lnsales	7170	19.14	1.500	6.490	24.07	16466	19.69	1.470	9.020	25.08
industry	7231	0.040	0.200	0	1	16488	0.0500	0.220	0	1
labor	7220	7.010	1.330	1.100	12.12	16488	7.350	1.240	1.950	12.21
persale	7167	12.84	1.280	3.500	18.96	16466	13.06	1.160	5.250	18.84
lnwage	7188	16.62	1.270	4.610	22.15	16430	17.38	1.270	8.480	22.66
perwage	7178	9.610	0.820	4.330	16.49	16430	10.03	0.590	2.640	14.86
Size	6823	21.86	0.780	17.31	25.18	15317	22.61	0.830	20.35	26.62
Debt	7230	0.930	18.02	0.0510	1303	16488	0.410	0.480	0.0513	42.58
Intensity	7168	2.050	28.87	0	1526	16463	1.370	14.93	0	1635

Note：This table presents the summary statistics for the variables. The left-hand side of this table presents the summary statistics for the experimental group and the right-hand side presents the summary statistics for the control group.

Table 2B gives the summary statistics for firms without political connections. The left side is these before the introduction of the EPFC. The average value of the sales is 19.14, with a maximum value of 24.07 and a minimum value of 6.49. The right side of Panel A is those after the introduction of the EPFC. The average value of the logarithm of sales is 19.69, with a maximum value of 25.08 and a minimum value of 9.02.

4.4 Empirical model

We estimate how politically-connected companies are affected by the EPFC. Specifically, the EPFC has a significant impact on the five industries closely related to government consumption：accommodation, catering, liquor, automobile manufacturing and tobacco, which are closely associated with TPF. Hence, we introduce the $Pol \times Post \times Indus$ triple-interaction term to identify the industry heterogeneity of the impact of the EPFC on the sales, profitability, labor and wage. In other words, the EPFC, which aims to reduce government spending, affects the value of political connections in directly associated industries.

We run the following empirical model.

$$Y_{it} = \beta_0 + \beta_1 Pol_{it} \times Post \times Indus + \beta_2 Pol_{it} \times post + \beta_3 Pol_{it} \times Indus + \beta_4 Pol_{it}$$
$$+ \beta_5 post \times Indus + \beta_6 post + \beta_7 control + \tag{1}$$

In Eq. (1), we use Sales, ROA, Labor, Per-capita sales, and Wage as the dependent variable respectively to test Hypothesis 1, Hypothesis 2, Hypothesis 3. Pol is the dummy variable for political connection, Post is the dummy variable for EPFC enforcement, Indus is the dummy for associated industries, and control variables include the size, debt and intensity ratio of the firms. And we also control the time, industrial and province fixed effects.

5 Empirical results

5.1 The sales

Table 3 gives the empirical result of Hypothesis 1, where we control time and regional fixed effect in column 1 and 2, time and industrial effects in column 3 and 4, and time, regional and industrial fixed effects in column 5 and 6. Table 3 shows that the coefficient of the Post × Pol × Indus term is significantly negative, rejecting the null hypothesis at 1% level in column 1, 3 and 5, and remains significant in column 2, 4 and 6. This means that the EPFC significantly and negatively affects the sales of politically-connected firms in associated industries. The government procurement from these companies decreases significantly in associated industries. Our results show that after the introduction of the EPFC, the sales of politically-connected companies in associated industries is at least 32.9% lower than these of companies without political connections. We can also explain the result as the value of political connection such that politically-connected firms have at least extra 32.9% higher sales before EPFC.

Table 3　Sales

Variables	Dependent variable: Sales					
	(1)	(2)	(3)	(4)	(5)	(6)
Pol×Post×Indus	−0.842***	−0.654***	−0.314***	−0.284***	−0.365***	−0.329**
	(−4.862)	(−3.854)	(−2.846)	(−2.907)	(−2.977)	(−2.515)
Pol×Post	−0.00321	0.0302	−0.0144	0.0248	−0.0187	0.0212
	(−0.0508)	(0.537)	(−0.216)	(0.437)	(−0.291)	(0.383)
Pol×Indus	0.674***	0.555***	0.275**	0.283***	0.240*	0.250**
	(6.167)	(5.047)	(2.471)	(3.237)	(1.868)	(2.066)
Pol	0.366***	0.310***	0.361***	0.302***	0.368***	0.315***
	(3.755)	(3.739)	(3.686)	(3.578)	(3.491)	(3.485)
Post×Indus	0.0996	0.0617	−0.335**	−0.265*	−0.304**	−0.226
	(0.510)	(0.331)	(−2.538)	(−1.945)	(−1.992)	(−1.480)
Post	1.258***	0.634***	1.273***	0.641***	1.255***	0.645***
	(11.35)	(6.921)	(11.45)	(8.427)	(11.18)	(8.287)
Size		0.976***		1.017***		1.012***
		(25.02)		(26.29)		(26.79)
Debt		2.116***		2.212***		2.193***
		(8.325)		(16.08)		(17.94)
Intensity		−0.309***		−0.317***		−0.307***
		(−11.67)		(−10.18)		(−10.50)
Constant	19.03***	−2.458***	18.03***	−4.514***	18.35***	−4.150***
	(110.2)	(−3.128)	(205.5)	(−5.103)	(129.4)	(−5.036)
Time Fixed Effects	YES	YES	YES	YES	YES	YES
Regional Fixed Effect	YES	YES	NO	NO	YES	YES
Industry Fixed Effect	NO	NO	YES	YES	YES	YES
Observations	37,751	37,739	37,751	37,739	37,751	37,739
R-squared	0.0940	0.5699	0.1594	0.6320	0.1897	0.6461

Notes: This table presents the coefficients of our main regression of firms' sales. The control variables include firm size (Size), leverage (Debt), capital intensity (Intensity). We control time and regional fixed effect in column 1 and 2, and control time and industry effect in column 3 and 4. Column 5 and 6 control all these three fixed effects, and adjust the standard errors by clustering. The numbers in parentheses are t values. *, **, ***, represent the significant level of 10%, 5%, and 1%, respectively. The R^2 values in the following columns refer to Pseudo R^2.

Consider coefficients of control variables in Table 3. The coefficient of firm size is significantly positive, which means the company's market value has a significantly positive correlation with the sales. This indicates that the larger firms have higher sales revenue and profitability. The leverage has a positive impact on sales, and capital intensity positively affects the sales.

Table 3 gives solid empirical evidence to show that the EPFC significantly decreases sales of the politically-connected companies in associated industries, which is consistent with Hypothesis 1.

5.2 Profitability

Table 4 presents the results of Hypothesis 2. We control the fixed effect in the same way as in Table 3. Table 4 shows that the coefficient of Post $\times$ Pol $\times$ Indus is insignificant in any regression settings. The result indicates that EPFC has no impact on the ROA of politically-connected firms in associated industries. The profitability of the politically-connected firms has no significantly difference with that of firms without politically-connected firms in associated industries, even though politically-connected firms are suffering from the EPFC shocks in the sales. Thus, we find the EPFC has no impact on firms' profitability, which is consistent with Hypothesis 2. Why the EPFC policy affects negatively the sales while has no effect on ROA of politically connected companies in associated industries? We argue that affected companies immediately take corporate policies such as the layoff and the wage policies to smooth the EPFC shock.

Table 4   ROA (Profitability)

Variables	Dependent variable: ROA					
	(1)	(2)	(3)	(4)	(5)	(6)
Pol×Post×Indus	−1.274	−1.154	−1.156	−0.0849	−0.419	−0.214
	(−0.836)	(−1.357)	(−0.528)	(−0.0631)	(−0.161)	(−0.157)
Pol×Post	−0.383	0.0199	−0.441	−0.00428	−0.482	−0.0164
	(−0.645)	(0.103)	(−0.662)	(−0.0218)	(−0.743)	(−0.0814)
Pol×Indus	1.800	0.802	1.811	0.0453	1.364	0.0416
	(1.231)	(0.985)	(0.727)	(0.0325)	(0.553)	(0.0300)
Pol	0.620	0.0241	0.599	0.0270	0.557	0.0246
	(1.136)	(0.129)	(0.970)	(0.150)	(0.981)	(0.130)
Post×Indus	0.834**	0.648***	0.755	−0.441	0.106	−0.355
	(2.151)	(3.190)	(0.807)	(−0.991)	(0.0759)	(−0.763)
Post	2.591***	0.637*	2.538***	0.578	2.468***	0.600*

continued

Variables	Dependent variable：ROA					
	(1)	(2)	(3)	(4)	(5)	(6)
	(4.367)	(1.842)	(3.791)	(1.653)	(4.017)	(1.669)
Size		1.918***		1.889***		1.898***
		(14.87)		(16.80)		(16.72)
Debt		−7.688***		−7.647***		−7.665***
		(−15.07)		(−13.67)		(−14.63)
Intensity		−0.507***		−0.574***		−0.537***
		(−6.889)		(−7.155)		(−6.955)
Constant	1.987***	−36.06***	3.963***	−34.12***	4.306***	−33.73***
	(2.982)	(−13.77)	(7.158)	(−14.52)	(3.619)	(−14.12)
Time Fixed Effects	YES	YES	YES	YES	YES	YES
Regional Fixed Effect	YES	YES	NO	NO	YES	YES
Industry Fixed Effect	NO	NO	YES	YES	YES	YES
Observations	37,815	35,742	37,815	35,742	37,815	35,742
R-squared	0.0110	0.1559	0.0114	0.1635	0.0167	0.1672

Notes：This table presents the coefficients of our main regression of firms' ROA. The control variables include firm size (Size), leverage (Debt), capital intensity (Intensity). We control time and regional fixed effect in column 1 and 2, and control time and industry effect in column 3 and 4. Column 5 and 6 control all these three fixed effects, and adjust the standard errors by clustering. The numbers in parentheses are t values. *, **, ***, represent the significant level of 10%, 5%, and 1%, respectively. The R^2 values in the following columns refer to Pseudo R^2.

5.3 Firm response：Employment and wage adjustment

The above empirical evidence shows that EPFC negatively affects the sales, while has no effect on the profitability of politically-connected companies in associated industries. We argue that politically-connected firms disentangle effectively the suffer from the EPFC shock. We consider here the layoff and wage strategies that firms take.

5.3.1 Labor

Table 5 reports the empirical evidence of how firms use the layoff strategy to pass through the negative EPFC shock. Table 5 shows that the coefficient of the Pol × Post × Indus term is negative and significant at the 1% level in column 1, 3 and 5. And the coefficient in column 6 is -0.118, which is still significant. This means that politically-connected firms employ at least less 42.3% of labors than companies without political connection to deal with the impact of EPFC. This indicates that politically-connected companies have fewer employees than companies without political connections in the associated industry after the initiation of EPFC. Hence Table 5 gives solid evidence that politically-connected companies pass through the negative effects of EPFC to workers through the layoff policy, which is consistent with Hypothesis 3.

Table 5   Labor

Variables	Dependent variable: Labor					
	(1)	(2)	(3)	(4)	(5)	(6)
Pol×Post×Indus	−0.765***	−0.630**	−0.437**	−0.371	−0.462*	−0.423*
	(−3.833)	(−2.009)	(−2.033)	(−1.538)	(−1.855)	(−1.741)
Pol×Post	0.0269	0.115**	−0.0174	0.0813	−0.0229	0.0757
	(0.415)	(2.009)	(−0.267)	(1.569)	(−0.340)	(1.509)
Pol×Indus	0.651***	0.476*	0.393***	0.301	0.390**	0.307
	(6.019)	(1.874)	(2.965)	(1.178)	(2.282)	(1.220)
Pol	0.284***	0.0612	0.339***	0.101*	0.317***	0.0767
	(3.910)	(1.303)	(4.997)	(1.812)	(4.320)	(1.434)
Post×Indus	0.421**	0.449***	0.176	0.286	0.213	0.324*
	(2.241)	(2.728)	(0.756)	(1.523)	(0.875)	(1.743)
Post	0.581***	−0.209**	0.592***	−0.205***	0.589***	−0.196***
	(5.356)	(−2.360)	(5.543)	(−2.993)	(5.615)	(−2.899)
Size		0.784***		0.817***		0.818***
		(19.67)		(27.85)		(28.80)
Debt		0.870**		1.404***		1.374***
		(2.637)		(12.16)		(12.06)
Intensity		−0.0603**		−0.0705***		−0.0625***
		(−2.470)		(−5.719)		(−4.990)
Constant	7.102***	−10.09***	5.974***	−12.33***	6.238***	−12.09***
	(37.69)	(−11.61)	(70.41)	(−17.52)	(42.49)	(−17.56)
Time Fixed Effects	YES	YES	YES	YES	YES	YES
Regional Fixed Effect	YES	YES	NO	NO	YES	YES
Industry Fixed Effect	NO	NO	YES	YES	YES	YES
Observations	37,907	35,742	37,907	35,742	37,907	35,742
R-squared	0.0787	0.3487	0.1699	0.4833	0.1966	0.5030

Notes: This table presents the coefficients of the regression of firms' labor. The control variables include firm size (Size), leverage (D)ebt, capital intensity (Intensity). We control time and regional fixed effect in column 1 and 2, and control time and industry effect in column 3 and 4. Column 5 and 6 control all these three fixed effects, and adjust the standard errors by clustering. The numbers in parentheses are t values. ˙,˙˙,˙˙˙, represent the significant level of 10%, 5%, and 1%, respectively. The R2 values in the following columns refer to Pseudo R^2.

5.3.2 Per-capita sales

Next we further consider whether the per-capita sales of politically-connected companies change after the introduction of EPFC. If the per-capita sales is negatively related with the EPFC for politically-connected companies in associated industries, we argue that the pass-through using the layoff policy is partial.

For this purpose, we take the per-capita sales as the dependent variable in Eq. (1), and Table 6 reports the empirical evidence. In Table 6, the per-capita sales of politically-connected companies is significantly and negatively related with EPFC. The negative coefficient is −0.251, which means the per-capita sales of politically-connected companies in associated industries decrease significantly 25.1% more than companies that have no political connections in associated industries. Even though companies adopt the layoff policy to deal with the negative effects of EPFC, we still observe very large negative effect on the per-capita sales, which means that the pass-through is partial.

Table 6   Per-capita Sales

Variables	Dependent variable: Per-capita Sales					
	(1)	(2)	(3)	(4)	(5)	(6)
Pol×Post×Indus	−0.727˙˙˙	−0.462˙˙	−0.244˙˙	−0.224˙	−0.288˙˙˙	−0.251˙
	(−4.839)	(−2.152)	(−2.221)	(−1.695)	(−3.062)	(−1.876)
Pol×Post	−0.0102	0.0719˙˙	−0.0143	0.0859˙˙	−0.0182	0.0823˙˙
	(−0.178)	(2.018)	(−0.239)	(2.539)	(−0.315)	(2.550)
Pol×Indus	0.586˙˙˙	0.364	0.216˙	0.207	0.181	0.166
	(5.447)	(1.642)	(1.732)	(1.496)	(1.491)	(1.017)
Pol	0.329˙˙˙	0.0806˙˙	0.316˙˙˙	0.0503	0.326˙˙˙	0.0616
	(3.604)	(2.135)	(3.459)	(1.293)	(3.329)	(1.513)
Post×Indus	0.0356	0.0747	−0.367˙˙˙	−0.122˙˙˙	−0.343˙˙˙	−0.119˙˙
	(0.201)	(0.671)	(−3.968)	(−2.855)	(−3.088)	(−2.373)

continued

Variables	Dependent variable: Per-capita Sales					
	(1)	(2)	(3)	(4)	(5)	(6)
Post	1.172***	0.0550	1.186***	0.0100	1.168***	0.0177
	(11.59)	(0.976)	(11.81)	(0.186)	(11.50)	(0.323)
Size		0.876***		0.912***		0.907***
		(25.57)		(27.08)		(27.32)
Debt		2.009***		2.018***		2.005***
		(9.324)		(16.04)		(17.48)
Intensity		−0.300***		−0.306***		−0.297***
		(−11.85)		(−10.16)		(−10.50)
Constant	17.09***	−2.201***	16.24***	−3.943***	16.53***	−3.613***
	(110.2)	(−3.190)	(205.0)	(−5.155)	(127.7)	(−4.979)
Time Fixed Effects	YES	YES	YES	YES	YES	YES
Regional Fixed Effect	YES	YES	NO	NO	YES	YES
Industry Fixed Effect	NO	NO	YES	YES	YES	YES
Observations	37,747	35,681	37,747	35,681	37,747	35,681
R-squared	0.0912	0.5693	0.1603	0.6252	0.1902	0.6388

Notes: This table presents the coefficients of the regression of firms' per-capita sales (persale). The control variables include firm size (Size), leverage (Debt), capital intensity (Intensity). We control time and regional fixed effect in column 1 and 2, and control time and industry effect in column 3 and 4. Column 5 and 6 control all these three fixed effects, and adjust the standard errors by clustering. The numbers in parentheses are t values. *, **, ***, represent the significant level of 10%, 5%, and 1%, respectively. The R^2 values in the following columns refer to Pseudo R^2.

Consider the results in Table 5 and Table 6. Table 5 shows that politically-connected companies smooth the negative impact of EPFC through the layoff strategy, while Table 6 shows that the layoff strategy exhibit partial passthrough. Companies cannot perfectly smooth the negative effect of EPFC on sales by adjusting the employment. This is because companies do not rely only on the layoff strategy. They have at least the alternative strategy of wage adjustment to deal with the EPFC shock.

5.3.3 Wage

Consider the effect of wage adjustment strategy to cope with the EPFC shock. We take total wage as dependent variable, and Table 7 reports the empirical result.

Table 7 Wage

Variables	Dependent variable: Wage					
	(1)	(2)	(3)	(4)	(5)	(6)
Pol×Post×Indus	−0.832***	−0.681***	−0.343***	−0.328*	−0.373***	−0.368**
	(−5.886)	(−3.138)	(−3.738)	(−1.870)	(−3.780)	(−2.373)
Pol×Post	0.0444	0.148***	−0.0173	0.102*	−0.0143	0.101*
	(0.709)	(2.741)	(−0.277)	(1.882)	(−0.235)	(1.903)
Pol×Indus	0.684***	0.487**	0.275***	0.203	0.258***	0.196
	(10.03)	(2.208)	(3.089)	(1.144)	(2.756)	(1.092)
Pol	0.234***	−0.0220	0.288***	0.0130	0.285***	0.0122
	(2.764)	(−0.526)	(3.693)	(0.347)	(3.332)	(0.314)
Post×Indus	0.387***	0.421***	−0.0175	0.152***	0.00909	0.169***
	(2.961)	(4.041)	(−0.152)	(2.846)	(0.0875)	(3.398)
Post	1.354***	0.366***	1.390***	0.378***	1.374***	0.394***
	(13.65)	(4.563)	(13.82)	(5.412)	(13.77)	(5.382)
Size		0.910***		0.943***		0.936***
		(28.29)		(31.72)		(32.18)
Debt		1.061***		1.393***		1.413***
		(4.681)		(12.90)		(13.91)
Intensity		−0.0996***		−0.110***		−0.0971***
		(−4.839)		(−7.200)		(−6.653)
Constant	16.36***	−3.557***	15.58***	−5.297***	15.83***	−4.933***
	(98.29)	(−5.067)	(188.1)	(−7.636)	(100.6)	(−7.438)
Time Fixed Effects	YES	YES	YES	YES	YES	YES
Regional Fixed Effect	YES	YES	NO	NO	YES	YES
Industry Fixed Effect	NO	NO	YES	YES	YES	YES
Observations	37,791	35,641	37,791	35,641	37,791	35,641
R-squared	0.1426	0.4992	0.1909	0.5760	0.2177	0.5904

Notes: This table presents the coefficients of the regression of firms' total wage(wage). The control variables include firm size (Size), leverage (Debt), capital intensity (Intensity). We control time and regional fixed effect in column 1 and 2, and control time and industry effect in column 3 and 4. Column 5 and 6 control all these three fixed effects, and adjust the standard errors by clustering. The numbers in parentheses are t values. *,**,***, represent the significant level of 10%, 5%, and 1%, respectively. The R^2 values in the following columns refer to Pseudo R^2.

Table 7 shows that the coefficient of the Pol × Post × Indus term is negative and significant, and the coefficient in column 6 is − 0.368. This means that total wage of politically-connected firms is at least 36.8% fewer than companies without political connection in associated industries to pass through the shock of EPFC. This indicates that politically-connected companies pay lower wage to the staff than companies without political connections in associated industries.

The EPFC has significantly negative impact on firms' wage. The empirical results are consistent with Hypothesis 3.

In summary, we provide solid evidence that the politically-connected companies take the layoff and wage strategies to smooth the risk from the decline of sales to maintain the corporate profitability in associated industries when the EPFC is introduced as the anti-corruption policy.

5.4 Heterogeneity analysis

5.4.1 Regional heterogeneity

Firms in undeveloped regions depend more on the government than the firms in developed regions. Hence it is interesting to show empirical evidence whether the impact of EPFC on the corporate performance and policies exhibits heterogeneity across different regions.

For this purpose, we classify provinces into developed and underdeveloped regions, using the province-level marketization index given in Fan Gang's "China Market Index Report (Fan et al., 2011)"[1]. According to the registration place, we obtain 635 companies in developed regions, and 257 companies in underdeveloped regions. Table 8 reports the empirical results, where Table 8A for developed regions and Table 8B for underdeveloped regions respectively.

---

① The developed provincial regions include Beijing, Tianjin, Hebei, Liaoning, Shanghai, Jiangsu, Zhejiang, Fujian, Shandong, Guangdong, Hainan provinces. The less developed provinces include Shanxi, Jilin, Heilongjiang, Anhui, Jiangxi, Henan, Hubei, Hunan, Sichuan, Chongqing, Guizhou, Yunnan, Xizang, Gansu, Qinghai, Ningxia, Xinjiang, Guangxi, Inner Mongolia, Shaanxi provinces and autonomous regions.

Table 8A   Underdeveloped regions

Variables	(1) Sales	(2) ROA	(3) Labor	(4) Per-capita sale	(5) Wage
Pol×Post×Indus	−0.488***	1.297	−0.330	−0.386*	−0.437**
	(−3.185)	(1.234)	(−0.768)	(−1.913)	(−2.566)
Pol×Post	0.106	−0.258	−0.00735	0.107	0.109*
	(1.193)	(−0.771)	(−0.0787)	(1.338)	(1.985)
Pol×Indus	0.414***	−1.564	0.543	0.297***	0.311
	(2.797)	(−1.590)	(1.242)	(3.202)	(1.658)
Pol	0.125*	0.310	0.192**	0.0951	−0.0310
	(1.774)	(1.241)	(2.051)	(1.432)	(−0.756)
Post×Indus	−0.101	−1.040	0.223	−0.178	0.274***
	(−0.621)	(−1.461)	(0.773)	(−0.825)	(4.149)
Post	−0.0468	−0.239	−0.167	−0.0258	0.382***
	(−0.340)	(−0.422)	(−1.439)	(−0.201)	(5.292)
Size	1.062***	2.158***	0.835***	0.950***	0.929***
	(16.91)	(13.42)	(17.05)	(17.37)	(30.89)
Debt	2.035***	−8.022***	1.387***	1.838***	1.551***
	(9.732)	(−9.345)	(7.153)	(9.858)	(13.39)
Intensity	−0.297***	−0.684***	−0.0567***	−0.289***	−0.0957***
	(−9.211)	(−4.101)	(−3.021)	(−9.311)	(−6.261)
Constant	−4.899***	−38.79***	−12.34***	−4.217***	−4.974***
	(−3.412)	(−11.74)	(−10.65)	(−3.365)	(−7.143)
Fixed-effect	YES	YES	YES	YES	YES
Observations	10,277	10,299	10,272	10,272	10,257
R-squared	0.6613	0.1895	0.5289	0.6542	0.6005

Note: This table presents the regression results of the listed firms in China's underdeveloped regions. The control variables include firm size (Size), leverage (Debt), capital intensity (Intensity). We control for time, industry, and provincial fixed effects in all our regression models and adjust the standard errors by clustering. The numbers in parentheses are t values. *, **, ***, represent the significant level of 10%, 5%, and 1%, respectively. The R^2 values in the following columns refer to Pseudo R^2.

Table 8B   Developed regions

Variables	(1) Sales	(2) ROA	(3) Labor	(4) Per-capita sale	(5) Wage
Pol×Post×Indus	−0.365**	−0.970	−0.403***	−0.214	−0.241
	(−2.114)	(−0.577)	(−4.332)	(−0.764)	(−1.523)
Pol×Post	0.0621	0.0627	0.114***	0.0478	0.107
	(1.369)	(0.293)	(4.942)	(1.201)	(1.047)
Pol×Indus	0.267	1.157	0.220***	0.151	−0.0944
	(1.657)	(0.565)	(2.633)	(0.607)	(−0.741)
Pol	0.0781*	−0.0482	0.00814	0.0634	0.0704
	(1.670)	(−0.234)	(0.429)	(1.490)	(0.876)
Post×Indus	−0.0401	−0.0794	0.313***	−0.0770	−0.0803
	(−0.246)	(−0.222)	(4.419)	(−0.539)	(−0.812)
Post	0.399***	0.977**	−0.185**	0.0385	0.380***
	(5.807)	(2.257)	(−2.559)	(0.771)	(3.162)
Size	1.032***	1.826***	0.818***	0.885***	0.982***
	(24.74)	(14.15)	(98.65)	(28.74)	(16.74)
Debt	2.310***	−7.545***	1.435***	2.104***	0.0563*
	(15.93)	(−10.62)	(40.67)	(16.82)	(1.688)
Intensity	−0.0140***	−0.448***	−0.0578***	−0.308***	−0.0944***
	(−3.279)	(−9.691)	(−8.745)	(−9.576)	(−3.723)
Constant	−5.719***	−30.11***	−13.36***	−3.650***	−5.719***
	(−5.892)	(−8.993)	(−57.00)	(−5.360)	(−5.892)
Fixed-effect	YES	YES	YES	YES	YES
Observations	25,404	25,443	25,356	25,356	25,344
R-squared	0.6113	0.1713	0.4889	0.6421	0.6113

Note: This table presents the regression results of the listed firms in China's underdeveloped regions. The control variables include firm size (Size), leverage (Debt), capital intensity (Intensity). We control for time, industry, and provincial fixed effects in all our regression models and adjust the standard errors by clustering. The numbers in parentheses are t values. *, **, ***, represent the significant level of 10%, 5%, and 1%, respectively. The R^2 values in the following columns refer to Pseudo R^2.

Robust t-statistics in parentheses.

It is interesting to consider Table 8A, Table 8B together. In underdeveloped regions, the coefficients of Pol × Post × Indus for sales are significant negative in both Table 8A, Table 8B, which means that the sales of politically-connected firms decreases with respect to firms without political connection in associated industries in both underdeveloped and developed regions. More interestingly, the coefficient is -0.488 in underdeveloped regions, while it is -0.365 in developed regions. It implies the regional heterogeneity in terms of the impact of EPFC on politically-connected companies in associated industry. Underdeveloped provinces have more negative effects than developed provinces. The market economy is well-developed and the government involves less in developed regions than that in underdeveloped regions: Officials in underdeveloped regions are more likely to be corrupted, and the firms in underdeveloped regions are more likely interested in building connections with government officials than the firms in developed regions. So, the EPFC will have a greater impact in underdeveloped regions.

More importantly, there exists the regional heterogeneity in the corporate response to the EPFC shock. Companies take the layoff strategy more likely rather than the wage strategy in developed regions, while take the wage strategy rather than the layoff strategy in underdeveloped regions. In underdeveloped provinces, companies do not take the layoff strategy (the coefficient of Pol $\times$ Post $\times$ Indus term for labor is insignificant), hence the per-capita sales of politically-connected companies decrease dramatically by 38.6% with respect to that of companies without political connections in associated industries. In developed regions, companies do take the layoff strategy. Politically-connected companies shrink the employment by 40.3% with respect to companies without political connection, hence the per-capita sale does not decrease significantly, which means the developed regions just use layoff strategies to passthrough the shock of EPFC. The market economy is less developed and the labor market is weak in underdeveloped regions. It is hard for workers to find new jobs if they lose the current jobs. Hence firms are more flexible in adjusting the total wage rather than laying off the employees in underdeveloped regions. The labor market is quite mature and large in developed regions. Each worker knows his/her market value. When he/she loses the current job, because of either layoff or unsatisfied payment, he/she can easily find the new job in the labor market. Hence companies take the layoff rather than the wage strategies as a response to the EPFC shock.

5.4.2 Company size

Next We considered heterogeneity in company size. We divided the samples into two groups, the companies whose total assets are greater than the median are defined as large companies, and those whose total assets are smaller are considered as small companies. Table 9 reports the regression results, where Table 9A for large companies and Table 9B for small companies respectively.

Table 9A Large company

Variables	(1) Sales	(2) ROA	(3) Labor	(4) Per-capita sale	(5) Wage
Pol×Post×Indus	−0.376**	0.544	−0.561***	−0.270**	−0.287
	(−2.362)	(0.421)	(−4.472)	(−2.538)	(−1.314)
Pol×Post	0.0376	−0.0673	0.0354	0.0321	0.0426
	(0.723)	(−0.461)	(1.369)	(0.689)	(0.678)
Pol×Indus	0.288	−0.220	0.442***	0.204	0.149
	(1.634)	(−0.170)	(3.905)	(1.561)	(0.655)
Pol	0.0492	−0.0539	0.0854***	0.0363	0.0257
	(1.037)	(−0.268)	(4.062)	(0.788)	(0.551)
Post×Indus	0.0218	−0.873*	0.520***	−0.0716	0.119
	(0.411)	(−1.825)	(4.936)	(−1.089)	(1.169)
Post	0.344***	1.297***	0.0326	0.321***	0.655***
	(5.883)	(4.272)	(0.427)	(5.540)	(10.58)
Size	0.873***	1.708***	0.741***	0.781***	0.852***
	(24.02)	(12.66)	(80.66)	(24.22)	(27.17)
Debt	2.335***	−6.808***	1.429***	2.145***	1.575***
	(20.13)	(−17.06)	(33.94)	(19.40)	(12.15)
Intensity	−0.285***	−0.352***	−0.0563***	−0.276***	−0.0864***
	(−7.496)	(−9.172)	(−7.534)	(−7.621)	(−3.763)
Constant	−1.517*	−30.46***	−11.05***	−1.186*	−3.496***
	(−1.920)	(−10.16)	(−42.71)	(−1.701)	(−4.730)
Fixed-effect	YES	YES	YES	YES	YES
Observations	20,127	21,060	21,127	20,127	20,097
R-squared	0.6723	0.4043	0.5221	0.6612	0.6247

Note: This table presents the regression results of the listed firms in China's underdeveloped regions. The control variables include firm size (Size), leverage (Debt), capital intensity (Intensity). We control for time, industry, and provincial fixed effects in all our regression models and adjust the standard errors by clustering. The numbers in parentheses are t values. * , ** , *** , represent the significant level of 10%, 5%, and 1%, respectively. The R^2 values in the following columns refer to Pseudo R^2.

Table 9B   Small company

Variables	(1) Sales	(2) ROA	(3) Labor	(4) Per-capita sale	(5) Wage
Pol×Post×Indus	−0.278	−4.909	−0.164	−0.297	−0.476
	(−0.708)	(−1.200)	(−0.296)	(−0.898)	(−1.439)
Pol×Post	0.0791	−0.0268	0.0913	0.0724	0.134*
	(1.014)	(−0.0358)	(0.947)	(1.018)	(1.736)
Pol×Indus	0.0964	3.943	0.0378	0.138	0.336
	(0.234)	(0.938)	(0.0529)	(0.395)	(1.015)
Pol	0.0395	0.0138	0.0296	0.0264	−0.00941
	(0.541)	(0.0250)	(0.285)	(0.395)	(−0.129)
Post×Indus	−0.176	−0.739	0.0244	−0.181	0.181
	(−0.907)	(−0.906)	(0.0761)	(−1.193)	(1.271)
Post	−0.00470	−0.0379	−0.131	0.0216	0.436***
	(−0.0428)	(−0.0532)	(−0.988)	(0.215)	(3.535)
Size	0.523***	1.758***	0.402***	0.464***	0.541***
	(8.561)	(3.025)	(6.257)	(8.614)	(8.184)
Debt	0.603***	−10.27***	0.296	0.557***	0.329*
	(3.615)	(−5.800)	(1.568)	(3.886)	(1.890)
Intensity	−0.281***	−0.694***	−0.0411***	−0.275***	−0.0809***
	(−14.42)	(−3.680)	(−2.595)	(−14.15)	(−3.781)
Constant	7.964***	−28.53**	−1.948	7.320***	4.703***
	(5.934)	(−2.272)	(−1.369)	(6.241)	(3.127)
Fixed-effect	YES	YES	YES	YES	YES
Observations	16,707	16,592	16,729	16,707	16,671
R-squared	0.5050	0.1157	0.4132	0.4947	0.4472

Note: This table presents the regression results of the listed firms in China's underdeveloped regions. The control variables include firm size (Size), leverage (Debt)), capital intensity (Intensity). We control for time, industry, and provincial fixed effects in all our regression models and adjust the standard errors by clustering. The numbers in parentheses are t values. *, **, ***, represent the significant level of 10%, 5%, and 1%, respectively. The R^2 values in the following columns refer to Pseudo R^2.

Table 9A shows the coefficient of Pol×Post×Indus for sales is significant negative, which means that the sales of politically-connected firms decrease with respect to firms without political connection in associated industries for large firms. Large companies prefer to take the wage strategy rather than the layoff strategy to respond to the shock of EPFC (the coefficient is significantly negative for wage). In contrast, the regression results of small firms in Table 9B are completely different. We find the coefficients of Pol×Post×Indus are insignificant in any model setting we consider, which means the shock of the EPFC does not affect small firms' performance.

The reason for this difference may lie in the fact that the EPFC has a bigger impact on large companies. For example, the government set up the inspection groups to investigate the corruption cases. Because of the time and manpower constraints, the inspection group may only investigate the large firms. Thus, the EPFC has a bigger impact on the large companies.

6 Robustness tests

6.1 Propensity score matching

We give solid empirical evidence that the political connection attributes to the difference in corporate performance between companies in associated industries. Someone may argue that these results could also have other potential interpretations. One possible interpretation is that the officials might choose to build the political connection with different types of firms. In other words, officials may have superior selection abilities to identify firms with better performance to grab more private benefits. Hence the political connection has the endogeneity problem.

To avoid the endogeneity problem caused by selection, we conduct propensity score matching (PSM). Specifically, we use the nearest neighbor matching method. We define the treatment group as companies with political connections, and the control group as companies without political connections. For each firm in the treatment group, we match to a firm with the closest score in the control group. We use a firm size, asset-liability ratio, ROE, total profit, firm's age, fixed-assets ratio in the logit model to get the propensity score. The T-test for the average treatment effect on the treated (ATT) is 3.40, so the matching is reasonable. We run the regression using the matched samples, and Table 10 gives the empirical result.

Table 10　PSM test

Variables	(1) Sales	(2) ROA	(3) Labor	(4) Per-capita sale	(5) Wage
Pol×Post×Indus	−0.352***	−1.192	−0.594**	−0.315**	−0.419**
	(−3.616)	(−0.584)	(−2.213)	(−2.287)	(−2.517)
Pol×Post	0.0607**	−0.0760	0.0279	0.0509	0.0626
	(2.426)	(−0.721)	(0.520)	(1.200)	(1.012)
Pol×Indus	0.289***	1.139	0.472*	0.238	0.274
	(3.507)	(0.629)	(1.698)	(1.530)	(1.473)
Pol	0.00617	−0.190	0.0425	−0.000618	−0.0292
	(0.315)	(−1.453)	(0.771)	(−0.0157)	(−0.640)
Post×Indus	−0.0339	0.528	0.49**	−0.147**	0.216***
	(−0.453)	(0.510)	(2.295)	(−2.352)	(3.576)
Post	0.0392	1.547***	−0.132	0.368***	0.454***
	(0.659)	(7.243)	(−1.609)	(5.725)	(5.758)
Size	0.995***	1.633***	0.810***	0.932***	0.925***
	(119.5)	(14.52)	(27.59)	(23.73)	(29.45)
Debt	2.254***	−6.491***	1.483***	2.007***	1.517***
	(58.11)	(−19.06)	(12.75)	(15.58)	(14.56)
Intensity	−0.300***	−0.445***	−0.0584***	−0.0246***	−0.0960***
	(−32.17)	(−11.27)	(−3.975)	(−3.047)	(−5.091)
Constant	−3.933***	−28.74***	−11.95***	−4.729***	−4.852***
	(−18.33)	(−11.47)	(−17.50)	(−5.301)	(−6.560)
Fixed-effect	YES	YES	YES	YES	YES
Observations	21,822	21,822	21,788	21,822	21,781
R-squared	0.6727	0.3652	0.5219	0.6255	0.6112

Notes: This table presents the regression results of the PSM test. The control variables include firm size (Size), leverage (Debt), capital intensity (Intensity). We control for time, industry, and provincial fixed effects in all our regression models and adjust the standard errors by clustering. The numbers in parentheses are t values. *, **, ***, represent the significant level of 10%, 5%, and 1%, respectively. The R^2 values in the following columns refer to Pseudo R^2.

Table 10 shows that the coefficient of Pol $\times$ Post $\times$ Indus is significantly negative for sales in column 1, while insignificant for ROA in column 2. Furthermore, the coefficients for Labor, Per-capita sales, and Wage are significantly negative respectively. The result in Table 10 is consistent with the benchmark results. It means that the endogeneity problem does not affect our empirical results.

6.2 Placebo test

We consider other policies which may affect the benchmark results. The EPFC might be contemporaneous with other policies that affected firms in China, such as reform of the use of government car, which was conducted in July 2014 and the Document No. 18 by the Organization Department of CCP in October 2013, which prohibited officials taking part-time jobs in enterprises. It is possible that this policy decreases the firms' performance in the automobile industry, and makes the empirical results biased in the benchmark model.

Since we focus on the introduction of EPFC in December 2012, it is necessary to use Placebo test to investigate after ascertaining that the specific time is 2012 instead of other time. To exclude the possible impact of other policies, we push the variable Post backwards to the beginning of 2012, and push it forwards to the end of 2014, and use the sales as the dependent variable to redo our regression.

Table 11 presents the regression result, Table 11 shows the coefficient of Pol * Post * Indus term is negative and significant in the fourth quarter of 2012, and insignificant based on other quarterly periods before or after the promulgation of the EPFC. This shows that the sales of politically-connected companies in associated industries only changed significantly around the date of EPFC.

Table 11 Placebo test

Dependent variable: Sales

Time	2012Q1	2012Q2	2012Q3	2012Q4	2013Q1	2013Q2	2013Q3	2013Q4	2014Q1	2014Q2	2014Q3	2014Q4
Pol×Post×Indus	-0.234	-0.249	-0.270	-0.329**	-0.350	-0.305	-0.325	-0.338	-0.319	-0.295	-0.272	-0.221
	(-1.072)	(-1.314)	(-1.560)	(-2.515)	(-1.581)	(-1.276)	(-1.360)	(-1.408)	(-1.362)	(-1.301)	(-1.221)	(-1.011)
Pol×Post	0.119***	0.133***	0.134***	0.0935**	0.0909**	0.130***	0.128***	0.122***	0.116***	0.110**	0.100**	0.0824*
	(3.276)	(3.866)	(3.797)	(2.505)	(2.315)	(2.947)	(2.912)	(2.741)	(2.618)	(2.450)	(2.192)	(1.750)
Pol×Indus	0.0490	0.0440	0.0504	-0.0588	0.226	0.0420	0.0455	0.0440	0.0237	0.000618	-0.0179	-0.0487
	(0.177)	(0.184)	(0.228)	(-0.977)	(1.150)	(0.192)	(0.213)	(0.210)	(0.117)	(0.00317)	(-0.0949)	(-0.266)
Pol	0.0455	0.0426	0.0454	0.00154	0.0784*	0.0598	0.0650	0.0721*	0.0784*	0.0850**	0.0925**	0.103**
	(0.725)	(0.746)	(0.816)	(0.0259)	(2.062)	(1.338)	(1.477)	(1.652)	(1.825)	(2.004)	(2.203)	(2.458)
Post×Indus	-0.179***	-0.183***	-0.172***	-0.0588	-0.0324	-0.158	-0.141	-0.133	-0.132	-0.149	-0.148	-0.159
	(-3.030)	(-3.413)	(-3.225)	(-0.977)	(-0.261)	(-1.210)	(-1.102)	(-1.070)	(-1.086)	(-1.283)	(-1.315)	(-1.444)
Post	-0.162***	-0.166***	-0.166***	0.00154	0.00199	-0.164**	-0.163***	-0.161***	-0.159**	-0.156**	-0.153**	-0.147**
	(-2.792)	(-2.911)	(-2.926)	(0.0259)	(0.0373)	(-2.637)	(-2.629)	(-2.584)	(-2.555)	(-2.513)	(-2.466)	(-2.371)
Size	1.074***	1.074***	1.074***	1.012***	1.012***	1.074***	1.074***	1.074***	1.074***	1.074***	1.074***	1.074***
	(22.87)	(22.83)	(22.82)	(26.79)	(43.29)	(40.73)	(40.73)	(40.74)	(40.75)	(40.76)	(40.76)	(40.77)
Debt	0.217	0.217	0.217	0.217	0.217	0.217	0.217	0.217	0.217	0.217	0.217	0.217
	(1.306)	(1.306)	(1.306)	(1.318)	(1.320)	(1.328)	(1.328)	(1.329)	(1.329)	(1.329)	(1.330)	(1.330)
Intensity	-0.310***	-0.310***	-0.310***	-0.307***	-0.307***	-0.310***	-0.310***	-0.310***	-0.310***	-0.310***	-0.311***	-0.311***
	(-9.019)	(-9.030)	(-9.034)	(-10.50)	(-18.62)	(-17.97)	(-17.97)	(-17.97)	(-17.97)	(-17.97)	(-17.98)	(-17.98)
Constant	-4.600***	-4.602***	-4.603***	-4.150***	-4.153***	-4.612***	-4.615***	-4.617***	-4.619***	-4.621***	-4.620***	-4.619***
	(-4.484)	(-4.490)	(-4.491)	(-5.036)	(-7.746)	(-7.149)	(-7.153)	(-7.156)	(-7.159)	(-7.160)	(-7.160)	(-7.157)
Fixed-effect	YES	YES	YES	YES	YES	YES	YES	YES	YES	YES	YES	YES
Observations	37,739	37,739	37,739	37,739	37,739	37,739	37,739	37,739	37,739	37,739	37,739	37,739
R-squared	0.5751	0.5753	0.5754	0.6461	0.6461	0.5755	0.5755	0.5754	0.5754	0.5753	0.5752	0.5751

Notes: This table presents the regression results of Placebo test. The control variables include firm size (Size), leverage (Debt), capital intensity (Intensity). We control for time, industry, and provincial fixed effects in all our regression models and adjust the standard errors by clustering. The numbers in parentheses are t values. "*", "**", "***", represent the significant level of 10%, 5%, and 1%, respectively. The R^2 values in the following columns refer to Pseudo R^2.

6.3 Baidu index

Baidu Search is the most popular search engine for Chinese users. Based on this engine, Baidu index shows what search scale a certain keyword has in Baidu. As Fig. 1(A) shows, the search frequency of the keyword "anti-corruption" dramatically increased since 2012. We use "anti-corruption" as the keyword to get the Baidu index of "anti-corruption", denoted as "Baidu", and use it as an alternative measure of EPFC.

Table 12 shows the sales of politically-connected companies is influenced significantly and negatively after the EPFC. And the coefficient of Pol×Baidu ×Indus term for ROA is insignificant, which means EPFC has no impact on firms' profitability. The coefficients of Labor, Per-capita sales and Wage are all significantly negative, which means the politically-connected companies in associated industries use the layoff and wage strategies to pass through the negative impact. In general, these results are consistent with our hypothesis, and our benchmark results are robust.

Table 12　Baidu index

Variables	(1) Sales	(2) ROA	(3) Labor	(4) Per-capita sale	(5) Wage
Pol×Baidu× Indus	−9.45e-06***	−1.17e-05	−9.68e-06**	−7.92e-06*	−9.13e-06***
	(−3.027)	(−0.323)	(−2.452)	(−1.864)	(−2.723)
Pol×Baidu	3.00e-06***	9.53e-06	2.81e-06**	2.83e-06**	3.06e-06***
	(3.347)	(1.019)	(2.528)	(2.220)	(2.932)
Pol×Indus	0.307***	0.322	0.309	0.219*	0.231**
	(2.605)	(0.237)	(1.631)	(1.688)	(2.336)
Pol	0.0387	−0.369	0.0408	0.0287	−0.0151
	(1.222)	(−1.364)	(0.834)	(0.542)	(−0.288)
Baidu×Indus	4.18e-06*	4.97e-07	6.15e-06**	2.71e-06	5.63e-06*
	(1.846)	(0.0301)	(1.980)	(1.024)	(1.675)
Baidu	0.000207***	−2.03e-05***	4.44e-05***	2.56e-05***	3.70e-05***
	(3.511)	(5.888)	(−5.172)	(7.179)	(6.505)
Size	1.035***	1.752***	0.842***	0.972***	0.955***
	(131.6)	(15.11)	(29.22)	(22.30)	(29.09)

continued

Variables	(1) Sales	(2) ROA	(3) Labor	(4) Per-capita sale	(5) Wage
Debt	2.163***	−7.129***	1.363***	1.901***	1.400***
	(61.20)	(−13.46)	(11.69)	(12.56)	(12.77)
Intensity	−0.291***	−0.453***	−0.0587***	−0.0103**	−0.0958***
	(−38.28)	(−8.856)	(−4.912)	(−2.189)	(−6.119)
Constant	−5.136***	−36.75***	−11.97***	−6.707***	−5.778***
	(−23.10)	(−13.21)	(−17.57)	(−6.230)	(−8.143)
Fixed-effect	YES	YES	YES	YES	YES
Observations	29,482	29,525	29,503	29,482	29,447
R-squared	0.6420	0.1755	0.5154	0.5886	0.5701

Notes: This table presents the regression results of Baidu index. The control variables include firm size (Size), leverage (D)ebt, capital intensity (Intensity). We control for time, industry, and provincial fixed effects in all our regression models and adjust the standard errors by clustering. The numbers in parentheses are t values. *, **, ***, represent the significant level of 10%, 5%, and 1%, respectively. The R^2 values in the following columns refer to Pseudo R^2.

6.4 Private vs state-owned companies

State-owned companies have natural political connections. We argue that state-owned companies have weaker political connections than private companies, which means the EPFC has smaller impact on state-owned companies than private companies in associated industries. We use the triple-interaction term Soe × Post × Indus to consider the effect of EPFC on the natural political connections that state-owned firms are endowed, and compare with that of the political connection of private firms. Table 13 gives the empirical evidence.

Table 13　Private vs state-owned companies

Variables	Dependent variable: Sales		
	(1)	(2)	(3)
Soe×Post×Indus	−0.280**		−0.188
	(−2.331)		(−1.200)
Soe×Post	−0.163***		−0.205***
	(−3.392)		(−3.793)

continued

Variables	Dependent variable: Sales		
	(1)	(2)	(3)
Soe×Indus	0.219		0.231
	(0.745)		(0.645)
Soe	−0.483***		−0.500***
	(−11.44)		(−9.833)
Pol×Post×Indus		−0.418***	−0.251*
		(−5.239)	(−1.684)
Pol×Post		0.0904**	0.138***
		(2.181)	(3.224)
Pol×Indus		0.0655	−0.0826
		(0.946)	(−0.319)
Pol		−0.210***	0.0649
		(−3.828)	(0.976)
Post×Indus	−0.103	−0.116	−0.102
	(−0.771)	(−0.740)	(−0.758)
Post	1.722***	1.490***	1.739***
	(24.17)	(19.94)	(23.29)
Size	1.105***	1.139***	1.101***
	(33.13)	(32.76)	(35.09)
Debt	0.270	0.415	0.370
	(1.226)	(1.329)	(1.318)
Intensity	−0.0141***	−0.0143***	−0.0139***
	(−3.816)	(−3.903)	(−3.839)
Constant	−5.007***	−5.847***	−4.975***
	(−6.557)	(−7.500)	(−6.893)
Fixed-effect	YES	YES	YES
Observations	71,275	71,275	71,275
R-squared	0.6838	0.6649	0.6862

Note: This table presents the regression results of the sample, including private and state-owned companies. The control variables include firm size (Size), leverage (Debt), capital intensity (Intensity). We control for time, industry, and provincial fixed effects in all our regression models and adjust the standard errors by clustering. The numbers in parentheses are t values. *, **, *** , represent the significant level of 10%, 5%, and 1%, respectively. The R^2 values in the following columns refer to Pseudo R^2.

In Table 13, both the coefficients of Soe×Post×Indus and Pol×Post×Indus for the sales are negative and significant at 1% level, which means the

EPFC affects the sales of both the state-owned companies, which have natural political connections, and the politically-connected private companies in associated industries. More interestingly, the coefficient of Soe×Post×Indus-0. 280 is less than that of Pol×Post×Indus-0. 418, which suggests that state-owned firms are less negatively affected by EPFC than politically-connected private firms in associated industries. When we put the natural political connection and the political connection in the private sector in one regression, the evidence shows that the coefficient of Pol×Post×Indus is significant while the coefficient of Soe × Post × Indus is less significant. Furthermore, the coefficient of Soe×Post×Indus is less negative. State-owned companies have natural political connections and hence have more protection from the natural political connections than that from the private firms' political connections after the EPFC. The evidence suggests the EPAR targets more likely the corruption in the private sector.

7 Conclusions

Both central and local governments play an indispensable role in China's economic development. Governments affect resource allocation. Similar to other developing countries, China has a history of economic corruption. Consequently, companies have high incentive to seek rent from the political connections of their senior executives (e. g., CEOs and chairmen of the board). Entrepreneurs must enhance firms' profits and obtain resources, such as talent, capital and investment opportunities, by taking advantage of their political resources. Government expenditure brings companies benefit through such political connections. Government procurement favors politically-connected companies. Hence, political connections affect corporate sales and profitability.

The EPFC was introduced in December 2012, we investigate the corporate response to the negative shock from EPFC through political connections in Chinese listed firms. We construct political connection variables for both private and state-owned companies and empirically test the effect of EPFC and the corporate response using the quarterly data of private listed companies in China.

The empirical results show that the sales decrease significantly for politically-connected companies in industries associated with the EPFC. However, the profitability of these companies changes insignificantly after the EPFC shock. These companies pass through the negative impact of EPAR to the labor market by laying off employees and reducing the wage. It seems that the negative effects of EPFC are offset by adjusting labor costs.

Furthermore, we find evidence of regional heterogeneity. The decrease in sales after the EPFC is more serious for politically-connected companies in underdeveloped regions than those in developed regions. More importantly, companies take the wage strategy rather than the layoff strategy in underdeveloped regions, whereas companies in developed regions adopt more likely the layoff strategy rather than the wage adjustment under the shock of EPFC.

Corporate size heterogeneity also exists. For large politically-connected companies, the sales decreases significantly while ROA has no significant change. The corporate policies, measured as either per-capita sales, or labor are significantly negative whereas the wage does not change after the EPAR. For small politically-connected firms, EPFC does not change the sales, and hence companies have no reaction. It seems that small companies are not significantly affected.

The EPFC affects the sales both of the state-owned companies, who have natural political connections, and of the politically-connected private companies in associated industries. More interestingly, state-owned firms have weaker negative effect from EPFC than politically-connected private firms in associated industries.

Acknowledgments

We acknowledge the financial support from the National Natural Science Foundation of China (Grant No. 71673249), the NSFC-RCUK-ESRC Joint

Research Project (Grant No. 71661137002), the MOE project of Key Research Institute of Humanities and Social Sciences at Universities (Grant No. 16JJD790052), and the Fundamental Research Funds for the Central Universities (Grant No. 201853-9).

Appendix 1: Marketisation index of China's provinces (2011)

Provinces	Marketisation index
Zhejiang	11.8
Jiangsu	11.54
Shanghai	10.96
Guangdong	10.42
Beijing	9.87
Tianjin	9.43
Fujian	9.02
Shandong	8.93
Liaoning	8.76
Chongqing	8.14
Henan	8.04
Anhui	7.88
Jiangxi	7.65
Hubei	7.65
Sichuan	7.56
Hunan	7.39
Hebei	7.27
Jilin	7.09
Hainan	6.4
Inner Mongolia	6.27
Guangxi	6.17
Shanxi	6.11
Heilongjiang	6.11
Yunnan	6.06
Ningxia	5.94

	continued
Provinces	Marketisation index
Shanxi	5. 65
Guizhou	5. 56
Xinjiang	5. 12
Gansu	4. 98
Qinghai	3. 25
Xizang	0. 38

Appendix 2: EPFC

The eight-point frugality code (EPFC) is a document adopted in a meeting of the Political Bureau of the Communist Party of China (CPC) Central Committee, the country's top-ruling body, on Tuesday, Dec 4, 2012. The document makes explicit requirements on how Political Bureau members should improve their work style in eight aspects, focusing on rejecting extravagance and reducing bureaucratic visits, meetings and empty talk.

The requirements, which are the first detailed guidance for a new working style adopted after the election of the Political Bureau members in Nov 2012, were issued to strengthen ties between the people and officials, whose malpractice including corruption and power abuse have distanced them from ordinary citizens.

The Political Bureau, which has 25 members, includes the top decision-makers, such as State leaders, Party chiefs of several key provincial-level regions, ministers and top army officials.

1. Leaders must keep in close contact with the grassroots. They must understand the real situation facing society through in-depth inspections at grassroots. Greater attention should be focused on places where social problems are more acute, and inspection tours must be carried out more thoroughly. Inspection tours as a mere formality should be strictly prohibited. Leaders should work and listen to the public and officials at the grassroots, and people's practical problems must be tackled. There should be no welcome banner, no red carpet, no floral arrangement or grand receptions for officials' visits.

2. Meetings and major events should be strictly regulated，and efficiency improved. Political Bureau members are not allowed to attend ribbon-cutting or cornerstone-laying ceremonies，or celebrations and seminars，unless they get approval from the CPC Central Committee. Official meetings should get shortened and be specific and to the point，with no empty and rigmarole talks.

3. The issuing of official documents should be reduced.

4. Officials' visits abroad should only be arranged when needed in terms of foreign affairs with fewer accompanying members，and on most of the occasions，there is no need for a reception by overseas Chinese people，institutions and students at the airport.

5. There should be fewer traffic controls when leaders travel by cars to avoid unnecessary inconvenience to the public. It should be fewer traffic controls arranged for the leaders' security of their trips to avoid unnecessary inconvenience to the public.

6. The media must not report on stories about official events unless there is real news value. The regulations also ban worthless news reports on senior officials' work and activities and said such reports should depend on work needs，news value and social effects.

7. Leaders should not publish any works by themselves or issue any congratulatory letters unless an arrangement with the central leadership has been made. Official documents without substantial contents and realistic importance should be withheld. Publications regarding senior officials' work and activities are also restricted.

8. Leaders must practice thrift and strictly follow relevant regulations on accommodation and cars.

References

Acemoglu D，Johnson S，Kermani A，et al，2013. The value of connections in turbulent times：Evidence from the united states[J]. Journal of Financial Economics，121(2)：368-391.

Akcigit U，Baslandze S，Lotti F，2023. Connecting to power：Political connections, innovation, and firm dynamics[J]. Econometrica, 91(2): 529-564.

Allen F, Qian J, Qian M, 2005. Law, finance, and economic growth in china [J]. Journal of Financial Economics, 77(1): 57-116.

An H, Chen Y, Luo D, et al, 2016. Political uncertainty and corporate investment: Evidence from China[J]. Journal of Corporate Finance, 36:174-189.

Asiedu E, Freeman J, 2010. The effect of corruption on investment growth: Evidence from firms in Latin America, Sub-Saharan Africa, and transition countries[J]. Review of Development Economics, 13(2): 200-214.

Balsvik R, Jensen S, Salvanes K G, 2015. Made in China, sold in Norway: Local labor market effects of an import shock [J]. Journal of Public Economics, 127: 137-144.

Bernal R, Eslava M, Melendez M, et al, 2017. Switching from payroll taxes to corporate income taxes: Firms' employment and wages after the 2012 Colombian tax reform [J]. Economia Journal of the Latin American & Caribbean Economic Association, 18(1): 41-74.

Cai H, Fang H, Xu L C, 2011. Eat, drink, firms, government: An investigation of corruption from the entertainment and travel costs of Chinese firms[J]. The Journal of Law and Economics, 54(1): 55-78.

Chen L, Randall M, Yin Y B, et al, 2016. Anti-corruption reforms and shareholder valuations: Event study evidence from China[J]. NBER Working Papers:1-54.

Claessens S, Feijen E, Laeven L, 2008. Political connections and preferential access to finance: The role of campaign contributions[J]. Journal of Financial Economics, 88(3):554-580.

Cruces G, Galiani S, Kidyba S, 2010. Payroll taxes, wages and employment: Identification through policy changes[J]. Labour Economics, 17(4): 0-749.

Faccio M, 2006. Politically connected firms [J]. The American Economic Review, 96(1):369-386.

Faccio M, Masulis R W, Mcconnell J J, 2006. Political connections and corporate bailouts[J]. Journal of Finance, 61: 2597-2635.

Fan G，Wang X，Zhu H，2011. NERI index of marketization of China's provinces 2011 report[M]. Beijing：Economic Science Press.

Fan J P H，Wong T J，Zhang T，2007. Politically connected CEOs，corporate governance，and post-IPO performance of China's newly partially privatized firms[J]. Journal of Financial Economics，84：330-357.

Fisman R，2001. Estimating the value of political connections[J]. American Economic Review，91(4)：1095-1102.

Fisman R，Svensson J.，2007 Are corruption and taxation really harmful to growth? firm level evidence[J]. Journal of Development Economics，83(1)：63-75.

Haselmann R F H，Schoenherr D，Vig V，2018. Rent-seeking in elite networks[J]. Journal of Political Economy，126(4)：1638-1690.

Hu Q，Schaufeli W B，2011. Job insecurity and remuneration in chinese family—owned business workers[J]. Career Development International，16(1)：6-19.

Ko K，Weng C，2012. Structural changes in chinese corruption[J]. The China Quarterly，211(211)：718-740.

Ku H，Schönberg U，Schreiner R C，2018. How Do Firms Respond to Place-Based Tax Incentives? [J]. Journal of Public Economics，CPD11/18：1-46.

Leff N H，1964. Economic development through bureaucratic corruption[J]. American Behavioral Scientist，8(3)：8-14.

Li H，Meng L，Wang Q，et al，2008. Political connections，financing and firm performance：Evidence from Chinese private firms [J]. Journal of Development Economics，87(2)：0-299.

Liu L X，Shu H，Wei K J，2017. The impacts of political uncertainty on asset prices：Evidence from the Bo scandal in China [J]. Journal of Financial Economics，125(2)：286-310.

Mauro P，1995. Corruption and growth[J]. Quarterly Journal of Economics，110 (3)：681-712.

Mauro P，1998. Corruption and the composition of government expenditure [J]. Journal of Public Economics，69 (2)：263-279.

Mironov M，Zhuravskaya E，2011. Corruption in procurement and the political cycle in tunneling: Evidence from financial transactions data[J]. Social Science Electronic Publishing, 8(2):287-321.

Pan X, Tian G G, 2017. Political connections and corporate investments: Evidence from the recent anti-corruption campaign in China[J]. Journal of Banking & Finance, 119: 1-15.

Qian N, Wen J, 2015. The impact of Xi Jinping's anti-corruption campaign on luxury imports in China (Preliminary Draft)[R]. Working Paper: 1-37.

Schoenherr D, 2019. Political connections and allocative distortions[J]. Journal of Finance, 74(2):543-586.

Shleifer A, Vishny R W, 1993. Corruption[J]. Social Science Electronic Publishing, 108(3): 599-617.

Shleifer A, Vishny R W, 1994. Politicians and firms[J]. Quarterly Journal of Economics, 109(4): 995-1025.

Wang Y, Chen C R, Sophie Y, 2014. Economic policy uncertainty and corporate investment: Evidence from China[J]. Pacific Basin Finance Journal, 26: 227-243.

Wang Y, Yao C, Kang D, 2018. Political connections and firm performance: Evidence from government officials ' site visits[J]. Pacific-Basin Finance Journal, 57: 101021.

Wedeman A, 2012. Double paradox: Rapid growth and rising corruption in China[M]. Ithaca:Cornell University Press.

Wei Y, Wang M, Jin X, 2012. Political connection and Financing constraint: Information effect and resource effect[J]. Economic Research Journal, 9:125-139.

Wu W, Wu C, Rui O M, 2012. Ownership and the value of political connections: Evidence from China[J]. European Financial Management, 18: 695-729.

Wu W, Wu C, Zhou C, et al, 2012. Political connections, tax benefits and firm performance: Evidence from China[J]. Journal of Accounting & Public Policy, 31(3):277-300.

Stock Name Length and High Visibility Premium[①]

Abstract   High stock visibility reduces the cost of capital and creates high firm value. In China's A-share market, only 427 stocks have a three-character name, while almost 3000 stocks have four-character names; we use posts read and reply at BBS to verify the high visibility of former. We then use stock name length as the measure of stock visibility and examine abnormally high returns of stocks with high visibility. We find that the premiums of three-character length name stocks exist after controlling for systematic risks, and that premiums could decrease when the information environment for stocks improves.

Key words   Stock name; Stock visibility; Investor base; Information environment

1   Introduction

Individual stock selection is becoming increasingly difficult as China's A-share market continues to expand. There were 8 listed companies in 1990, a number that rose to 1381 in 2005, and 3757 in 2019. Large amounts of securities suggest that investors could not observe certain stocks, and consequently, do

---

①   Originally published in *Finance Research Letters* (vol39, 2020) by Jin Xuejun, Shen Yifan and Yu Bin.

not invest them. Worse, this problem is aggravated in China's A-share market because individuals account for the vast majority of investors. Investor recognition theory introduced by Merton (1987) shows that incomplete information influences the trading behaviour of investors and the relevant firm values. Specifically, as more securities are traded per potential investor, it becomes less possible that a stock will be observed by the whole market, and more likely it would need certain event to increase its visibility. Kaniel et al. (2012) use highly positive trading volume shocks to measure the increased visibility of stocks and show that for a stock to achieve increased visibility, and consequently, increase investors who observed the stocks, and then reduce the cost of capital and increase the stock value. The findings of Kaniel et al. (2012) are pervasive across many countries, except for several emerging countries, including China. One potential explanation for the insignificant results in developing countries is that the data from DataStream are incomplete.

In this study, we used complete A-share data and proposed a new and natural measure of stock visibility, that is, the abbreviation of listed firms' names. Similar to the US stock market, stocks in China have two official names in the security exchange. We obtained these two names from the widely used China A-share database, CSMAR (China Stock Market & Accounting Database). In CSMAR, the variable 'Stknme' is the abbreviation of a company's name, and is displayed prominently in stock trading software. Furthermore, all analysts' reports and media reports use stock codes and abbreviations when relevant news is published. The variable 'conme' is the full name of the company; however, this full name is only visible after clicking on the company information. Most importantly, there are two primary types of 'Stknme' in the A-share market; specifically, only 427 stocks have a three-character 'Stknme', while the remaining 3000 stocks have a four-character name. Therefore, the three-character name is highly visible to investors.

As Table 1 shows, a company with an abbreviated three-character name is much more striking to investors than a four-character abbreviation. This is similar to teachers who always remember the names of students with uncommon names when calling roll. It is natural to think shorter names with one or two characters would be even more prominent; however, there are only two types of names in the market: either three or four characters. [1]A possible reason may be that one or two characters could not convey a firm's basic information, and such a name would not be adopted by firms or approved by the China Securities Regulatory Commission (CSRC).

Table 1   Examples of China's A shares: "Stkcd" is the stock code of listed firm, "Stknme" is the abbreviation of a company's name, we use the capital letter "X" to represent the Chinese characters

Stkcd	Stknme
002,001	X
002,002	X
002,003	X
002,004	X
002,005	X
002,006	X
002,007	X
002,008	X
002,009	X

Based on Merton's (1987) investor recognition hypothesis and previous literature, we expect a stock with a three-character name will command a premium because of its high visibility. In contrast, stocks with four-character names are more likely to suffer from an insufficient investor base. As a result, the lack of complete information about a firm would raise its cost of capital and cause the firm's market value to be underestimated.

Besides the visibility explanation to the mispricing of stocks, there are

---

[1]   We exclude the special treatment stocks which have delisting risk. Noticeably, our sample only cover pure A-share stocks, which do not issue H-shares in Hongkong Stock Exchange at the same time, since the microstructure for dual A and H shares is largely different.

also many researches on investor attention and asset prices. Da et al. (2011) use search frequency in google to proxy investor attention and show that it generates abnormal high return of IPO stocks in the short run. In contrast, Hou and Moskowitz (2005) use institutional ownership, analyst coverage, number of employees, and number of shareholders to measure attention, and find that high investor attention could reduce price delay of stocks and therefore reduce the relevant premium in U. S market. However, Qian et al. (2017) find opposite result that high investor attention (proxy by turnover) has a negative impact on price efficiency in A-shares market. Therefore, we distinguish different impacts on stock return between name length and traditional investor attention measures in our research.

Furthermore, Frieder and Subrahmanyam (2005) show investors have a preference on strong brands stocks, which affects their returns; hence, it is also necessary to examine whether there is an overlap between three-character name stocks and stocks that are well known. Furthermore, psychology research suggests the fluency of stock names may affect investors' decisions; people look favourably upon stocks whose names are short and easy to pronounce, and this favourability will increase the value of these firms (Green & Jame, 2013). Besides the name's fluency, stock names with popular meanings also raise firm values. For instance, Cooper et al. (2001) also find the market capitalization of firms with dotcom names was inflated in the Internet boom. Therefore, name fluency and popular name meanings might also explain the difference of returns between three-character and four-character stocks.

Using a sample from July 2004 to December 2017, our empirical results show that stocks with three-character names generate a monthly return of 0. 246% more than stocks with four-character names. This return difference increases to 0. 449% in a bear market with a low investor base. Moreover, after eliminating systematic risk, strong brands, and psychological factors, the premium is significant. The results also show that a high proportion of holdings by national social security funds, large analyst followings, and bull market conditions could reduce the premium. This suggests measures that improve the information environment could increase the visibility of other stocks, and reduce the investor awareness of stocks with three-character names, as well as their corresponding abnormal returns.

The rest of the paper proceeds as follows. Section 2 describes our data and variables. Section 3 reports the empirical results, and Section 4 concludes.

2 Sample and variables

We used the CSMAR database to collect A-share data from 2004 to 2017. We obtained firm trading data, firm characteristics, analyst coverage, financial annual report data, and institutional holdings from CSMAR. We crawled the posts read and reply data from Eastmoney Securities. Since individual stock liquidity is a major variable in our study, we required our sample stocks to have returns for 60 months (at least 36 months). We also excluded the port industry, because all 16 listed port firms have names that are three characters long in the Chinese language. ①Moreover, we also excluded data for which the relevant variable information is unavailable. The final sample includes 2421 stocks. Table 2 presents the summary statistics for the sample.

Table 2 Summary statistics of China's A shares stocks

	Mean	Median	Std	Q1	Q3
EXCESS	0.0218	0.0029	0.2188	−0.0731	0.0881
SIZE	12179.4825	4276.3081	54054.0162	2165.7415	8825.1901
BM	0.4346	0.3685	0.5293	0.2217	0.5738

---

① Port firms' names consist of the city name and the word that represents harbor. All 16 of the listed port firms are located in cities with two character names and the Chinese word for harbor is one character; hence, all 16 port firms have three-character names. A four-character port firm would be strikingly different; however, no such firm actually exists in the market. Moreover, 16 firms account for only 3.7% of the three-character sample. Thus, including the port firms would not change the empirical results but would conflict with the intention to investigate premiums of high visibility stocks.

continued

	Mean	Median	Std	Q1	Q3
MOM	0.2058	0.0213	0.6699	−0.2063	0.4010
INV	0.3917	0.1019	8.8637	0.0109	0.2389
GP	0.0478	0.0313	1.0991	0.0032	0.0737
ILLIQ	0.0018	0.0006	0.0042	0.0002	0.0015
SFH	2.1978	1.6556	1.9919	0.9311	2.7943
IO	4.61%	2.60%	6.10%	0.43%	6.70%
ANA	5.4094	2.0000	7.0081	0.0000	8.0000
EMP	6,605	2,200	24,580	980	5000
SH	63876	39000	91690	22000	70000

Table 2 reports summary statistics of A-share at the end of April from 2004 to 2017. From May (Year $t-1$) to April (Year t) during 2004 to 2017, we required our sample A-share to have at least 180 trading days and positive book equity in the latest annual report. EXCESS is the monthly stock return in excess of the risk free rate. SIZE is a firm's market floating size at the end of April in year t. BM is a stock's book value on market value ratio at the end of December in year $t-1$. GP is a firm's gross profitability defined as dividing the difference between sales and cost of goods sold by the lagged total asset at the end of December in year $t-1$. INV is a firm's asset growth rate at the end of December in year $t-1$. MOM is a firm's cumulative monthly return from May (Year $t-1$) to March (Year t). ILLIQ is a firm's daily average Amihud (2002)'s illiquidity ratio. SFH is a firm's average social security funds holdings in year $t-1$. IO is a stock's institutional ownership. ANA is a stock's number of following analysts in year $t-1$. EMP is the employee number. SH is the shareholder number.

We also constructed measures of name fluency, good name meanings, and strong brands. First, to distinguish between the length of a stock's name and psychological factors, we follow Green and Jame (2013) and introduced name fluency scores; specifically, we counted the number of words in the firm name. Firm names of one word are given a score of 3, two words are given a score of 2, three words are given a score of 1, and four words are given a score of 0. Since the maximum number of characters in a firm name abbreviation is four, four is also the maximum number of words. Moreover, to measure the popular meanings of firm names, we manually examined whether the firm names contain popular or traditionally lucky words (e. g. words relevant to wealth or health, etc.). If we determined that they do, we assigned a value of 1; otherwise, the value is 0. Finally, we used goodwill as reported in the annual announcements as a proxy for the value of firm brands.

3 Empirical analysis

We first examined the industry distribution of stocks with three-character names. As Fig. 1 shows, such stocks account for 11% of the sample across 14 industries. The bar chart shows that such stocks are not concentrated in any single industry, eliminating the possibility that industry is the cause of the difference in returns between the two types of stocks. We notice the relatively low proportion of three-character names in two industries, electricity and heat (D) and transportation (G), compared to the average. However, this appears to be simply factual, and not systematic.

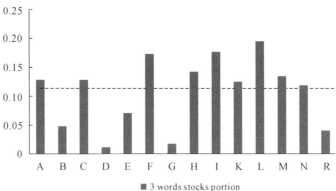

Fig. 1 Three-character stocks potion across industries

Based on the industry classification guidance of listed companies of CSRC, A represents agriculture, B represents mining and relevant, C represents manufacturing, D represents electricity and heat, E represents construction, F represents wholesale and retail trade, G represents transportation, H represents accommodation and catering, I represents hardware and software, K represents real estate, L represents business service, M represents technical services, N represents utility, R represents media.

Table 3 reports the average firm characteristics of stock portfolios sorted by name length for our sample. For risk characteristics, the SIZE, GP and INV present no significant difference between stocks with three-character and four-character names. The BM of three-character name stocks are significant lower than four-character name group, indicating that three-character name stocks tend to be growth stock. Moreover, even if the return previous year skips one month, MOM is also almost significantly higher than control group, showing that three-character name stocks tend to be stocks which perform better in the past year. As for investor attention variables, three-character name stocks tend to have higher institution holdings and following analysts, suggesting that three-character name stocks overlap with high investor attention stocks to some extent.

Table 3　Report on summary statistics of A-share at the end of April from 2004 to 2017

Panel A: Risk Characteristics

	SIZE	BM	GP	INV	MOM
3 character	7255. 367	0. 394	0. 116	0. 748	0. 251
4 character	7238. 409	0. 424	0. 039	0. 328	0. 229
Difference	16. 958	−0. 030**	0. 077	0. 421	0. 022
t-Value	0. 10	−2. 80	1. 29	0. 90	1. 75

Panel B: Investor Attention

	IO	ANA	EMP	SH	
3 character	0. 047	5. 820	3750. 844	43267. 311	
4 character	0. 044	4. 547	3756. 357	46044. 013	
Difference	0. 003*	1. 273*	−5. 514	−2776. 702	
t-Value	1. 84	2. 06	−0. 02	−0. 96	

Note: The variable definitions are same as table 2.

To empirically explore the high visibility of stocks with three-character names, the regression formula for table 4 is shown in Eq. (1). We regress the number of Postings read at the largest Chinese stock BBS (Eastmoney securities) on name dummy, we control for the top 3 best performance industries dummy and number of Postings read last month, the stocks with three-character names attract more posts read at 5% significance level. After controlling for firm investor attention features (size, book to market value, gross profit, institutional holdings and number of investors), Model 2 shows that the name dummy still demonstrates significant explanatory power for number of posts read. We further use number of posts reply as dependant variable in models 3 to 4. The results show that the name dummy is also an important determinant that arouses investors' discussion.

$$\log(Read_{i,t}) = \alpha + \beta_1 \times name \cdot lummy + \beta_2 TopIND_{i,t-1} + \beta_3 (Read_{i,t-1})$$
$$+ \beta_4 \times \log(SIZE_{i,y}) + \beta_5 \times \log(BM_{i,y}) + \beta_6 \times GP_{i,y} + \beta_7$$
$$\times IO_{i,y} + \beta_8 \times \log(SH_{i,y}) + \beta_9 \times Excessreturn_{i,t-1} + e_{i,t} \quad (1)$$

where $\log(Read_{i,t})$ is a stock's average daily read number in month t, and the t denotes month and the y denotes year. We use stock feature variables in April of year y to predict stocks' monthly number of reads from May in year y to April in year $y+1$.

Table 4 reports the Fama-MacBeth results of monthly posts read and reply on Name_Dummy. LOG_READ/REPLY is logarithm of the post read/reply at the Eastmoney BBS, the Name_Dummy is 1 when the stocks have a name of 3 characters length, is 0 when the stocks have a name of 4 characters length. Top_Ind3 is the top 3 best performance industries dummy. Log (SIZE) is logarithm of the stock's market size at end of April (Year t). Log (BM) is logarithm of the book value on market value at the end of December (Year $t-1$). GP is the gross profit. IO is the institutional holdings. Log (SH) is logarithm of the investors number at the end of April (Year t). EXCESS($-1, -1$) is the lagged stock return. Newey-West adjusted t-statistics (with lag=4) are reported in the parenthesis.

Table 4   Fama-MacBeth regressions of posts read and reply on Name_Dummy

VARIABLES	(1) LOG_READ	(2) LOG_READ	(3) LOG_REPLY	(4) LOG_REPLY
Name_Dummy	0.0090**	0.0064*	0.0229***	0.0176**
	(2.07)	(1.81)	(3.01)	(2.27)
Top_Ind3	0.0438***	0.0370***	0.0661***	0.0559***
	(5.97)	(5.36)	(5.44)	(5.20)
LOG_READ_{t-1}	0.7043***	0.7036***		
	(36.66)	(32.39)		
LOG_REPLY_{t-1}			0.7537***	0.7330***
			(75.90)	(77.15)
Log_SIZE		0.0469***		0.0631***
		(6.83)		(5.84)
Log_BM		−0.0082		−0.0090
		(−1.66)		(−1.43)
GP		0.0018		−0.0016
		(0.44)		(−0.30)
IO		−0.0014***		−0.0018***
		(−6.67)		(−6.07)
Log_SH		0.0406***		0.0876***
		(11.06)		(13.63)
$Excess_{t-1}$		0.4326***		0.8205***
		(5.68)		(6.34)
Constant	3.2009***	1.8079***	0.5095***	−1.6506***
	(14.62)	(6.66)	(8.59)	(−7.47)
Observations	71,587	56,700	71,480	56,691
R-squared	0.537	0.618	0.590	0.641

After verifying the high visibility of three-character stocks, we investigated portfolio differences based on a buy-and-hold strategy to examine whether the three-character portfolio outperforms the four-character portfolio. Panel A of Table 5 presents the raw returns of the two portfolios. Both generate positive returns and are significant higher than zero; however, the three-character portfolio generates an equally weighted monthly return that is 0.25% more than that of the four-character portfolio. The premium difference remains when valued-weighted returns are used. In Panel B of Table 5, we further compared the six-factor alphas of the two portfolios. The three-character portfolio still significantly outperforms the four-character portfolio by 0. 29% per month at the 5% significance level; the value-weighted adjusted return difference is similar, although not statistically significant. Furthermore, the six-factor model analysis shows that the portfolio of three-character stocks has lower factor loadings on HML and higher factor loadings on UMD than the four-character stock portfolio. This shows that stocks with three-character names tend to have lower book to market equity ratios and better stock performance from the past year, and this result is consistent to the results of table 3. Noticeably, for stocks with three-character names, the slope on UMD for equal weighted portfolio is insignificant (0. 0318) while highly significant for value weighted portfolio (0. 1347): The possible explanation is that stocks with larger market value in the portfolio have more significant positive past returns. Moreover, the slope on UMD is negative for equal weighted four-character portfolio, while it becomes positive for value-weighted portfolio, which is also because the stocks with larger market value in the portfolio have more positive past returns and therefore change the sign of the coefficient.

Table 5 reports raw returns and risk adjusted returns of three-character portfolio and four-character portfolio. $MKTRF$ is excess market return of A-share. SMB, HML, RMW, CMA is size, value, profitability and investment factors which follow Fama and French (2015). UMD is the momentum factor following Carhart (1997). Newey and West (1987) corrected for the 6-factor model analysis with 4 lags t-statistics which are reported in the parenthesis below the mean value.

Table 5　Three-character and Four-character portfolios' return comparison: raw return and six-factor model analysis

	Equal weighted			value weighted		
Panel A: Raw return						
	3characters	4characters	difference	3characters	4characters	difference
Raw return	0. 0260***	0. 0235***	0. 0025*	0. 0240***	0. 0215***	0. 0025*
	(19. 32)	(51. 49)	(1. 74)	(17. 84)	(47. 07)	(1. 76)

continued

Panel B: 6-factor model analysis

Intercept	0.0091***	0.0062***	0.0029**	0.0153***	0.0130***	0.0023
	(4.89)	(5.37)	(2.11)	(7.10)	(12.39)	(1.15)
MKTRF	1.0092***	1.0373	−0.0280*	1.0318***	1.0345***	−0.0026
	(44.62)	(1.04)	(−1.68)	(39.55)	(81.52)	(−0.11)
SMB	0.5849***	0.6171***	−0.0322	0.0292	0.1227***	−0.0935
	(7.07)	(12.05)	(−0.53)	(0.31)	(2.64)	(−1.05)
HML	−0.4461***	−0.2024***	−0.2437***	−0.5150***	−0.1448***	−0.3702***
	(−7.04)	(−5.16)	(−5.21)	(−7.04)	(−4.07)	(−5.41)
RMW	−0.0158	0.0121	−0.0279	−0.0492	0.0344	−0.0836
	(−0.19)	(0.23)	(−0.45)	(−0.50)	(0.72)	(−0.92)
CMA	0.1080	0.0489	0.0591	0.1244	0.0861*	0.0384
	(1.22)	(0.89)	(0.90)	(1.22)	(1.73)	(0.40)
UMD	0.0318	−0.0348	0.0665***	0.1347***	0.0183	0.1164***
	(0.93)	(−1.64)	(2.63)	(3.40)	(0.95)	(3.14)
ADJ-RSQ	0.9556	0.983	0.2366	0.9311	0.9826	0.2448

To further test the premiums of stocks with three-character names, we run the Fama-Macbeth (1973) regression to regress the future monthly returns on traditional return prediction determinants. The regression formula for table 6 is shown in Eq. (2).

$$Excessret_{i,t} = \alpha + \beta_1 \times namedummy + \beta_2 \times \log(SIZE_{i,y}) + \beta_3 \times \log(BM_{i,y})$$
$$+ \beta_4 \times MOM_{i,y} + \beta_5 \times Excessreg_{i,t-1} + \beta_7 \times GP_{i,y}$$
$$+ \beta_8 \times ILLIQ_{i,y} + \beta_9 \times IO_{i,y} + \beta_{10} \times \log(EMP_{i,y})$$
$$+ \beta_{11} \times \log(ANA_{i,y}) + e_{i,t} \tag{2}$$

where $Excess\ ret_{i,t}$ is a stock's monthly return in month t, and the t denotes month and the y denotes year. We use stock feature variables in April of year y to predict stocks' monthly excess returns from May in year y to April in year $y+1$.

Table 6 reports the Fama-MacBeth results of excess monthly returns on *Name_Dummy*. *Name_Dummy* is 1 when the stocks have a name of 3 characters length, is 0 when the stocks have a name of 4 characters length. Log($SIZE$) is logarithm of the stock's market size at the end of April (Year t). Log(BM) is logarithm of the book value on market value at the end of December (Year $t-1$). $EXCESS(-1,-1)$ is the lagged stock return. Other variable definitions are same as table 2. Newey-West adjusted t-statistics (with lag＝4) are reported in the parenthesis.

Table 6 Fama-MacBeth regressions of excess returns on Name_Dummy

Variables	(1) excess	(2) excess	(3) excess	(4) excess
Name_Dummy	0.0021**	0.0018**	0.0019**	0.0015*
	(2.04)	(1.98)	(2.10)	(1.70)
Log_SIZE		−0.0041**	−0.0033**	−0.0056***
		(−2.24)	(−2.02)	(−3.21)
Log_BM		0.0052	0.0066	0.0054
		(1.02)	(1.37)	(1.15)
MOM		−0.0003	−0.0009	−0.0017
		(−0.12)	(−0.35)	(−0.66)
EXCESS(−1,−1)		−0.0753***	−0.0756***	−0.0730***
		(−7.94)	(−7.48)	(−8.17)
INV			−0.0006	
			(−0.81)	
GP			0.0150*	
			(1.96)	
ILLIQ			3.7342**	
			(2.45)	
IO				0.0006
				(0.08)
Log_EMP				0.0004
				(0.90)
Log_ANA				0.0026**
				(2.52)
Constant	0.0091	0.0397*	0.0303	0.0474**
	(0.99)	(1.88)	(1.59)	(2.51)
Observations	256,183	204,939	198,352	204,491
R-squared	0.001	0.076	0.085	0.090
Number of sample periods	174	168	168	168

In Table 6, Model 1 shows that the three-character dummy significantly and positively predicts future excess stock returns. Even after controlling for size, the book to market equity ratio, a one month reversal, and momentum in Model 2, the results still suggest a name dummy premium for China's A-share. For Model 3, we further controled firm investment, gross profit, and Amihud's (2002) illiquidity ratio. The results continue to show that stocks with three-character names generate significantly positive future premiums. For the control variables, the results show that smaller-sized stocks, with lower previous month returns, higher gross profit, and lower liquidity have significantly more positive returns in subsequent months, which is consistent with the existing literature. For model 4, we controled the traditional investor attention variable other than the risk factors to distinguish the impact of name dummy from traditional investor attention variables. The institutional ownership and number of employees are positively relevant to future returns, however, each coefficient is significant. The number of analysts could generate positive return, which proves that high investor attention could earn abnormal return in A-shares market. Finally, the name dummy still maintains its predictive power on stock returns, showing that traditional investor attention variables could not subsume the name premium.

To investigate whether three-character name premiums could be explained by other factors relevant to company name, the regression formula is shown in Eq. (3), and the regression specification is similar as in Eq. (2). Table 7 presents the results of regressing future excess stock returns on strong brands, name fluency, and lucky names. The first column shows a significantly positive relationship between strong brands and subsequent returns, which is consistent with previous results that stocks with strong brands tend to generate positive firm value. The second and third columns show that firms with higher name fluency scores and lucky names, respectively, have positive abnormal returns, but neither coefficient is significant. Furthermore, the results indicate that the coefficient of the three-character name dummy remains positive and significant after controlling for the name variables, indicating that strong brands, name fluency, and lucky names could not subsume the three-character name premium.

$$Excessret_{i,t} = \alpha + \beta_1 \times namedummy + \beta_2 \times Brand + \beta_3 \times Fluencysocre$$
$$+ \beta_4 \times Luckyname + \beta_5 \times \log(SIZE_{i,y}) + \beta_6 \times \log(BM_{i,y})$$
$$+ \beta_7 \times MOM_{i,y} + \beta_8 \times Excessret_{i,t-1} + \beta_9 \times INV_{i,y} + \beta_{10} \times GP_{i,y}$$
$$+ \beta_{11} \times ILLIQ_{i,y} + e_{i,t} \tag{3}$$

Table 7 reports the Fama-MacBeth regression results of excess returns on *Name_Dummy*. *Name_Dummy* is 1 when the stocks have a name of 3 characters length，is 0 when the stocks have a name of 4 characters length. *Strong Brand* is the logarithm of the stock's goodwill at the end of year t. *Fluency_Score* equals to 4 minus the number of words in a company name. *Lucky_Name* equals to 1 when the company name contains traditional lucky characters. Controls are the same as in table 4. Newey-West adjusted t-statistics (with lag=4) are reported in the parenthesis.

Table 7 Fama-MacBeth regressions of excess returns on Strong Brand, Name Fluency and Lucky Nanme

Variables	(1) excess	(2) excess	(3) excess	(4) excess
Name_Dummy				0.0018**
				(2.13)
Strong Brand	0.0001*			0.0001
	(1.67)			(1.61)
Fluency_Score		0.0001		−0.0001
		(0.21)		(−0.24)
Lucky_Name			0.0001	−0.0002
			(0.06)	(−0.23)
Log_SIZE	−0.0036**	−0.0035**	−0.0035**	−0.0036**
	(−2.09)	(−2.07)	(−2.08)	(−2.10)
Log_BM	0.0081	0.0083	0.0083	0.0084
	(1.48)	(1.53)	(1.52)	(1.55)
MOM	−0.0006	−0.0006	−0.0006	−0.0006
	(−0.26)	(−0.23)	(−0.23)	(−0.25)
EXCESS(−1,−1)	−0.0762***	−0.0760***	−0.0762***	−0.0760***
	(−7.57)	(−7.49)	(−7.52)	(−7.57)
INV	−0.0007	−0.0007	−0.0007	−0.0007
	(−0.87)	(−0.84)	(−0.86)	(−0.83)

continued

Variables	(1) excess	(2) excess	(3) excess	(4) excess
GP	0.0155**	0.0153**	0.0154**	0.0156**
	(2.04)	(2.01)	(2.02)	(2.03)
ILLIQ	3.5114**	3.4997**	3.5071**	3.5438**
	(2.44)	(2.43)	(2.42)	(2.45)
Constant	0.0322	0.0316	0.0316	0.0319
	(1.63)	(1.61)	(1.63)	(1.62)
Observations	198,352	198,352	198,352	198,352
R-squared	0.086	0.086	0.086	0.090
Number of sample periods	168	168	168	168

In Table 8, we investigate how certain characteristics of the firm's and market's information environment affect the return premium of high visibility stocks. The results show that for stocks with analysts' reports, the premium difference is not significant for either type of stock; however, premium differences exist in stocks that analysts do not follow. Moreover, since stocks held by national social security funds have always attracted investors, we also examine the difference in returns between the group of stocks held by social security funds and those they do not hold. The results confirm that stock holdings by social security funds can increase stock visibility and reduce the related premiums. Finally, the information environment and potentially active investors are different in bull and bear markets. The high visibility premiums are still significantly positive in the bear market, which has a worse information environment and fewer active investors, while the premium differences disappear in the bull market.

Table 8 reports raw returns of three-character and four-character portfolio in different stocks subsamples.

Table 8   Three-character and four-character portfolios' return comparison in different information environment

	ANA		SFH		BULL	
	yes	no	yes	no	1	0
3character	0.0203	0.0247	0.0224	0.0340	0.0873	−0.0545
4character	0.0190	0.0207	0.0205	0.0301	0.0860	−0.0590
Difference	0.0013	0.0040*	0.0019	0.0038**	0.0013	0.0045**
T-Value	0.8251	1.9573	0.9928	2.1387	0.6787	2.4438

4   Conclusions

Using a sample of China's A-share, we examined the high visibility premiums of stocks, and the evidence supports Merton's (1987) investor recognition hypothesis. Specifically, in this market, there are fewer stocks with three-character names, making it easier for investors to observe them; therefore, we use a name dummy as a natural measure of stock visibility levels, and prove the existence of stock visibility premiums in China's A shares market. Furthermore, it is not possible to explain these premiums by traditional systematic risk factors and psychological factors. Moreover, as expected, the premium decreased with some measures for firm visibility, such as a high proportion of national social security fund holdings, a large analyst following, and bull market conditions. One possible question that might be raised is: If the three-character name generates premiums, why do listed firms not change their four-character names to three-character names? The answer is simple: the abbreviation of a listed firm's name has been reported and recorded in the IPO procedure. It is an official name acknowledged by the China SEC, and cannot be changed except in unusual cases (e. g. the firm was acquired by another firm). Thus, even if the three-character name premiums are gradually recognized by the market, firms cannot change their firm name abbreviation.

We demonstrate and explain the premium for stocks in China's A-share market with three-character names. Because similar findings might prevail in developing countries, potential investors could purchase highly visible stocks when facing a wide range of options in markets with worse information environments.

References

Amihud Y, 2002. Illiquidity and stock returns: Cross-section and time-series effects[J]. Journal of Financial Markets, 5: 31-56.

Carhart M M, 1997. On persistence in mutual fund performance[J]. Journal of Finance, 52(1): 57-82.

Cooper M J, Dimitrov O, Rau P R, 2001. A rose. com by any other name[J]. The Journal of Finance, 56(6): 2371-2388.

Fama E F, French K R, 2015. A five-factor asset pricing model[J]. Journal of Financial Economics, 116: 1-22.

Fama E, MacBeth J, 1973. Risk, return, and equilibrium: Empirical tests [J]. Journal of Political Economy, 71: 607-636.

Frieder L, Subrahmanyam A, 2005. Brand perceptions and the market for common stock[J]. Journal of Financial and Quantitative Analysis, 40(1): 57-85.

Green T C, Jame R, 2013. Company name fluency, investor recognition, and firm value[J]. Journal of Financial Economics, 109(3): 813-834.

Hou K, Moskowitz T J, 2005. Market frictions, price delay, and the cross-section of expected returns[J]. Review of Financial Studies, 18 (3): 981-1020.

Kaniel R, Ozoguz A, Starks L, 2012. The high volume return premium: Cross-country evidence[J]. Journal of Financial Economics, 103(2): 255-279.

Merton R C, 1987. A simple model of capital market equilibrium with incomplete information[J]. Journal of Finance, 42: 483-510.

Newey W, West K, 1987. A simple, positive semi-definite, hetero-skedasticity and autocorrelation consistent covariance matrix [J]. Econometrica, 55: 703-708.

Pastor L, Stambaugh R F, 2004. Liquidity risk and expected stock returns

[J]. Journal of Political Economy, 111: 64- 685.

Qian M, Sun P W, Yu B, 2017. High turnover with high price delay? Dissecting the puzzling phenomenon for China's A-shares [J]. Finance Research Letters, 22: 105-113.

Zhi D A, Engelberg J, Gao P, 2011. In search of attention[J]. Journal of Finance, 66(5):1461-1499.

Estimating the Reaction of Bitcoin Prices to the Uncertainty of Fiat Currency[①]

Abstract   Recent studies have found that investors move from fiat currencies to Bitcoin cryptocurrency in environments with low trust and high uncertainty. This paper investigates the reaction of Bitcoin prices to uncertainty concerning fiat currencies by introducing a complete ensemble empirical mode decomposition with adaptive noise (CEEMDAN)-based event analysis approach. The 2013 Cyprus bailout is used as an event over the uncertainty of fiat currencies. With the proposed approach, the original Bitcoin price series is decomposed into high-frequency, low-frequency, and trend components, thus disentangling the short-, medium-, and long-term effects of the events on Bitcoin prices, respectively. We find that the low-frequency component is dominant and has increased because of the event. In addition, the announcement significantly increased the intensity of short-term fluctuations in Bitcoin prices. However, there was no structural change in Bitcoin prices in the long-term trend. This paper provides a way to show the reaction of Bitcoin prices to the uncertainty of fiat currencies at different time scales and suggests that the reaction is mainly captured by the medium-term trend.

Key words   Bitcoin; Fiat currency; Empirical mode decomposition; Event analysis

---

① Originally published in *Research in International Business and Finance* (vol. 58, 2021) by Jin Xuejun, Zhu Keer and Wang Shouyang.

1 Introduction

Bitcoin, a fully decentralized cryptocurrency based on blockchain technology, was proposed by Satoshi Nakamoto after the 2008 financial crisis. [1] Unlike traditional currency, Bitcoin operates on a decentralized peer-to-peer network independent of governments or agencies (Weber, 2016; Demir et al. , 2018).

Fiat currency, which is issued and controlled by central banks and governments, has value because people place trust and responsibility in governments to properly oversee it and avoid economic instability.

However, since the 2008 financial crisis, a lingering feature of the financial markets has been the increase of general uncertainty, which has caused increasing distrust toward central banks and governments. Several crises, such as the European sovereign debt crisis, Cypriot banking crisis, and the Turkish currency crisis suggest that banks could fail and put savings at risk.

A currency's value is based on trust and belief; when people lose trust, typically they switch to another currency that they consider more valuable. Bitcoin is regarded as an alternative to fiat currencies because of its unique feature that no central authority guarantees or controls it. In an environment of low trust and high uncertainty, investors are moving from fiat currencies and turning to Bitcoin (Bouri et al. , 2017b). Reportedly, there is a flight from fiat currency to Bitcoin during periods of crisis, especially in geographic locations most affected by the European sovereign debt crisis and Cypriot banking crisis. [2] Luther and Olson (2015) note that by making traditional deposit accounts seem less secure, the 2013 Cyprus bailout announcement could have encouraged some users to consider Bitcoin. They confirm the

---

[1] https://bitcoin. org/en/bitcoin-paper.

[2] https://www. cnbc. com/id/100597242; http://money. cnn. com/2013/03/28/investing/bitcoin-cyprus/; http://www. forbes. com/sites/petercohan/2013/04/02/are-bitcoins-safer-than-cyprus/#42f9ceef3c7a; http://abcnews. go. com/Business/cyprus-crisis-boosting-unique-currency-bitcoin/story? id=18792763.

hypothesis that Bitcoin-related apps have become popular in countries with troubled banking systems.

As the uncertainty of fiat currency creates additional demand for Bitcoin, this uncertainty could substantially increase Bitcoin prices. Some researchers have revealed a negative relationship between traditional currency and Bitcoin prices (Bouri et al., 2018). This paper aims to investigate whether the uncertainty of fiat currency causes short-term fluctuations or long-term trend changes for Bitcoin prices by measuring the pure effect of the uncertainty-inducing event over a particular period by eliminating the noise and long-term trend contained in the original Bitcoin price series. This task is addressed from a multiscale perspective by applying empirical mode decomposition (EMD, Huang et al., 1998) and a complete ensemble EMD with adaptive noise (CEEMDAN)-based event analysis approach.

With CEEMDAN, the original Bitcoin price series to be analyzed is decomposed into several independent and concretely implicational intrinsic modes using small to large time scales. Then, the intrinsic modes are reconstructed into high-frequency, low-frequency, and trend components based on fine-to-coarse reconstruction, thus disentangling the short-, medium-, and long-term effects of a specific event on Bitcoin prices. Normally, there is a dominant component that is caused purely by the event and can be used to approximate the magnitude and pattern of the change in the original Bitcoin price series. Additionally, other components provide information about changes caused by the event at different time scales, such as how the event influences the short-term market fluctuations or the long-term trend.

The CEEMDAN-based event analysis approach has some advantages over traditional approaches. First, it is suitable for nonlinear and nonstationary data, while having been shown to be promising for analyzing the effect of extreme events on crude oil price variations (Zhang et al., 2009). Second, it provides a multiscale framework to analyze the effects of a specific event at different time scales and can provide much information.

Understanding how the Bitcoin price reacts to the uncertainty of fiat currency at different time scales is important. First, the debate regarding whether Bitcoin and other cryptocurrencies could be regarded as alternatives to the fiat currency remains controversial. To answer this, it is necessary to explore whether the fundamentals of Bitcoin are affected by the fiat currency. However, with the traditional method, it is difficult to measure these fundamentals because Bitcoin does not generate a return, unlike stock and other traditional assets. With the approach proposed in this paper, the Bitcoin price serials are decomposed into high-frequency, low-frequency, and trend components, which could be regarded as the fundamental values. Second, as the market capitalization of Bitcoin has reached more than \$180 billion in September, 2020, and Bitcoin has become more important, it is meaningful to investigate its drivers at different time scales. Numerous researchers have studied the drivers of the Bitcoin price but few studies reveal whether these drivers affect the long-term price or just increase short-term fluctuations. This paper investigates the short-, medium-, and long-term effects of the uncertainty-inducing event on Bitcoin prices and provides solutions to understand the factors that determine Bitcoin prices. Third, some countries have taken steps toward legalizing Bitcoin as a payment system, while more governments are working on government-run cryptocurrencies [such as the United States (U. S.), Russia, China, and Canada]. Thus, understanding the relationship between cryptocurrency and fiat currency is important.

The frequency of currency and sovereign debt crises increased after the 2008 financial crisis, and Bitcoin has been attracting attention from mainstream investors since 2013. To investigate the reaction of Bitcoin prices to the uncertainty of fiat currency, this paper analyzes the 2013 Cyprus bailout announcement, which introduced Bitcoin into public focus.

The remainder of the paper is structured as follows: Section 2 provides a detailed overview of the related literature, Section 3 describes the EMD algorithm and details of the CEEMDAN approach, Section 4 analyzes the effects of the 2013 Cyprus bailout announcement on Bitcoin prices, and Section 5 concludes the paper.

2 Related studies

Cryptocurrency represents a nascent but growing force within the financial world. Bitcoin, a popular decentralized cryptocurrency (Briere et al. , 2015), has attracted the most attention in research, primarily over concerns regarding technical, legal, and safety aspects and price manipulation of cryptocurrency (Reid & Harrigan, 2011; Barber et al. , 2012; Karame et al. , 2015; Anceaume et al. , 2016; Gandal et al. , 2018; Eyal & Sirer, 2018). [1] Recently, the economics and finance debates around Bitcoin have intensified because of its dramatic price fluctuations, high-return opportunities, and potential safe haven properties.

The determinants of Bitcoin prices have attracted considerable attention from scholars. Ciaian et al. (2016) pointed out that the market forces of demand and supply are major contributors to Bitcoin prices; Kristoufeck (2013), however, argued that Bitcoin's value is unaffected by demand and supply fundamentals. He claimed that it is only speculation that drives Bitcoin prices and found a positive and significant relationship between investor attention (using Google Trends and Wikipedia as proxies) and Bitcoin prices. Garcia et al. (2014) extended these studies and suggested that growing public attention drives the value of Bitcoin.

Because of its unique pricing characteristics, Bitcoin is often considered to have similar properties to gold, especially hedging and safe haven characteristics (Dyhrberg, 2016a, 2016b). Several studies have found evidence that Bitcoin can serve as a hedge against uncertainty and risk in extreme periods. Bouri et al. (2017a, 2017b, 2017c, 2017d) examined the hedging capabilities of Bitcoin under global uncertainty using the VIXs of 14 equity markets as a proxy. Using the results of wavelet and quasi-in-quantile estimates, the authors show that Bitcoin returns are negatively related to

---

[1] For a complete review of the literature, see Merediz-Solà et al. (2019) and Klarin et al. (2020), who provided a comprehensive systematic review of the cryptocurrency and blockchain literature through bibliometric studies.

uncertainty, and it does have hedging features during globally uncertain periods at the upper quantiles, especially on shorter investment horizons. Furthermore, Bouri et al. (2018) applied copula-based techniques to examine the quantile conditional dependence and causality between Bitcoin and the global financial stress index, finding that Bitcoin can help hedge against global financial stress. Demir et al. (2018) first analyzed the effect of the economic policy uncertainty (E)PU index on Bitcoin. In particular, the authors claimed that the uncertainties in economic policy decisions may decrease the trust in fiat currencies and affect Bitcoin returns. They tested the relationship between EPU and Bitcoin returns and found Bitcoin returns to be negatively associated with EPU, although EPU's effect is positive and significant in low and high quantiles. These results indicate that Bitcoin can serve as a hedging tool against uncertainty. From a different perspective, Fang et al. (2019) focused on how the global EPU affects the correlation between traditional assets and Bitcoin. They found that the global EPU has a significant negative impact on the Bitcoin-bonds correlation and a positive impact on Bitcoin-commodities and Bitcoin-equities correlations, indicating the possibility of Bitcoin acting as a hedge in periods of extreme economic uncertainty.

Recent studies have found that investors move from main-state economies and turn to Bitcoin in environments of low trust and high uncertainty. Both Dahir et al. (2018) and Arbaa and Varon (2019) concluded that exchange rate fluctuations in the BRICS (Brazil, Russia, India, China, and South Africa) economies, spillover effects among European commercial banks, and currency crises promote cryptocurrency investment. Wang et al. (2019) reported that many Turkish investors shifted their holdings to cryptocurrencies during Turkey's currency crisis. Additionally, Luther and Salter (2017) found that attention to Bitcoin rose following the 2013 Cyprus bailout announcement. Urquhart and Zhang (2019) implemented the non-temporal Hansen (2000) test to examine the safe haven properties of Bitcoin and suggested that it is a safe haven in extreme market turmoil periods for the CAD, CHF, and GBP.

While the safe haven properties of Bitcoin during extreme uncertainty have been extensively investigated, there are no studies considering whether the uncertainty of fiat currency causes short-term fluctuations or long-term trend changes for Bitcoin prices or how to measure the pure effect of the event of uncertainty over a particular period. Thus, it is necessary to explore these questions from a multiscale perspective.

Among the tools for multiscale analysis, the most popular are the auto-regressive conditional heteroscedasticity (ARCH) and wavelet-transform-based methods (Aggarwal et al., 2020). However, both methods have limitations; ARCH models are highly model-specific, while wavelet transform analysis depends on a priori assumption about the function. Unlike these methods, EMD is an intuitive, empirical, direct, and self-adaptive data processing method, specially designed for nonlinear and nonstationary data (Huang et al., 1998). By decomposing a time series into a small number of independent intrinsic modes based on scale separation, EMD provides a multiscale framework to analyze the effects of different factors on the original time series.

EMD was initially applied to studying ocean waves and then successfully applied to solve problems in various research areas, such as finance, medicine, and earthquakes (Huang et al., 2003; Loutridis, 2004; Pachori & Bajaj, 2011). Huang et al. (2003) first introduced this method into financial time-frequency analysis. Wu and Huang (2004) proposed ensemble empirical mode decomposition (E)EMD to overcome EMD's main drawback, i. e., its mode mixing problem. Lin et al. (2012) proposed a hybrid time series LSSVR model based on EMD to forecast the foreign exchange rate and found that decomposing the foreign exchange rate index by EMD improved forecasting. Similarly, Cheng and Wei (2014) proposed the EMD-SVR model for forecasting TAIEX. Li et al. (2016) proposed the EEMD-APSO-RVM model for predicting crude oil prices. Zhou et al. (2018) analyzed stock market contagion under time-varying frequencies by using a CEEMDAN model. Zhou et al. (2019) proposed combining CEEMDAN and extreme gradient boosting (XGBOOST) to forecast crude oil prices. The authors' extensive experiments demonstrate that the proposed CEEMDAN-XGBOOST method outperforms some state-of-the-art models. In addition, Li et al. (2020) proposed integrating improved complete ensemble empirical mode decomposition with adaptive noise (ICEEMDAN), GWO, and multiple kernel ELM (ICEEMDAN-GWO-MKELM) with short-term load forecasting (STLF) and demonstrated that the ICEEMDAN-GWO-MKELM is very promising for STLF. Aggarwal et al. (2020) used complete empirical ensemble mode decomposition to analyze the nature of Bitcoin price series.

The most relevant research to this paper is Zhang et al. (2008), which used EEMD and fine-to-coarse reconstruction to identify the short-, medium-, and long-term trends in crude oil price series. Additionally, Zhang et al. (2009) proposed an EMD-based event analysis method, indicating that this method was promising for analyzing the effect of extreme events on crude oil price variation from a multiscale perspective. With a similar methodology, we apply CEEMDAN and fine-to-coarse reconstruction to Bitcoin prices, which can enable a better understanding of the reaction of Bitcoin prices to the uncertainty of fiat currency at different time scales.

3 Methods

The nonlinear and nonstationary characteristics of a volatile price series—especially Bitcoin prices—which include non-periodicity, randomness, and scaling components in the series (El Alaoui et al., 2019) are too complicated to process. The complexity of such series is best analyzed using nonlinear models.

3.1 Empirical mode decomposition

EMD, proposed by Huang et al. (1998), is an adaptive and efficient method of analyzing nonlinear and nonstationary series. Its basic principle is to decompose the original time series into a finite number of intrinsic mode functions (IMFs) and residue. An IMF should satisfy two criteria: (1) it has the same number of extrema and zero-crossings or these differ by at most one; (2) it is axially symmetric with zero mean, i. e., the mean value of the envelopes defined by the local maxima and minima is equal to zero at all points.

With the above definition, any complicated time series $x(t)(t=1,2,\cdots,n)$ can be decomposed by

1) Confirming all the local extrema (maxima and minima) of $x(t)$ and then using the cubic spline function to generate the upper envelope $e_{max}(t)$ and lower envelope $e_{min}(t)$;

2) Calculating the local mean value of the envelopes:

$$m_1(t)=(e_{max}(t)+e_{min}(t))/2;\tag{1}$$

3) Subtracting the local mean $m_1(t)$ $from$ x(t):

$$h_1(t)=x(t)-m_1(t);\tag{2}$$

Replacing $x(t)$ with $h_1(t)$ and repeating this step until the obtained time series is an IMF, designating it as $IMF_1(t)$;

Then, separating $IMF_1(t)$ from $x(t)$ to obtain a new residue $r_1(t)=x(t)$ $-IMF_1$, taking $r_1(t)$ as a new data point and repeating steps $(1)-(4)$ until the residue $r_n(t)$ satisfies (1) the number of extrema of $r_n(t)$ being less than 3; and (2) the amplitudes of $r_n(t)$ being much smaller than the amplitudes of $r_{n-1}(t)$ at each point.

Therefore, the original time series can be represented by IMFs and a residue as follows:

$$x(t) = \sum_{j=1}^{N} IMF_j + r_n,\tag{3}$$

where N is the number of IMFs, and r_n is the residue.

However, EMD's shortcoming is mode mixing (Wu & Huang, 2008), which involves a single IMF consisting of signals of dramatically disparate or similar scales appearing in different IMF components. The ensemble EMD/ (EEMD) method is proposed to overcome this by defining the final IMFs as the means of an ensemble of trials (Wu & Huang, 2009). The EEMD method first adds various white noise to the original time series in several trials. Then, it decomposes these new series into several IMFs. Finally, the ensemble means of the corresponding IMFs of the decompositions is calculated.

Although the EEMD method overcomes the mode mixing problem, it cannot eliminate the added white noise, which results in a high reconstruction error that can gradually decrease as the number of trials increases, but its computational cost also increases rapidly. To solve these problems, there is CEEMDAN (Torres et al., 2011).

CEEMDAN is an improved EEMD method. Unlike EEMD, CEEMDAN adds noise to residuals from previous iterations. It eliminates mode mixing more effectively, the reconstruction error is almost zero, and the computational complexity is greatly reduced. Recently, CEEMDAN has been used in financial studies (Cao et al., 2019; Aggarwal et al., 2020) and because of its advantages, it is adopted in this paper.

Let the k th mode obtained by EMD be $E_k(\cdot)$, the white noise with normal on $N(0,1)$ be $w^i(t)$, and the noise coefficient be ε_k. The CEEMDAN decomposition process is as follows:

1) Add the white noise $w^i(t)$ to the original time series $x(t)$; the first mode is obtained by the EMD method:

$$IMF_1 = \frac{1}{I} \sum_{i=1}^{I} E_1(x(t) + \varepsilon_0 w^i(t)), \tag{4}$$

where I is the number of trials, $i = 1, 2, \cdots, I$;

2) The first residue $r_1(t)$ is calculated as $r_1(t) = x(t) - IMF_1$;

3) Decompose residue $r_1(t) + \varepsilon_1 E_1(w^i(t))$ to obtain the second mode:

$$IMF_2 = \frac{1}{I} \sum_{i=1}^{I} E_1(r_1(t) + \varepsilon_1 E_1(w^i(t))); \tag{5}$$

4) The j th residue is calculated as $r_j(t) = r_{j-1}(t) - IMF_j$ The $(j+1)$-th mode can be obtained as

$$IMF_{j+1} = \frac{1}{I} \sum_{i=1}^{I} E_1(r_j(t) + \varepsilon_j E_j(w^i(t))); \tag{6}$$

5) Repeat step (4) until the value of the residue is less than the two extremes. The final residue is

$$r(t) = x(t) - \sum_{j=1}^{N} IMF_j, \tag{7}$$

The original time series is

$$x(t) = r(t) + \sum_{j=1}^{N} IMF_j, \tag{8}$$

where N is the number of IMFs, and $r(t)$ is the residue.

3.2 Fine-to-coarse reconstruction

With CEEMDAN, the original time series can be decomposed into a finite number of independent IMFs and a residue. These IMFs can be separated into several categories by duration, frequency, and amplitude. This paper reconstructs the IMFs as high-frequency, low-frequency, and trend components based on the fine-to-coarse reconstruction algorithm (see Zhang et al., 2008). The reconstruction algorithm is as follows:

1) Calculate the mean value of the superposition sequences from IMF_1 to IMF_i:

$$Q_i(t) = \sum_{k=1}^{i} IMF_k(t) \tag{9}$$

2) Identify IMF_1 to IMF_{i-1} as high-frequency if the mean of the $Q_i(t)$ significantly departs from zero according to a t-test and identify the others as low-frequency;

3) Define the sum of all high-frequency IMFs as the high-frequency component, the sum of all low-frequency IMFs as the low-frequency component, and the residue $r_n(t)$ as the trend component.

3.3 CEEMDAN-based event analysis

The steps of the CEEMDAN-based event analysis approach are described as follows.

Step 1: *Identifying the events of interest*

Determine the events of interest.

Step 2: *Defining the analysis window*

The analysis window includes the estimation and event windows. The estimation period should be immediately before the event window, and the event window is a period that covers the effects of the event.

In addition, recently, search queries provided by Google Trends and Wikipedia have proven to be useful sources of information in financial applications (Kristoufek, 2013; Georgoula et al., 2015; Dastgir et al., 2018). Therefore, we used Google Trends to verify that our analysis window length selection was reasonable.

Step 3: *Decomposition and reconstruction*

Decompose the original price series into IMFs and a residue by CEEMDAN and then reconstruct them into high-frequency, low-frequency, and trend components based on the reconstruction algorithm.

Step 4: *Analyzing the intrinsic modes*

The average period, correlation coefficients, and variance ratio of each of the three components were calculated. According to the results, the dominant component with the highest variance ratio can be identified in the event window, which may give a clear evaluation of the magnitude and pattern of the change caused by the event. Additionally, other components that represent the effects at different time scales were analyzed. For the high-frequency component, the Mann-Whitney test was adopted to examine whether the event significantly amplifies the price volatility.

Step 5: *Testing whether the effect is temporary or permanent*

The structure breakpoint test (Bai & Perron, 2003) was applied to verify whether the effect of the event was temporary (eliminated soon after the event) or permanent. Furthermore, a wide data range was required because a structure breakpoint can be identified as a true breakpoint only over a long period of the time.

Step 6: *Economic analysis*

Through steps 1-5, the magnitude and pattern of the changes in Bitcoin prices caused by the event were summarized. Then, economic explanations were given.

The steps of the CEEMDAN-based approach are illustrated in Fig. 1.

3.4 Data

Bitcoin price index: we used the daily U. S. dollar closing price data for Bitcoin at Bitstamp, accessed at https://bitcoincharts. com/. This exchange rate pair was adopted because Bitcoin prices are mainly quoted in U. S. dollars (Demir et al. , 2018). In addition, Bitstamp is an old and popular cryptocurrency exchange.

Bitcoin attention: Google Trends has proven to be an intuitive and useful proxy for attention to Bitcoin (Kristoufek, 2013). We used the weekly data on Google Trends to represent Bitcoin attention. The data was obtained from http://trends. google. com.

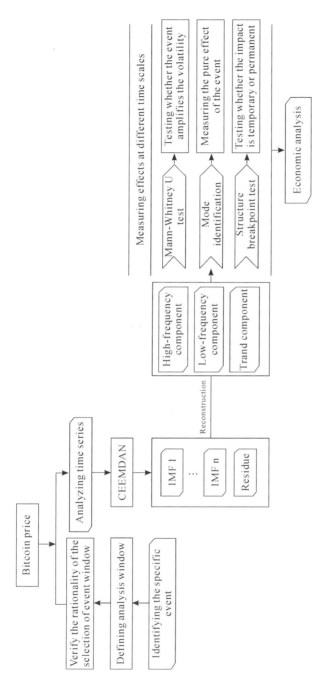

Fig. 1. Diagram of the CEEMDAN-based event analysis approach.

4 Event analysis: Estimating the effects of the uncertainty of fiat currency on Bitcoin prices

4.1 Identify events of interest

Our event of interest is the 2013 Cyprus bailout announcement. On March 16, 2013, Cyprus suddenly announced that it would accept a € 10 billion bailout by the Euro group, European Commission, European Central Bank, and International Monetary Fund to fortify the Cypriot economy. Among the bailout's conditions was a sizable levy collected from most bank accounts with holdings over the € 100,000 cutoff—a serious concern for wealthy Cypriots and many internationals—as the nation's favorable policies had made Cyprus a popular global tax haven, attracting domestic and overseas investors. To preserve their holdings before the bailout's conditions came into effect, many account holders bought Bitcoin, driving a price surge through early April that brought the value of a Bitcoin from approximately $80 to over $260. Furthermore, Luther and Salter (2017) found evidence that the interest in Bitcoin increased immediately after the announcement.

4.2 Defining the analysis window

The literature is not unanimous on the length of the estimation window, which is usually approximately 250 days (MacKinlay, 1997). Fig. 2 shows the event day, that is, March 16, 2013, is defined as $T_0 = 0$, and the event window is March 6, 2013, to May 5, 2013, i. e. , $[-10, 50]$. The estimation window is 240 trading days before the event window, from July 9, 2012, to March 5, 2013, i. e. , $[-250, -11]$ and 50 trading days after March 6, 2013, to June 24, 2013, i. e. , $[50, 100]$.

Here, the Bitcoin price at the daily time scale is considered a major indicator that reflects the effects of the event on the Bitcoin market. Fig. 3 shows the daily Bitcoin prices during the analysis window.

As noted, Luther and Salter (2017) found that attention to Bitcoin rose

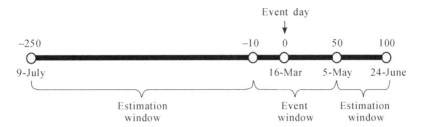

Fig. 2 Illustration of the analysis window

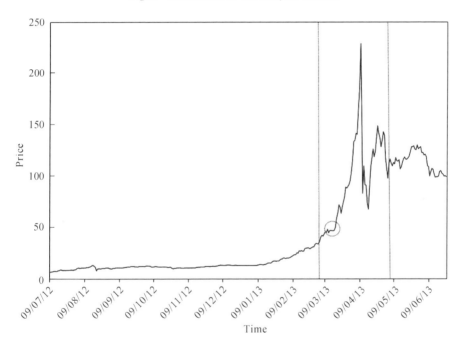

Fig. 3 Daily Bitcoin price series (USD) from July 9, 2012, to June 24, 2013

following the bailout announcement. Notably, recent research in the field of behavioral finance demonstrates that investor attention affects asset prices. For example, Kristoufek (2013) and Glaser et al. (2014) used internet searches (Google Trends and Wikipedia) as a proxy for investor attention and found that online searches significantly affect Bitcoin prices.

Therefore, we used Google Trends to examine whether the 2013 Cyprus bailout announcement caused a structural change in investor attention to Bitcoin. Google Trends provides values between 0 and 100, where 100 represents the highest relative number of searches made using a given keyword and 0 represents the fewest. A structure breakpoint test method by Bai and Perron (2003) was used to test the breakpoints at weekly global Google Trends search frequency for the phrase "Bitcoin" from July 9, 2012, to June 24, 2013. The Bayesian information criterion (B)IC detected two breakpoints: March 17, 2013, and April 21, 2013. [①] A breakpoint was identified for March 17, 2013, showing that the bailout announcement did cause a structural change in investor attention.

Fig. 4 illustrates the weekly global Google Trends search frequency for the phrases "Cyprus bailout" and "Bitcoin" around our event window. Both search terms significantly increase in frequency in the event window, while Google searches for "Cyprus bailout" increase first.

In sum, the above analysis provides evidence that our selection of the event window is reasonable in capturing the effect of the Cyprus bailout on Bitcoin prices.

4.3 Decomposition and reconstruction

In CEEMDAN, the added white noise in each ensemble member had a standard deviation of 0.2, and an ensemble size of 100 was used. Through CEEMDAN, the Bitcoin price series was decomposed into eight IMFs and a residue (Fig. 5). The frequency of the IMFs was arranged from high to low, and the last frequency was the residue.

According to the fine-to-coarse reconstruction method, the t-test used to identify i, the mean of the sum of IMF_1 to IMF_i, significantly departed from zero. The mean and p-value of the fine-to-coarse reconstruction method are presented in Fig. 6. The horizontal axis represents i. The mean of the sum of IMF_1 to IMF_4 did not significantly depart from zero but the mean of the sum of IMF_1 to IMF_5 did.

---

① The "breakpoints" tool available through the "strucchange" package was used. The model in which the breakpoints are estimated is a linear regression model that contains only a constant. The minimal segment size, given as a fraction relative to the sample size in each segment, was 0.1. The other parameters were set to the default values with the "breakpoints" method.

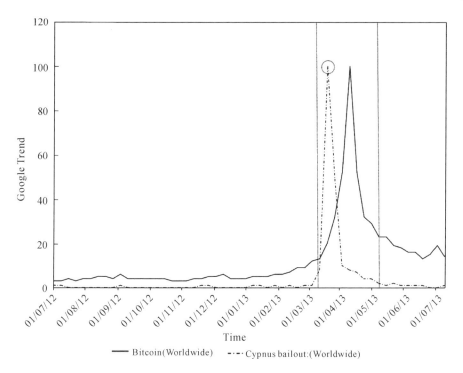

Fig. 4　The weekly global Google Trends search frequency from July 1, 2012, to July 7, 2013

The IMFs were divided into a high-frequency (the sum of IMF_1 to IMF_4) and low-frequency component (the sum of IMF_5 to IMF_8) (Fig. 7). The high-frequency component oscillates quickly around the value zero, representing the short-term fluctuations in the Bitcoin price series. The low-frequency component has a longer period and greater amplitude, representing the effects of medium-term fluctuations in the Bitcoin price series.

The residue reflects the overall trend of Bitcoin prices in the long run. In stock markets, the stock price usually has a fundamental price to fall back on. Similarly, Fig. 7 shows that although Bitcoin prices fluctuate dramatically because of medium-term trends, they normalize after the influence of the event ceases. Therefore, the long-term component could be regarded as the fundamental value of Bitcoin.

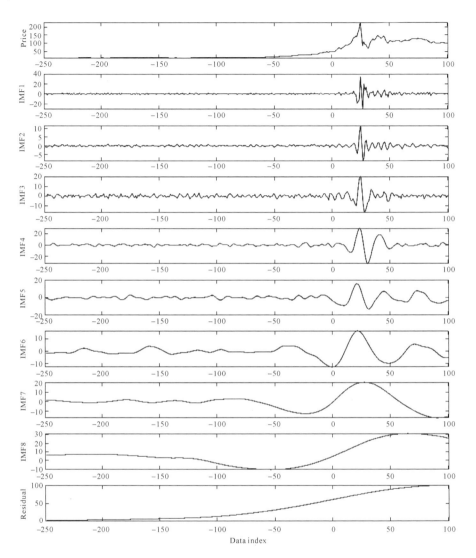

Fig. 5   IMFs and residue for the daily Bitcoin price series from July 9, 2012, to June 24, 2013, obtained through CEEMDAN

4.4   Analyzing the intrinsic modes in the event window

Table 1 shows the reconstruction results in the event window, including the average period, correlation coefficients, and variance ratio. The average period is the ratio of the total number of observations to the number of peaks for each component (Ming et al., 2016). The peaks are the significant spikes in the

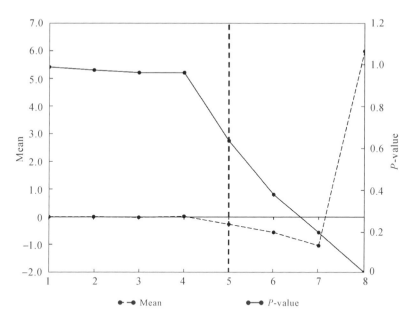

Fig. 6　The mean and p-value of the fine-to-coarse reconstruction method

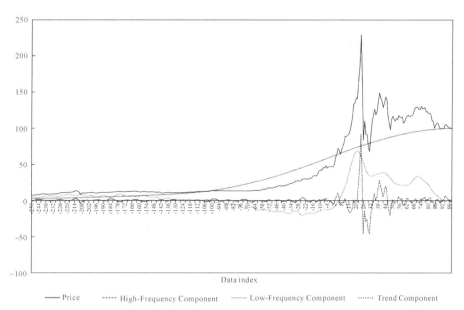

Fig. 7　The three components of the daily Bitcoin price series from July 9, 2012, to
June 24, 2013

given time series and are the largest occurring local maxima. Two correlation
coefficients, the Spearman correlation, and Kendall rank correlation,

measured the relationship between each component and the original price series.

Table 1 **The correlation and variance of the components of the daily Bitcoin price series from March 6,2013, to May 5, 2013**

	Average period	Spearman correlation	Kendall correlation	Variance	Variance as a % of observed components	Variance as a % of Σ components
Observed				1696.450		
High-frequency component	4.692	0.388***	0.292***	405.419	23.90%	34.00%
Low-frequency component	20.33	0.868***	0.716***	684.457	40.35%	57.41%
Trend component		0.767***	0.612***	102.452	6.04%	8.59%
Sum					70.28%	100.00%

*, **, and *** denote statistical significance at the 10%, 5%, and 1% levels, respectively. Variance as a % of observed components is the percentage of a component's variance of the observed variance. Variance as a % of Σ components is the percentage of a component's variance of the sum of the variances of three components.

In addition, the IMFs were independent of each other alongside the three components. We defined the variance ratio as the percentage of a component's variance relative to the total variance of the original price series. The variance ratio can explain the relative contribution of each component to the total volatility of the original price series. The component that explains the most variance in the total volatility is the dominant component (Zhang et al., 2009). However, as a result of a round-off error, the nonlinearity of the observed series, and the introduction of variance by the cubic spline (Peel et al., 2005), the sum of the variances of the components was not always equal to the observed variance (a −29.72% difference is shown in Table 1). Therefore, two types of variance ratios are presented: variance as a % of observed components and as a % of Σ components.

4.4.1 The dominant component in the event window

Table 1 indicates that the variance ratios of the low-frequency component are higher than those of the other two components, implying that it is the dominant component and can explain a much larger proportion of the Bitcoin price during the event window. The average period of the low-frequency component is approximately 20 days. In addition, the correlation coefficients of the low-frequency component and the original price reach a high level, above 0.7, at the 5% level during the event window.

The low-frequency component and original price series were normalized to the interval [0, 1] (Fig. 8). The low-frequency component matches the shape of the original price series almost perfectly. The low-frequency component began to rise from a local minimum on March 16, 2013 (day 0), reached a local maximum on April 5, 2013 (day 21), and then fell into another minimum on April 16, 2013 (day 32). Parameters such as the stopping criterion and the spline technique used in EMD may slightly affect the locations of extremes in IMFs (Zhang et al., 2009). However, the distance between the nearest local minimum and maximum remains relatively stable. Thus, the pure effect in the medium-term of the bailout announcement on Bitcoin prices can be measured by the distance from the first local minimum and the next local maximum of the dominant component (see Zhang et al., 2009). More specifically, the pure effect is \$82.57. The magnitude and pattern of the pure effect of the event are seen by analyzing the dominant component because the long-term trend and noise in the original price series are eliminated.

4.4.2 Results based on the high-frequency component

The high-frequency component represents the effects of short-term factors, such as market sentiment and speculative behavior. Table 1 shows a significant correlation between the high-frequency component and the original price series in the event window. Additionally, the high-frequency component accounts for more than 30% of the variability, indicating that short-term factors are important in determining Bitcoin prices during the event window.

However, the average period of the high-frequency component is less than five days, implying that the duration of the effects of short-term factors may be short.

In Fig. 7, most of the large and sudden jumps in the original price series are captured by the high-frequency component, i.e., the large changes in the

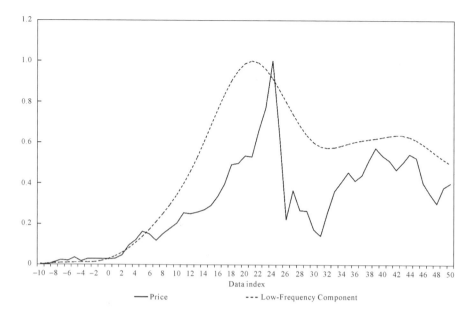

Fig. 8   The normalized price and low-frequency component from March 6, 2013, to May 5, 2013

original price series correspond to large amplitudes of the high-frequency component. This indicates that a sharp rise/descent always follows a sharp descent/rise. Therefore, in the shortterm, the Bitcoin market has a mean-reversion trend.

4.4.3   Did the event amplify the volatility?

We used the Mann-Whitney U test method to estimate whether the event amplified the volatility of Bitcoin prices. Table 2 supports the idea that the amplitudes of the high-frequency component in the event window are significantly larger than those in the estimation window. Hence, we conclude that the Cyprus bailout increased the volatility of the Bitcoin market.

Table 2   The Mann-Whitney test of the amplitudes of the high-frequency component

	High-frequency component
Mann-Whitney U	812.000
Wilcoxon W	29732.000
Z	−10.722
Progressive Sig. (bilateral)	0.000

4.5　Testing whether the impact is temporary or permanent

A structure breakpoint test method by Bai and Perron (2003) was adopted to test whether there is a breakpoint during the event window. The "strucchange" package in the *R* software (Zeileis et al., 2002) was used to test the breakpoints at monthly average Bitcoin prices from January 2012 to April 2020. The BIC detected six breakpoints: May 2017, October 2017, March 2018, October 2018, April 2019, and September 2019. ① There was no breakpoint in 2013, illustrating that the bailout announcement did not cause a structural change in Bitcoin prices (this event had no serious effects in the long run).

4.6　Comparing the event window with the analysis window

The analysis window is from July 9, 2013, to June 24, 2013, i. e., [−250, 100], which included the event window. To show the effect of the event, the results of the decomposition and reconstruction of the Bitcoin price series in the analysis window can be used as a benchmark for comparison.

Fig. 9 compares the variance as a % of Σ components of the daily Bitcoin price series between the event and analysis windows. Both the high- and low-frequency components exhibit a stronger impact in the event window than in the analysis window.

Moreover, Fig. 10 shows that the correlation of the high- or low-frequency component with the original price is significantly higher in the event window.

These differences illustrate that the bailout announcement increased the effects of short-term factors on the price of Bitcoin. Moreover, the announcement was the fundamental impetus that pushed prices up during the

---

① The "breakpoints" method in the "strucchange" package was used. The model in which the breakpoints are estimated is a linear regression model that contains only a constant. The minimal segment size, given as a fraction relative to the sample size in each segment, was defined as 0.05. The other parameters were set to the default values in the "breakpoints" method itself.

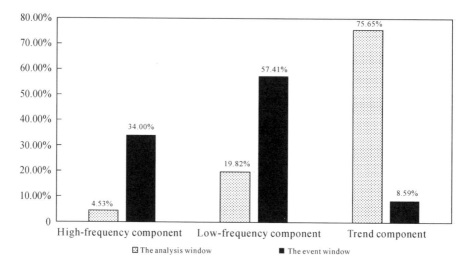

Fig. 9   The variance of the components of the daily Bitcoin price series

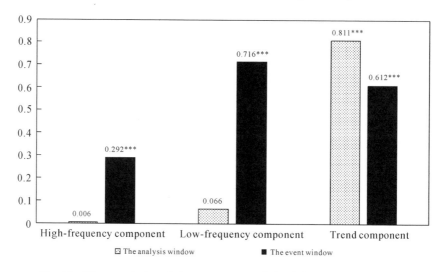

Fig. 10   The correlation of the components of the daily Bitcoin price series

event window.

4.7 Economic analysis

From the above analysis, some interesting findings and implications regarding the 2013 Cyprus bailout can be summarized:

The bailout announcement had two types of effects on Bitcoin prices: (i) short-term fluctuations with narrow amplitudes and short durations within five days; and (ii) a significant medium-term trend change lasting for approximately 20 days.

Short-term fluctuations, brought by market sentiment and speculative behavior, are in the high-frequency component. We find evidence that the bailout announcement increased the Bitcoin market's volatility. However, such short-term fluctuations were eliminated quickly within five days.

The low-frequency component reflects the medium-term trend of the change in Bitcoin prices, which is like a delta impulse. This component explains a much larger proportion of the Bitcoin prices during the event window. Therefore, the large change in Bitcoin prices during the event window was triggered by the 2013 Cyprus bailout announcement because the low-frequency component was almost unchanged before this event.

Bitcoin prices first went up after the event and then fell following the uncertainty being resolved. This finding illustrates that the bailout announcement caused mistrust in the domestic monetary authorities and fiat currency.

4.8 Model comparison

To test the performance of the CEEMDAN-based event analysis approach, we compared CEEMDAN with EEMD. For EEMD, an ensemble size of 100 was used, as the standard deviation of added white noise to each ensemble member is 0.2. Through EEMD, the Bitcoin price series was decomposed into seven IMFs and a residue (Fig. 11). According to the fine-to-coarse reconstruction method, the IMFs were divided into a high-frequency (the sum of IMF_1 to IMF_2) and a low-frequency component (the sum of IMF_3 to IMF_7) (Fig. 12).

Fig. 13 and Fig. 14 show the reconstruction error for CEEMDAN and EEMD, respectively. The reconstruction error is measured as the difference between the original Bitcoin price series and the sum of the IMFs and the residual. We found that the reconstruction errors of CEEMDAN were less than 3×10^{-14}, (maximum value of 2.84×10^{-14} and standard deviation of 5.87×10^{-15}), while they were much larger for EEMD (maximum value of 2.70 and standard deviation of 0.92). Therefore, CEEMDAN is more robust

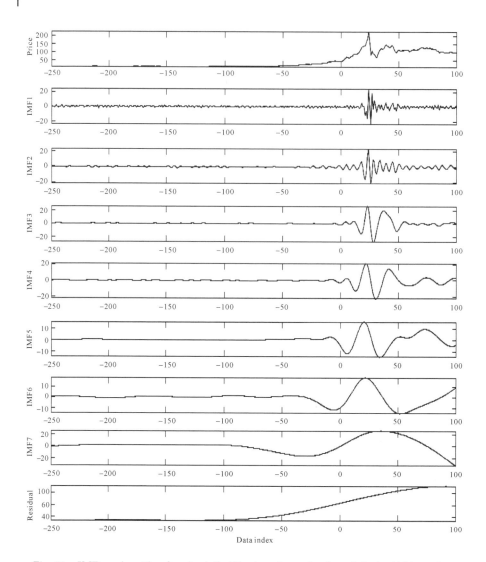

Fig. 11　IMFs and residue for the daily Bitcoin price series from July 9，2012，to June 24，2013，obtained through EEMD

than and superior to EEMD in our analysis.

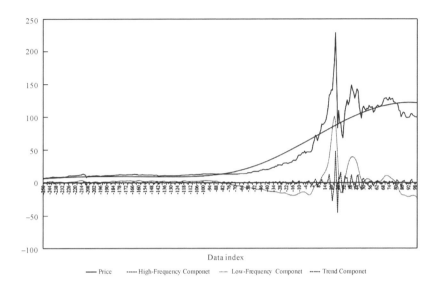

Fig. 12　The three components of the daily Bitcoin price series from July 9, 2012, to June 24, 2013, obtained through EEMD

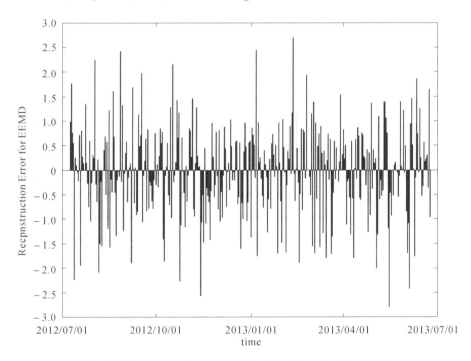

Fig. 13　Reconstruction error of Bitcoin price series for EEMD

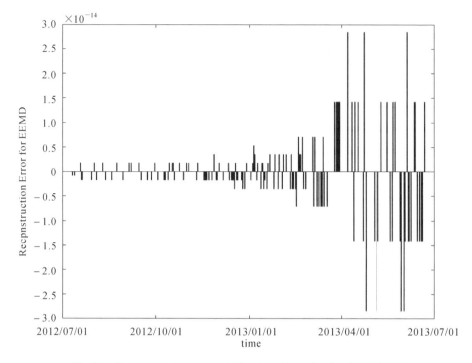

Fig. 14   Reconstruction error of Bitcoin price series for CEEMDAN

5   Concluding remarks

This paper proposes a CEEMDAN-based event analysis approach to estimate the effects of uncertainty from fiat currencies on Bitcoin prices from a multiscale perspective. The event of interest is the 2013 Cyprus bailout announcement. The empirical results show that this approach provides a feasible solution for measuring the effects, at different time scales, of specific events on Bitcoin prices. We also demonstrate that CEEMDAN is more robust and superior to EEMD.

With CEEMDAN, the fluctuations in the Bitcoin price series are decomposed into different time scales based on the local characteristics of the series itself. Furthermore, they are reconstructed into high-frequency, low-frequency, and trend components by fine-to-coarse reconstruction. In this paper, the low-frequency component is dominant in the event window, which shows the magnitude and pattern of the change caused by the event without noise or the long-term trend. The bailout announcement did drive Bitcoin prices up in the medium-term but did not cause a structural change in prices in the long-term. The low-frequency component gradually fell back to zero after the uncertainty was eliminated. In addition, we find that this event increased the volatility of the Bitcoin market.

These results provide evidence regarding the relationship between Bitcoin and fiat currencies. During the periods of analysis, the long-term component was dominant, and Bitcoin prices converged to the long-term component as stock prices converged to the fundamental value estimated over time. However, the low-frequency component was dominant during the event window. Significant short and medium-term changes due to the shock of the crisis were observed. However, the long-term component, which represents the fundamental value, was not significantly affected by the fiat currency crisis. The results demonstrate that although the uncertainty from the fiat currency created additional demand for Bitcoin, this demand could not be treated as the determinant of the fundamental value during the evolution of Bitcoin prices. Hedging the risk of fiat currencies might not be the key motivation for investing in Bitcoin.

This paper has some limitations. First, in the CEEMDAN-based event analysis approach, the decomposition results rely heavily on stopping criteria, and standard evaluation criteria have not been established. Second, only one case of fiat currency crises was used when more cases may help explore how currency crises affect different components. Lastly, this paper only provides a way to understand the effects of the uncertainty of fiat currency on Bitcoin prices, although using this approach to forecast Bitcoin prices is a more interesting topic for markets. Our future research will continue to address these issues.

Acknowledgments

This work was supported by the Natural Science Foundation of China (No.

71873089; No. 71988101; No. G030202). We wish to express our gratitude to John W. Goodell (the Editor) and anonymous referees for their valuable comments and suggestions on the earlier version of this paper. All remaining errors are solely ours.

References

Aggarwal D, Chandrasekaran S, Annamalai B, 2020. A complete empirical ensemble mode decomposition and support vector machine-based approach to predict Bitcoin prices[J]. Journal of Behavioral and Experimental Finance, 27:1-12.

Alaoui M E, Bouri E, Roubaud D, 2019. Bitcoin price-volume: A multifractal cross-correlation approach[J]. Finance Research Letters, 31: 374-381.

Anceaume E, Lajoie-Mazenc T, Ludinard R, et al, 2016. Safety analysis of Bitcoin improvement proposals[C]//IEEE Computer Society. 2016 IEEE 15th International Symposium on Network Computing and Applications (NCA). New York: IEEE.

Arbb O A, 2019. Turkish currency crisis——Spillover effects on European banks[J]. Borsa Istanbul Review, 19(4):372-378.

Bai J, Perron P, 2003. Computation and analysis of multiple structural change models[J]. Journal of Applied Econometrics, 18 (1): 1-22.

Barber S, Boyen X, Shi E, et al, 2012. Bitter to better—How to make Bitcoin a better currency[C]//International Conference on Financial Cryptography and Data Security. Berlin: Springer.

Bouri E, Azzi G, Dyhrberg A, 2017c. On the return-volatility relationship in the Bitcoin market around the price crash of 2013[J]. Economics, 11(2): 1-16.

Bouri E, Gupta R, Lau C K M, et al, 2018. Bitcoin and global financial stress: A copula-based approach to dependence and causality in the quantiles [J]. The Quarterly Review of Economics and Finance, 69: 297-307.

Bouri E, Gupta R, Tiwari A, et al, 2017b. Does Bitcoin hedge global uncertainty? Evidence from wavelet-based quantile-in-quantile regressions[J].

Finance Research Letters, 23:87-95.

Bouri E, Jalkh N, Molnar P, et al, 2017d. Bitcoin for energy commodities before and after the December 2013 crash: Diversifier, hedge or safe haven? [J]. Applied Economics, 49(50): 5063-5073.

Bouri E, Molnár P, Azzi G, et al, 2017a. On the hedge and safe haven properties of Bitcoin: Is it really more than a diversifier? [J]. Finance Research Letters, 20: 192-198.

Briere M, Oosterlinck K, Szafarz A, 2015. Virtual currency, tangible return: Portfolio diversification with Bitcoin[J]. Journal of Asset Management, 16 (6): 365-373.

Cheng C H, Wei L Y, 2014. A novel time-series model based on empirical mode decomposition for forecasting taiex[J]. Economic Modelling, 36: 136-141.

Ciaian P, Rajcaniova M, Kancs D, 2016. The economics of Bitcoin price formation[J]. Applied Economics, 48(19): 1799-1815.

Dahir A M, Mahat F B, Ali N A B, 2018. Funding liquidity risk and bank risk-taking in BRICS countries: An application of system GMM approach[J]. International Journal of Emerging Markets, 13 (1): 231-248.

Dastgir S, Demir E, Downing G, et al, 2018. The causal relationship between Bitcoin attention and Bitcoin returns: Evidence from the copula-based granger causality test[J]. Finance Research Letters, 28: 160-164.

Demir E, Gozgor G, Lau C K M, et al, 2018. Does economic policy uncertainty predict the Bitcoin returns? An empirical investigation[J]. Finance Research Letters, 26: 145-149.

Dyhrberg A H, 2016a. Bitcoin, gold and the dollar——A GARCH volatility analysis[J]. Finance Research Letters, 16: 85-92.

Dyhrberg A H, 2016b. Hedging capabilities of Bitcoin. Is it the virtual gold? [J]. Finance Research Letters, 16: 139-144.

Eyal I, Sirer E G, 2018. Majority is not enough: Bitcoin mining is vulnerable [J]. Communications of the ACM, 61 (7): 95-102.

Fang L, Bouri E, Gupta R, et al, 2019. Does global economic uncertainty matter for the volatility and hedging effectiveness of Bitcoin? [J].

International Review of Financial Analysis, 61: 29-36.

Gandal N, Hamrick J T, Moore T, et al, 2018. Price manipulation in the Bitcoin ecosystem[J]. Journal of Monetary Economics, 95: 86-96.

Garcia D, Tessone C J, Mavrodiev P, et al, 2014. The digital traces of bubbles: Feedback cycles between socio-economics signals in the Bitcoin economy[J]. Journal of the Royal Society Interface, 11: 1-28.

Giaglis G M, Georgoula I, Pournarakis D, et al, 2015. Using time-series and sentiment analysis to detect the determinants of Bitcoin prices[J]. SSRN Electronic Journal:1-13.

Glaser F, Zimmermann K, Haferkorn M, et al, 2014. Bitcoin——Asset or currency? Revealing users' hidden intentions[C]//European Conference on Information Systems 22th European Conference on Information Systems, Tel Aviv.

Hansen B E, 2000. Sample splitting and threshold estimation [J]. Econometrica, 68 (3): 575-603.

Huang N E, Shen Z, Long S R, et al, 1998. The empirical mode decomposition and the Hilbert spectrum for nonlinear and non-stationary time series analysis [J]. Proceedings Mathematical Physical & Engineering Sciences, 454(1971):903-995.

Huang N E, Wu M L, Qu W, et al, 2010. Applications of Hilbert-Huang transform to non-stationary financial time series analysis [J]. Applied Stochastic Models in Business & Industry, 19(3):245-268.

Karame G O, Androulaki E, Roeschlin M, et al, 2015. Misbehavior in Bitcoin: A study of double-spending and accountability[J]. Acm Transactions on Information & System Security, 18(1):1-32.

Kristoufek L, 2013. Bitcoin meets Google trends and Wikipedia: Quantifying the relationship between phenomena of the internet era[J]. Scientific Reports, 3(1): 3.

Lin C S, Chiu S H, Lin T Y, et al, 2012. Empirical mode decomposition——Based least squares support vector regression for foreign exchange rate forecasting[J]. Economic Modelling, 29(6):2583-2590.

Li T Y, Qian Z J, He T, 2020. Short-term load forecasting with improved

CEEMDAN and GWO-based multiple kernel ELM[J]. Complexity, 3: 1-20.

Li T Y, Zhou M, Guo C Q, et al, 2016. Forecasting crude oil price using EEMD and RVM with adaptive PSO-based kernels[J]. Energies, 9 (12): 1014.

Loutridis S J, 2004. Damage detection in gear systems using empirical mode decomposition[J]. Engineering Structures, 26(12):1833-1841.

Luther W J, Olson J, 2015. Bitcoin is memory[J]. Journal of Prices & Markets, 3 (3): 22-33.

Luther W J, Salter A W, 2017. Bitcoin and the bailout[J]. Quarterly Review of Economics & Finance, 66(nov.):50-56.

Mackinlay A C, 1997. Event studies in economics and finance[J]. Journal of Economic Literature, 35 (1): 13-39.

Ming L, Yang S, Cheng C, 2016. The double nature of the price of gold——A quantitative analysis based on ensemble empirical mode decomposition[J]. Resources Policy, 47: 125-131.

Pachori R B, Bajaj V, 2011. Analysis of normal and epileptic seizure eeg signals using empirical mode decomposition [J]. Computer Methods and Programs in Biomedicine, 104 (3): 373-381.

Reid F, Harrigan M, 2013. An analysis of anonymity in the Bitcoin system [M]. New York: Springer:197-223.

Urquhart A, Zhang H, 2019. Is Bitcoin a hedge or safe-haven for currencies? An intraday analysis[J]. International Review of Financial Analysis, 63: 49-57.

Wang G J, Xie C, Wen D, et al, 2018. When Bitcoin meets economic policy uncertainty(EPU): Measuring risk spillover effect from EPU to Bitcoin[J]. Finance Research Letters, 31: 489-497.

Weber B, 2016. Bitcoin and the legitimacy crisis of money[J]. Cambridge Journal of Economics, 40 (1): 17-41.

Wu Z, Huang N E, 2004. A study of the characteristics of white noise using the empirical mode decomposition method [J]. Proceedings Mathematical Physical & Engineering Sciences, 460(2046):1597-1611.

Wu Z, Huang N E, 2009. Ensemble empirical mode decomposition: A noise-assisted data analysis method[J]. Advances in Adaptive Data Analysis, 1(1): 1-41.

Zeileis A, Leisch F, Hornik K, et al, 2002. Strucchange: A R package for testing for structural change in linear regression models [J]. Journal of Statistical Software, 7(2): 1-38.

Zhang X, Lai K K, Wang S Y, 2008. A new approach for crude oil price analysis based on Empirical mode decomposition[J]. Energy Economics, 30 (3): 905-918.

Zhang X, Yu L, Wang S, et al, 2009. Estimating the impact of extreme events on crude oil price: An EMD-based event analysis method[J]. Energy Economics, 31(5): 768-778.

Zhou Z, Lin L, Li S, 2018. International stock market contagion: A ceemdan wavelet analysis[J]. Economic Modelling, 72: 333-352.

Zhou Y, Li T, Shi J, et al, 2019. A CEEMDAN and XGBOOST-based approach to forecast crude oil prices[J]. Complexity, 5:1-15.

Why Are the Prices of European-style Derivatives Greater Than the Prices of American-style Derivatives?[①]

Abstract　The prices of European-style derivative warrants in Hong Kong are generally higher than those of identical American-style options. We show that liquidity differences have strong explanatory power for this overpricing behavior, especially for low moneyness and long-term derivatives. Other causative factors include counterparty credit risk, investor preference, information asymmetry, volatility discovery, exercise style, market makers' behavior, and investor sentiment. We also find a big gap in market-wide liquidity between the two markets. Specifically, lower liquidity results in the weaker efficiency of the options market compared with the derivative warrants market.

Key words　Derivative warrants; Exercise style; Liquidity; Price difference

1　Introduction

Derivative warrants are actively traded in Hong Kong, China. Li and Zhang (2011) find that derivative warrants are generally more expensive than otherwise identical options due to liquidity differences by using daily Hang

---

①　Originally published in *Journal of Futures Markets* (vol. 9, 2022) by Jin Xuejun, Zhao Jingyu and Luo Xingguo.

Seng Index (HSI) derivative data. However, for derivative warrants and options written on individual stocks, the exercise styles differ: i. e. , the derivative warrants are European style, but the options are American style in Hong Kong. Theory says a European-style option should be priced no higher than an identical American-style option, which contradicts the reality. To explain this paradox and extend the conclusions of Li and Zhang (2011), we explore what causes the overpricing behavior between the European-style derivative warrants and the American-style options by focusing on intraday individual stocks.

Price differences between derivative warrants and options are little explored in the literature. The phenomenon of derivative warrants being more expensive than otherwise identical options is common in regions where these two markets coexist, such as in Hong Kong, China (Duan & Yan, 1999; Li & Zhang, 2011; Fung & Zeng, 2012; Li & Zhang, 2019), the Netherlands (Horst & Veld, 2006), and Australia (Chan & Pinder, 2000). Using daily quote data on derivative warrants and options written on the HSI for the 2002-2007 period, Li and Zhang (2011) find that the liquidity premiums of derivative warrants over options reflect the better liquidity of warrants, while clientele effects explain how warrants and options can coexist in the markets. Fung and Zeng (2012) extend the work of Li and Zhang (2011) to show that short-selling restrictions and a high proportion of unsophisticated investors lead to overpriced derivative warrants with overestimated implied volatility. Li and Zhang (2019) show that in addition to liquidity, counterparty credit risk and investor gambling preferences can explain the price differences between derivative warrants and options. Using data from the Netherland, Horst and Veld (2006) find that call derivative warrants are priced higher than call options with the same underlying stocks and strike price but longer maturity, which is attributed to issuers' marketing strategies. Using data from the Australian Exchange, Chan and Pinder (2000) show that derivative warrants are more expensive than comparable options and that liquidity differences can explain this overpricing. Using data for matched warrants and options with different exercise styles in the German markets, Bartram and Fehle (2007) find that competition between the derivative warrants market and the options market significantly improves liquidity in either market. In controlling for exercise-style derivatives and other factors similarly affecting prices, much of the literature on price differences between derivative warrants and options acknowledges the strong explanatory power of liquidity differences. However, few studies are concerned with whether overpricing remains in different exercise-style derivatives, which is important in evaluating the law of option pricing. Some important variables are omitted, including the differences in information asymmetry, volatility discovery, market makers' behavior, and investor sentiment between the two markets; therefore, there are imperfections in the model specifications.

This paper explains the phenomenon in Hong Kong where European-style derivative warrants are more expensive than American-style options. Hong Kong has one of the most active derivative warrants and options markets in the world. Because of their special markets and product design, the American-style options traded on the stock options exchange of the Hong Kong Exchanges and Clearing Limited (HKEX) also have counterpart European-style derivative warrants traded on the HKEX's securities market. The Hong Kong markets' high-frequency tick-by-tick data available for the period from July 2012 to November 2016 present unique advantages when studying price differences between homogeneous derivatives with different exercise styles. We use a matched sample of derivative warrants and options both written on individual stocks to address this puzzle by controlling for strike prices, maturity, underlying stocks, trading times, and call or put types. We divide the full sample into several subsamples based on moneyness, maturity, and option type. Liquidity plays an important role in both stocks (Amihud & Mendelson, 1986; Amihud et al. , 1997; Hua et al. , 2020; Amihud & Noh, 2021) and derivative pricing (Brenner et al. , 2001; Deuskar et al. , 2011; Christoffersen et al. , 2018; Muravyev & Pearson, 2020). We explain the overpricing of derivative warrants with three high-frequency liquidity measures as our core explanatory variables. In addition to liquidity, we follow Li and Zhang (2019) and add the measures of counterparty credit risk and investor preference to our model. We explore more factors in our novel perspective: for example, information asymmetry, volatility discovery, exercise style, market makers' behavior, and investor sentiment. We discuss these factors in detail in Section 2.3.

We conduct our main analysis in three steps. First, we document overpricing and compare the liquidity differences for each subsample. We find that European-style derivative warrants are more expensive than the corresponding American-style options with high premium proportions and premium values. However, we find that this effect tends to be nonsignificant or even reversed in the subsample of in-the-money (ITM) and short-term (ST) derivative pairs. In addition, derivative warrants show better liquidity than matched options. The results confirm the overpricing behavior between derivative warrants and options written on individual stocks in Hong Kong, which is consistent with the findings for derivatives written on the HSI (Li & Zhang, 2011; Fung & Zeng, 2012). Next, we use linear panel regression to examine whether liquidity differences and other relevant factors can explain this overpricing behavior. Liquidity differences provide strong explanatory power for overpricing. However, variables such as counterparty credit risk, investor preference, information asymmetry, volatility discovery ability, exercise style, market makers' behavior, and investor sentiment also significantly affect the price differences. Finally, we re-estimate our benchmark model using subsamples divided by moneyness, maturity, and call or put type, which shows that the model is robust except for the ITM group. The model also provides greater power for low moneyness and long-term (LT) derivatives. We also repeat our analysis using different derivative samples and sampling frequencies to avoid sample choice and sampling frequency bias.

We conduct a series of additional analyses to deepen our understanding of the liquidity differences between the derivative warrants market and the options market in Hong Kong. Inspired by Chordia et al. (2001), we study aggregate market-wide liquidity and trading activity for these two markets. We construct daily time series indices of market-wide liquidity measures over the period from July 2012 to November 2016, which enable a further comparison of the liquidity differences between derivative warrants and options from a market-wide perspective. We find a big gap in liquidity indicators; i. e. , the market-wide liquidity of the derivative warrants market is usually much better than that of the options market.

The phenomenon of more expensive derivative warrants does not necessarily mean that the warrants are overvalued (Fung & Zeng, 2012); thus, we test their pricing efficiency and explain what causes the difference in pricing efficiency between the derivative warrants and options markets. Following Chordia et al. (2008), we use variance ratios and return predictability from order flows to examine the efficiency of each market. The literature emphasizes the relationship between liquidity and market efficiency (Chowdhry & Nanda, 1991; Amihud et al. , 1997; Chordia et al. , 2008); therefore, it is natural to ask whether the liquidity differences affect the efficiency differences between the two markets. Our matched sample of derivative warrants and options offers us an ideal way to examine the impact of liquidity differences on market efficiency because we control for most variables affecting market efficiency, except for the liquidity differences between the two markets. As a result, the level of efficiency in the derivative warrants market is higher than in the options market because of higher liquidity. In addition, the subsample for derivatives written on small-cap stocks has lower efficiency.

We are motivated by Li and Zhang (2011), who show that liquidity differences explain the liquidity premium for derivative warrants over identical options. While Li and Zhang (2011) focus on European-style derivative warrants and options written on the HSI, we extend their conclusions to include derivative warrants and options written on individual stocks, in which exercise styles differ. Li and Zhang's (2011) model also omits critical variables such as counterparty credit risk, investor preference, information asymmetry, volatility discovery ability, exercise style, market makers' behavior, and investor sentiment. We improve their findings with a more comprehensive consideration of impact factors and include these critical variables in our model. In addition, the higher frequency of data enables us to evaluate the intraday patterns for the price differences between derivative warrants and options. We construct most variables, including measures of the underlying stock and futures markets as well as derivative warrants and options markets, based on high-frequency tick-by-tick data.

More generally, this paper contributes new evidence to the option pricing literature. To the best of our knowledge, we are the first to discover and explain the phenomenon in which European-style derivatives are more expensive than American-style derivatives with similar terms. Differing from Figlewski (2021) who emphasizes on illiquidity discount for European exercise, we find liquidity premium in the pricing of European-style derivatives. Besides, we intuitively compare liquidity differences between derivative warrants and options from a market-wide perspective. Moreover, we use return predictability from order flows to examine market efficiency and confirm the positive relationship between liquidity and market efficiency, which contributes to empirical studies of liquidity and market efficiency.

The rest of this paper is organized as follows. Section 2 compares Hong Kong's derivative warrants market and options market, and then describes the data and main variables used in our empirical analysis. Section 3 presents our main empirical findings regarding the price differences between derivative warrants and options traded in Hong Kong and conducts robustness tests. Section 4 provides additional empirical results to better understand the liquidity differences between the two markets. Finally, Section 5 concludes the paper.

2　Markets

2.1　Overview of the markets

We must obtain an overview of Hong Kong's derivative warrants and options markets to improve our understanding of the causes underlying the price differences. Both derivative warrants and options are traded on the HKEX, which is made up of the securities and derivatives markets. The HKEX's futures and stock options exchanges consist of the derivatives market, while securitized derivatives, including derivative warrants, are traded on the HKEX's securities market like common stocks, with the largest trading volume in the world over the past decade. According to data from the World Federation of Exchanges, the total trading volume of securitized derivatives on the HKEX (more than 50% are derivative warrants) is US $ 532.3 billion from January 2019 to November 2019, which is nearly three times the sum of the second to tenth places combined! Hong Kong's fast-developing options market coexists with its derivative warrants market. Options written on the HSI are traded on the HKEX's futures exchange, while those written on individual stocks are traded on the HKEX's stock options exchange. With over 20 years of development, 107 types of stock options have been sold in Hong Kong, with an average daily contract turnover of more than 520,000 according to 2020 HKEX's annual market report.

Although the expected payoff for financial products is almost equal, we cannot neglect the differences in design and structure between the two markets. Concerning market participants, market makers are more active suppliers of liquidity in the derivative warrants market because of multiple competing issuers for each underlying stock, while liquidity providers in the options market face slack liquidity requirements. Investor structures also differ. For example, retail investors are major buyers in the warrants market, while institutional investors are clustered in the options market (SFC, 2005).

Considering the products traded on these two markets, other than the differences in exercise style, derivative warrant contracts are more flexible for various underlying assets, maturities, and strike prices, while options contracts are standardized.

In terms of differences in trading rules in these markets, the central clearing house and margin system almost remove counterparty credit risk in the options market, while investors in derivative warrants must consider the credit risk of issuers. Short-selling restrictions where only issuers of derivative warrants can take a short position are present in the warrants market, but when investors open a margin account, they can short their options at any time. The market threshold for the warrants market is lower than for the options market because a futures account is needed and the minimum trading size is higher in the options market. These differences help to understand the price gap between the derivative warrants and options markets in Hong Kong.

2.2　Data

We use high-frequency tick-by-tick trade data for derivative warrants and options written on individual stocks listed on the HKEX. We also use tick-by-tick trade data for the underlying stocks and futures to construct the relevant variables. The full sample spans the period from July 3, 2012 to November 30, 2016. The high-frequency data in our sample are provided by the HKEX, while other daily data are from the Chinese Stock Market and Accounting Research (CSMAR) website. We exclude trading records for warrants, options, and underlying stocks that are time-stamped before 9:30 a. m. or after 4:00 p. m. The sampling frequency for the high-frequency data is 5 minutes, which is the most commonly used frequency (Hansen & Lunde, 2006) to consider an increasing sample size and reduce market microstructure noise.

We differentiate and match derivative warrants and options by strike price, maturity, underlying assets, trading time, and option type (call or put). We regard warrants and options with the same characteristics mentioned above as the same product so they constitute a set of derivative pairs. Finally, we obtain 266,828 derivative pairs from 59 underlying individual stocks (see Table A1). We then divide our full matched sample into 18 subsamples based on moneyness, maturity, and option type (Li & Zhang, 2011). Moneyness is divided into three groups: $k \leqslant -0.03$ (out-of-the-money [OTM]), $-0.03 < k \leqslant 0.03$ (at-the-money [ATM]), and $k > 0.03$ [ITM]).[①] Maturity is also divided into three groups: ST with maturity no more than 60 days, medium term (MT) with maturity more than 60 days and no more than 120 days, and long term (LT) with maturity more than 120 days. Finally, the types of

---

　　① Call group, $k = 1 - X/S(t)$; put group, $k = X/S(t) - 1$. k, X, and $S(t)$ indicate moneyness, strike price, and underlying stock price at time t, respectively.

options are divided into call and put groups.

2.3   Variables

The price data for derivative warrants and options are normalized by the underlying stock prices, $S/100$, to be comparable across time. In addition, the price of derivative warrants is multiplied by the entitlement ratio[①] to ensure that the prices of warrants and options are comparable. Let P^w and P^o respectively denote the price of warrants and the price of options after normalization and adjustment, DP denotes the price difference for each pair; thus, the price premium ratio of the ith pair at time t can be written as

$$DP_{i,t} = \frac{P^w_{i,t} - P^o_{i,t}}{P^o_{i,t}} \tag{1}$$

Liquidity plays an important role in overpricing; therefore, three variables to measure liquidity are considered as our core explanatory variables. We quantify three dimensions of liquidity: i. e. , market width, depth, and resiliency. These dimensions are respectively measured by Roll spread (Roll, 1984), trading volume, and Amihud illiquidity measure (Amihud, 2002).

To measure market width, we use Roll spread as a substitute for the bid-ask spread because we could not precisely compute the bid-ask spread with the lack of high-frequency quote data. We define Roll spread, $Rolls_{i,t}$, as follows:

$$Rolls_{i,t} = \begin{cases} \dfrac{2\sqrt{-\mathrm{Cov}(\Delta P_{i,t}, \Delta P_{i,t-1})}}{S_{i,t}/100}, & \mathrm{Cov}(\Delta P_{i,t}, \Delta P_{i,t-1}) < 0 \\ 0, & \mathrm{Cov}(\Delta P_{i,t}, \Delta P_{i,t-1}) \geqslant 0 \end{cases} \tag{2}$$

Like the earlier price measure, we express Roll spread as a percentage of the underlying stock price. We use $DRolls_{i,t}$ to approximate the differences in the bid-ask spread, which are given by:

$$DRolls_{i,t} = \frac{Rolls^w_{i,t} - Rolls^o_{i,t}}{Rolls^o_{i,t}} \tag{3}$$

The second liquidity measure that we consider is trading volume measured by the share of transactions. Let Vol^w and Vol^o denote the trading volume of warrants and options, respectively, then the trading volume difference for the

---

① The number of warrants needed to buy one share of common stock.

i^{th} option pair at time t, $DVol_{i,t}$, can be written as

$$DVol_{i,t} = Vol_{i,t}^w - Vol_{i,t}^o \qquad (4)$$

We used the popular Amihud illiquidity measure to scale resiliency; that is, $A_{i,t}^w$ for warrants and $A_{i,t}^o$ for options are defined as

$$A_{i,t} = \frac{1}{11} \sum_{i=-5}^{5} \frac{|R_{i,t}|}{Vol_{i,t}} \qquad (5)$$

where $R_{i,t}$ is the 5-minute return for warrants or options. Thus, we could describe the difference in Amihud illiquidity measure of the ith option pair at time t, $DA_{i,t}$, as

$$DA_{i,t} = \ln(A_{i,t}^w) - \ln(A_{i,t}^o) \qquad (6)$$

We not only documented the impact of illiquidity differences between warrants and options on their price differences, but also investigated if there are other factors that may affect the price differences. We added these factors as control variables in our model. Considering the control variables, we refer to Li and Zhang (2019), who identified counterparty credit risk and behavioral biases in addition to liquidity as the major determinants of price differences. Compared with options, derivative warrants are subject to the credit risk of issuers or guarantors and the lottery-like trading behavior of retail investors. We used daily iTraxx Asia ex-Japan credit default swaps (CDS) index data with logarithm CDS_t to measure counterparty credit risk. We used moneyness ($k_{i,t}$) and maturity ($m_{i,t}$) to control for investor preference. From a new perspective, we then proposed to consider more factors, such as the underlying stock's liquidity and volatility, theoretical price differences, liquidity providers' behavior, and investor sentiment, to better understand the causes of price differences and make our model more robust.

We used the trading volume of the underlying stocks at 5-minute intervals, $Vol\_Ud_{i,t}$, to measure the trading activity of the underlying stocks as a proxy for information asymmetry. We computed daily volatility, $\sigma_{i,t}$, as the sum of intraday squared 5-minute returns, excluding overnight returns (Martens, 2002):

$$\sigma_{i,t} = (1+c) \sum_{n=1}^{N} (r_{t,n}^i)^2 \qquad (7)$$

where $r_{t,n}^i$ is the 5-minute return on the ith underlying stock. The constant is equal to $\frac{98}{81}$ in our estimation (Martens, 2002).

Remarkably, trading warrants and options on the HKEX use different exercise styles. Derivative warrants are all European style, while individual stock options are all American style. Therefore, we must control for the differences in their theoretical prices, which reflect their value differences based on different exercise styles. We used the standard Black-Scholes-Merton (BSM) option pricing model to estimate the theoretical price of warrants denoted by $\hat{P}_{i,t}^{w}$. We used a simplified American option pricing model (Alghalith, 2020) to estimate the theoretical price of options, which is given by

$$\hat{P}_{i,t}^{o} = e^{0.5 \, (e^{r_t m_{i,t}} - 1) \, (1 - r_t) m_{i,t}} \hat{P}_{i,t}^{BS} \tag{8}$$

where r_t is the risk-free interest rate at time t according to the daily overnight Hong Kong Interbank Offered Rate (HIBOR), while $\hat{P}_{i,t}^{BS}$ is the theoretical price of options from the BSM model. In theory, the price of American-style options is always higher than that of European-style options when we control for other factors similarly. Likewise, we express the theoretical price as a percentage of the underlying stock price. We define the difference in theoretical prices as

$$D\hat{P}_{i,t} = \frac{\hat{P}_{i,t}^{w} - \hat{P}_{i,t}^{o}}{S_{i,t}/100} \tag{9}$$

Market makers' behavior is another plausible causative candidate. In the Korean derivative warrant market, Chae et al. (2012) find that liquidity providers only provide limited liquidity and earn profits through information advantages. In Germany, Baule et al. (2018) find that warrant liquidity providers are inclined to increase their quotes compared with providers in the options markets to generate additional profits. Similarly, SFC (2005a) finds that market makers in Hong Kong's derivative warrants market actively provide liquidity, which contributes to the 73% trading volume. Chow et al. (2007) suggest that market makers in Hong Kong's derivative warrants market do not always provide liquidity to the market. We constructed our proxy for liquidity providers' behavior using the warrant/option order imbalance (OI) inspired by Christoffersen et al. (2018), which reflects the inventory risk of liquidity providers. We used a method to calculate OI following Bernile et al. (2016) and Luo et al. (2020). [①] Thus, the variables measuring liquidity providers' behavior, $Lp_{i,t}^w$ and $Lp_{i,t}^o$, are equally given by

$$Lp_{i,t} = |OI_{i,t}| = \frac{\left| \sum_{n=1}^{N} Vol\,\$_{i,n}^{Buy} - \sum_{n=1}^{N} Vol\,\$_{i,n}^{Sell} \right|}{\sum_{n=1}^{N} Vol\,\$_{i,n}} \quad (10)$$

where $Vol\,\$_{i,n}^{Buy}$ and $Vol\,\$_{i,n}^{Sell}$ refer to the trading volume of warrants and options in Hong Kong dollars, respectively. The time interval is 5 minutes and N is the total number of trading records from time $t-1$ to time t. We used these indicators to measure the behavior of market makers. When market makers conduct negative feedback trading[②], $Lp_{i,t}$ falls because these market makers provide liquidity to mitigate OI. When market makers conduct positive feedback trading, $Lp_{i,t}$ increases because these market makers are trading for profit or to manage inventory risk, which aggravates OI. We define the difference in liquidity providers' behavior, $DLp_{i,t}$, as

$$DLp_{i,t} = Lp_{i,t}^w - Lp_{i,t}^o \quad (11)$$

Additionally, we included a measure of investor sentiment, which may affect the prices of the two markets heterogeneously because of the differing investor structures in the two markets. That is, investors in the warrants market are mainly retail investors, while those in the options market are mainly institutional investors. Building on the work of Han (2008), we used the net position of speculators in futures written on individual stocks in Hong Kong to measure investor sentiment, which we construct by using the number of long contracts minus the number of short contracts, excluding hedging transactions. Let Ftp_t denote investor sentiment in the derivatives market at

---

① The data are not labeled as buyer- or seller-initiated transactions; therefore, we use the tick rule classification to flag the direction. That is, a transaction is initiated by the buyer (seller) if the transaction price is higher (lower) than the latest price. If the price between the two transactions is still unchanged, the earlier transaction will be marked as the same trade.

② Negative feedback trading means selling calls (buying puts) when the underlying price goes up (down), while positive feedback trading means buying calls (selling puts) when underlying price goes up (down).

time t. The measurement frequency is also 5 min (Table 1).

Table 1   Summary statistics

	Mean	St. Dev.	Median	Min	Max	N
DP	0.206	0.331	0.159	−0.396	1.212	266,828
$DRolls$	−0.066	0.267	−0.018	−22.608	5.981	266,828
$DVol$	0.149	0.456	0.020	−0.200	2.582	266,828
DA	−2.826	2.218	−2.756	−14.060	8.142	266,828
CDS	4.785	0.134	4.759	4.561	5.086	266,625
k	−0.056	0.054	−0.048	−0.209	0.043	266.828
m	0.196	0.120	0.178	0.022	0.561	266,828
Vol_Ud	12.715	1.198	12.680	10.150	15.658	266,828
σ	0.171	0.177	0.111	0.020	0.891	260,061
$D\hat{P}$	0.042	0.077	0.012	0.000	0.393	266,824
DLp	−0.103	0.321	0	−1	1	266,828
Ftp	0.025	0.575	0.010	−17.890	16.960	240,620

Notes: This table reports the descriptive statistics for the variables we constructed in Section 2.3. We winsorized all variables at the 2% and 98% levels. DP denotes the price premium ratio of the derivative pair; $DRolls$, $DVol$, and DA measure the liquidity differences in Roll spread, trading volume, and Amihud illiquidity measure, respectively. CDS is the measure of counterparty credit risk. k is moneyness and m is maturity, and both measure investor preference. Vol_Ud and σ are the trading volume and volatility of the underlying stock and measure information asymmetry and volatility discovery ability, respectively. $D\hat{P}$ denotes the theoretical value differences for derivative pairs and measures the differences in exercise style. DLp measures market makers' behavior and is the difference in absolute OI. Ftp denotes investor sentiment measured by futures net positioning. The sample period is from July 3, 2012 to November 30, 2016.

3   Empipical results

3.1   Overpricing and liquidity differences

We assessed whether the derivative warrants written on individual stocks were more expensive than the matched options and documented their liquidity differences. As a result, the prices of derivative warrants are significantly higher than the corresponding options, but tend to be nonsignificant or even reversed in the ITM-ST group. Considering liquidity differences, the liquidity of derivative warrants is generally higher than the liquidity of matched options.

Table 2 shows the overpricing behavior of derivative warrants compared with that of options. In Panel A of Table 2, we present the proportion of observations for which the trading price of warrants is higher than that of their matched options. In the full sample, for example, 73.5% of the derivative warrants are more expensive than their matched options. The OTM-LT group shows the highest overpricing, with 94.3% and 98% for calls and puts, respectively, which indicates that almost all warrants in the group have higher prices than the matched options. The ITM-ST group shows the lowest overpricing, with 42.8% and 50.5% for calls and puts, respectively. The price premium proportions of the LT group are higher than those of the ST group, while those of the OTM group are higher than those of the ITM group, which is consistent with earlier findings based on derivative warrants and options written on the HSI (Fung & Zeng, 2012; Li & Zhang, 2011). [1] However, the proportions should have been 0 in theory because the price of American-style options is always higher than that of European-style options when we control for other factors similarly. Thus, our empirical results are inconsistent with option pricing theory.

In Panels B and C of Table 2, we present the average price premium and the average price premium ratio for each moneyness and maturity group separately. Regardless of the average price premium value or ratio, they are all significantly greater than 0 at the 5% level, except in the ITM-ST group. Overall, the overpricing behavior of the put group is more obvious than that of the call group, which is inconsistent with the finding of Li and Zhang (2011). Panel D shows the number of observations for the matched pairs of warrants

---

[1] The HSI is the benchmark index for the HKEX, on which the warrants and options written on the HSI are both European style.

and options in each group. ①

Table 2   Overpricing

Group	Call			Put		
	ST	MT	LT	ST	MT	LT
Panel A: Proportion						
OTM	0.618	0.849	0.943	0.821	0.906	0.980
ATM	0.523	0.668	0.879	0.628	0.729	0.871
ITM	0.428	0.528	0.728	0.505	0.644	0.740
Panel B: Average premium						
OTM	0.184	0.445	0.882	0.340	0.533	0.877
ATM	0.079	0.329	0.879	0.234	0.495	1.075
ITM	−0.069*	0.157	0.463	0.055*	0.379	0.777
Panel C: Average premium ratio						
OTM	0.223	0.285	0.311	0.399	0.379	0.410
ATM	0.064	0.106	0.121	0.110	0.116	0.142
ITM	−0.014*	0.015	0.045	0.008*	0.048	0.053
Panel D: Observations						
	53,103	71,404	19,840	9749	14,932	4054
	47,985	24,188	4674	4710	2557	730
	5731	1767	551	529	194	130

Notes: This table shows the overpricing behavior of derivative warrants compared with options in each moneyness-maturity group for calls and puts separately. OTM, ATM, and ITM denote out-of-the-money, at-the-money, and in-the-money, respectively. ST, MT, and LT refer to short, medium, and long terms, respectively. Panel A reports the premium proportion of the observations. Panels B and C show the average price premium and average price premium ratio, respectively, while Panel D presents the number of observations for the matched derivative pairs.

* Denotes a nonsignificant difference from 0 at the 5% level.

---

① The pairs of derivative warrants and options are matched at 1-h intervals to obtain the sample. We also compare the price and liquidity using synchronous trading records to ensure the robustness of our findings.

In Panel A of Table 3, we outline the proportion of observations for which the liquidity of derivative warrants is better than that of matched options. For all liquidity measures in all groups, the proportion is greater than 50%. Panel B of Table 3 shows the average liquidity differences for each moneyness and maturity group. Overall, the findings in Table 3 indicate that the liquidity of derivative warrants is generally higher than that of matched options. There is only one nonsignificant t-statistic in the premiums from all groups.

Table 3 Liquidity differences

		Call			Put		
	Group	ST	MT	LT	ST	MT	LT
Panel A: Proportion							
$Rolls_{i,t}^{w}$ $>Rolls_{i,t}^{O}$	OTM	0.538	0.608	0.656	0.548	0.597	0.627
	ATM	0.529	0.611	0.682	0.545	0.664	0.564
	ITM	0.563	0.664	0.673	0.573	0.572	0.573
$Vol_{i,t}^{w}>Vol_{i,t}^{O}$	OTM	0.717	0.759	0.716	0.748	0.776	0.736
	ATM	0.665	0.688	0.619	0.672	0.675	0.599
	ITM	0.616	0.599	0.579	0.522	0.546	0.504
$A_{i,t}^{w}>A_{i,t}^{w}$	OTM	0.810	0.905	0.938	0.833	0.952	0.985
	ATM	0.823	0.917	0.936	0.767	0.892	0.962
	ITM	0.875	0.954	0.962	0.908	0.961	0.980
Panel B: Average							
$-(Rolls_{i,t}^{w}$ $-Rolls_{i,t}^{O})$	OTM	0.061	0.136	0.294	0.059	0.172	0.323
	ATM	0.076	0.192	0.473	0.089	0.335	0.593
	ITM	0.230	0.549	0.648	0.074	0.311	0.531
$Vol_{i,t}^{w}$ $-Vol_{i,t}^{O}$	OTM	0.073	0.281	0.249	0.051	0.120	0.150
	ATM	0.053	0.166	0.144	0.018	0.060	0.045
	ITM	0.027	0.056	0.048	0.043	0.032	0.029*
$-(A_{i,t}^{w}-A_{i,t}^{w})$	OTM	0.041	0.044	0.067	0.029	0.062	0.088
	ATM	0.023	0.033	0.066	0.038	0.063	0.105
	ITM	0.029	0.051	0.105	0.548	0.086	0.108

    Notes: This table shows the liquidity differences between derivative warrants and options
in each moneyness-maturity group for calls and puts separately. OTM, ATM, and ITM
denote out-of-the-money, at-the-money, and in-the-money, respectively. ST, MT, and LT
refer to short, medium, and long terms, respectively. Superscripts ^{w} and ^{O} denote derivative
warrants and options, respectively. DRolls, DVol, and DA measure the liquidity differences
in Roll spread, trading volume, and Amihud illiquidity measure, respectively. Panels A and
B report the proportion and the average value of the derivative warrant liquidity measure,
which are greater than the values of the matched option.
    * Denotes a nonsignificant difference from 0 at the 5% level.

3.2 Regression results

We used a series of panel regression models to empirically evaluate the effects
of the liquidity differences between derivative warrants and options on their
price differences. The benchmark model is as follows:

$$DP_{i,t} = \alpha_i + \beta_1 DRolls_{i,t} + \beta_2 DVol_{i,t} + \beta_3 DA_{i,t} + \beta_4 CDS_t + \beta_5 k_{i,t} + \beta_6 m_{i,t}$$
$$+ \beta_7 Vol\_Ud_{i,t} + \beta_8 \sigma_{i,t-1} + \beta_9 D\hat{P}_{i,t} + \beta_{10} DLp_{i,t} + \beta_{11} Ftp_{t-1} + \varepsilon_{i,t} \quad (12)$$

    where $DP_{i,t}$ is the price difference in percentage between matched
warrants and options. $DRolls_{i,t}$, $DVol_{i,t}$, and $DA_{i,t}$ are the differences in
liquidity measures for Roll spread, trading volume, and Amihud illiquidity
measure, respectively. CDS_t measures the counterparty credit risk of
derivative warrants. $k_{i,t}$ refers to moneyness, while $m_{i,t}$ refers to maturity,
which controls for investor preference. $Vol\_Ud_{i,t}$ and $\sigma_{i,t-1}$ are the trading
volume of the underlying stock and one-period lagged volatility, respectively,
which control for asymmetric information and volatility discovery ability.
$D\hat{P}_{i,t}$ is the theoretical value difference between matched warrants and
options, which controls for the effect of different exercise styles (i. e.,
European for warrants and American for options). $DLp_{i,t}$ reflects the different
OI levels between the derivative warrants market and the options market, and
controls for the difference in liquidity providers' behavior. Ftp_{t-1} is the one-
period lagged net position of speculators in futures written on individual stocks
listed on the HKEX, which controls for investor sentiment in Hong Kong's

derivatives market. In addition, we controlled for both individual and time effects[①] in the regression (Table 4).

Table 4　Basic panel regressions

	(1)	(2)	(3)	(4)	(5)
DRolls	−0.077***			−0.071***	−0.057***
	(−12.02)			(−11.01)	(−8.83)
DVol		0.040***		0.029***	0.026***
		(29.65)		(21.75)	(19.60)
DA			−0.014***	−0.012***	−0.008***
			(−28.49)	(−24.72)	(−17.73)
CDS					−0.291***
					(−10.56)
k					−1.892***
					(−44.79)
m					0.454***
					(9.25)
Vol_Ud					−0.010***
					(−10.82)
σ					−0.025***
					(−3.52)
$D\hat{P}$					−0.092**
					(−2.54)
DLp					−0.005***
					(−3.28)
Ftp					0.005***
					(7.47)
Individual effect	Yes	Yes	Yes	Yes	Yes
Time effect	Yes	Yes	Yes	Yes	Yes
Observations	266,828	266,828	266,828	266,828	234,380
R^2	0.010	0.008	0.018	0.031	0.142

Notes: This table reports the basic panel regression results:

$$DP_{i,t} = \alpha_i + \beta_1 DRolls_{i,t} + \varepsilon_{i,t},\qquad(1)$$

$$DP_{i,t} = \alpha_i + \beta_1 DVol_{i,t} + \varepsilon_{i,t},\qquad(2)$$

---

① The time variables are monthly because of the daily CDS, which is equal for the ith pair. Meanwhile, our panel data are extremely imbalanced. When we adjust the time variables to 5 minutes, the robustness of our liquidity measures is unchanged.

$$DP_{i,t} = \alpha_i + \beta_1 DA_{i,t} + \varepsilon_{i,t}, \tag{3}$$

$$DP_{i,t} = \alpha_i + \beta_1 DRolls_{i,t} + \beta_2 DVol_{i,t} + \beta_3 DA_{i,t} + \varepsilon_{i,t}, \tag{4}$$

$$DP_{i,t} = \alpha_i + \beta_1 DRolls_{i,t} + \beta_2 DVol_{i,t} + \beta_3 DA_{i,t} + \beta_4 CDS_t + \beta_5 k_{i,t} + \beta_6 m_{i,t} + \beta_7 Vol\_Ud_{i,t}$$
$$+ \beta_8 \sigma_{i,t-1} + \beta_9 D\hat{P}_{i,t} + \beta_{10} DLp_{i,t} + \beta_{11} Ftp_{t-1} + \varepsilon_{i,t}, \tag{5}$$

where DP denotes the price premium ratio of the derivative pair; $DRolls$, $DVol$, and DA measure the liquidity differences in Roll spread, trading volume, and Amihud illiquidity measure, respectively; CDS is the measure of counterparty credit risk; k is moneyness and m is maturity, which both measure investor preference. Vol_Ud and σ are trading volume and underlying stock volatility, which measure information asymmetry and volatility discovery ability, respectively; $D\hat{P}$ denotes the theoretical value differences for derivative pairs, which measures the difference in exercise style; DLp measures market makers' behavior and is the difference in absolute OI; Ftp denotes investor sentiment measured by futures net positioning. The sample period is from July 3, 2012 to November 30, 2016. ***, **, and* denote statistical significance at the 1%, 5%, and 10% levels, respectively. The t statistics (in brackets) are adjusted for 12-period autocorrelation lags using the Newey-West (1987) procedure.

Models (1) to (3) in Table 4 show the univariate regression results to assess the impact of each liquidity indicator on the price differences. Model (4) combines three liquidity indicators, while Model (5) is based on Model (4), with all control variables added. Each liquidity indicator is statistically and economically significant and has the expected sign in univariate or multivariate regressions. The results indicate that the liquidity differences also explain the price differences between derivative warrants and options written on individual stocks to a certain extent, which extends earlier results in the literature (Li & Zhang, 2011; Fung & Zeng, 2012; Li & Zhang, 2019). The coefficients of $DRolls$ and DA are negative, while those of $DVol$ are positive. This suggests that higher liquidity leads to a premium price for derivative warrants. CDS is negatively and significantly related to DP, which is consistent with the finding of Li and Zhang (2019). This result shows that the counterparty credit risk of derivative warrants leads to a discounted price. Moneyness k and maturity m are also both significant, which suggests that the preference of warrant investors also influences the price. The coefficient of k is negative, but the coefficient of m is positive, which contradicts the literature (Li & Zhang, 2011; Li & Zhang, 2019).

The coefficient of *Vol_Ud* is negatively and significantly related to *DP*, which suggests that liquidity and trading activity on the underlying stock explain *DP* to a certain extent. An explanation for this finding is that warrant investors have less information than option investors and this information asymmetry is mitigated when trading stocks with high liquidity. The coefficient of volatility σ is significantly negative, which shows that the price of options is more sensitive to volatility changes. The German options market plays a leading role in volatility discovery compared with the German warrants market; in a way, this explains the difference in volatility sensitivity (Baule, 2018). $D\hat{P}$ is significant with the expected negative sign, which means that the differences in exercise style explain the price differences. Specifically, the European-style warrants should have been cheaper than the American-style options. The proxy for market makers' behavior, *DLp*, is negatively and significantly related to *DP*, which suggests that market makers in the warrants market trade more actively to provide liquidity to the market and mitigate OI. This behavior improves the price of the warrants market compared with that of the options market. *Ftp* measures investor sentiment in the derivatives market, and its positive and significant relationship with *DP* shows that investors in the derivative warrants market are more susceptible to market sentiment. *Ftp* and *Vol_Ud* together imply the different investor structures between the derivative warrants and options markets because the warrants market is designed for retail investors, while the options market is dominated by institutional investors.

3.3 Robustness tests

We conducted several robustness tests to ensure the robustness of the benchmark model. First, we re-estimated our model using different groups, considering the critical factors that may simultaneously influence the prices and liquidity in the derivative warrants and options markets. Considering our extremely imbalanced data set, we deleted firms with less than 1,000 observations to avoid sample choice bias. Moreover, we repeated our analysis using data sampled at a 10-min frequency to address any concerns about our results being dependent on the choice of sampling frequency.

Considering the obvious overpricing and liquidity difference among the groups (see Section 3. 1), it is natural to ask whether our empirical results are robust when we focus our analysis on each group individually. Table 5 reports our subsample panel regression results. Models (1) to (3) focus on the OTM, ATM, and ITM groups, respectively. The results show that the level of moneyness had an effect on all groups. The three liquidity measures in the OTM group have the strongest explanatory power, with an absolute average value of t reaching 14. 31 and a R^2 value above 10%. The measures lose explanatory power in the ITM group; however, the theoretical value difference $D\hat{P}$ (in that it is mostly significant and negatively related to DP) suggests that in the case of warrants or options ITM, investors are more sensitive to the gap in exercise opportunities resulting from the exercise style. Therefore, the price of options tends to be higher than that of derivative warrants. The subsample results for maturity are estimated using Models (4) to (6) for the LT, MT, and ST groups, respectively. The results are similar with full sample regression, the core explanatory variables are still significant, and the sign of the coefficients is unchanged. The explanatory power of the model is strongest in the LT group ($R^2 = 0. 27$). Models (7) and (8) focus on the call and put groups, respectively. The results show that the liquidity measures are useful in explaining price differences regardless of call or put transactions. However, some variables perform differently in the Put group. Maturity m loses explanatory power and its sign is negative, which suggests that LT European-style put warrants are not preferred by investors. In addition, $D\hat{P}$ loses power in the put group. The likely positive θ of long-term put may explain these findings in the Put group. Ftp is negatively and significantly related to DP, which makes sense because when market sentiment increases, investors in the warrants market will reduce their purchases of put warrants more aggressively because of their optimism about the future.

Table 5 Robustness tests: Group panel regressions

	OTM (1)	ATM (2)	ITM (3)	LT (4)	MT (5)	ST (6)	Calls (7)	Puts (8)
$DRolls$	−0.066***	−0.042***	−0.030**	−0.036*	−0.058***	−0.066***	−0.052***	−0.089***
	(−12.09)	(−3.91)	(−2.20)	(−1.67)	(−17.47)	(−6.61)	(−8.17)	(−4.99)
$DVol$	0.024***	0.022***	−0.003	0.012***	0.014***	0.038***	0.026***	0.014***
	(16.67)	(9.26)	(−0.50)	(6.09)	(11.83)	(8.54)	(18.68)	(3.37)
DA	−0.008***	−0.006***	0.000	−0.004***	−0.006***	−0.006***	−0.008***	−0.007***
	(−14.18)	(−8.76)	(0.13)	(−3.90)	(−11.82)	(−7.70)	(−16.46)	(−5.75)
CDS	−0.437***	−0.029	0.003	−0.248***	−0.387***	−0.150***	−0.258***	−0.507***
	(−11.78)	(−0.70)	(0.04)	(−4.18)	(−11.16)	(−3.50)	(−8.40)	(−8.01)
k	−2.075***	−2.381***	−1.753***	−2.090***	−2.079***	−1.817***	−1.843***	−1.561***
	(−33.66)	(−21.71)	(−2.80)	(−22.80)	(−35.01)	(−24.80)	(−38.23)	(−14.15)
m	0.513***	0.213**	0.412***	0.375***	0.898***	0.653***	0.564***	−0.049
	(7.87)	(2.57)	(3.44)	(3.34)	(12.20)	(6.01)	(10.27)	(−0.46)
Vol_Ud	−0.010***	−0.007***	−0.005**	−0.006***	−0.009***	−0.010***	−0.009***	−0.014***
	(−8.91)	(−5.45)	(−2.06)	(−3.01)	(−7.90)	(−7.21)	(−9.24)	(−6.99)
σ	−0.056***	0.000	0.019**	−0.045***	−0.038***	−0.029***	−0.017**	−0.037*
	(−5.96)	(0.02)	(2.06)	(−3.06)	(−4.20)	(−2.65)	(−2.15)	(−1.82)
$D\hat{P}$	0.045	0.065	−0.362***	0.038	0.039	0.413	−0.199***	−0.003
	(0.99)	(0.99)	(−3.14)	(0.89)	(0.78)	(1.38)	(−5.02)	(−0.04)
DLp	−0.005***	−0.004**	−0.004	−0.001	−0.002	−0.005**	−0.005***	−0.005
	(−2.76)	(−2.18)	(−1.03)	(−0.45)	(−1.40)	(−2.47)	(−3.20)	(−1.39)
Ftp	0.003***	0.009***	0.001	0.000	0.003***	0.009***	0.007***	−0.011***
	(3.84)	(9.12)	(0.51)	(0.00)	(3.89)	(7.62)	(9.73)	(−5.12)
Individual effect	Yes	Yes	Yes	Yes	Yes	Yes	Yes	Yes
Time effect	Yes	Yes	Yes	Yes	Yes	Yes	Yes	Yes
Observations	151,488	74,836	8056	25,099	100,630	108,651	201,752	32,628
R^2	0.119	0.069	0.019	0.271	0.196	0.093	0.130	0.128

Notes: This table reports the group panel regression results:

$$DP_{i,t} = \alpha_i + \beta_1 DRolls_{i,t} + \beta_2 DVol_{i,t} + \beta_3 DA_{i,t} + \beta_4 CDS_t + \beta_5 k_{i,t} + \beta_6 m_{i,t} + \beta_7 Vol\_Ud_{i,t}$$
$$+ \beta_8 \sigma_{i,t-1} + \beta_9 D\hat{P}_{i,t} + \beta_{10} DLp_{i,t} + \beta_{11} Ftp_{t-1} + \varepsilon_{i,t},$$

We repeated the benchmark regression in different moneyness and maturity groups for calls and puts separately. OTM, ATM, and ITM denote out-of-the-money, at-the-money, and in-the-money, respectively. ST, MT, and LT refer to short, medium, and long terms, respectively. DP denotes the price premium ratio of the derivative pair; $DRolls$, $DVol$, and DA measure the liquidity differences in Roll spread, trading volume, and Amihud illiquidity measure, respectively; CDS is the measure of counterparty credit risk; k is moneyness and m is maturity, which both measure investor preference. Vol_Ud and σ are the trading volume and underlying stock volatility, which measure information asymmetry and volatility discovery ability, respectively; $D\hat{P}$ denotes the theoretical value differences for derivative pairs, which measures the difference in exercise style; DLp measures the market makers' behavior and is the difference in absolute OI; Ftp denotes the investor sentiment measured by futures net positioning. The sample period is from July 3, 2012 to November 30, 2016. ***, **, and * denote statistical significance at the 1%, 5%, and 10% levels, respectively. The t statistics (in brackets) are adjusted for 12-period autocorrelation lags using the Newey-West (1987) procedure.

In our sample, the 44 firms with less than 1,000 observations represent 74.6% of the full sample. Considering our extremely imbalanced data set, we removed these firms and repeated the regressions from Section 3.2 (Table 6). The results are still robust and the significance of the liquidity measures improves.

Table 6   Robustness tests: Deleting firms with few observations

	(1)	(2)	(3)	(4)	(5)
DRolls	−0.085***			−0.077***	−0.062***
	(−16.33)			(−14.80)	(−12.01)
DVol		0.040***		0.029***	0.026***
		(29.64)		(21.72)	(19.56)
DA			−0.014***	−0.012***	−0.008***
			(−28.24)	(−24.39)	(−17.48)
CDS					−0.295***
					(−10.58)
k					−1.884***
					(−44.01)
m					0.449***
					(9.02)
Vol_Ud					−0.010***
					(−11.15)
σ					−0.026***
					(−3.48)
D$\hat{P}$					−0.082**
					(−2.21)
DLp					−0.004***
					(−3.12)
Ftp					0.005***
					(7.11)
Individual effect	Yes	Yes	Yes	Yes	Yes
Time effect	Yes	Yes	Yes	Yes	Yes
Observations	259,922	259,922	259,922	259,922	228,674
R^2	0.010	0.009	0.018	0.031	0.141

Notes: This table reports the panel regression results. The sample excludes firms with less than 1000 observations. The sample period is from July 3, 2012 to November 30, 2016. ***, **, and * denote statistical significance at the 1%, 5%, and 10% levels, respectively. The t statistics (in brackets) are adjusted for 12-period autocorrelation lags using the Newey-West (1987) procedure.

To address any concerns about sampling frequency bias, we repeated the analysis in Section 3.2 using data sampled at a 10-minute frequency. Table 7 reports the regression results. All of the variables retain their explanatory power and the expected sign of the coefficients; however, the significance level of the liquidity measures decreases slightly.

Table 7   Robustness tests: 10-min sampling frequency

	(1)	(2)	(3)	(4)	(5)
$DRolls$	-0.078^{***}			-0.072^{***}	-0.056^{***}
	(-10.06)			(-9.27)	(-7.21)
$DVol$		0.040^{***}		0.029^{***}	0.027^{***}
		(24.50)		(17.89)	(16.34)
DA			-0.014^{***}	-0.012^{***}	-0.008^{***}
			(-25.82)	(-22.42)	(-15.78)
CDS					-0.300^{***}
					(-9.48)
k					-1.904^{***}
					(-38.47)
m					0.475^{***}
					(8.45)
Vol_Ud					-0.009^{***}
					(-9.21)
σ					-0.023^{***}
					(-2.62)
$D\hat{P}$					-0.080^{*}
					(-1.89)
DLp					-0.005^{***}
					(-2.63)
Ftp					0.006^{***}
					(6.75)
Individual effect	Yes	Yes	Yes	Yes	Yes
Time effect	Yes	Yes	Yes	Yes	Yes
Observations	133,974	133,974	133,974	133,974	118,530
R^2	0.011	0.008	0.018	0.032	0.142

Notes: This table reports the panel regression results. The sampling frequency is 10 min rather than 5 min. The sample period is from July 3, 2012 to November 30, 2016. ***, **, and * denote statistical significance at the 1%, 5%, and 10% levels, respectively. The t statistics (in brackets) are adjusted for 12-period autocorrelation lags using the Newey-West (1987) procedure.

4 Understanding liquidity differences

4.1 Aggregate market liquidity

We move on from discussing individual derivative warrants or options with short-time interval data to exploring aggregate market liquidity using three dimensions (i. e. , width, depth, and resiliency) for the derivative warrants and options markets using one-day interval data. We are inspired by Chordia et al. (2001), who study aggregate liquidity and trading activity in US equities.

For the warrants or options markets, we define the following liquidity measures roughly the same as in earlier sections:

Rolls: Daily market-wide average for Roll spread.

A: Daily market-wide average for Amihud illiquidity measure.

Vol: Daily market-wide aggregate trading volume in Hong Kong dollars.

AveVol: Daily market-wide aggregate trading volume (*Vol*) divided by the daily number of trading products in the warrants or options markets.

We winsorized the trading records at 2% for the warrant and option samples. ① We cut the period from July 3, 2012 to November 30, 2016. April 2016 is eliminated because of missing data. We adopted the following principles to fill the time series: (i) for trading volume or average trading volume, nontrading dates are assigned a value of 0; (ii) for Roll spread or Amihud illiquidity measure, we fill in nontrading dates using an average value from the past 10 trading days. Figures 1-4 illustrate the time series averages of each of the cross-sectional average liquidity differences, while Figure 5

---

① At 5-minute intervals, there are approximately 8. 6 million transaction records for derivative warrants and 1. 2 million transaction records for options.

illustrates the difference in the number of daily product transactions. Panels A and B of Table 8 report the descriptive statistics for the derivative warrant and option samples, respectively. All of the variables pass the augmented Dickey-Fuller test, which ensures stationarity.

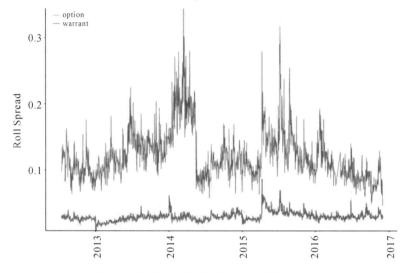

Fig. 1　Market-wide Roll spread differences

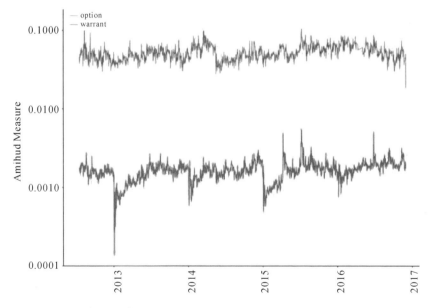

Fig. 2　Market-wide Amihud illiquidity measure differences

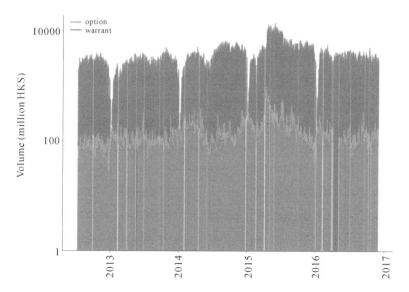

Fig. 3   Market-wide trading volume differences in millions of Hong Kong dollars

Panels A and B of Table 8 report the summary statistics for the market-wide liquidity measures of derivative warrants and options, respectively. Figures 1-5 plot the market-wide liquidity and trading activity differences between the warrants and options markets. While the numbers of products available for trading in these two markets are similar, we found a big gap in liquidity indicators, with the daily average trading volume of warrants roughly 26 times higher than that of options, Roll spread roughly 4 times smaller, and Amihud illiquidity measure roughly 26 times smaller. However, the liquidity differences in the average daily changes between these two markets are small. Figures 1-4 show a positive correlation between the daily changes in liquidity in these two markets; i. e., the correlation coefficients of Roll spread, Amihud illiquidity measure, and trading volumes between the two markets are 0. 59, 0. 25, and 0. 21, respectively.

Table 8 Summary statistics for market-wide liquidity

	Mean	St. Dev.	Min	Median	Max
Panel A：Warrants market					
Rolls	0.030	0.007	0.020	0.028	0.086
ΔRolls	0.010	0.141	−0.292	−0.004	0.499
A	0.002	0.0005	0.001	0.002	0.006
ΔA	0.012	0.153	−0.281	0.003	0.411
Vol	3876.599	1841.178	66.659	3472.71	9378.99
ΔVol	0.025	0.185	−0.453	0.005	0.864
AveVol	514.151	236.804	105.757	429.1	1,121.712
ΔAveVol	0.009	0.147	−0.325	−0.002	0.532
NumPdt	817.272	299.757	4	852	1583
Panel B：Options market					
Rolls	0.121	0.035	0.029	0.113	0.205
ΔRolls	0.019	0.194	−0.292	−0.006	0.499
A	0.052	0.011	0.018	0.051	0.076
ΔA	0.015	0.166	−0.281	−0.001	0.411
Vol	150.212	92.826	66.659	124.7	982.611
ΔVol	0.044	0.310	−0.453	−0.0004	0.864
AveVol	28.56	8.86	18.584	26.35	75.635
ΔAveVol	0.021	0.202	−0.325	−0.013	0.532
NumPdt	502.359	152.529	94	470	1380

Notes：Table 8 reports the descriptive statistics for market-wide liquidity and trading activity. Rolls，A，and Vol are Roll spread，Amihud illiquidity measure，and trading volume，which represent market width，resiliency，and depth，respectively. NumPdt represents the number of daily product transactions. The Δ prefixes denote the daily change in percentage. Panels A and B report the results for the derivative warrants and options markets separately.

4.2 Liquidity and market efficiency

Market efficiency may be strongly related to liquidity. The benefits of liquidity will theoretically endogenously improve market efficiency（Chowdhry &

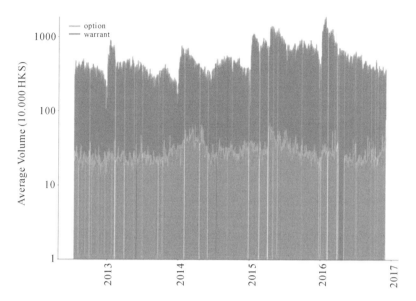

Fig. 4　Market-wide average trading volume differences in 10,000 Hong Kong dollars

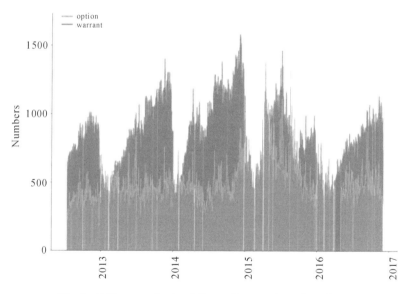

Fig. 5　Differences in the daily trading number of products

Nanda, 1991). Chordia et al. (2008) empirically examine changes in the market efficiency of the New York Stock Exchange and find that improvements in the exchange's liquidity will enhance its market efficiency.

Using data from the Tel Aviv Stock Exchange, Amihud et al. (1997) also empirically show that liquidity is positively correlated with market efficiency. We assess the differences in market efficiency between the derivative warrants and options markets following the methodology of Chordia et al. (2008). Using our matched sample of warrants and options, we simply focus on the interaction between liquidity and market efficiency in the two markets, controlling for other factors affecting market efficiency.

First, we used return predictability from order flows to identify the level of market efficiency. The models used to estimate return predictability are as follows:

$$r_t = \alpha + \beta_1 OI_{t-1} + \beta_2 OI_{t-1} \times ILQ + \varepsilon_t \tag{1}$$

$$r_t = \alpha + \beta_1 OI_{t-1} + \beta_2 OI_{t-1} \times wo + \beta_3 OI_{t-1} \times ILQ + \varepsilon_t \tag{2}$$

where r_t denotes the 5-minute returns of warrants or options at time t and OI_{t-1} is the one-period lagged OI calculated above. The low-liquidity dummy, ILQ, which measures market-wide liquidity, takes a value of 1 if the two markets' daily Roll spread is simultaneously at least one standard deviation above the average level, and otherwise 0. The dummy wo indicates a derivative warrant when equals to 1 and an option when equals to 0. We then separately assessed return predictability from order flows in the warrant and option samples using Model (13). We used Model (14) to examine the performance of the full sample. Considering the positive relationships between efficiency and firm size or liquidity and firm size, we stratified the samples into three firm size groups by a firm's market value, as firm size may have a much greater impact on information efficiency for investors because of the high leverage characteristics of trading derivative warrants and options.

Table 9 reports the results for return predictability from order flows. First, we show that for the derivative warrants and options markets, one-period lagged OI positively and significantly predicts 5-minute ahead returns because the coefficients of OI_{t-1} are all positively and significantly related to return r_t in regression (1). Second, we find that the level of efficiency of the warrants market is better than that of the options market because of its higher liquidity. The coefficients of $OI_{t-1} \times ILQ$ are positive and highly significant for the full sample and the option sample, which shows that OI's return predictability improves during periods of illiquidity. Therefore, illiquidity weakens market efficiency, which is consistent with the finding of Chordia et al. (2008). The significance and explanatory power of OI for the option sample are stronger than for the warrant sample because of larger coefficients, t-statistics, and R^2. The significantly negative coefficients of $OI_{t-1} \times wo$ indicate lower predictability for OI in the warrants market than in the options market. We suggest that the level of market efficiency is higher for warrants and options written on the stocks of larger firms. The regression results show that the explanatory power of OI increases with firms' shrinking market value.

Table 9 Return predictability regressions

	All	Large-cap	Mid-cap	Small-cap
OI_{t-1}	0.001 ***	0.001 *	0.001 ***	0.002 ***
	(6.862)	(1.740)	(4.116)	(5.656)
$OI_{t-1} \times ILQ$	0.000	−0.002 *	0.002 **	0.000
	(0.681)	(−1.817)	(2.401)	(0.215)
Constant	0.002 ***	0.001 ***	0.002 ***	0.004 ***
	(15.590)	(4.552)	(9.344)	(12.573)
Observations	266,828	88,936	88,931	88,961
R^2	0.0002	0.00001	0.0004	0.0004
OI_{t-1}	0.004 ***	−0.001	0.003 ***	0.009 ***
	(10.092)	(−1.106)	(4.829)	(11.943)
$OI_{t-1} \times ILQ$	0.009 ***	0.004 ***	0.009 ***	0.015 ***
	(11.391)	(2.935)	(7.230)	(8.596)
Constant	0.005 ***	0.004 ***	0.005 ***	0.007 ***
	(15.596)	(7.317)	(9.321)	(10.194)
Observations	266,828	88,936	88,931	88,961
R^2	0.002	0.00001	0.002	0.004
OI_{t-1}	0.005 ***	−0.000	0.00 ***	0.010 ***
	(16.184)	(−0.508)	(7.684)	(18.530)
$OI_{t-1} \times wo$	−0.004 ***	0.000	−0.003 ***	−0.010 ***
	(−10.639)	(0.550)	(−4.626)	(−12.804)
$OI_{t-1} \times ILQ$	0.006 ***	0.002 **	0.007 ***	0.008 ***
	(11.623)	(2.105)	(8.293)	(8.451)
Constant	0.004 ***	0.002 ***	0.004 ***	0.005 ***
	(20.638)	(8.521)	(12.497)	(14.260)
Observations	533,656	177,872	177,862	177,922
R^2	0.001	0.000	0.001	0.003

Notes：This table presents the results of return predictability from order flows：

$$r_t = \alpha + \beta_1 OI_{t-1} + \beta_2 OI_{t-1} \times ILQ + \varepsilon_t , \tag{i}$$

$$r_t = \alpha + \beta_1 OI_{t-1} + \beta_2 OI_{t-1} \times wo + \beta_3 OI_{t-1} \times ILQ + \varepsilon_t , \tag{ii}$$

We use Model (i) for estimations of the derivative warrant or option sample. We use Model (ii) for full sample estimations. We stratify the samples into three firm size groups by a firm's market value as large-cap, mid-cap, and small-cap samples. The dependent variable is the 5-min return of warrants or options at time t. OI_{t-1} is one-period lagged OI. ILQ takes a value of 1 if the two markets' daily Roll spread is at least one standard deviation above the average level simultaneously, and otherwise 0. The dummy variable wo takes a value of 1 for warrants and 0 for options. Panels A-C report the results for the samples of warrants, options, and both, respectively. The sample period is from July 3, 2012 to November 30, 2016. ˙˙˙, ˙˙, and ˙ denote statistical significance at the 1%, 5%, and 10% levels, respectively.

Furthermore, we used variance ratios and autocorrelation to ensure the robustness of the above results by suggesting that the price of derivative warrants is closer to a random walk benchmark than that of options (Table 10). Five-minute daily variance ratios are calculated as the variance of 5-minute returns plus q divided by the variance of daily returns, where q is the number of 5-minute intervals in a 1-day horizon. This measure would converge to 1 for a random walk. Thus, Panel A of Table 10 suggests that the price of warrants is closer to a random walk than that of options. The per hour open/close variance ratios are constructed as (per hour) open/close return variances divided by (per hour) close/open variances. The higher this measure, the more the price reflects private information. Panel B of Table 10 shows that these ratios are higher for the warrant sample, suggesting greater efficiency in the warrants market than in the options market. Panel C of Table 10 shows that the one-period lagged price change leads to stronger explanatory power for the options markets. Thus, the efficiency of the options market is inferior to that of the warrants market.

Table 10   Variance ratios and autoregressions

Panel A: 5-min/daily variance ratios

	Large-cap	Mid-cap	Small-cap
Warrants	7. 16	6. 19	5. 72
Options	32. 06	33. 16	43. 40

Panel B: Per hour open/close variance ratios

	Large-cap	Mid-cap	Small-cap
Warrants	7. 82	10. 98	7. 36
Options	1. 68	1. 58	1. 28

Panel C: First-order autoregressions of daily price change

	Coefficient	t statistics	R^2
Warrants	−0. 21	−6. 79	0. 04
Options	−0. 27	−8. 99	0. 07

Notes: This table shows the variance ratios and autoregression results of derivative warrants and options in each firm size group. Panel A reports the ratio of 5-min return variance to open-to-close return variance. Panel B presents (open-to-close) ÷ (close-to-open) per hour return variance ratios. Panel C reports the regression outcome of first-order autoregressions of daily price change.

5   Conclusions

This study uses a matched sample of derivative warrants and options written on individual stocks listed on the HKEX to explain the paradox that European-style derivative warrants are more expensive than American-style options given that other elements affecting prices can be controlled. The samples used in previous studies (Li & Zhang, 2011; Fung & Zeng, 2012; Li & Zhang, 2019) exclude derivative warrants and options with different exercise styles and concentrate on derivative warrants and options written on stock indices. We use high-frequency tick-by-tick trade data for individual stock warrants and options to explain this paradox. Our findings provide additional knowledge for option-type derivative pricing.

Our results demonstrate that liquidity differences significantly explain the overpricing behavior of different exercise-style derivatives. In addition, their explanatory power is stronger for the OTM and LT groups. Many other variables have explanatory power, which indicates that the price differences between derivative warrants and options reflect at least the following factors: Counterparty credit risk, investor preference, information asymmetry, volatility discovery ability, exercise style, market makers' behavior, and investor sentiment. Our findings add to the literature on the price determinants of derivative assets.

We conduct additional empirical analyses to better understand the liquidity differences between the derivative warrants and options markets. We compare the liquidity differences from a daily market-wide perspective, which suggests that from three dimensions (i. e. , width, depth, and resiliency), the liquidity of the derivative warrants market is far better than that of the options market most of the time. Furthermore, we use return predictability from order flows and variance ratios to confirm empirically that the level of efficiency in the derivative warrants market is higher than in the options market because of its higher liquidity.

Data availability statement

The data used in this study are available from the Hong Kong Exchanges and Clearing Limited [HKEX (www. hkex. com. hk)] and the Chinese Stock Market and Accounting Research (CSMAR) (http://cndata1. csmar. com/). The data can be acquired by paying a license fee or receiving permission.

References

Alghalith M, 2020. Pricing the american options: A closed-form, simple formula[J]. Physica A: Statistical Mechanics and its Applications, 548: 1-4.
Amihud Y, 2002. Illiquidity and stock returns: Cross-section and time-series effects[J]. Journal of Financial Markets, 5(1): 31-56.

Amihud Y, Mendelson H, 1986. Asset pricing and the bid-ask spread[J]. Journal of Financial Economics, 17: 223-249.

Amihud Y, Mendelson H, Lauterbach B, 1997. Market microstructure and securities values evidence from the Tel Aviv Stock Exchange[J]. Journal of Financial Economics, 45(3): 365-390.

Amihud Y, Noh J, 2021. Illiquidity and stock returns II: Cross-section and time-series effects[J]. Review of Financial Studies, 34(4): 2101-2123.

Bartram S M, Fehle F, 2007. Competition without fungibility: Evidence from alternative market structures for derivatives [J]. Journal of Banking & Finance, 31: 659-677.

Baule R, Frijns B, Tieves M E, 2018. Volatility discovery and volatility quoting on markets for options and warrants[J]. Journal of Futures Markets, 38(7): 758-774.

Bernile G, Hu J, Tang Y, 2016. Can information be locked up? Informed trading ahead of macro—news announcements [J]. Journal of Financial Economics, 121(3): 496-520.

Brenner M, Eldor R, Hauser S, 2001. The price of options illiquidity[J]. Journal of Finance, 56(2): 789-805.

Chae J, Khil J, Lee E J, 2013. Who makes markets? Liquidity providers versus algorithmic traders[J]. Journal of Futures Markets, 33(5): 397-420.

Chan H W, Pinder S M, 2000. The value of liquidity: Evidence from the derivatives market[J]. Pacific-Basin Finance Journal, 8: 483-503.

Chordia T, Roll R, Subrahmanyam A, 2001. Market liquidity and trading activity[J]. Journal of Finance, 56(2): 501-530.

Chordia T, Roll R, Subrahmanyam A, 2008. Liquidity and market efficiency [J]. Journal of Financial Economics, 87(2): 249-268.

Chow Y, Li J, Liu M, 2007. Making the derivative warrants market (working paper)[R]. Hong Kong: Chinese University of Hong Kong, 2007:1-27.

Chowdhry B, Nanda V, 1991. Multi-market trading and market liquidity[J]. Review of Financial Studies, 3: 483-511.

Christoffersen P, Goyenko R, Jacobs K, et al, 2018. Illiquidity premia in the equity options market[J]. Review of Financial Studies, 31(3): 811-851.

Deuskar P，Gupta A，Subrahmanyam M G，2011. Liquidity effect in OTC options markets：Premium or discount? [J]. Journal of Financial Markets，14：127-160.

Duan J，Yan Y，1999. Semi-parametric pricing of derivative warrants (working paper)[R]. Hong Kong SAR：Hong Kong University of Science and Technology：1-27.

Easley D，O'Hara M，Srinivas P S，1998. Option volume and stock prices：Evidence on where informed traders trade[J]. Journal of Finance，53(2)：431-465.

Figlewski S，2022. An American call is worth more than a European call：The value of American exercise when the market is not perfectly liquid[J]. Journal of Financial and Quantitative Analysis，57(3)：1023-1057.

Fung J K W，Zeng T Z X，2012. Are derivative warrants overpriced? [J]. Journal of Futures Markets，32(12)：1144-1170.

Han B，2008. Investor sentiment and option prices[J]. Review of Financial Studies，21(1)：387-414.

Hansen P R，Lunde A，2006. Realized variance and market microstructure noise[J]. Journal of Business & Economic Statistics，24(2)：127-161.

Horst J T，Veld C，2008. An empirical analysis of the pricing of bank issued options versus options exchange options[J]. European Financial Management，14(2)：288-314.

Hua J，Peng L，Schwartz R A，et al，2020. Resiliency and stock returns[J]. Review of Financial Studies，33(2)：747-782.

Li G，Zhang C，2011. Why are derivative warrants more expensive than options? An empirical study [J]. Journal of Financial and Quantitative Analysis，46(1)：275-297.

Li G，Zhang C，2019. Counterparty credit risk and derivatives pricing[J]. Journal of Financial Economics，134(3)：647-668.

Luo X，Yu X，Qin S，et al，2020. Option trading and the cross—listed stock returns：Evidence from Chinese A-H shares[J]. Journal of Futures Markets，40(11)：1665-1690.

Martens M，2002. Measuring and forecasting S&P 500 index-futures volatility using high-frequency data[J]. Journal of Futures Markets, 22(6): 497-518.

Muravyev D, Pearson N D, 2020. Options trading costs are lower than you think[J]. Review of Financial Studies, 33(11): 4973-5014.

Pan J, Poteshman A, 2006. The information in option volume for future stock prices[J]. Review of Financial Studies, 19: 871-908.

Roll R, 1984. A simple implicit measure of the effective bid-ask spread in an efficient market[J]. Journal of Finance, 39(4): 1127-1139.

The Securities and Futures Commission (SFC). A healthy market for informed investors? A report on the derivative warrants market in Hong Kong (working paper) [R]. Hong Kong: Hong Kong Securities and Futures Commission, 2005.

Data Citation

[dataset] HKEX; 2012-2016; Warrants and options data; HKEX; www. hkex. com. hk

[dataset] CSMAR; 2012 — 2016; Stock data; CSMAR; http://cndata1. csmar. com/

Appendix A

Table A1 Observations and premium proportions for the matched pairs
of derivative warrants and options written on each individual stock

UnderlyCode	Prod_name	Obs.	Prem%
00700. HK	Tencent Holdings Limited	58692	73. 26%
00941. HK	China Mobile Ltd.	51297	72. 21%
00005. HK	HSBC Holdings Plc	37058	75. 44%
00388. HK	Hong Kong Exchanges and Clearing Ltd.	33383	72. 30%
02318. HK	Ping An Insurance (Group) Co. of China Ltd.	32292	71. 45%
02628. HK	China Life Insurance Company Ltd.	14389	75. 68%
01299. HK	AIA Group Limited	7178	74. 99%
00027. HK	Galaxy Entertainment Group Ltd.	6513	78. 17%
00939. HK	China Construction Bank Corp.	4797	68. 79%
01928. HK	Sands China Ltd.	4438	86. 89%

continued

UnderlyCode	Prod_name	Obs.	Prem%
00016. HK	Sun Hung Kai Properties Ltd.	2376	84.43%
00386. HK	China Petroleum & Chemical Corp.	2271	72.26%
00857. HK	Petrochina Company Limited	1863	72.25%
00001. HK	CK Hutchison Holdings Ltd.	1858	73.20%
01398. HK	Industrial and Commercial Bank	1517	65.59%
03988. HK	Bank of China Ltd.	956	66.63%
00688. HK	China Overseas Land & Investment Limited	770	79.87%
03323. HK	China National Building Material Company Limited	735	64.90%
00267. HK	CITIC Ltd.	476	72.69%
00914. HK	Anhui Conch Cement Company Limited	429	89.28%
03968. HK	China Merchants Bank Co.	395	56.46%
01088. HK	China Shenhua Energy Company Limited	379	91.03%
01988. HK	China Minsheng Banking Corp.	344	50.29%
01211. HK	BYD Company Limited	281	53.38%
03888. HK	Kingsoft Corporation Ltd.	222	85.14%
01171. HK	Yanzhou Coal Mining Company Limited	214	84.11%
03328. HK	Bank of Communications Co.	174	43.10%
00992. HK	Lenovo Group Ltd.	162	90.74%
00998. HK	China CITIC Bank Corporation Limited	127	61.42%
02601. HK	China Pacific Insurance (Group) Co.	117	94.02%
00728. HK	China Telecom Corporation Ltd.	115	82.61%
02388. HK	BOC Hong Kong (Holdings) Limited	107	74.77%
00358. HK	Jiangxi Copper Company Limited	103	90.29%
02888. HK	Standard Chartered PLC	76	82.89%
06837. HK	Haitong Securities Co.	69	100.00%
00762. HK	China Unicom (Hong Kong) Limited	68	91.18%
00902. HK	Huaneng Power International Inc.	63	93.65%
01898. HK	China Coal Energy Company Limited	56	55.36%
01800. HK	China Communications Construction Company Limited	54	90.74%
01359. HK	China Cinda Asset Management Co.	50	36.00%
00012. HK	Henderson Land Development Co. Ltd.	45	97.78%
00017. HK	New World Development Co. Ltd.	41	53.66%
02333. HK	Great Wall Motor Company Ltd.	38	89.47%
06030. HK	CITIC Securities Co. Ltd.	37	100.00%
01288. HK	Agricultural Bank of China Ltd.	33	78.79%
02328. HK	PICC Property and Casualty Company Limited	26	100.00%
00019. HK	Swire Pacific Ltd.	22	100.00%

continued

UnderlyCode	Prod_name	Obs.	Prem%
01339. HK	People's Insurance Co. (Gp) of China Ltd.	22	63. 64%
00011. HK	Hang Seng Bank Ltd.	20	80. 00%
01186. HK	China Railway Construction Corporation Limited	17	100. 00%
00006. HK	Power Assets Holdings Ltd.	13	100. 00%
00066. HK	MTR Corporation Limited	12	100. 00%
00002. HK	CLP Holdings Ltd.	11	100. 00%
00135. HK	Kunlun Energy Co. Ltd.	8	62. 50%
00494. HK	Li & Fung Limited	6	100. 00%
00023. HK	The Bank of East Asia Ltd.	4	100. 00%
02899. HK	Zijin Mining Group Company Limited	4	75. 00%
01113. HK	Cheung Kong Property Holdings Ltd.	3	33. 33%
01109. HK	China Resources Land Ltd.	2	50. 00%

Notes: This table lists the underlying stocks for the matched pairs of derivative warrants and options in our sample, including the codes for the underlying stocks, names of underlying firms, and the observations and premium proportions for the matched pairs of derivative warrants and options written on each individual stock.

Does Prospect Theory Explain Mutual Fund Performance? Evidence From China[①]

Abstract　We empirically investigated the role of prospect theory in explaining mutual fund performance. Using a comprehensive open-ended equity fund dataset in China covering a period from 2004 to 2017, we constructed a fund-level prospect theory value (TK) measure and find that it positively and significantly predicts future fund performance. This predictive power cannot be explained by existing risk factors or other fund characteristics. High TK funds also attract higher net fund inflows. Both performance persistence and price impact contribute to the fund performance predictability. Comprehensive robustness checks support our main findings.

Keywords　Mutual fund performance; Fund flow; Prospect theory; China

1　Introduction

Mutual fund is one of the largest and rapidly evolving financial markets in the world. According to the 2020 Investment Company Fact Book, the total net asset value of world-regulated mutual funds at the end of 2019 was 54.9 trillion USD.[②] Understanding what drives mutual fund performance is a long-

---

　　① Originally published in *Pacific-Basin Finance Journal* (vol. 73 2022) by Yu Bin, Shen Yifan, Jin Xuejun and Xu Qi.

　　② https://www.icifactbook.org/ch1/20_fb_ch1.

standing question that dates back to Jensen (1968). Previous studies have documented that fund size, age, skills, as well as a set of fund-level and market-level variables are informative about future fund performance. ① In contrast to other major asset classes, mutual funds are primarily held by *individual investors*. By the end of 2019, households (or retail investors) held 89% of mutual funds' total net assets in the US. ② This distinctive feature implies that fund investors have a particularly high propensity to trade speculatively. While it is true that fund managers' skills play a dominant role in fund performance, whether fund investor behavior may reveal important information about future fund performance remains unclear. ③

Prospect theory, developed by Kahneman and Tverskey (1979) and Tverskey and Kahneman (1992), provides a realistic decision-making framework for describing investor behaviour. Early studies on prospect theory mainly employ theoretical or experimental approaches. Recently, Barberis, Mukherjee, and Wang (2016) empirically examined the use of prospect theory to explain the cross-sectional variations in individual stock returns. The prospect theory framework is general and has been applied to investors in different financial markets and even to agents in a non-financial market environment when making decisions. ④

Mutual funds offer a unique research venue for understanding how irrational trading behaviors affect asset prices, given the dominance of

---

① For example, Kacperczyk, Van Nieuwerburgh, and Veldkamp (2014) show that time-varying managerial skills are related to future performance.

② https://www.icifactbook.org/ch3/20_fb_ch3.

③ Previous studies, such as Adebambo and Yan (2016), have investigated the role of the behavioral bias of fund managers, e. g. , overconfidence. Instead, in this paper, we focus on fund investor behaviors. Bailey, et al. (2011) use brokerage data to understand the behavioral bias of mutual fund investors. Different from their paper, we are interested in how fund investor behavior may reveal useful information to understand fund performance.

④ Besides the equity market evidence, Zhong and Wang (2018) and Xu et al. (2020) show that prospect theory value also predicts the cross-section of corporate bond returns and currency returns respectively. Levy (2003), for instance, considers the application of prospect theory in political sciences. Clark and Lisowski (2017) apply prospect theory to understand residential migration decisions.

individual investors. Prior studies extensively consider the impact of behavioral bias on mutual fund investors. For instance, Barber et al. (2005) show that mutual fund investors are influenced by salient and attention-grabbing information. This finding indicates that fund investors are likely to be attracted by the lottery-like features of fund performance. Bailey et al. (2011) document that behavioral biased fund investors make poor investment decisions and exhibit trend-chasing behaviors. Li et al. (2017) show that fund investors put higher weight on the worst signal when information uncertainty is high. Akbas and Genc (2020) find that fund investors tend to overweight the probability of extreme payoffs. These studies support the notion that fund investors are subject to behavioral bias. Therefore, prospect theory might be a useful framework to summarise their behaviors and hence may reveal important fund performance information.

However, empirical evidence on the potential role of prospect theory in explaining mutual fund performance remains lacking. Our study addresses this literature gap. We empirically investigate whether prospect theory contributes to understanding fund performance. Unlike existing fund studies, which mainly focus on the US market, our empirical investigation centers on Chinese mutual funds for at least two main reasons. First, the investor base in China differs substantially from that in the US and other developed countries. Chinese stock markets are dominated by unsophisticated and irrational individual investors. According to the 2019 Chinese Stock Market Investor Status Investigation Report, by the end of 2019, individual investors has accounted for 99.76% of all stock investors in China.[①] In particular, these unsophisticated investors in China generate extremely high turnover ratios. As documented by Pan et al. (2016), the turnover ratio in Chinese stock markets was as high as 500% in the 1990s while it remains at around 200% recently. Instead, turnover ratios in the US and other developed markets rarely exceed 100%. The constantly high turnover ratio in China implies that Chinese investors are in general more speculative than their pairs in developed

---

① https://www.sac.net.cnhyfwhydyt/202003/t20200330_142269.html.

markets. According to the 2019 Chinese Asset Management Industry Annual Report, by the end of 2018, individual investors had accounted for over 99.98% of all investors in mutual funds in China. ① As a result, we expect that speculative trading by fund investors in China should be more pronounced than that in developed markets. Barberis et al. (2016) suggest the effects of prospect theory on stock returns are stronger for stocks with lower institutional holdings. Namely, unsophisticated individual investors are more likely to rely on historical performance, e. g. , price charts and hence technical trading rules, to evaluate the attractiveness of stock, in line with prospect theory. Therefore, Chinese mutual funds provide us an ideal empirical setting to understand the effects of investor irrational trading behavior described by prospect theory on asset prices in a speculative market dominated by individual investors.

Second, the Chinese mutual fund industry saw rapid development in the past decades. Based on the 2019 Chinese Asset Management Industry Annual Report, by the end of 2018, the total net asset value for all mutual funds in China had exceeded 13 trillion RMB (or about 1.85 trillion USD). This number was below 1 trillion RMB (or about 0.14 trillion USD) in 2006. The total number of all types of mutual funds had approached 6,000 by the end of 2018, while the number was only about 500 in 2006. In our sample of actively traded open-ended equity funds, the number was only 18 in 2008, while the number jumped to 421 in 2017. The fast growth of the mutual fund industry both in terms of the number of funds and market capitalizations allows us to observe the time evolution of fund performance and the potential variations of predictability over time.

In our empirical analysis, we constructed a novel measure of fund-level

---

① www. amac. org. cn/researchstatistics/publication/zgzqtzjjynb/202001/t20200102_5414. html. By the end of 2018, total mutual fund accounts in China had exceeded 600,000, 000, of which 125,700 accounts belonged to institutional investors, while the rest are all individual investors. 99.98% is calculated as 1-(125,700/600,000,000). Moreover, the average account size was only 9,500 RMB (or about 1358.5 USD).

prospect theory value (*TK*) based on historical fund performance. [①]
Analogous to Barberis, et al. (2016), we assumed that fund investors
mentally represent the attractiveness of a fund based on its price chart; hence,
they rely on the historical return distribution to form the prospect theory value
of a fund. Following their study, we constructed our fund-level prospect
theory value by using a rolling window of 60 months of past fund returns. A
high-TK fund is more appealing to speculative individual investors. Our
sample period covers up to 421 open-ended equity funds in China from January
2004 to December 2017.

Our empirical results support the use of the prospect theory to explain
mutual fund performance. By grouping funds according to their TK values, we
observe an increasing pattern in fund performance from low-TK (less
appealing) to high-*TK* (more attractive) funds. The return spread between
high- and low-*TK* funds is not only statistically significant but also
economically meaningful (24 basis points per month or 2.8% per year).
Conventional systematic risk factors such as the three factors by Fama and
French (1993), four factors by Carhart (1997), or five factors by Fama and
French (2015) do not explain the return spread. We further account for other
commonly used fund-level characteristics using Fama and Macbeth (1973)
regressions. *TK* still positively and statistically significantly predicts the
subsequent month's fund performance. Collectively, our findings support the
predictive power of prospect theory value for future fund performance. High
TK funds are also associated with higher net inflows in the following quarter.
This observation is consistent with our prediction that prospect theory value
attracts the excess demands of irrational investors. Our results hold for each
prospect theory's value component. The economic magnitude is larger when
the convexity/concave component is used compared with the loss aversion or
probability weighting components.

At first sight, the positive *TK*-fund performance relation appears to be
distinct from the negative *TK*-stock return relation, as documented in

---

[①] The prospect theory value is constructed using the Tverskey and Kahneman (1992)
formula (and hence TK hereafter). Section 2 provides a detailed description of the formula.

Barberis, et al. (2016). We suggested that the institutional features of mutual funds help reconcile these differences. In stock markets, irrational investors are more likely to hold high-TK stocks. Their excess demand for these high-TK stocks cause overpricing, and hence these stocks earn lower returns in the future. For mutual funds, high-TK funds are also more likely to be held by irrational investors. However, their purchases (and net inflows) of these funds do not necessarily cause their overvaluation, given the absence of a commonly agreed *intrinsic value* of a fund. Moreover, even if irrational traders indeed push a high-TK fund to a high value, reversal is not necessarily expected, given the lack of tools (and hence virtually impossible) for rational arbitragers to "short" these "overvalued" funds. Therefore, our fund-level findings are not necessarily inconsistent with the existing evidence in stock markets.

What drives the positive TK-fund performance relationship? We considered two plausible explanations for this: performance persistence and price impact. These two explanations are not mutually exclusive, and both receive empirical support. First, since fund-level prospect theory value is constructed based on historical fund performance, the positive relationship may be due to persistent fund performance. Namely, high-TK funds may be those funds with historically better performance, and they tend to continue performing well in the future. We found that fund-level TK is positively correlated with stock-level TK as well as stock-picking skills and the fund gap, while it is negatively correlated with the Churn rate. Hence, our results confirm that high-TK funds indeed have historically better performance, supporting explanation of performance persistence. The predictive power of TK cannot be captured by existing fund persistence indicators such as fund momentum. Reference-dependent preference or disposition effect does not fully account for this predictability.

Second, we investigated whether the price impact generates this positive relationship. Since high-TK funds have higher future net fund inflows, the strong future performance of high-TK funds may be due to the use of newly injected money. One plausible explanation is that funds with high market power use these new cash inflows to reinvest in those stocks they already hold. Buying pressure pushes these stock prices higher and hence improves the fund performance[①]. The price impact explanation requires two premises. Initially, the fund should indeed use the new money to buy the stocks they hold. Moreover, the fund should have the market power to influence the stock prices. Our empirical results are in line with both conditions. High-TK funds indeed buy high TK stocks that they have already held. The TK-performance relation is also stronger for funds with a higher average purchase size, and hence, more likely to influence stock prices. These findings support the price impact explanation. We additionally documented that the predictive pattern persists up to nine months ahead, then becomes insignificant, and eventually reverses. Therefore, although both effects matter, the performance persistence effect dominates.

We conducted a battery of robustness checks and additional analyses. Our results remain robust when considering alternative performance measures, alternative estimation windows, non-crisis periods, lottery features, and fund momentum orthogonalized measures, as well as a fund style-adjusted measure. This positive relationship is also stronger when fund cash holdings and fund risk are low. Using stock portfolio-level prospect theory value does not replicate the main finding, highlighting the distinctive information at the fund level. In short, our findings are robust across different specifications.

The overall contribution of this study is two-fold. First, we extend the literature on mutual fund performance by introducing a new fund return predictor motivated by a behavioral theory. Previous studies (e. g. , Jenson, 1969; Henriksson, 1984; Treynor Mazuy, 1966) suggest that fund performance is linked to fund managers' stock-picking and market timing skills. Grinblatt and Titman (1992) find that past fund performance contains useful information for investors seeking funds with high future abnormal returns. Jordan and Riley (2015) show that the past volatility of mutual fund

---

① Fund managers often use the above means to improve performance ranking at the end of the quarter or year, also known as portfolio pumping, which has been observed and widely studied by scholars (e. g. Li & Wu, 2019).

returns predicts future performance. Dong et al. (2019) and Karagiannis and Tolikas (2019) document that liquidity risk and and tail risks predict mutual fund performance. [1] Our study is among the first in the literature to consider a new fund performance predictor motivated by prospect theory. We find that the new measure has non-redundant predictive power for fund performance.

Several recent studies are related to our study. Akbas and Genc (2020) show that mutual fund investors overweight the probability of extreme outcomes using the maximum monthly return (Max) by Bali et al. (2011). Heuson et al. (2020) suggest that the skewness of hedge fund returns is associated with managerial skills and future performance. While both MAX and skewness are related to our measure, we show that the predictive power of our prospect theory value goes beyond the existing proxies for lottery-like properties. Our results suggest that the function form of the total prospect theory value plays a more critical role than the probability weighting component alone.

A concurrent study by Guo and Schonleber (2021) examines prospect theory in US mutual funds. [2] They also show that prospect theory value positively predicts fund flow, consistent with our China evidence. However, our paper differs from theirs in several important aspects. First, we aim to investigate whether prospect theory can help to understand fund performance in an emerging mutual fund industry in China while they primarily focus on

---

[1]   Other studies show that fund holding data is also informative about future fund performance (Cremers & Petajisto, 2009; Petajisto, 2013). Kacperczyk et al. (2014) construct managers' timing and picking ability measures based on holding information and find that skilled managers could generate persistent good performance for up to one year. Bollen and Busse (2004) find superior performance from mutual fund managers is short-lived. Another stream of studies also considers the use of different performance measures. Goetzmann et al. (2007) suggest that fund managers may manipulate traditional performance measures for the motivation of window dressing. They propose a manipulation-proof performance measure (MMPM) to better evaluate fund performance. Chen et al. (2018) confirm that using MMPM could help to select the superior managers who can outperform their counterparts for up to six months.

[2]   We thank an anonymous referee for informing us about this parallel paper.

using prospect theory to explain fund flows in the well-developed industry in the US. Second，we provide robust evidence that prospect theory value positively predicts Chinese fund performance while significant evidence on performance in the US sample is lacking. The fund-level prospect theory value and the stock portfolio-level prospect theory value are positively correlated in China while such link is weak in the US. We attribute these differences in results to differences in investor base in the two markets. Unlike the US mutual fund industry，which is relatively mature，the Chinese mutual fund industry is still developing. Given the overall speculative nature of the Chinese stock market，Chinese mutual fund managers might be more subjective to behavioral bias. [1] As a result，prospect theory may play a more important role in Chinese mutual funds，in line with its stronger predictive power for performance. Third，we provided additional evidence that performance persistence and price impact are plausible explanations for the positive TK-fund performance relation we uncovered in China. Overall，this paper and Guo and Schonleber（2021）contribute to the literature in different ways and collectively support the application of prospect theory in the mutual fund industry.

---

[1] Several previous studies have already shown that mutual fund managers are subject to behavioral bias. For instance，O'Connell and Teo（2009）show that institutional investors aggressively reduce risk following the loss and mildly increase risk following the gain，consistent with the dynamic loss aversion. Goetzmann et al.（2015）find that professional investors are subject to investor moods induced by the weather. Edelen et al.（2016）show that institutional investors have a strong tendency to buy overvalued stocks. Adebambo and Yan（2016）suggest that fund managers overconfidence and self-attribution bias contribute to explaining the momentum effect. Du et al.（2021）document that fund managers' trading experience tends to bias their stock repurchase decisions. These prior studies show that fund managers could present behavioral bias，in line with our analysis. Therefore，even these sophisticated professional investors are also likely to make their investment decisions based on the prospect theory framework，albeit probably to a less extent compared to individual investors. We suggest that the effect tends to be particular pronounced in the Chinese mutual fund industry. For instance，a recent work on Chinese mutual funds by Jin et al.（2021）finds that high-performing funds experiencing high abnormal inflow tend to buy risky stocks and past-winner stocks.

Second, our study also enriches the literature on the asset pricing implications of prospect theory in general by providing new evidence from the mutual fund industry, an important financial market dominated by individual investors. Several studies have applied this theoretical framework to understand asset prices. [①] Empirical studies such as Kumar (2009), Boyer et al. (2010), Bali et al. (2011), and Conrad, et al. (2013) provide evidence that different measures of skewness and extreme returns predict the cross-section of stock returns. Barberis et al. (2016) construct individual stock-level prospect theory value and find that prospect theory value negatively predicts the cross-section of stock returns. Our study complements existing studies that apply prospect theory to equity markets and other asset classes. This study provides new empirical insights into the positive relationship between prospect theory value and fund performance.

The remainder of this paper is organised as follows. Section 2 highlights the main features of prospect theory, introduces the construction of the fund-level prospect theory value, and describes the main dataset and other variables. Section 3 reports the main empirical findings on the role of prospect theory value in explaining fund performance and fund flow. Section 4 provides additional empirical results to understand potential explanations for predictability. Section 5 summarizes the results of comprehensive robustness checks and additional analyses. Section 6 concludes the paper.

2 Data and methodology

2.1 Prospect theory and fund-level prospect theory value

In this section, we briefly describe the major features of prospect theory and then introduce the empirical procedures to construct prospect theory value at the fund level.

---

① Barberis et al. (2001) provide a framework based on prospect theory to explain equity premium, excess volatility, and predictability puzzles. Barberis and Huang (2008) show theoretically that prospect theory predicts the pricing of skewness in stock returns.

Prospect theory deviates from the conventional and rational expected utility (EU) framework from two main aspects. Initially, prospect theory replaces the utility function from the EU framework with a value function. The value function has some unique properties such as loss aversion and concaves in the gain while convex in the loss regions. Therefore, the value function is expected to better capture more realistic decision-making for investors in the real world. Moreover, prospect theory also has a probability weighting function. In the EU framework, the expected utility is computed based on the weighted average of utility value under different states of the world. Therefore, the weight is a linear function of the true probability for each state realization. In contrast, prospect theory allows for a nonlinear probability weighting function. Specifically, investors tend to overweight extreme tail events with small probability due to the lottery-like preference. In short, prospect theory provides a more realistic decision-making framework to describe the way investors evaluate the risk they faced.

We assume a non-trivial proportion of fund investors think in line with prospect theory. These prospect theory fund investors mentally represent the risk of a fund using the historical performance or the price chart. Hence, we use the historical fund performance to construct the empirical measure of fund-level prospect theory value. Analog to Barberis et al. (2016), we consider a vector of K consecutive fund return series r and sort them in increasing order,

$$\left(r_{-m},\frac{1}{k};r_{-m+1},\frac{1}{k};\cdots;r_{-1},\frac{1}{k};r_1,\frac{1}{k};\cdots;r_{n-1},\frac{1}{k};r_n,\frac{1}{k}\right) \quad (1)$$

There are m negative observations and n positive observations each with a probability of $\frac{1}{K}$. According to Tverskey and Kahnman (1992), prospect theory value (TK) can be defined as follows,

$$TK \equiv \sum_{i=-m}^{n} \pi_i v(r_i) \quad (2)$$

where π_i is the probability weighting function and $v(r_i)$ is the value function for the gain or loss of a gamble, i. e. , the vector of return in our case. The probability weighting function is defined as,

$$\pi_i = \begin{cases} w^+(p_i + \cdots + p_n) - w^+(p_{i+1} + \cdots + p_n), & 0 \leq i \leq n \\ w^-(p_{-m} + \cdots + p_i) - w^-(p_{-m} + \cdots + p_{i-1}), & -m \leq i \leq 0 \end{cases} \quad (3)$$

where probability weighting functions for gain and loss are defined separately,

$$w^+(P) = \frac{P^\gamma}{(P^\gamma + (1-P)^\gamma)^{1/\gamma}}, \quad w^-(P) = \frac{P^\delta}{(P^\delta + (1-P)^\delta)^{1/\delta}} \tag{4}$$

The value function is defined as,

$$v(r) = \begin{cases} r^a & r \geqslant 0 \\ -\lambda(-r)^a & r < 0 \end{cases} \tag{5}$$

In summary, the prospect theory value (TK) can be rewritten as

$$TK \equiv \sum_{j=-m}^{-1} v(r_j) \left[w^- \left(\frac{j+m+1}{K} \right) - w^- \left(\frac{j+m}{K} \right) \right]$$
$$+ \sum_{j=1}^{n} v(r_j) \left[w^+ \left(\frac{n-j-1}{K} \right) - w^+ \left(\frac{n-j}{K} \right) \right] \tag{6}$$

α, λ, γ, and δ are four parameters characterizing the probability weighting and the value functions. α measures the curvature of the value function. λ governs the severity of kink. The higher the value of λ, the more loss-averse the investor is. γ, and δ capture the overweight of tails. Lower values refer to higher overweighting of tails. In this paper, we follow the original parameter values as shown in Tversky and Kahnman (1992), i. e. (α, λ, γ, δ) is (0.88, 2.25, 0.61, 0.69). These parameters are also used by Barberis et al. (2016) in their study of individual stocks. In the robustness check part, we also consider different components of the total TK that can turn off some parameters.

In our paper, we used the monthly fund raw return, which is the simple return of fund net asset value (NAV) over the month as our main input for the TK formula. We compute monthly TK for each fund using a rolling window with a size of 60 months. [1]

2.2 Data and fund Characteristics

Our data is collected from the Chinese Stock Market and Accounting Research

---

[1] We follow Barberis et al. (2016) and use the rolling window with the size of the past 60 months to compute prospect theory value in our study. In the robustness check, we show that our results are unaffected when other window sizes (Table A5 in Internet Appendix) or fund style-adjusted return (Table A11 in Internet Appendix) are considered in constructing the fund-level prospect theory value.

(CSMAR) database and the WIND database from January 2004 to December 2017.[①] We collect the net asset values (NAV) of mutual funds from the CSMAR. Mutual funds' stock holding, funds size, funds age, and other stock-level data are obtained from the WIND. Our main empirical analysis focuses on the monthly frequency. Mutual funds in China only disclose their top ten stock holdings in each quarter while they are required to disclose their all holdings at the end of June and December. Therefore, variables involving stock holdings, such as the portfolio-level TK (the stock-level TK aggregating to the fund level)[②], stock picking, and market timing, are available at the semi-annual frequency. Hence, we used the latest values of these variables until the information about fund holding is updated.

We focus on actively managed open-end equity mutual funds, excluding index funds, ETFs, and QFIIs. The final sample in our empirical analysis includes up to 421 funds from December 2008 to December 2017[③], while the exact number of funds varies over time. Since Chinese funds grow rapidly over the past two decades and they are very rare to cease to operate, survivorship bias is virtually negligible when using Chinese mutual fund data (Chen et al., 2018). In addition to conventional mutual fund level characteristics, we also construct variables related to lottery properties, such as skewness and MAX, for comparisons and control purposes. We describe all of the main variables in Appendix A.

---

① The starting date is chosen given the data available consideration. Before 2004, the number of funds in China is too small to conduct powerful empirical analysis, especially in portfolio analysis.

② We use the stock-level TK (aggregating to the fund level) or the portfolio-level TK interchangeably. To notice, the fund-level TK is computed from historical fund performance, while the portfolio-level TK is calculated as the weighted average of the stock-level TK based on stock historical performance, where the weight is based on each fund's stock holding information. We provide more details in Section 4.5.

③ Our fund-level TK measure is calculated using the past five years (60 months) observations, therefore, our final sample starts from December 2008, where the first TK observation is available.

3 Empirical findings

3.1 Summary Statistics

This section presents the main empirical findings. Table 1 provides the descriptive statistics. In Panel A, we observed the rapid growth in the number of funds from 18 to 421 from 2008 to 2017. The average size of each fund is relatively stable over time. The fund age is also relatively stable, indicating that many new funds are launched. The average fund raw return varies across time from − 2.3% to 3.9%. Skewness is almost all negative for different years, indicating that fund performance surffers from crash risk. Our main variable fund-level prospect theory value (TK) is negative on average across time and it ranges from − 0.069 to − 0.027. Summary statistics of the main fund-level variables by pooling all observations and pairwise correlations of these variables are reported in Panel B and Panel C.

3.2 Univariate portfolio sorting

We then report our main empirical results on the link between prospect theory value and mutual fund performance. We used a cross-sectional portfolio-sorting approach to understand the predictive relationship between TK and fund performance. [1] At the beginning of each month, we sorted all funds into five portfolios according to their latest TK values. Portfolio 1 contains funds with the lowest TKs, whereas Portfolio 5 includes funds with the highest TKs. We hold each portfolio for one month, record portfolio returns, and

---

[1] Portfolio sorting is a conventional tool used in the empirical asset pricing literature to understand the cross-sectional return predictive power. We used it to examine the link between TK and fund performance. The long-short return fund performance spread can be viewed as a hypothetical strategy employed by a fund of fund (FOF) manager who buys high TK funds while shorts low TK funds. In practice, we recognized that it is virtually impossible to short a mutual fund. Instead, we used the long-short return spread to quantify the economic value of the predictive power of TK for fund performance.

rebalance portfolios every month to reflect the updated TK values.

Table 2 reports portfolio sorting results. Panel A reports the portfolio performance. We report raw return and risk-adjusted return using CAPM, Fama and French (1993) three-factor model, Carhart (1997) four-factor model, Fama and French (2015) five-factor model, as well as a six-factor model augmenting the five-factor with a momentum factor. We observed an increase while not a strictly monotonic pattern for returns from low-TK funds to high-TK funds. Average raw returns range from 96 basis points to 120 basis points per month. A high minus low return spread is 24 basis points per month (or 2.8% annually). The return spread is both economically meaningful and statistically significant. This finding is also illustrated in Figure 1. We observe that funds with the highest TK consistently outperform their low TK counterparts over time. Our results hold for both raw return and risk-adjusted return. Therefore, the predictive power is unlikely to be driven by exposures to well-known systematic risk factors in the literature. Our findings support the predictive power of fund-level prospect theory value for future fund performance. In Panel B, we report the average values of characteristics for each portfolio. We find that conventional characteristics do not present significant spreads between high and low prospect theory value sorted portfolios. Therefore, the predictive power of fund-level prospect theory value is unlikely driven by these existing characteristics. ①

In short, our portfolio sorting analysis shows that prospect theory value positively and significantly predicts one-month ahead fund returns. The predictability is not due to the exposure to the commonly known systematic risk factors.

3.3 Multivariate tests for fund performance

Then, we explored the relationship between fund-level prospect theory value and fund performance by controlling for a set of fund characteristics. We

---

① In addition to the average characteristics, we also considered which type of stocks will those high (low) TK funds buy in Table 9 in Section 4. We find that high TK funds tend to buy stocks with higher stock TK.

measured fund performance using the rank return in the spirit of Sirri and Tufano (1998) and Huang et al. (2007). Specifically, we assigned continuous scores or fractional performance ranks (rank return hereafter) from zero (the lowest performance) to one (the highest performance) to the cross-section of funds according to their current month fund raw returns. We defined this performance rank score as the rank return and use it as the dependent variable in our multivariate regression analysis. ① We employed the conventional Fama and Macbeth (1973) approach by regressing one-month ahead fund performance on the current month TK and other fund characteristics. We consider the following baseline model specification,

$$RankReturn_{i,t+1} = const + \beta_{tk} TK_{i,t} + \gamma' Z_{i,t} + \varepsilon_{i,t+1} \tag{7}$$

Table 1 Descriptive statistics

Panel A: average fund characteristics										
	2008	2009	2010	2011	2012	2013	2014	2015	2016	2017
No. of funds	18	48	78	133	177	213	259	314	367	421
TK	−0.029	−0.027	−0.030	−0.043	−0.069	−0.054	−0.042	−0.031	−0.047	−0.038
Log(Size)	21.470	21.907	22.024	21.996	21.944	21.797	21.381	20.961	20.554	20.478
Log(Age)	1.748	1.750	1.816	1.857	1.887	1.971	2.031	2.075	2.113	2.151
Log(Co_Size)	23.778	24.008	23.968	23.794	23.624	23.611	23.460	23.374	23.162	23.197
Log(Co_Age)	2.066	2.110	2.164	2.219	2.306	2.400	2.474	2.536	2.600	2.662
EXP(%)	2.761	2.780	2.783	2.783	2.788	2.787	2.783	2.781	2.779	2.748
Net flow	0.084	−0.031	−0.002	0.010	−0.010	−0.026	−0.062	−0.108	0.035	0.004

---

① Using the rank return helps to mitigate the potential impact of outliers on estimation results. Previous studies also use the past 12-month returns to calculate performance rank. We focus on the current month return in the regression analysis, as our fund-level prospect theory value TK is computed using past 60-month returns. Therefore, using the cumulative return as a dependent variable may generate artificially high correlations due to the overlapping of observations. Instead, this issue does not exist in our current empirical specification. Our main results remain qualitatively unchanged when the raw return and the excess return relative to the market are used as dependent variables. We also replace our dependent variable by other performance measures including CAPM alpha, Fama-French three-factor alpha, Carhart four-factor alpha, Fama-French five-factor alpha, and six-factor alpha controlling for Fama-French five-factor and momentum factor. Our results remain unaffected. Therefore, our findings are not due to specific investment style or existing systematic risk factors. These results are provided in the Internet Appendix Table A1.

continued

Panel A: average fund characteristics

	2008	2009	2010	2011	2012	2013	2014	2015	2016	2017
Max	−0.005	0.028	0.051	0.051	0.059	0.067	0.059	0.106	0.083	0.045
Skewness	0.151	0.128	−0.180	0.118	−0.275	0.279	−0.365	0.161	0.072	0.056
Raw return	0.028	0.039	0.007	−0.023	0.005	0.011	0.018	0.036	−0.008	0.012

Panel B: summary statistics.

	Mean	Median	Std	Q1	Q3
Net flow	−0.021	−0.031	0.2	−0.082	−0.004
Raw return	0.011	0.012	0.074	−0.023	0.044

	Mean	Median	Std	Q1	Q3
Log($Size$)	21.122	21.372	1.338	20.365	22.09
Log(Age)	2.038	2.02	0.272	1.809	2.249
Log(Co_Size)	23.409	23.582	1.037	22.787	24.111
Log(Co_Age)	2.49	2.512	0.275	2.319	2.682
EXP(%)	2.775	2.75	0.091	2.75	2.75
TK	−0.044	−0.042	0.016	−0.054	−0.033
Max	0.067	0.058	0.047	0.037	0.086
Skewness	0.012	0.021	0.682	−0.358	0.417

Panel C: correlation matrix.

	Net flow	Raw return	Log ($Size$)	Log (Age)	Log (Co_Size)	Log (Co_Age)	EXP (%)	TK	Max	Skewness
Net flow	1.000									
Raw return	−0.052	1.000								
Log($Size$)	0.056	0.002	1.000							
Log(Age)	−0.055	0.010	0.091	1.000						
Log(Co_Size)	−0.022	0.071	0.552	0.047	1.000					
Log(Co_Age)	0.022	−0.025	−0.094	0.418	0.259	1.000				
EXP(%)	−0.012	−0.011	0.113	−0.018	0.052	−0.046	1.000			
TK	0.019	0.165	−0.013	0.093	0.114	0.168	−0.048	1.00		
Max	0.025	−0.019	0.047	0.142	−0.002	0.045	0.082	0.089	1.00	
Skewness	0.015	0.018	−0.034	0.010	−0.006	0.048	0.001	0.081	0.138	1.00

This table reports summary statistics of China's open-end equity mutual funds (excluding index funds, ETFs, and QFIIs) in the year-end from 2008 to 2017. Stock funds are required to hold at least 60% net asset value in stocks at any time. Panel A reports average fund characteristics over time. Panel B reports mean, median, standard deviation, Q1 (bottom 25%), and Q3 (top 25%) value of fund characteristics. Panel C reports a pairwise correlation matrix of these fund characteristics. We consider the following fund characteristics: TK (TK is the prospect theory value of a fund's historical return distribution), fund size, fund age, fund company size, fund company age, total expense (management expense plus loads), average quarterly flow per fund, Max and Skewness of monthly style-adjusted return in the last 12 months, monthly fund raw return.

where $RankReturn_{i,t+1}$ is our dependent variable rank return for fund i in month $t+1$, and $TK_{i,t}$ is our main independent variable prospect theory value for fund i in month t. $Z_{i,t}$ refers to a vector of fund characteristics for fund i in month t, including fund size, fund age, fund company size, fund company age, total expense (management expense plus load), churn rate, lagged rank return, net fund flow, Max, and skewness. We obtained the time-series average of cross-sectional regression coefficients and use Newey and West (1987)'s heteroskedasticity and serial correlated corrected standard errors to make the inference.

Table 2　Univariate portfolio sorting

	Low	2	3	4	High	High-Low	t-statistics
Panel A: Portfolio performance							
Raw Return	0.010	0.011	0.011	0.012	0.012	0.002**	(2.09)
Alpha CAPM	−0.002	−0.001	0.000	0.001	0.002	0.003**	(2.53)
Alpha FF3F	−0.002	−0.001	0.000	0.001	0.001	0.004**	(2.51)
Alpha Cahart4F	−0.002	−0.001	0.000	0.001	0.001	0.004***	(2.67)
Alpha FF5F	−0.003	−0.001	−0.001	−0.001	0.000	0.003**	(2.36)
Alpha FF5F+UMD	−0.003	−0.001	−0.001	0.000	0.000	0.003**	(2.54)
Panel B: Portfolio characteristics							
TK	−0.055	−0.046	−0.041	−0.037	−0.028	0.027***	(11.36)
P_Size	22.671	22.715	22.664	22.607	22.627	−0.043	(−0.64)
P_BM	0.641	0.661	0.638	0.644	0.646	0.004	(0.35)
P_GP	0.243	0.252	0.248	0.252	0.252	0.009	(1.50)
P_TK	−0.034	−0.034	−0.034	−0.034	−0.035	−0.001	(−0.60)
P_Max	0.047	0.047	0.047	0.047	0.047	0.000	(0.45)
P_Skewness	0.180	0.199	0.187	0.201	0.206	0.026	(0.82)
P_Mom	0.226	0.218	0.224	0.218	0.210	−0.016*	(−1.74)

This table reports portfolio sorting results through ranking funds by their monthly TK. Panel A reports portfolio performance. We consider raw returns, and returns adjusted by CAPM, Fama and French three-factor model, Carhart four-factor model, Fama and French five-factor model, and a sixfactor model include momentum. Those six factors are MKTRF, SMB, HML, RMW, CMA, and UMD. Newey-West t-statistics are reported in the parenthesis. ***, **, and * denote significance at the 1%, 5%, and 10% level, respectively. Panel B reports average values of portfolio characteristics when forming these *TK* sorted portfolios.

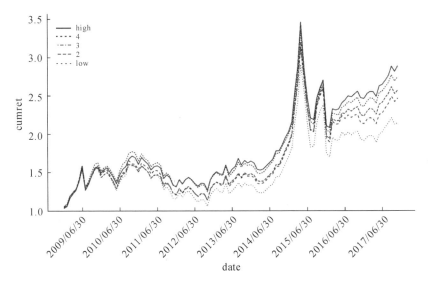

Fig. 1   This figure plots the cumulative returns of five fund-level prospect theory value (*TK*) sorted fund portfolios over our sample period

Table 3 reports the regression results. We find that *TK* consistently predicts fund performance in the next month with and without controlling for other characteristics. The predictive relation is statistically significant and economically sizeable. An increase of one standard in *TK* is associated with a 1.77% increase in the subsequent month's fund rank return.[①] Max and skewness have also been used in extant studies to measure lottery-like properties and predict stock returns. In our analysis, the predictive power of *TK* dominates Max and skewness for future fund performance. When *TK* is included, fund age and churn rate remain statistically significant, while fund size and net fund flow only marginally relate to performance. Fund company size and age, and total expense are insignificantly correlated with future performance when *TK* is considered. We also controled for fund selectivity using fund *R*-squared as in Amihud and Goyenko (2013) and take account of

---

① 1.77% is calculated as 1.108 (coefficient) times 0.016 (standard deviation of the independent variable).

Table 3 Cross-sectional regression analysis for fund performance

	(1)	(2)	(3)	(4)	(5)	(6)	(7)	(8)	(9)	(10)
TK	1.1080**	1.1314**	1.0980**	1.0849**	1.3392***	1.3846***	1.1324**	1.0845**	1.0770**	1.2287**
	(2.16)	(2.09)	(2.05)	(2.45)	(2.84)	(2.91)	(2.57)	(2.08)	(2.42)	(2.51)
Log(Size)		−0.0030	−0.0092**	−0.0074*	−0.0115**	−0.0123**	−0.0078**	−0.0076*	−0.0108**	−0.0114**
		(−0.67)	(−2.04)	(−1.84)	(−2.23)	(−2.55)	(−2.14)	(−1.90)	(−2.30)	(−2.22)
Log(Age)		−0.0915***	−0.0855***	−0.0916***	−0.0885***	−0.0938***	−0.0980***	−0.1077***	−0.0908***	−0.0906**
		(−2.79)	(−2.72)	(−3.02)	(−2.89)	(−3.01)	(−2.78)	(−2.80)	(−2.75)	(−2.56)
Log(Co_Size)		0.0063	0.0062	0.0042	0.0058	0.0070	0.0056	0.0065	0.0042	0.0049
		(1.36)	(1.31)	(1.05)	(1.38)	(1.65)	(1.34)	(1.57)	(0.72)	(1.17)
Log(Co_Age)		0.0243	0.0178	0.0264*	0.0213	0.0192	0.0257*	0.0269*	0.0203	0.0214
		(1.41)	(1.09)	(1.82)	(1.47)	(1.38)	(1.79)	(1.89)	(1.44)	(1.51)
EXP		0.0420	0.0339	0.0283	0.0412	0.0338	0.0058	−0.0033	0.0246	0.0347
		(0.91)	(0.76)	(0.73)	(0.91)	(0.87)	(0.21)	(−0.13)	(0.66)	(0.76)
Churn rate			−1.1589***	−1.0984***	−1.2984***	−1.1938**	−1.0466**	−0.8457**	−1.2746***	−1.1770**
			(−2.65)	(−2.64)	(−2.71)	(−2.59)	(−2.54)	(−2.03)	(−2.84)	(−2.37)
Rank return				0.0374	0.0309	0.0399	0.0373	0.0453	0.0284	0.0281
				(1.42)	(1.17)	(1.40)	(1.40)	(1.57)	(1.08)	(1.07)
Net flow					0.0800*	0.0801**	0.1023**	0.1040**	0.0952**	0.0727*
					(1.94)	(2.02)	(2.03)	(2.11)	(2.02)	(1.77)
Max						0.1251		0.1577		
						(0.90)		(1.08)		
Skewness							−0.0012	−0.0025		

	(1)	(2)	(3)	(4)	(5)	(6)	(7)	(8)	(9)	(10)
R^2							(−0.21)	(−0.39)		
MOM									0.0033	0.0579
									(0.06)	(1.36)
Constant	0.5518***	0.4679***	0.6458***	0.6368***	0.6763***	0.6881***	0.6925***	0.6861***	0.7371***	0.6990***
	(28.70)	(2.73)	(3.77)	(3.90)	(4.65)	(4.70)	(4.59)	(4.57)	(4.30)	(4.49)
Observations	21,515	21,283	21,266	21,266	21,236	21,236	21,196	21,196	21,236	21,236
R-squared	0.0315	0.113	0.130	0.199	0.218	0.238	0.233	0.252	0.241	0.236

This table reports results about the predictive power of fund-level prospect theory value for the subsequent month fund performance using Fama and Macbeth (1973) regressions, as shown in Eq. (7). Fund performance is measured using rank return in month $t+1$, which is calculated by assigning ranking scores from zero (low performance) to one (high performance) to the cross-section of funds according to their fund raw returns in each month. TK and other control variables are in month t. TK is the prospect theory value of a fund's historical return distribution. The control variables include the logarithm of fund size, the logarithm of fund age, the logarithm of fund company size, the logarithm of fund company age, total expense (management expense plus loads), the churn rate of fund portfolio introduced by Yan and Zhang (2009), the lagged monthly ranked return, the lagged quarterly net fund flow, the max and skewness of fund return, the fund R squared, and fund momentum. Time-series average coefficients and the Fama-Macbeth t-statistics (in parentheses) calculated with Newey-West robust standard errors are reported. *, **, and *** denote significance at the 10%, 5%, and 1% levels, respectively.

fund persistence using fund momentum. ① Our main results remain valid when these variables are controlled.

In summary, our multivariate regression results confirm the aforementioned portfolio-level results. We show that fund TK can predict fund performance and that the predictive power is not subsumed by existing fund characteristics.

3.4　Effects on fund flow

In addition to the effect of prospect theory value on fund performance, we further investigate the relationship between prospect theory value and fund flow. Intuitively, funds with higher prospect theory values attract investors to hold, in the absence of other news. Therefore, we expect that prospect theory value should be positively associated with fund net inflow in the subsequent period. Since Chinese mutual funds only disclose fund flow quarterly, we check whether the prospect theory value predicts the subsequent quarter fund net inflow.

We considered the same Fama and Macbeth (1973) regression specification as above, except that we replace the dependent variable from fund performance to fund net inflow. We controled for fund characteristics as before. The specification is as follows,

$$NetFlow_{i,q+1} = const + \beta_{tk} TK_{i,q} + \gamma' Z_{i,q} + \varepsilon_{i,q+1} \tag{8}$$

where $NetFlow_{i,q+1}$ is the dependent variable net fund inflow for fund i in quarter q. Since our TK measure is on the monthly frequency, to match with the net flow at the quarterly frequency, we took the monthly average value within a quarter to obtain the quarterly measure of TK. Besides fund size and age, we also controlled for the lagged value of net flow and quarterly fund raw return in the quarter q. As before, we corrected for heteroskedasticity and serially correlated issues in standard errors.

Table 4 reports results on fund flow. We find that fund prospect theory

---

① Fund R-squared is calculated based on a 36-month rolling window estimation by regressing fund return on the CAPM model. Fund momentum is calculated using the cumulative fund return over the past 12 months and skipping the most recent month.

value positively and significantly predicts the next quarter fund net inflow. Hence our finding is consistent with the evidence using Max by Akbas and Genc (2020). A high value of *TK* indeed leads to the excess demands for this type of fund. The effect is not only statistically significant but also economically meaningful. An increase of one standard in fund *TK* is associated with a 1.48% increase in fund net inflow next quarter. [1] The effect cannot be subsumed by other fund variables that are associated with future inflow. [2] Controlling for skewness and Max does not affect the positive *TK*-net flow relation.

Table 4 Effects on fund flows

	(1)	(2)	(3)	(4)	(5)
TK	0.9247**	0.9958**	0.8529**	0.8033**	0.8027*
	(2.35)	(2.59)	(2.16)	(2.13)	(1.84)
Log(*Size*)		0.001	0.0012	0.0015	0.0019
		(0.36)	(0.39)	(0.47)	(0.90)
Log(*Age*)		−0.0328	−0.0182	−0.0236	−0.0317
		(−1.59)	(−0.96)	(−1.11)	(−1.30)
Log(*Co_Size*)		−0.0077*	−0.0076*	−0.0082**	−0.0106
		(−1.88)	(−1.88)	(−2.12)	(−1.37)
Log(*Co_Age*)		0.0185	0.0094	0.0102	0.0058
		(1.25)	(0.79)	(0.86)	(0.31)
EXP		0.0354*	0.0258	0.0219	0.0195
		(1.92)	(0.91)	(0.74)	(0.74)
Lagged net flow		0.1040***	0.0353	0.0412	0.0289
		(3.49)	(0.89)	(1.19)	(0.59)
L_ret			0.0097	0.0016	0.0044
			(0.28)	(0.04)	(0.11)
M_ret			0.0538***	0.0542***	0.0653**
			(2.85)	(2.90)	(2.53)

---

[1] 1.48% is calculated as 0.9247 (coefficient) times 0.016 (standard deviation of the independent variable).

[2] In addition to the regression analysis，we also conducted portfolio sorting analysis in the Internet Appendix Table A2 to understand the effect of *TK* on past and future fund flows. We find that *TK* is positively associated with both past and future fund net inflows. Therefore，the effect of *TK* seems to be persistent.

continued

	(1)	(2)	(3)	(4)	(5)
H_ret			0. 3595***	0. 3679***	0. 3907***
			(3. 59)	(3. 66)	(3. 43)
Skewness				0. 0036	−0. 0022
				(1. 08)	(−0. 68)
Max					0. 2781**
					(2. 29)
Constant	0. 0158	0. 1061	0. 0821	0. 1072	0. 1798
	(0. 66)	(1. 29)	(1. 09)	(1. 36)	(1. 51)
Observations	6722	6643	6643	6643	6591
R-squared	0. 02	0. 124	0. 174	0. 183	0. 196

This table reports the results of Fama and Macbeth (1973) regressions by regressing net inflow in the subsequent quarter on fund TK, as shown in Eq. (8). Net flow is calculated by Inflow minus Outflow in quarter $q+1$. TK and other control variables are in quarter q. TK is the prospect theory value of a fund's historical return distribution. The control variables include the logarithm of fund size, the logarithm of fund age, the logarithm of fund company size, the logarithm of fund company age, total expense (management expense plus loads), lagged net flow, quarterly return in the current quarter, and fund skewness and Max. Time-series average coefficients and the Fama-Macbeth t-statistics (in parentheses) calculated with Newey-West robust standard errors are reported. *, **, and *** denote significance at the 10%, 5%, and 1% levels, respectively.

Our results suggest that fund-level TK is positively associated with future fund performance and flow. Berk and Green (2004) document that fund performance and flow present a convex relationship. [①] Therefore, it is interesting to explore whether the convex relation holds in our sample and whether the TK-flow relation can be attributed to the documented convex relation. Specifically, we follow Sirri and Tufano (1998) and Huang et al. (2007) to construct fractional performance rank for funds to capture the convex flow-performance relationship. We define as follows: $L\_ret = Min (Rank\_ret, 0. 2)$, $M\_ret = Min (0. 6, Rank\_ret-L\_ret)$, and $H\_ret = Rank\_ret - L\_ret - M\_ret$, where $Rank\_ret$ is the funds' performance percentile. This

---

[①] We thank an anonymous referee for the suggestion to consider the convex relationship.

partition allows us to explore the flow sensitivity to the performance of different ranges. We included these variables in the fund flow regression. We find that funds with the best performance can attract additional flows, while those with poor performance have weak flow sensitivity. This finding confirms the convex flow-performance relationship in our sample, in line with the previous literature. Moreover, we show that the effect of TK on flow remains robust. Hence the effect of TK on fund flows cannot be fully attributed to this convex relationship.

In short, our results suggest that fund-level prospect theory value predicts not only future fund performance but also fund net inflows.

3.5 Prospect theory value components

Thus far, our results have focused on total prospect theory value. In this section, we consider different prospect theory value components, that is, loss-aversion (LA), convexity/concave (CC), and probability weighting (PW). We follow Barberis et al. (2016) and construct these prospect theory value components using different sets of parameters. Specifically, we use the set of parameters (α, λ, γ, δ) with the values of (1, 2.25, 1, 1), (0.88, 1, 1, 1)., and (1, 1, 0.61, 0.69) to obtain the LA, CC, and PW components respectively.

Table 5 replicates our main regression analysis results using different prospect theory value components. Two observations are noteworthy. First, we find that all components matter, indicating that the positive predictive relationship holds for all three types of behavioral bias. Second, we find that the economic magnitude of the CC component is slightly larger than that of other components. CC captures the asymmetric risk preference patterns in that investors are risk-averse at the gain region while they are risk-taking at the loss region. A larger magnitude of CC implies a potential disposition effect, in which investors tend to sell winning funds while holding losing funds. Previous studies, such as Grinblatt and Han (2005) show that investors with prospect theory preferences may generate a disposition effect, which can lead to an underreaction to news, and hence the momentum effect. The performance

Table 5 Prospect theory components

	LA	LA	LA	CC	CC	CC	PW	PW	PW
TK	2.0638***	2.1076***	1.8525**	3.2623***	2.8057***	2.3872***	1.9357***	1.8915***	1.8043***
	(2.82)	(2.84)	(2.13)	(3.26)	(2.92)	(2.66)	(2.90)	(2.71)	(2.78)
Log(Size)	-0.0016	-0.0108**	-0.0075*	-0.0026	-0.0111**	-0.0080**	-0.0023	-0.0122**	-0.0091**
	(-0.39)	(-2.21)	(-1.95)	(-0.60)	(-2.16)	(-2.06)	(-0.57)	(-2.28)	(-2.21)
Log(Age)	-0.0938***	-0.0850***	-0.1042***	-0.0685**	-0.0632**	-0.0775**	-0.0809***	-0.0702**	-0.0809***
	(-2.91)	(-2.74)	(-2.65)	(-2.50)	(-2.30)	(-2.43)	(-2.78)	(-2.55)	(-2.68)
Log(Co_Size)	0.0015	0.0040	0.0041	0.0012	0.0043	0.0045	0.0054	0.0079*	0.0080*
	(0.40)	(1.04)	(1.06)	(0.32)	(1.14)	(1.10)	(1.31)	(1.89)	(1.77)
Log(Co_Age)	0.0351*	0.0243*	0.0282**	0.0348**	0.0235	0.0248*	0.0308**	0.0184	0.0206
	(2.26)	(1.67)	(2.01)	(2.19)	(1.60)	(1.78)	(2.00)	(1.24)	(1.49)
EXP	0.0324	0.0386	-0.0018	0.0395	0.0449	0.0013	0.0427	0.0519	0.0067
	(0.83)	(0.91)	(-0.07)	(0.92)	(0.99)	(0.05)	(0.99)	(1.03)	(0.24)
Rank return	0.0362	0.0307	-0.8458**	0.0296	0.0274	-0.8933**	0.0390	0.0343	-0.9847**
	(1.35)	(1.16)	(-2.00)	(1.05)	(0.99)	(-2.19)	(1.43)	(1.25)	(-2.53)
Churn rate		-1.1866**	0.0427		-1.1441**	0.0425		-1.2781***	0.0480
		(-2.60)	(1.51)		(-2.56)	(1.48)		(-2.83)	(1.63)
Net flow		0.0829*	0.1071**		0.0870**	0.1020**		0.0830**	0.0949**
		(1.97)	(2.14)		(2.12)	(2.22)		(2.08)	(2.15)
Max			0.1665			0.1347			0.1289
			(1.22)			(1.02)			(0.91)
Skewness			-0.0032			-0.0041			-0.0033
			(-0.50)			(-0.68)			(-0.56)
Constant	0.5137***	0.6670***	0.7081***	0.3774**	0.5204***	0.5829***	0.3463**	0.5086***	0.5593***
	(3.33)	(4.60)	(4.52)	(2.50)	(3.60)	(3.72)	(2.31)	(3.44)	(3.65)

	LA	LA	LA	CC	CC	CC	PW	PW	PW
Observations	21,283	21,236	21,196	21,283	21,236	21,196	21,283	21,236	21,196
R-squared	0.184	0.219	0.251	0.178	0.212	0.244	0.173	0.209	0.242

This table reports results about the predictive power of fund TK on the subsequent month fund performance using different components of TK. Fund performance is measured using rank return in month t+1, which is calculated by assigning ranking scores from zero (low performance) to one (high performance) to the cross-section of funds according to their fund raw returns in each month. Prospect theory components and other control variables are in month t. We considered prospect theory value components, namely loss aversion (LA), convexity/concave (CC), and probability weighting (PW). Following Barberis et al. (2016), we compute these components by changing original total prospect theory value parameter values (α, λ, γ, δ) to (1,2.25,1,1) for LA, (0.8,1,1,1) for CC, and (1,1,0.61,0.69) for PW. The control variables include the logarithm of fund size, the logarithm of fund age, the logarithm of fund company size, the logarithm of fund company age, total expense (management expense plus loads), the churn rate of fund portfolio introduced by Yan and Zhang (2009), the lagged monthly ranked return, the lagged quarterly net fund flow, the max and skewness of fund return. Time-series average coefficients and the Fama-Macbeth t-statistics (in parentheses) calculated with Newey-West robust standard errors are reported. ``*``, ``**``, and ``***`` denote significance at the 10%, 5%, and 1% levels, respectively.

of the *CC* component in our case along with the positive predictive relationship, is broadly consistent with this reasoning. However, since other components, i. e. , loss-aversion and probability weighting also contribute to the predictive pattern, we suggest that the disposition effect is unlikely to be the sole mechanism driving the predictive relation. We conducted formal empirical analysis in Section 4 to further investigate potential explanations for the positive TK-performance relation.

4   Potential explanations

In this section, we attempt to shed light on the potential sources of predictability. We first discuss why the positive *TK*-fund performance relationship that we uncovered is not necessarily inconsistent with the negative TK-stock return relation shown in the literature. We then empirically explore two potential explanations for this positive relationship: performance persistence and price impact.

4.1   On the positive *TK*-performance relation: A discussion

Why do *TK*-sorted portfolios produce a positive return spread in mutual funds while the spread is negative when individual stocks are used as shown in the literature? We reconcile these different patterns by acknowledging and highlighting the distinctive institutional features of these two markets.

In stock markets, rational arbitragers can remove mispricing by profiting from potential arbitrage opportunities. Therefore, when irrational traders bid a high-*TK* stock price to a higher level and cause overpricing, rational arbitragers rush into the market and correct mispricing by shorting these overvalued stocks. Consequently, high-*TK* stocks earn lower returns on average because of the reversal effect.

In contrast, similar arbitrage and reversal are difficult in mutual funds. Initially, while it is possible to rank different funds according to various performance measures, it is extremely difficult to identify the intrinsic value of a fund. Consequently, it is not easy to define an overpriced fund. Moreover, the net value of a fund or the fund "price" can hardly be influenced by the trading of fund investors directly in the same way as stock investors affect stock price. The net value of a fund is determined by fund performance, rather than by the demand or supply for fund issuance. Therefore, even if a high-TK fund may attract more investment from irrational investors, these investors offer more cash inflows to fund managers, but do not necessarily bid the fund's net asset value to be higher. Furthermore, unlike stock investors, fund investors can be virtually impossible to "short" a fund. Therefore, even though high-TK funds have higher fund values, their subsequent reversals are still not expected.

In short, our positive TK-performance relation in mutual funds does not necessarily contradict the documented negative TK-stock return relation in the literature. We refer to the following empirical analysis to further understand what might drive this positive relationship.

4.2 Potential explanation I: Performance persistence

The first plausible explanation for the positive relation is fund performance persistence. As the fund-level prospect theory value is constructed using historical fund returns, the measure contains information about historical fund performance and, hence, may be informative about future fund performance. If some fund managers have superior skills, funds with historically better performance tend to persist in the future. Therefore, the better performance of high-TK funds indicates that TK could be correlated with existing performance measures. Hence, a positive predictive relationship may reflect persistent performance. To verify this explanation, we consider three sets of empirical exercises. First, we investigate whether fund-level TK is correlated with existing performance measures. Second, we analyse whether TK contains information beyond fund momentum, a conventional indicator of performance persistence. Third, since the disposition effect may drive the momentum effect and our existing results indicate the importance of the convexity/concave component of prospect theory value, we check whether the positive relationship can be attributed to the disposition effect.

4.2.1 Performance measure and other determinants

We investigate whether TK is correlated with existing fund performance measures in the literature. We ran the Fama-Macbeth regression as before; however, the dependent variable is the fund-level prospect theory value, while the independent variables are a set of fund performance measures, the portfolio-level prospect theory value, and other fund characteristics. Unlike the predictive regressions above, we now run contemporaneous regressions to understand the determinants of the fund-level prospect theory value. [1] We consider the following model,

$$TK_{i,t} = const + \beta_{ptk} P\_TK_{i,t} + \gamma' Z_{i,t} + \varepsilon_{i,t} \qquad (9)$$

where $P\_TK_{i,t}$ refers to the portfolio-level prospect theory value by aggregating stock-level prospect theory value to the fund level using fund holding information. $Z_{i,t}$ refers to a vector of fund characteristics plus three additional fund performance measures: stock-picking skills, market timing skills, and fund gap.

Table 6 reports the determinants of the fund-level prospect theory values. We show that the fund-level TK is positively associated with the portfolio-level TK, indicating that those more attractive funds indeed hold more attractive stocks. [2] In terms of performance measures, TK is positively associated with stock-picking skills and fund gap while negatively associated with Churn rate. The relation between TK and market timing skills is

---

[1] In addition to the regression analysis, we also conduct portfolio sorting to check the relation between TK and alternative performance measures in the Internet Appendix Table A3. In line with our regression results, we show that high TK funds indeed have higher values across different performance measures including alphas relative to different factor models, stock-picking skills, and fund gaps.

[2] In an unreported analysis, we also replicate our results using a US mutual fund sample. We find that fund TK remains positively and significantly associated with future fund flow, but its effect on performance becomes positive and insignificant. We also find that the fund-level TK is positive but insignificantly correlated with the portfolio-level TK and positive and significantly correlated with skewness. These observations are consistent with a parallel paper by Guo and Schoenleber (2020). We attribute the different results by differences in investor base between US and Chinese mutual fund industries.

insignificant. The linkage between prospect theory value and performance measure is broadly consistent with the evidence of hedge fund skewness by Heuson et al. (2020). We find that *TK* is positively correlated with both skewness and Max, in line with their lottery-like properties, and its correlation with Max is also significant. Our results in Table 3 have already shown that the predictive power of *TK* is robust after controlling for skewness and Max. Therefore, the information content of the fund-level *TK* goes beyond existing lottery-related proxies.

Table 6   Prospect theory value and performance measures

	(1)	(2)	(3)	(4)	(5)	(6)	(7)
P_TK	0.0913**	0.0769**	0.0738**	0.0747**	0.0708**	0.0444	0.0857**
	(2.31)	(2.20)	(2.19)	(2.24)	(2.07)	(1.43)	(2.45)
Log(*Size*)		0.0001	0.0002	0.0001	0.0002	0.0001	0.0003
		(0.54)	(0.63)	(0.25)	(0.79)	(0.47)	(0.89)
Log(*Age*)		0.0044***	0.0042***	0.0042***	0.0043***	0.0026*	0.0033
		(2.89)	(2.93)	(2.89)	(3.12)	(1.92)	(1.56)
Log(*Co_Size*)		0.0018***	0.0017***	0.0016***	0.0017***	0.0016***	0.0016***
		(8.06)	(7.94)	(6.78)	(8.73)	(8.43)	(8.45)
Log(*Co_Age*)		0.0026***	0.0026***	0.0022***	0.0024***	0.0028***	0.0032***
		(4.63)	(4.43)	(3.68)	(4.28)	(4.87)	(4.91)
EXP		−0.0044**	−0.0042**	−0.0052***	−0.0047**	−0.0054***	−0.0044***
		(−2.58)	(−2.42)	(−2.94)	(−2.57)	(−3.24)	(−2.64)
Churn rate		−0.1034***	−0.1054***	−0.1047***	−0.1012***	−0.1079***	−0.0918***
		(−3.69)	(−3.64)	(−3.93)	(−3.80)	(−3.96)	(−2.77)
Picking			0.0053***				
			(2.69)				
Timing				0.0552			
				(0.97)			
Fund gap					0.0185***		
					(5.99)		
Max						0.0502***	
						(6.73)	
Skewness							0.0005
							(0.94)
Constant	−0.0394***	−0.0855***	−0.0843***	−0.0725***	−0.0842***	−0.0802***	−0.0842***
	(12.11)	(10.53)	(10.73)	(−7.77)	(−10.78)	(−10.44)	(−10.22)
Observations	14,267	14,139	14,133	14,133	14,133	14,139	14,099
R-squared	0.038	0.205	0.221	0.230	0.220	0.249	0.224

This table reports results of Fama and Macbeth (1973) regressions by regressing monthly fund *TK* (*TK*) on holding portfolio *TK* (*P_TK*) and various fund ability measures and control characteristics contemporaneously in month t, as shown in Eq. (9). *TK* is the prospect theory value of a fund's historical return distribution. *P_TK* is the prospect theory value of a stock's historical return distribution aggregated to the portfolio using a fund's stock portfolio holding information. Market timing and stock picking measures are defined by Kacperczyk et al. (2014) for the past 6-month. Return gaps are calculated based on Kacperczyk et al. (2008) by using the difference between fund returns and holding returns. The control variables include the logarithm of fund size, the logarithm of fund age, the logarithm of fund company size, the logarithm of fund company age, total expense (management expense plus loads), the churn rate of fund portfolio introduced by Yan and Zhang (2009), the max and skewness of fund return. Timeseries average coefficients and the Fama-Macbeth t-statistics (in parentheses) calculated with Newey-West robust standard errors are reported. *, **, and *** denote significance at the 10%, 5%, and 1% level, respectively.

In summary, we find that TK is significantly correlated with a set of performance measures. [1] Our evidence indicates that the strong predictive power of TK may come from its role as a performance measure, especially in selecting better-performing funds in the cross-section. Therefore, our findings are consistent with the explanation of performance persistence.

4.2.2 Fund prospect theory value and fund momentum

If the predictive power is mainly due to fund performance persistence, a natural concern is whether the fund-level prospect theory value contains incremental predictive information beyond existing performance persistence indicators. Cahart (1997) shows that US fund returns over the past year predict fund returns in the next year, and performance persistence is mainly due to the momentum effect. To check whether fund-level prospect theory value contains information beyond existing measures of performance persistence, we explicitly controlled for fund momentum. The baseline regression analysis in Table 3 demonstrates that the predictive power of TK is robust after controlling for fund momentum. In this section, we use a double-sorting portfolio approach to further understand this relationship.

Specifically, we first sorted all funds into five momentum portfolios according to fund momentum. Then within each momentum portfolio, we

---

[1] Besides the contemporaneous correlation and predictive sorts, we also compare TK with other performance measures by holding portfolios for the next 6 months in the Internet Appendix Table A4. We find that TK outperforms a set of performance measures in the magnitude of high minus low return spread, and it is second only to the six-factor alpha. This observation supports the role of fund TK as a powerful performance measure, hence supporting the performance persistence explanation for the positive TK-performance relation.

further sorted funds into five TK portfolios according to their fund-level *TK*. Therefore, we produced 25 momentum and *TK* double-sorted portfolios. If *TK* indeed carries predictive information for fund returns beyond momentum, we expect that the return spreads of *TK*-sorted portfolios will remain strong across different momentum portfolios. In contrast, if the information content of *TK* largely overlaps with or is subsumed by momentum, we expect the *TK* portfolio return spread to be insignificant or to be significant only in specific momentum portfolios.

Table 7 reports results about portfolios double sorted by momentum and *TK*. We find that *TK* sorted portfolios present monotonic increasing patterns for average returns across all momentum portfolios. We observe significant return spreads of *TK* sorted portfolios regardless of whether fund momentum is high or low. Therefore, our findings suggest that the predictive power of TK for future fund performance cannot be fully captured by fund momentum. Meanwhile, the fund momentum return spreads are also significant after the experiment for *TK*, indicating these two types of signals for future fund performance are not completely overlapped, despite their similarity in using historical fund performance.

Table 7   Prospect theory value and fund momentum

		TK						
		Low	2	3	4	High	High-Low	t-statistics
MOM	Low	0.002	0.005	0.007	0.009	0.014	0.011***	(3.85)
	2	0.004	0.009	0.011	0.013	0.016	0.012***	(4.88)
	3	0.005	0.009	0.010	0.012	0.016	0.009***	(3.77)
	4	0.008	0.011	0.011	0.013	0.017	0.009***	(3.86)
	High	0.008	0.014	0.015	0.016	0.018	0.009***	(2.95)
	High-Low	0.006**	0.008***	0.008***	0.007***	0.005**		
	t-statistics	(2.40)	(3.90)	(3.66)	(3.07)	(2.19)		

This table reports the *TK* premium of funds sorted by fund performance persistence using fund momentum (*MOM*). Within each quintile portfolio sorted by performance persistence, we further sort funds into quintile portfolios based on *TK*. Next, we calculate subsequent 12 monthly equally weighted portfolio returns of those 25 portfolios. *TK* is the prospect theory value of a fund's historical return distribution. *MOM* is a fund's cumulative monthly return in the previous year skipping the lagged month. Numbers in brackets are *t*-statistics using Newey-West robust standard errors. *, **, and *** denote significance at the 10%, 5%, and 1% level, respectively.

4.2.3 Disposition effect and reference-dependent preference

The results above show that the positive TK-fund performance relation is consistent with performance persistence and the information content of TK is beyond momentum. In Section 3.5, we also show that the economic magnitude of the convexity/concave component of prospect theory value is slightly larger than that of other components, although all prospect theory value components matter at the predictable relation. Since the convexity/concave component captures asymmetric risk preference (risk aversion in the gain region and risk-seeking in the loss region), it might imply a disposition effect, that is, investors sell stocks when they gain profits while holding stocks when they lose money. Previous studies, such as Grinblatt and Han (2005), show that the disposition effect explains momentum as selling winning stocks leads to an underreaction to good news. Although we provide evidence that the predictive power of TK is beyond momentum, the mechanism generating momentum through the disposition effect may still possibly contribute to the TK-performance relation.

We are interested in whether the disposition effect also explains the positive TK-performance relationship. [1] We follow Grinblatt and Han (2005) and use capital gain overhang (CGO) to capture the disposition effect. If the disposition effect fully captures the positive TK-performance relation, we expect that the regression coefficient before CGO is positive and significant, while TK is insignificant. Moreover, a recent study by An et al. (2020) points out the importance of reference-dependent preference (RDP) in explaining lottery-related anomalies. The reference point is a critical element in prospect theory. According to prospect theory, investors tend to be more risk-seeking when they experience loss. Therefore, they are more likely to

---

[1] We recognize the difficulty to fully disentangle prospect theory from disposition effect. Previous studies are more mixed regarding their relationships, including Barberis and Xiong (2009), Kausita (2010), Li and Yang (2013), Meng and Weng (2018), Li et al. (2020) among others. In this paper, we resort to the CGO to understand the effect of disposition effect on the TK-performance relation for simplicity.

gamble assets with lottery-like properties. If the predictive relation is mainly due to the reference-dependent preference, we expect the TK-performance relation to be stronger when investors face losses, i. e. , when CGO is low. [1] We resort to the Grinblatt and Han (2005) formula and use the past three-year rolling window to compute the monthly CGO at the fund level. [2] Similar to the above empirical specifications, we included the interaction of CGO and TK into our baseline model.

$$RankReturn_{i,t+1} = const + \beta_{tk}TK_{i,t} + \beta_{CGO}CGO_{i,t}$$
$$+ \beta_{tk \times cgo}TK_{i,t} * CGO_{i,t} + \gamma'Z_{i,t} + \varepsilon_{i,t+1} \quad (10)$$

where $CGO_{i,t}$ is a measure of fund-level capital gain overhang. $TK_{i,t} \times CGO_{i,t}$ is the interaction term. Since CGO measures the unrealized gain, we expect the coefficient of CGO to be positive and significant, if the disposition effect captures the predictive relation. We also expect the interaction term to be negative and significant, i. e. , the positive TK-performance relation is stronger at the loss region if reference-dependent preference plays a role.

Table 8 provides the results for the disposition effect and reference-dependent preference. Initially, we find that the coefficient of CGO is negative but insignificant. Hence prior losses are followed by higher fund performance, which is inconsistent with the disposition effect explanation. Therefore, despite the larger economic magnitude of the convexity/concave component in

---

[1] In An et al (2020), they focus on the effect of RDP on lottery-related anomalies in stock markets. The interaction term between lottery proxy and CGO is positive and significant as the negative lottery-return relation is stronger when CGO is more negative. Instead, our main results show a positive TK-performance relation. If TK plays the same role as lottery proxies, we expect the positive relation to be stronger when investors faced prior losses, i. e. , when CGO is low, hence the interaction is expected to be negative.

[2] One empirical challenge to construct CGO at the fund level is the absence of the fund turnover ratio data. By definition, the stock turnover ratio is the ratio of trading volume to total share outstanding. Therefore, we use an analogous measure based on the net inflow ratio, which is the ratio of net inflow amount to the total asset value at the time. We recognize that the net inflow ratio at the fund level is not exactly the same as the turnover at the stock level. However, in the absence of other possible measures, it still provides a rough weighting measure to obtain the weighted average of past prices to reflect the average buying price as the reference price.

prospect theory value, the disposition effect alone does not adequately account for the positive *TK*-fund performance relationship. Moreover, we show that the interaction term is negative, which is broadly consistent with reference-dependent preference, as the effect is mainly from the prior loss region when investors are more likely to gamble. However, the interaction is only marginally significant and it then becomes insignificant once more control variables are included. Hence reference-dependent preference is unlikely to be the main driving force behind the positive TK-fund performance relationship.

Table 8 Reference-dependence preference and the TK-performance relation

	(1)	(2)	(3)
TK	11.9316*	4.0831	3.5453
	(1.92)	(0.83)	(0.63)
CGO	−0.2686	−0.0986	0.0196
	(−1.38)	(−0.65)	(0.12)
CGO * *TK*	−10.6134*	−2.9122	−2.1811
	(−1.75)	(−0.64)	(−0.401)
Rank return	0.0423	0.0414	0.0357
	(1.60)	(1.53)	(1.33)
Log(*Size*)		−0.0017	−0.0113**
		(−0.42)	(−2.35)
Log(*Age*)		−0.0984***	−0.0922***
		(−2.87)	(−2.84)
Log(*Co_Size*)		0.0043	0.0053
		(1.04)	(1.23)
Log(*Co_Age*)		0.0369**	0.0255*
		(2.18)	(1.73)
EXP		0.0343	0.0282
		(0.89)	(0.67)
Churn rate			−1.3046***
			(−2.77)
Net flow			0.1007**
			(2.53)
Constant	0.8029***	0.5685**	0.6939**
	(4.03)	(2.19)	(2.60)
Observations	21,443	21,232	21,232
R-squared	0.135	0.203	0.235

This table reports results about the role of reference-dependent preference on the relation between fund *TK* and future fund performance on the monthly frequency using Fama and Macbeth (1973) regressions, as shown in Eq. (10). Fund performance is measured using rank return in month $t+1$, which is calculated by assigning ranking scores from zero (low performance) to one (high performance) to the cross-section of funds according to their fund raw returns in each month. *TK*, *CGO*, interaction term, and other control variables are in month t. *TK* is the prospect theory value of a fund's historical return distribution. *CGO* refers to capital gain overhang, computed based on Grinblatt and Han (2005). An interaction between *TK* and *CGO* is included. The control variables include the logarithm of fund size, the logarithm of fund age, the logarithm of fund company size, the logarithm of fund company age, total expense (management expense plus loads), the churn rate of fund portfolio introduced by Yan and Zhang (2009), the lagged monthly ranked return, the lagged quarterly net fund flow. Time-series average coefficients and the Fama-Macbeth t-statistics (in parentheses) calculated with Newey-West robust standard errors are reported.

In summary, our results show that fund-level prospect theory value is correlated with a set of performance measures. Therefore, we provide evidence to support a performance persistence explanation for the positive *TK*-performance relation. The predictive power of TK is beyond fund momentum. Neither the disposition effect nor reference-dependent preference sufficiently explains this predictive relationship.

4.3 Potential explanation II: Price impact

Price impact is another possible explanation for the positive *TK*-fund performance relationship. Our findings show that high *TK* is followed by higher fund performance and net inflows. Therefore, besides *TK* selecting historically better-performing funds, it is also possible that the better performance is due to the increased net inflows. Funds may use the newly injected money to reinvest in stocks they have already held. [1] Excessive demand then pushes the stock price up, which boosts future fund performance.

---

[1] The trading activities of mutual funds may affect stock prices for different reasons. For instance, including stocks into a fund's portfolio or removing stocks from the portfolio could have an immediate effect of stock prices through buying or selling pressures. Besides, herding of mutual funds may also affect stock prices. Wermers (1999) show that herding by growth-oriented funds is related to positive feedback trading: funds herd on the buy (sell) side for high (low) past-return stocks.

The price impact explanation builds on two important conditions: reinvestment and market power. First, funds need to use newly injected money to re-invest the stocks that they have already held. Second, funds' trading activities should have critical impacts on stock prices. We empirically investigate these two conditions to understand the price impact channel.

First, we checked whether funds indeed reinvest their holding stocks. Table 6 shows that fund TK is contemporaneously correlated with stock TK. That is, funds with high TK generally hold high-TK stocks. Table 9 reports the average stock characteristics of portfolio changes for high-TK funds. As Chinese mutual funds disclose their stock holdings semi-annually, we consider the change in trading portfolios for these funds from the previous reporting date to the current date and from the current date to the next reporting date. We show that high-TK funds *continue* to buy stocks with high stock TK. These funds also tend to invest in high Max stocks, given the similar lottery-like properties. Therefore, our findings imply that these funds are very likely to reinvest those stocks they hold using new cash inflows, consistent with the first condition.

Table 9　Characteristics of trading portfolios ranked by fund *TK*

	Panel A: Portfolio change between T-1 and T			
	Buy	Sell	Buy-Sell	t-statistics
P_Size	23.377	23.424	−0.047	(−1.18)
P_BIM	0.570	0.547	0.023	(1.37)
P_GP	0.296	0.296	0.000	(0.01)
P_TK	−0.033	−0.036	0.003***	(3.47)
P_Max	0.042	0.041	0.001***	(3.67)
$P\,Skewness$	0.108	0.105	0.002	(0.30)
P_Mom	0.268	0.272	−0.004	0.59)
	PanelB: Portfolio change between T and $T+1$			
	Buy	Sell	Buy-Sell	t-statistics
P_Size	23.426	23.447	−0.021	(−0.64)
P_BIM	0.535	0.540	−0.006	(−0.64)
P_GP	0.278	0.304	−0.026**	(−2.00)
P_TK	−0.033	−0.035	0.002**	(2.13)
P_Max	0.041	0.040	0.001***	(3.06)
$P\,Skewness$	0.111	0.111	0.000	(0.03)
P_Mom	0.255	0.261	−0.006	(−0.48)

This table reports the average characteristics of trading portfolios (buy, sell, and the difference) for funds with high fund-level TK values. We first obtained funds with the high fund-level TKs (funds ranked at the top 20%). Then we formed buy and sell portfolios separately based on holding stocks of these funds and their stock holding change information from WIND. We calculated stock characteristics and aggregate them to the buy/sell portfolio levels. We also calculate the buy and sell difference. We report average characteristic values for these portfolios. Since Chinese mutual funds disclose their stock holdings every half year, we focus on the semi-annual horizons. Panel A reports average characteristics of portfolio change between the current reporting date and the previous reporting date. Panel B reports the average characteristics of portfolio change between the current report date and the next reporting date. Our sample includes China's open-end equity mutual funds (excluding index funds, ETFs, and QFIIs) in the month-end from Dec 2008 to Dec 2017. Size (in millions) is the semi-annually-end market capitalization of the stock. Book to market ratio is the most recent semi-annually-end book equity value to divide by fiscal quarterly-end market equity value. Gross profit is calculated by revenue minus the cost of goods sold. Stock TK is the average monthly holding TK per semi-annual. Max, skewness, and Mom are the return characteristics of holding stocks. Newey West t-statistics are reported in the parenthesis below the mean value. * * * , * * , and * denote significance at the 1%, 5%, and 10% level.

Second, we examined whether these funds have the market power to influence stock prices. Intuitively, if the trading activities of funds are negligible and they are price takers, then even though they use new funds to reinvest old stocks, they can hardly benefit from trading. In contrast, if funds have market power, then their trading may influence stock price directly or their trading may attract followers to mimic, which subsequently bids up the prices of stocks they hold and hence enhance their fund performance. We expect the positive TK-performance relation to be stronger for funds with large purchase sizes, and hence a stronger price impact.

Empirically, we used the average purchase size of a fund to measure its market power. Unlike individual stock investors, which are price takers, major institutional investors, such as funds with large purchases, are expected to have a non-negligible influence on stock prices. ①

We consider the following empirical specification,

$$RankReturn_{i,t+1} = const + \beta_{tk} TK_{i,t} + \beta_{pur} Fund\_PUR_{i,t}$$
$$+ \beta_{tk \times pur} TK_{i,t} \times Fund\_PUR_{i,t} + \gamma' Z_{i,t} + \varepsilon_{i,t+1} \quad (11)$$

where $Fund\_PUR_{i,t}$ equals to the average purchase size of the fund. $TK_{i,t} \times Fund\_PUR_{i,t}$ is the interaction term. We expect the interaction term to be positive and significant. Namely, the TK effect should be more pronounced for those funds with higher fund purchasing sizes.

Table 10 reports regression results about fund purchasing power. We find that the interaction terms are indeed positive and significant across different specifications. That is, the predictive power of prospect theory value is stronger for funds with high average purchase size and hence with the market power to influence stock prices. Combining this finding with the trading portfolio results obtained above, we suggest that our results are consistent with both the re-investment condition and the market power condition. Therefore, our results support the price impact explanation for the TK-fund performance relation.

Table 10 Fund purchase power and the TK-performance relation

	(1)	(2)	(3)
TK	0.4758	0.6586	0.9108
	(0.79)	(1.02)	(1.44)
Fund_PUR	0.0395***	0.0446***	0.0442***
	(3.02)	(2.67)	(3.30)
*Fund_PUR * TK*	0.7574**	0.7510*	0.6132**
	(2.61)	(1.77)	(2.16)
Rank return	0.0435*	0.0339	0.0297
	(1.69)	(1.35)	(1.19)
Log(*Size*)		-0.0081	-0.0220***
		(-1.30)	(-3.04)

① In an unreported analysis, we also used the market share of the fund company as a proxy for market power. Our results remain qualitatively unchanged. Compared with fund market share, fund purchase provides a more direct measure of purchase power, and hence we use fund purchase size in the main analysis.

continued

	(1)	(2)	(3)
Log(Age)		-0.1061^{**}	-0.0825^{**}
		(-2.50)	(-2.31)
Log(Co_Size)		0.0052	0.0059
		(1.40)	(1.52)
Log(Co_Age)		0.0340^{**}	0.0191
		(2.16)	(1.30)
EXP		0.0385	0.0477
		(0.87)	(0.98)
Churn rate			-1.7220^{***}
			(-3.67)
Net flow			0.0682^{*}
			(1.87)
Constant	0.4950^{***}	0.5618^{***}	0.8437^{***}
	(17.18)	(3.18)	(5.55)
Observations	21,479	21,250	21,236
R-squared	0.144	0.215	0.243

This table reports results about the role of fund market power on the relation between fund TK and future fund performance on the monthly frequency using Fama and Macbeth (1973) regressions, as shown in Eq. (11). Fund performance is measured using rank return in month $t+1$, which is calculated by assigning ranking scores from zero (low performance) to one (high performance) to the cross-section of funds according to their fund raw returns in each month. TK, $Fund\_PUR$, interaction term, and other control variables are in month t. TK is the prospect theory value of a fund's historical return distribution. Fund_PUR equals the purchase of the fund. An interaction between TK and $Fund\_PUR$ is included. The control variables include the logarithm of fund size, the logarithm of fund age, the logarithm of fund company size, the logarithm of fund company age, total expense (management expense plus loads), the churn rate of fund portfolio introduced by Yan and Zhang (2009), the lagged monthly ranked return, the lagged quarterly net fund flow. Time-series average coefficients and the Fama-Macbeth t-statistics (in parentheses) calculated with Newey-West robust standard errors are reported.

4.4 Long-term performance

Our results provide supportive evidence for both the performance persistence and price impact explanations. These two explanations are not mutually exclusive, and they both contribute to the TK-performance relation. A natural question is which effect is dominant. Identifying these two effects separately is empirically challenging, as they can be intertwined. Instead, we employ long-term portfolio performance to determine which effect plays a stronger role. Intuitively, performance persistence tends to have long-lasting effects, whereas price impact concentrates on the short horizon. If high-TK funds are funds with better-skilled managers, we expect the performance to persist for longer horizons. In contrast, if high-TK funds generate better future performance mainly through re-investing stocks they held, the effect cannot be sustainable. Hence, the price impact effect tends to reverse relatively quickly.

In Table 11, we held TK-$sorted$ portfolios for longer horizons. We find that the positive TK-performance relation held up to 9 months ahead. Therefore, the predictive power of prospect theory value for future fund performance is not transitory. We also show that the predictive relationship eventually reverses in the long run. The long-horizon predictive power indicates that the performance persistence effect is stronger than the price impact effect, though both explanations contribute to predictability.

Table 11 Persistence of TK sorted portfolios

	$R_{t+1,t+3}$	$R_{t+4,t+6}$	$R_{t+7,t+9}$	$R_{t+10,t+12}$	$R_{t+13,t+24}$	$R_{t+25,t+36}$	$R_{t+37,t+48}$	$R_{t+49,t+60}$
Low	0.010	0.008	0.008	0.008	0.007	0.008	0.012	0.013
2	0.010	0.009	0.008	0.008	0.008	0.008	0.012	0.012
3	0.011	0.009	0.008	0.007	0.006	0.008	0.012	0.012
4	0.011	0.010	0.008	0.008	0.007	0.008	0.013	0.013
High	0.012	0.011	0.009	0.009	0.008	0.009	0.012	0.013
High-Low	0.002**	0.003***	0.002**	0.001	0.001	0.001	0.000	0.000
t-statistics	(1.98)	(3.71)	(2.18)	(1.20)	(1.73)	(1.16)	(0.43)	(−0.38)

This table reports accumulative raw returns for the subsequent month, month 1 to month 3, month 4 to 6, month 7 to 9, month 10 to 12, month 13 to 24, month 25 to 36, month 37 to 48, and month 49 to 60 for equity mutual funds ranked by Fund TK. Newey-West t-statistics are reported in the parenthesis below the mean value. ***, **, and * denote significance at the 1%, 5%, and 10% level.

5 Robustness checks and additional analyses

In this section, we summarize the results of a set of comprehensive robustness checks and further analyses. Detail results are provided in the Internet Appendix Table A5 to Table A11.

Firstly, we considered alternative measures of prospect theory value. We consider alternative estimation windows of 3 years (36 months) and 4 years (48 months) to construct prospect theory value. Table A5 shows that our results remain valid when alternative measures are used. Hence our findings are not restricted to a particular choice of the estimation window.

Secondly, we analyzed whether our results are driven by extreme market conditions. Table A6 reports regression results when we remove the crisis period in Chinese financial markets (June 2015 to January 2016). We find that our results remain strong. Consequently, our results cannot be solely attributed to the crisis period.

Thirdly, we conducted additional cross-sectional analyses. We check the role of cash holding and fund risk in the TK-performance relation. Cash holding may affect fund performance in two potential ways. Initially, funds with higher performance may have lower cash holding, as fund managers optimally use cash to invest in new projects. Moreover, funds in shortage of cash may be more likely to benefit from the excess inflow, as their investment opportunity is no longer restricted by the financial constraint. In both situations, we expect the TK-performance relation to be stronger for funds with lower cash holdings. We interacted TK with a dummy variable equal to one if a fund is in the bottom decile of cash holding and zero otherwise. Table A7 shows that the interaction term is positive and significant, consistent with the above prediction. Hence the effect is stronger for funds with lower cash holdings.

Fund risk may affect the TK-performance relation in different manners. [①] If the strong performance of high TK funds is because they are riskier, then the relation is expected to be stronger for funds with higher risk. If the predictability is mainly due to limits to arbitrage, the performance should be stronger for funds with higher idiosyncratic volatility. If learning from fund performance plays a role, then the relationship tends to be weaker when uncertainty is high. We constructed three measures of fund risk including total risk, systematic risk, and idiosyncratic risk, and interact each of them with TK. Table A8 shows that the interaction term is negative and significant when total and systematic risks are used and negative but insignificant when idiosyncratic risk is used. Therefore, our results do not support risk-based or limits to arbitrage explanations. Instead, we show that the lower flow-performance sensitivity when uncertainty is high may depress fund performance.

Fourthly, we checked whether the predictive power simply stems from the stock-level measure of prospect theory value. We constructed a stock-level measure and then calculate the weighted average value at the fund level (portfolio level) based on the stock portfolio holding information for each fund. We then replicated our baseline regression analysis by using the stock portfolio-level measure. Table A9 reports results using the portfolio-level TK. Unlike our main results, we do not find significant predictive relation using the portfolio-level TK. While in Table 6, we did show that the fund-level TK and the portfolio-level TK are positively correlated. The superior predictive power indicates the incremental information at the fund level, which could be related to managerial skills.

[①] Huang et al. (2011) suggest that managerial risk-taking affects fund performance. Starks and Sun (2016) suggest that fund flow-performance sensitivity decreases in uncertainty. While they use the economic policy uncertainty index at the aggregate market level to measure uncertainty, we focus on total fund risk, systematic risk, and idiosyncratic risk at the fund level, given our empirical setting of the fund-level Fama-Macbeth regressions. Barberis et al. (2016) show that the predictive power of prospect theory value in stock returns is stronger when stocks are more difficult to arbitrage.

Finally, we further checked the incremental predictive power of *TK*. We regressed the fund-level *TK* on the *MAX* and fund momentum respectively to control for existing lottery and performance persistence indicators and retrieve regression residuals. We then re-produce our baseline regression analysis using these residuals, i. e. , orthogonal versions of *TK*. Table A10 reports that these orthogonalized TKs still positively and significantly predict fund performance. Therefore, empirical results support that the predictive power of *TK* is incremental to existing characteristics related to lottery-like features or fund performance. Table A11 shows that our main results remain unaffected when a fund style-adjusted *TK* measure is employed.

In summary, these robustness and additional analyses further support our main findings.

6 Conclusions

Our study empirically investigates the role of prospect theory in explaining mutual fund performance. Using Chinese open-ended equity fund data, we construct a measure of prospect theory value at the fund level. We provide evidence that prospect theory value is positively associated with future fund performance using both portfolio sorting and regression analysis. Controlling for well-known systematic risk factors and existing fund characteristics does not fully account for this predictability. High-*TK* funds also have higher net fund inflows in the future, consistent with the properties of these funds to attract the excess demand of irrational investors. We show that all three prospect theory value components contribute to predictable return patterns, and the economic magnitude is slightly larger for the convexity/concave component.

We then consider potential explanations for this predictability. We suggest that the positive *TK*-fund performance relation is not necessarily inconsistent with the negative *TK*-stock return relation shown in the equity market literature, given the distinctive institutional features of the mutual fund industry. We then formally investigate two plausible explanations for this predictability: performance persistence and price impact. However, these two explanations are not mutually exclusive. We provide empirical support for both explanations.

High-TK funds have superior stock-picking skills, which is consistent with the explanation of performance persistence. Neither fund momentum nor reference-dependent preferences fully account for the predictability. Hence, the predictive power of fund TK goes beyond existing indicators of performance persistence. We also show that high-TK funds continue to buy the high-TK stocks they hold. Moreover, the TK-performance relation is stronger for funds with higher fund-purchasing sizes. These results suggest that high-TK funds can use newly injected cash to reinvest in stocks they have already held, thus boosting fund performance. Therefore, our results are consistent with the explanation of the price impact. Portfolio performance persists up to nine months ahead, then becomes insignificant, and eventually reverses. Hence, the performance persistence effect generally dominates the price impact effect, although both explanations contribute to the predictability.

Our main results are unaffected when we consider different performance measures as dependent variables, use different window sizes to estimate prospect theory value, or remove the financial crisis periods. Additional cross-sectional analyses show that the predictability is stronger for funds with lower fund risk and lower cash holdings. Replacing the fund-level prospect theory value with the stock portfolio-level prospect theory value does not reproduce the main findings, supporting the unique predictive information content of the fund-level prospect theory value. Using the orthogonal versions of fund-level prospect theory value controlling for existing measures of fund persistence or lottery-like features does not change our main findings. Results remain strong when a fund style-adjusted TK measure is used.

Overall, this paper provides novel empirical evidence from China that prospect theory plays an important role in understanding mutual fund performance.

Acknowledgements

We are grateful for insightful and constructive comments from Wenfeng Wu (Guest Editor) and an anonymous referee. We also thank Xin Hong, Ying Sophie Huang, Jeong-Ho (John) Kim, Meifen Qian, Rina Ray, Youchang Wu, and conference participants at 2020 China International Risk Forum for their helpful comments. Bin Yu gratefully acknowledges the financial support from the National Social Science Fund of China (No. 18BJY241). All remaining errors are ours.

Appendix A: Variable definitions

Symbol	Description
TK	A measure of the fund-level prospect theory value based on the past fund performance; more detail is shown in section 2.
P_TK	A measure of the portfolio-level prospect theory value by first calculating the individual stock-level TK and then aggregating the stock-level measure with stock portfolio holding information for each fund to obtain a fund-level measure.
TK_Style	A measure of TK calculated by using the monthly fund style-adjusted returns over the previous 36 months. We classify funds into three categories depending on different investment styles (Growth, Balance, Value) and then subtract investment style benchmarks from fund returns to calculate the style-adjusted return.
TK_O1	The residual term of regressing TK on Max, which eliminates the fund's lottery feature from the original TK.
TK_O2	The residual term of regressing TK on fund momentum, which eliminates the fund's past returns from the original TK.
Log(Size)	The natural logarithms of mutual funds' total net assets (TNA) at the end of each quarter.
Log(Age)	The natural logarithms of mutual funds age since it is set up at the end of each quarter.

continued

Symbol	Description
$Log(Co\_Size)$	The natural logarithms of fund companies' total net assets (TNA) at the end of each quarter.
$Log(Co\_Age)$	The natural logarithms of fund companies' age since it sets up at the end of each quarter.
$EXP(\%)$	The sum of operating expense ratio and front-end-load fees (in ratio), following Sirri and Tufano (1998).
Churn Rate	A measure of mutual funds' turnover rate in each quarter, following Yan & Zhang (2009) using the aggregate purchase and sale, a high value of churn rate represents that the fund trades more frequently
Raw Return	The simple return of net asset value (NAV) of the fund over the month.
Rank Return	The fractional performance rank scores range from zero (the lowest performance) to one (the highest performance) assigned to the cross-section of funds according to their current month fund raw returns.
Alpha CAPM	The monthly risk-adjusted return using the CAPM.
Alpha FF3F	The monthly risk-adjusted return using the Fama and French (1993) three-factor model.
Alpha Cahart4F	The monthly risk-adjusted return using the Carhart (1997) four-factor model.
Alpha FF5F	The monthly risk-adjusted return using the Fama and French (2015) five-factor model
Alpha FF5F+ UMD	The monthly risk-adjusted return using the six-factor (Fama and French (2015) five-factor model plus momentum) model.
Net Flow	The net fund flow of a mutual fund in each quarter. The net flow is the difference between inflow and outflow.
Max	The maximum monthly style-adjusted return over the last 12 months. We classify funds into three categories depending on different investment styles (Growth, Balance, Value), and then subtract investment style benchmarks from fund returns to calculate the style-adjusted return.
Skewness	The skewness of monthly style-adjusted return over the previous year. We classify funds into three categories depending on different investment styles (Growth, Balance, Value), and then subtract investment style benchmarks from fund returns to calculate the style-adjusted return.

continued

Symbol	Description
Mom	The fund momentum using the past twelve-month fund return, skipping for one month.
R^2	R-squared is obtained from regressing fund return on CAPM using a rolling window of 36 months.
Picking	A measure of a fund's stock-picking ability at the end of the quarter, following Kacperczyk et al. (2014)
Timing	A measure of a fund's market timing ability at the end of the quarter, following Kacperczyk et al. (2014)
Fund Gap	A measure of a fund's ability. The gap refers to the difference between the fund return and holding return according to the fund's portfolio.
Cash	A dummy variable equals 1 if cash holding percentage ranked in the bottom quintile during our sample period, and 0 otherwise.
Fund_PUR	The average purchase size of the fund for each semi-annual.
Risk	One of the three measures of fund risk. Total risk is based on the standard deviation of daily fund return over the month. Idiosyncratic risk is based on the standard deviation of residual obtained by the Carhart four-factor model. Systematic risk is the difference between total risk and idiosyncratic risk.
CGO	A measure of capital gains overhang (CGO) based on the difference between the reference price and the real fund net asset value (NAV), where the reference price is obtained by fund flow and fund performance over the past three years, in the spirit of the stock-level measure by Grinblatt and Han (2005)
P_Size	A measure of fund holding style on size, using the stock holdings and stock size to get the portfolio-level size.
P_BM	A measure of fund holding style on value, using the stock holdings and stock book-to-market ratio to get the portfolio-level book-to-market ratio.
P_GP	A measure of fund holding style on value, using the stock holdings and stock gross profits to get the portfolio-level gross profits.
P_Max	A measure of fund holding style on maximum return, using the stock holdings and stock maximum daily return of the month to get the portfolio-level maximum daily return.

continued

Symbol	Description
P_Skewness	A measure of fund holding style on skewness, using the stock holdings and the stock-level monthly skewness to get the portfolio-level skewness.
P_Mom	A measure of fund holding style on momentum, using the stock holdings and the stock-level monthly momentum (cumulative return from t-12 to t-2) to get the portfolio-level momentum.

Appendix B: Supplementary data

Supplementary data to this article can be found online at https://doi. org/ 10. 1016/j. pacfin. 2022. 101766.

References

Adebambo B N, Yan X, 2016. Momentum, reversals, and fund manager overconfidence[J]. Financial Management, 45(3): 609-639.

Akbas F, Genc E, 2018. Do mutual fund investors overweight the probability of extreme payoffs in the return distribution? [J]. Journal of Financial and Quantitative Analysis, 55(1):1-86.

Amihud Y, Goyenko R, 2013. Mutual fund's R2 as predictor of performance [J]. Review of Financial Studies, 26(3): 667-694.

An L, Wang H, Wang J, et al, 2020. Lottery-related anomalies: The role of reference-dependent preferences[J]. Management Science, 66: 473-501.

Baber B M, Odean T, Zheng L, 2005. Out of sight, out of mind: The effects of expenses on mutual fund flows[J]. The Journal of Business, 78(6): 2095-2120.

Bailey W, Kumar A, Ng D, 2011. Behavioral biases of mutual fund investors [J]. Journal of Financial Economics, 102: 1-27.

Bali T G, Cakici N, Whitelaw R, 2011. Maxing out: Stocks as lotteries and the cross- section of expected returns[J]. Journal of Financial Economics, 99: 427-446.

Barberis N，Huang M，Santos T，2001. Prospect theory and asset prices[J]. Quarterly Journal of Economics，116：1-53.

Barberis N，Huang M，2008. Stocks as lotteries：The implications of probability weighting for security prices[J]. American Economic Review，98：2066-2100.

Barberis N，Mukherjee A，Wang B，2016. Prospect theory and stock returns：An empirical test[J]. Review of Financial Studies，29：3068-3107.

Barberis N，Xiong W，2009. What drives the disposition effect? An analysis of a long-standing preference-based explanation[J]. Journal of Finance，64 (2)：751-784.

Berk J B，Green R C，2004. Mutual fund flows and performance in rational markets[J]. Journal of Political Economy，112(6)：1269-1295.

Bollen N，Busse J，2004. Short-term persistence in mutual fund performance [J]. Review of Financial Studies，18：569-597.

Boyer B，Mitton T，Vorkink K，2010. Expected idiosyncratic skewness[J]. Review of Financial Studies，23：169-202.

Carhart M M，1997. On persistence in mutual fund performance[J]. Journal of Finance，52：57-82.

Chen F，Qian M，Sun P，et al，2018. In search for managerial skills beyond common performance measures[J]. Journal of Banking & Finance，86：224-239.

Chen R，Gao Z，Zhang X，et al，2018. Mutual fund managers' prior work experience and their investment skill[J]. Financial Management，47(1)：3-24.

Clark W，Lisowski W. Prospect theory and decision to move or stay[J]. Proceedings of the National Academy of Science，2017，114 (36)：7432-7440.

Conrad J，Dittmar R，Ghysels E，2013. Ex-ante skewness and expected stock returns[J]. Journal of Finance，68：85-124.

Cremers M，Petajisto A，2009. How active is your fund manager? A new measure that predicts performance[J]. Review of Financial Studies，22：3329-3365.

Dong X，Feng S，Sadka R，2019. Liquidity risk and mutual fund performance [J]. Management Science，65：955-1453.

Du M, Nieesen-Ruenzi A, Odean T, 2001. Stock repurchasing bias of mutual funds[J]. SSRN Working Paper.

Edelen R, Ince O, Kadlec G, 2016. Institutional investors and stock market anomalies[J]. Journal of Financial Economics, 119 (3): 472-488.

Fama E F, French K R, 1993. Common risk factors in the returns on stocks and bonds[J]. Journal of Financial Economics, 33: 441-465.

Fama E F, French K R, 2015. A five-factor asset pricing model[J]. Journal of Financial Economics, 116: 1-22.

Fama E F, MacBeth J, 1973. Risk, return, and equilibrium: Empirical tests [J]. Journal of Political Economy, 71: 607-636.

Goetzmann W, Ingersoll J, Spiegel M, et al, 2007. Portfolio performance manipulation and manipulation-proof performance measures[J]. Review of Financial Studies, 20: 1503-1546.

Goetzmann W N, Kim D, Kumar A, et al, 2015. Weather-induced mood, institutional investors, and stock returns[J]. Review of Financial Studies, 28 (1): 73-111.

Grinblatt M, Han B, 2005. Prospect theory, mental accounting, and momentum[J]. Journal of Financial Economics, 78: 311-339.

Grinblatt M, Titman S, 1992. The persistence of mutual fund performance [J]. Journal of Finance, 47: 1977-1984.

Guo J, Schoenleber L, 2021. Investor behavior under prospect theory: Evidence from mutual funds [J]. Social Science Electronic Publishing: 3754814.

Henriksson R, 1984. Market timing and mutual fund performance: An empirical investigation[J]. The Journal of Business, 57: 73-96.

Heuson A J, Hutchinson M C, Kumar A, 2020. Predicting hedge fund performance when fund returns are skewed[J]. Financial Management, 4: 1-20.

Huang J, Sialm C, Zhang H, 2011. Risk shifting and mutual fund performance[J]. Review of Financial Studies, 24: 2575-2616.

Huang J C, Yan H, Wei K D, 2007. Participation costs and the sensitivity of fund flows to past performance[J]. Journal of Finance, 62 (3): 1273-1311.

Jensen M, 1968. The performance of mutual funds in the period 1945—1964 [J]. Journal of Finance, 23: 389-416.

Jin X, Shen Y, Yu B, et al, 2022. Flow—driven risk shifting of high—performing funds[J]. Accounting & Finance, 62(1):71-100.

Jordan B D, Riley T B, 2015. Volatility and mutual fund manager skill[J]. Journal of Financial Economics, 118: 289-298.

Kacperczyk M, Sialm C, Zheng L, 2008. Unobserved actions of mutual funds [J]. Review of Financial Studies, 21: 2379-2416.

Kacperczyk M, Van Nieuwerburgh S, Veldkamp L, 2014. Time-varying fund manager skill[J]. Journal of Finance, 69: 1455-1484.

Kahneman D, Tverskey A, 1979. Prospect theory: An analysis of decision under risk[J]. Econometrica, 47: 263-291.

Karagiannis N, Tolikas K, 2019. Tail risk and the cross-section of mutual fund expected returns[J]. Journal of Financial and Quantitative Analysis, 54: 425-447.

Kaustia M, 2010. Prospect theory and the disposition effect[J]. Journal of Financial and Quantitative Analysis, 45(3):791-812.

Kumar A, 2009. Who gambles in the stock market? [J]. Journal of Finance, 64: 1889-1933.

Levy J, 2003. Applications of prospect theory to political science[J]. Decision Theory, 135(2): 215-241.

Li C, Tiwari C, Tong L, 2017. Investment decisions under ambiguity: Evidence from mutual fund investor behavior[J]. Management Science, 63 (8): 2509-2528.

Li Y, Yang L, 2013. Prospect theory, the disposition effect, and asset prices [J]. Journal of Financial Economics, 107(3):715-739.

Li Z, Seiler M J, Sun H, 2019. Prospect theory and a two-way disposition effect: Theory and evidence from the housing market[J]. SSRN Working Paper: 2939186.

Meng J, Weng X, 2008. Can prospect theory explain the disposition effect? [J]. Management Science, 64 (7): 3331-3351.

Newey W K, West K D, 1987. A simple, positive semi-definite, heteroskedasticity and autocorrelation consistent covariance matrix [J]. Econometrica, 55(3): 703-708.

O'Connell P, Teo M, 2009. Institutional investors, past performance, and dynamic loss aversion[J]. Journal of Financial and Quantitative Analysis, 44 (1): 155-188.

Pan L, Tang T, Xu J, 2016. Speculative trading and stock returns[J]. Review of Finance, 20 (5): 1835-1865.

Petajisto A, 2013. Active share and mutual fund performance[J]. Financial Analysts Journal, 69: 73-93.

Sirri E R, Tufano P, 1998. Costly search and mutual fund flow[J]. Journal of Finance, 53(5): 1589-1622.

Starks L, Sun S, 2016. Economic policy uncertainty, learning and incentives: Theory and evidence on mutual funds[C]. Austin: University of Texas at Austin.

Treynor J L, Mazuy K K. Can mutual funds outguess the market? [J]. Harvard Business Review, 1966, 44: 131-136.

Tverskey A, Kahneman D, 1992. Advances in prospect theory: Cumulative representation of uncertainty[J]. Journal of Risk and Uncertainty, 5: 297 - 323.

Wermers R, 1999. Mutual fund herding and the impact on stock prices[J]. Journal of Finance, 54(2): 581-622.

Xu Q, Kozhan R, Taylor M P, 2020. Prospect theory and currency returns: Empirical evidence[J]. Social Science Electronic Publishing:3629061.

Yan X S, Zhang Z, 2009. Institutional investors and equity returns: Are short-term institutions better informed? [J]. Review of Financial Studies, 22: 893-924.

Zhong X, Wang J, 2018. Prospect theory and corporate bond returns: An empirical study[J]. Journal of Empirical Finance, 47: 25-48.

The Day-of-the-month Effect and the Performance of the Dollar Cost Averaging Strategy:Evidence From China^①

Abstract   Dollar cost averaging (DCA) is a popular strategy adopted by investors who recognize the difficulty in consistently timing the market. Using a sample of open-ended equity mutual funds in China from 2004 to 2020, this study investigates a calendar anomaly not yet documented——the day-of-the-month effect for monthly mutual fund DCA investment. We find that DCA investment in the first five days of each month could generate an annualized style-adjusted return of 0.35% more than in the remaining days. The results hold for sub-samples of different fund styles, especially for growth funds. Moreover, the effects of earnings announcements, holidays, and fund tournaments contribute to the DCA calendar anomaly. Robustness checks support our main findings.

Keywords   dollar cost averaging; calendar anomaly; Chinese mutual fund

1   Introduction

Using samples across stock markets in developed and emerging countries,

---

①   Originally published in *Accounting & Finance* in Marth, 2023, by Jin Xuejun, Li Hongze and Yu Bin, thanks to the financial support from the National Social Science Foundation of China (Program No. 18BJY241).

extant research has extensively tested trading rules and complicated strategies aimed at outperforming the market. These ambitious technologies have proved effective only in the short term, constrained by the lack of professional knowledge and investment tools for average individual investors. An innovation that has recently gained in popularity among traders is dollar cost averaging (DCA). ① DCA does not require investors to have the ability of timing investments, which is a particularly attractive feature: It is well documented that investment timing is difficult to achieve even for experienced traders and professionals. A 2021 research report② conducted jointly by Galaxy Securities and Fuguo fund found the average return of fund investors with DCA strategy is 2.94% higher than that of non-DCA investment customers every year; they can effectively avoid large losses of more than 30%. Tomlinson (2012) documents how DCA enables investors to use "no timing" strategy when facing the risk of price fluctuations. There has been new theoretical and practical evidence on DCA and average investment timing strategy (Kirkby et al., 2020; Milevsky & Posner 2003; Vanduffel et al., 2012). However, some studies believe that DCA lacks flexibility to make appropriate adjustments to the new information carried over time and argue that it is suboptimal (Constantinides 1979; Knight & Mandell 1992; Williams & Bacon 2004).

This study does not attempt to settle any of the differences between practice and theory; nor do we address behavioral theory in explaining the popularity of DCA for individual investors. Instead, we concede that DCA has been welcomed by ordinary investors and has shown its advantages in many research and practice. Given this environment, we will determine the optimal starting day to maximize returns.

---

① DCA, which is also known as automatic investment plan (AIP), is defined as a strategy in which a fixed amount of cash flow is invested in a risky asset (e. g. exchange traded funds (ETF) or mutual funds) regularly within the scheduled time period.

② Research Report on mutual funds released by Fuguo fund and Galaxy Securities, using a sample of 46.82 million fund investors from 2004 to February 2021. https://weibo. com/ttarticle/p/show? id=2309404414355654443184.

Although DCA is considered an investment method that does not need timing skills, this conclusion is based on the assumption that the time of DCA is long enough. However, according to aforementioned Fuguo Fund-Galaxy Securities report, 27.47% of the investors have a DCA term of 1-3 years, while only 11.73% of the investors have a term of more than 3 years; the remaining DCA investors did not even last for a year. Therefore, if the frequency of monthly fixed investment is adopted, and the investment is made on the fixed day of each month, it may also affect the return on DCA with limited length of time. Therefore, DCA investors need to decide which is the "auspicious day" to start the fixed investment. To the best of our knowledge, this is the first attempt to investigate the calendar effect of DCA.

The literature has focused on two main topics. The first is the seasonality effects in the equity market, which refer to various calendar "anomalies". The most extensively studied calendar effect is the day-of-the-week effect (e. g., Monday effect, Friday effect and weekend effect). The stock returns on Monday are significantly lower than those on other days, while the returns on Friday are significantly higher (Birru, 2016; Cao et al., 2021; Doyle & Chen, 2009). Wang et al. (1997) document that the day-of-the-week effect is the most significant in the fourth and fifth weeks. Moreover, evidence of the month-of-the-year effect (e. g., January effect, May-to-October or Halloween effect) is also documented globally. For example, the average return of stocks in January is lower than that in other months (Ogden, 1990). Kang (2010) finds that the January effect is more apparent in small cap stocks. The May-to-October effect indicates that the equity market significantly underperforms in terms of returns during May to October relative to the other months (Bouman & Jacobsen, 2002; Jacobsen & Marquering, 2008). The week-of-the-month and week-of-the-year effects exist too; Wang et al. (1997) find that the return rate in the first week of a month is often significantly positive, while the return rate in the remaining weeks is statistically no different from zero. Cao et al. (2021) document that the prediction of future monthly earnings by heterogeneous volatility is related to a particular week of each month. Using a sample covering 20 markets, Levy and Yagil (2012) empirically proved that the week-of-the-year effect exists widely. Finally, in China, there are seasonal anomalies relevant to the lunar calendar. Traditionally, some Chinese lunar calendar days are considered fortuitous for obtaining wealth. Empirical research shows that in markets using the lunar calendar, such as China, Singapore and Korea, the individual investor's trading behavior is more aggressive on lucky lunar calendar days; however, sentiment-driven trading yields a loss on average. (Huang et al. , 2022; Liu, 2013).

The second topic that has been intensively studied concerns potential explanations of calendar anomalies. Relevant explanations mainly relate to the trading pattern of individual investors and institutional investors. Miller (1988) conjectures that the Monday effects can be attributed to individual investors' weekday trading patterns. Lakonishok and Edwin (1990) document that individuals tend to trade (sell) stocks more on Monday, putting pressure on prices. Subsequent studies have inferred the motivation behind the trading patterns of individual investors. Ogden (1990) argues that since investors normally receive salaries at the end of the month, the enhanced returns are a reflection of the price pressure resulting from the reinvestment of that money. Birru (2016) found that mood played a role in investors' trading decision, improving over Monday to Friday and leading to a gradual increase in purchase transactions, pushing up the stock prices. This is consistent with the investor psychology findings that their mood improves from Thursday to Friday and deteriorates on Monday. Interestingly, some studies argue that the calendar effect is driven by informed traders. Foster and Viswanathan (1990) show that informed traders pre-empt trading after trading suspension, which causes abnormal stock prices after weekends and holidays. Kang (2010) documents that the probability of informed trading (PIN) in small stocks is more severe, which means a high level of informed trading would lead to an increase in their returns due to the 'information risk effect' in January. Finally, Ulku and Rogers (2018) use data on institution trading data to investigate their impact with regard to the Monday effect. They find that as large-sized trades require an analysis and decision process, institutions trade (buy) less on Mondays and increase net buying in the remaining week. As a result, the aggregate net demand for stocks temporarily declines in the beginning of the week, bringing down stock prices; the opposite happens for the rest of the week.

Our study uses the disclosed holdings of a sample of 764 Chines equity funds from 2004 to 2020 to document that annual fund returns with monthly DCA investment fluctuate from -3.52% to -2.90% according to the DCA start date, since the average fund expense is around 3.25% ①(management expense plus load), that is, as long as the annualized rate of return is greater than -0.0325, it means that the return of the DCA is positive (before deducting expense). We find that the DCA annual return in the first five days of the month is the highest, 0.35% higher than in the remaining days. It is unexpected that the difference in returns using the same DCA strategy is so large simply because the start dates are different. Therefore, this research aims to shed light on the "auspicious" (correct) day for the funds to start DCA investments, the reasons for obtaining the highest DCA income on that day, whether the same day is auspicious for all types of funds, and whether the difference in returns is robust for DCA investments in different periods.

Our primary finding is that DCA for mutual funds in the first five days of each month demonstrate better performance than for others in groups of five days in our sample period. Specifically, DCA returns are calculated as the difference between fund returns and corresponding benchmark returns. The annual benchmark adjusted returns reach the maximum when starting on the 2nd of every month (-2.90%) and the minimum when starting on the 28st (-3.52%) day, and the difference in returns between these days equal 0.62%. Notably, the returns during the first five days of each month are significantly greater than the DCA investment starting on other dates. In contrast, the DCA returns on the final six days of each month are significantly less than the DCA investment starting on other dates. Moreover, when we classified different funds according to their investment style-value, growth and

---

① Specifically, the operating fee is divided into following parts, 1.5% of the management fee and 0.25% of the bank custody fee, the same for all funds, while the front end load fees range from 0.5% to 2% depending on the investment amount, with an average of 1%. On the whole, above three fees add up to 3.243% on average for full sample.

balance——we found that the day-of-the-month effect of DCA returns is still significant; this result is the most profound for the growth funds.

What drives the day-of-the-month effect for monthly mutual fund DCA investment? We considered four plausible explanations proposed in the literature on calendar anomaly: earnings announcement effect, holiday effect, fund tournament effect and Halloween effect. These effects cause concentrated selling or buying behaviour in investors in the corresponding months, thus causing the difference in the average returns on different days of certain months. We use a dummy variable measure to capture the four effects, and find that the differences in returns between the first five days (final six days) and the remaining days of each month, correlated to possible trading behaviour caused by different effects, might lead to calendar effects. Therefore, we provide evidence to support the four explanations for the calendar anomaly, the day-of-the-month effect, for DCA.

Finally, we empirically investigated whether the return differences are robust when the DCA terms are extended to longer periods. The results show that the day-of-the-month effect continues to shrink with the extension of the investment period and disappear in three years. This also conforms to the DCA principle that the effect of investment timing will become negligible as long as the period is long enough and the number of investments large enough. We also replicate the tests in the subsample classified by the bull-bear cycle, and the results show that calendar anomaly is more significant in the first cycle than in the second. This finding is consistent with the adaptive market hypothesis (AMH), which predicts that individuals learn from these anomalies and adapt, and this adaptation drives arbitrage opportunities to disappear (Urquhart & Mcgroarty, 2014). Doyle and Chen (2009) also report a wandering weekday effect in recent years, that is, the calendar effect changes over time and even disappears.

The study makes three contributions. First, this paper adds an important dimension to the research on calendar anomalies. While scholars have investigated various seasonality effects in different markets worldwide, few consider that DCA that does not need timing skills will also be affected by timing in a limited investment period. Therefore, our study enriches the research on calendar anomalies, as the differences in DCA returns due to different starting dates have not been considered and observed in the literature so far. Second, in addition to demonstrating the day-of-the-month effect about DCA, we construct measures to capture four potential explanations. We find that the earnings announcement, holiday, fund tournament, and Halloween effects could well explain calendar anomalies. Hence, our study enriches the research of the mechanism of how the DCA calendar anomaly forms. Finally, the results based on the China A shares sample give us a comprehensive understanding of the application of DCA in developing countries. Our analysis extend the research based in developed countries to developing countries with the help of the fast-growing funds sector in China.

The remainder of the paper is structured as follows. Section 2 describes summary of the data and variables. Section 3 presents the empirical analysis to confirm the calendar anomaly in mutual fund DCA, Section 4 provides additional empirical results as potential explanations for the anomaly, Section 5 tests the robustness of the results, and Section 6 concludes the paper.

2 Data & variables

To examine day of the month effect of DCA investment and the potential source of one-year term DCA investment anomaly induced by starting day within the month, the data are obtained from Wind database and the China Stock Market and Accounting Research (CSMAR) database for the period of 2004 − 2020. Specifically, the trading data of benchmark index and equity mutual fund data are obtained from the CSMAR, and the fund style information data are obtained from Wind. We excluded ETFs, index funds, and QFIIs and retain only active open-end equity funds in our analysis.

2.1 Dollar cost averaging

To study the performance of DCA investment, we first calculated the raw internal rate of return (IRR), of mutual fund in predefined holding period,

R_i, and then we select the Shanghai Composite Index as the benchmark of all fund, CSI 300 as the benchmark index of value funds, CSI 500 as the benchmark index of growth funds and CSI 800 as the benchmark index of balanced funds. For each DCA investment, we subtract the benchmark return from raw return. Hence, the benchmark adjusted return is calculated as the following expressions:

$$Adj\_R_i = R_i - Benchmark_i \qquad (1)$$

Specifically, we built DCA mutual fund investment strategy as follows: first, since people who use DCA investment method are primary individual investors and people' most salary payment frequency is monthly China, we set the DCA investment interval as monthly and the total DCA investment period as 12 months, that is, one year. There are 31 days at most in a month. Because we use the rolling window, the DCA investment can start in any month, so the possible DCA investment start date is 31 days. In particular, if the same date in the next month is a non-trading day for a DCA investment date, or there is no such date in the next month, the investment in the next month will be deferred to the next trading day. Therefore, for an investment whose time interval is monthly and the total date of DCA investment is one year, in fact, we calculated the total return of 12 cash flows occurring on the same date of each month; moreover, to simplify the research, we took all funds as a value weighted fund portfolio, and adopts the same method for the different fund style portfolio; finally, in order to verify the robustness of the results, we further extended the total DCA investment period to 18 months and 36 months in the follow-up tests.

Finally, according to the aforementioned Research Report on mutual funds released by Fuguo fund and Galaxy Securities, using a sample of 46. 82 million fund investors from 2004 to February 2021, it was found that the fixed investment fund investors account for 21. 49% of the total fund investors. For the fixed investment fund investors, 27. 47% of the investors have a fixed investment period of 1 to 3 years, which is the most common DCA period, while 11. 73% of the investors have a DCA period of more than 3 years. The investment period of the remaining investors with DCA patterns is less than one year, which could not be regarded as a DCA investor in the strict sense, because DCA needs enough fixed investment times to play a role. Therefore, we use 1 to 3 years as the term of DCA in the following empirical work, which is not only in line with the actual situation of China, but also in line with the definition of DCA.

2.2 Summary statistics

Table 1 presents the summary of our sample. The number of active mutual funds in China increases from 23 in 2004 to 742 in 2020. During the whole period, the number of growth funds is the largest and the number of value funds is the least, and value funds did not exist until 2009. Moreover, all funds in the sample belong to 91 fund companies. The average size of the fund has been declining since the bull market reached the maximum of 11.36 billion in 2007, dropped to 1.05 billion in 2018 and was back to 1.76 billion in 2020.

Table 1   Descriptive statistics

Year	Funds	Style			Company	Fund size		Fund Company size	
		Growth	Balance	Value		Total (10^{11})	Average (10^9)	Total (10^{12})	Average (10^{10})
2004	23	16	7	0	16	0.58	2.52	0.37	1.61
2005	52	39	13	0	30	0.80	1.53	0.89	1.71
2006	54	29	25	0	34	0.63	1.16	0.98	1.81
2007	126	93	33	0	51	14.32	11.36	9.79	7.77
2008	163	83	80	0	56	8.80	5.40	6.89	4.23
2009	206	14	182	10	58	10.89	5.29	11.00	5.34
2010	248	101	137	10	59	11.39	4.59	13.01	5.25
2011	302	129	156	17	61	9.68	3.20	14.67	4.86
2012	370	136	214	20	66	9.12	2.46	20.50	5.54
2013	406	264	133	9	67	9.67	2.38	25.68	6.32
2014	436	74	228	134	69	8.79	2.02	33.66	7.72
2015	536	235	273	28	70	7.47	1.39	76.76	14.32
2016	613	76	391	146	75	8.65	1.41	114.55	18.69
2017	654	71	438	145	78	8.88	1.36	135.95	20.79
2018	749	141	473	135	86	7.86	1.05	186.20	24.86
2019	764	326	350	88	93	8.68	1.14	176.91	23.16
2020	742	462	253	27	91	13.05	1.76	202.56	27.30

Note: This table reports the summary statistics of China's open-end equity mutual funds from

2004 to 2020. We exclude index funds, ETFs, bond mutual funds and QFIIs from our sample.

3　Empirical analysis

3. 1　The day of the month effect for mutual funds dollar cost averaging: sorting method

As shown in Panel A of Table 2, we present the one-year term benchmark adjusted return of the monthly DCA investment starting on each day on the month. The annual DCA investment return starting on the 2nd of each month is the highest at -2.902%. The second highest is the DCA investment starting on the 3rd of each month, with a benchmark adjusted return of -2.912%. The lowest return is the investment staring from the 28th of the month, at -3.516%, and the second lowest return is the DCA investment starting on the 30th, with a benchmark adjusted return of -3.473%. Noticeably, the results exhibit a bunching pattern, that is, the most profitable DCA starts in the first few days of the month, while the least profitable ones are concentrated at the end of the month.

To verify whether the performance of DCA investment dates have a bunching effect, that is, whether the optimal days are adjacent to each other, we divided a total of 31 DCA investment days into 6 groups: dates $1-5$ are in the 1st Group, $6-10$ in the 2nd Group, and so on, ending with dates $26-31$ in the 6th Group. The results are presented in Panel B of Table 2, where we observe an increasing monotonic pattern for returns from the 1st Group to the 6th Group. Average benchmark adjusted returns range from -2.971% to -3.408% per year. A high-minus-low return spread is 0.437% annually, which is economically meaningful. Noticeably, only the average return of the first group is significantly greater than -0.0325 (average of annual fund expense), that is, the raw return of the first group before deducting expenses is significantly greater than 0. Moreover, we classified funds into three sub-samples depending on their investment style - value, balance, and growth. For balance and growth subsamples, the 1st Group still generates the highest return, and the 6th Group is still the worst. The results for the value style subsamples do not present a significant difference between the date-sorted portfolios. In short, the preliminary analysis shows that the benchmark adjusted of one-year DCA will vary with the start date, and the results of the overall sample, growth subsample, and balance subsample show that the returns starting at the beginning of the month rank at the top, while those at the end of the month rank at the bottom.

Table 2 One-year term benchmark adjusted return of DCA

Panel A: Date-specific benchmark adjusted return of DCA

Date	Total	Style		
		Growth	Balance	Value
1	−0.03035	−0.14845	−0.14183	−0.15804
2	−0.02902	−0.14714	−0.14012	−0.15862
3	−0.02912	−0.14792	−0.14049	−0.15962
4	−0.03018	−0.14979	−0.14091	−0.15924
5	−0.02988	−0.14937	−0.14094	−0.15901
6	−0.03013	−0.14920	−0.14091	−0.15736
7	−0.03302	−0.15131	−0.14165	−0.15762
8	−0.03265	−0.15188	−0.14277	−0.15641
9	−0.03306	−0.15239	−0.14430	−0.15880
10	−0.03200	−0.15110	−0.14396	−0.15847
11	−0.03439	−0.15423	−0.14308	−0.15801
12	−0.03346	−0.15326	−0.14360	−0.15935
13	−0.03291	−0.15092	−0.14430	−0.16005
14	−0.03328	−0.15079	−0.14392	−0.16072
15	−0.03231	−0.14900	−0.14246	−0.15719
16	−0.03340	−0.15263	−0.14315	−0.15979
17	−0.03338	−0.15314	−0.14389	−0.15978
18	−0.03360	−0.15324	−0.14357	−0.15871
19	−0.03262	−0.15233	−0.14198	−0.15598
20	−0.03278	−0.15091	−0.14214	−0.15490
21	−0.03292	−0.15249	−0.14366	−0.15783
22	−0.03345	−0.15286	−0.14318	−0.15615
23	−0.03361	−0.15379	−0.14398	−0.15768
24	−0.03265	−0.15089	−0.14306	−0.15887
25	−0.03319	−0.15135	−0.14354	−0.15898
26	−0.03312	−0.15225	−0.14399	−0.15874

continued

Panel A: Date-specific benchmark adjusted return of DCA

Date	Total	Style		
		Growth	Balance	Value
27	−0. 03380	−0. 15380	−0. 14528	−0. 16025
28	−0. 03516	−0. 15458	−0. 14710	−0. 16032
29	−0. 03437	−0. 15385	−0. 14547	−0. 15842
30	−0. 03473	−0. 15273	−0. 14557	−0. 15740
31	−0. 03332	−0. 15232	−0. 14311	−0. 15901

Panel B: Group-specific benchmark adjusted return of DCA

Group	Total	Style		
		Growth	Balance	Value
1st	−0. 02971	−0. 14853	−0. 14086	−0. 15891
2nd	−0. 03217	−0. 15118	−0. 14272	−0. 15773
3rd	−0. 03327	−0. 15164	−0. 14347	−0. 15907
4th	−0. 03316	−0. 15245	−0. 14295	−0. 15783
5th	−0. 03317	−0. 15228	−0. 14348	−0. 15790
6th	−0. 03408	−0. 15326	−0. 14509	−0. 15902

Note: This table reports the one-year term benchmark adjusted return of DCA strategy starting from different day of the month. In panel A, we report benchmark adjusted return of DCA strategy from date the 1st to the 31st of the month for full sample and style-based subsamples. In panel B, we divide a total of 31 DCA investment days into 6 groups: dates 1 −5 are in the 1st Group, 6−10 in the 2nd Group, and so on, ending with dates 26−31 in the 6th Group, and report the performance of six groups for full sample and style-based subsamples.

Because our main interest is whether there is day-of-the-month effect for DCA investment and whether there is a bunching effect for the anomaly days, we used the portfolio-sorting method based on the preliminary results in Table 2 to compare the differences in returns between one-year monthly DCA of the top (bottom) group and other groups.

Table 3 reports the portfolio sorting results. Column 1 of Table 3 presents the differences in average bench mark-adjusted returns between the different five-day groups of each month. The difference is calculated by subtracting the average return of each group from those of other groups. The best performing group is the 1st, the group whose investment start dates are 1 to 5; its average benchmark adjusted return is greater than that of the other groups. Indeed, the 1st Group outperforms others by 0.348% on average per year. In particular, the return difference of the 1st Group is significantly higher, by 0.44%, than that of the 6th Group, which has the worst performance. Compared with other groups, its return differences are all significantly negative.

Using the same DCA investment, we divided funds into three groups based on investment styles to assess whether the results hold for the sub-groups. Column 2 to Column 4 of Table 3 report the results for growth funds, balance funds and value funds, respectively. For the growth funds portfolio in Column 2, the overall characteristics are still similar to those of the full sample and balance subsample. The performance of the 1st Group is better than the other five groups, with the 6th Group significantly worse off than all others. Column 3 reports the results of the portfolios of balance funds. Here, the performance of the 1st Group is still the best, 0.228% higher at 5% significance level than that of 2nd to 5th Groups, and 0.42% higher at 1% significance level than that of the 6th Group. The 6th Group's average return is still significantly lower than that of other groups, which is consistent with the results of full sample. For the value style fund portfolio (column 4), the performance of each group does not show the obvious characteristics as do the preliminary results in Table 2, possibly because the number of value funds is too small (less than 10% during half of the sample period) or the previously observed DCA calendar anomaly does not exist in value funds.

In summary, there are obvious outstanding performance differences attributable to DCA investment starting date. The 1st Group fares significantly better than other groups, while 6th Group significantly worse. If there can be optimal days for one-year term monthly DCA investment, it should be the first five days of every month.

Table 3 The day of the month effect for mutual funds DCA: Sorting method

Return difference of		(1)	(2)	(3)	(4)
ith and jth five-day		Total	Growth	Balance	Value
1st-jth	1 Minus 2	0.0025***	0.0026***	0.0018**	−0.0012**
		(6.32)	(5.65)	(2.89)	(−3.75)
	1 Minus 3	0.0036*	0.0031	0.0026***	0.0002
		(2.23)	(0.89)	(6.22)	(0.81)
	1 Minus 4	0.0034***	0.0039*	0.0021**	−0.0011
		(9.94)	(2.16)	(4.19)	(−0.36)
	1 Minus 5	0.0035***	0.0037**	0.0026***	−0.0010
		(12.16)	(3.36)	(15.22)	(−1.98)
	1 Minus 6	0.0044***	0.0047***	0.0042***	0.0001
		(15.30)	(5.66)	(7.46)	(0.17)
6th−jth	6 Minus 1	−0.0044***	−0.0047***	−0.0042***	−0.0001
		(−15.30)	(−5.66)	(−7.46)	(−0.17)
	6 Minus 2	−0.0019***	−0.0021***	−0.0024*	−0.0013
		(−40.45)	(−5.31)	(−2.57)	(−1.55)
	6 Minus 3	−0.0008**	−0.0016*	−0.0016***	0.0000
		(−2.32)	(−2.21)	(−7.44)	(0.12)
	6 Minus 4	−0.0009**	−0.0008**	−0.0021**	−0.0012*
		(−2.58)	(−2.72)	(−3.57)	(−2.20)
	6 Minus 5	−0.0009**	−0.0010**	−0.0016**	−0.0011
		(−2.76)	(−2.59)	(−2.99)	(−1.11)

Note: This table reports the benchmark-adjusted returns between the different groups of each month. We divide a total of 31 DCA investment days into 6 groups: dates 1−5 are in the 1st Group, 6−10 in the 2nd Group, and so on, ending with dates 26−31 in the 6th Group. In the first half of the table, we report the return difference between the 1st group and the other groups. In the second half of the table, we report the return difference between the 6th group and the other groups. T-statistics are calculated with Newey and West (1987) adjusted standard error. ***, **, and * indicate statistical significance at the 1%, 5%, and 10% levels.

3.2 The day of the month effect for mutual funds dollar cost averaging: AR(p)-GJR-GARCH (1,1) model

To comprehensively verify the results in Table 3, we used linear regression modelling. The earlier regression to analyse the day effects used OLS with daily returns as dependent variable and month-day dummy variables as independent variables. Moreover, recent studies adopt an AR (p)-GJR-GARCH(1,1) specification (Glosten et al., 1993) to assess the statistical significance of the calendar effect. Compared to the OLS method, the latter better captures the time-series properties of daily returns relevant to this analysis.

Specifically, following Doyle and Chen (2009) and Ulkua and Rogers (2018), we used 10 lagged (AR, or autoregressive) terms plus a single moving average (MA) term. The lagged AR terms constitute two full weeks of trading days. This model equation is:

$$Adj\_R_t = \sum_{i=1}^{6} \beta_i \, \text{Day\_Dummy} + \sum_{j=1}^{10} \rho_j \, \text{Adj\_R}_{t-j} + m\varepsilon_{t-1} + \gamma' Z_{i,t} + \varepsilon_t \tag{1}$$

Adj_R_t is the one-year term benchmark adjusted return of the monthly DCA investment starting on day t, assuming 31 days in a month, and t is in the range of $1-31$. All days are classified in groups of five or six days. Day_Dummy$_2$ is a dummy variable that equals 1 if Adj_R_t measure the DCA returns starting at dates $1^{st}-5^{th}$ in the month, and zero otherwise and so on[①]. $Z_{i,t}$ refers to a vector of semi-annual fund characteristics[②], including fund size, churn rate, fund flow. The system in Eq. (1) is estimated via ML using Student's t-distribution. The error term follows the GARCH (1,1) model with the following specification:

$$\varepsilon_t \sim N(0, \sigma_t^2), \text{ and } \sigma_t^2 = \omega + \alpha \varepsilon_{t-1}^2 + \gamma \sigma_{t-1}^2 \tag{2}$$

---

① Day_Dummy_3 is a dummy variable that equals 1 if Adj_R_t measures the DCA returns starting at dates $11-15$ in each month, and zero otherwise. Day_Dummy_4 is a dummy variable that equals 1 if Adj_R_t measures the DCA returns starting at dates $16-20$, and zero otherwise. Day_Dummy_5 is a dummy variable that equals 1 if Adj_R_t measure the DCA returns starting at dates $21-25$, and zero otherwise. Day_Dummy_6 is a dummy variable that equals 1 if Adj_R_t measures the DCA returns starting at dates $26-31$, and zero otherwise.

② Our data source CSMAR database updates the fund holdings for half a year, so the relevant fund variables are at the semi-annual frequency. To measure turnover rate of fund, we follow Yan and Zhang (2009) method to use the total sale and purchase: The higher value the measure, more frequent trading occurs.

Since we observed that first five days' DCA performance is higher than the other groups. After we obtain coefficients from equation (1), we formed our hypothesis as follows.

$$H_0 1 : \beta_1 > (\beta_2 + \beta_3 + \beta_4 + \beta_5 + \beta_6)/5$$

We simplify the hypothesis to

$H_0 1 : \beta_1 - (\beta_2 + \beta_3 + \beta_4 + \beta_5 + \beta_6)/5 > 0$ (null for the first five days of the month effect)

Moreover, since we also observed that DCA performances starting from last six days of the month are relatively lower compared to that on other days, we could also classify the last six days as the 6th Group and use it as the base of day dummies, forming the corresponding hypothesis:

$H_0 2 : \beta_6 - (\beta_1 + \beta_2 + \beta_3 + \beta_4 + \beta_5)/5 < 0$ (null for the last six days of the month effect)

Table 4 reports the results of Eq. (1). Since the 1st Group containing date 1—5 is the best group to start DCA investment with, the difference in the coefficients of the day dummy variables between the 1st group and the 2nd to 6th Groups should be positive. As expected, the difference in the coefficients of the dummy variables is positive at 1% significance level for the OLS regression model and at 5% significance level for model with ARMA, indicating that the return on DCA investment from the 1st Group is better than that on other days. Moreover, the difference in the coefficients of the day dummy variables between the 6th group and 1st to 5th Groups should be negative. The difference in the coefficients of the dummy variables is negative at 5% significance level for both the models, which is also consistent with our prediction that DCA starting from the last six days of month ranks the least of all choices.

Columns 2 to 4 of Table 4 report the results for the differences in the coefficients of the day dummy variables of three fund styles, the growth fund portfolio results being the most significant. For such funds, the difference in the coefficients of the day dummy variables between the 1st and 2nd to 6th Groups is significantly positive, while the difference between the 6th group and 1st to 5th Groups is significantly negative. For the balance and value funds, the results are similar, though not significant for all coefficient differences.

Table 4   The day of the month effect for mutual funds DCA：
Coefficients differences from Regression

	OLS (No AR-GJR-GARCH)		With AR-GJR-GARCH		Obs.
	β_1-Avg(β_2 to β_6)	β_6-Avg(β_1 to β_5)	β_1-Avg(β_2 to β_6)	β_6-Avg(β_1 to β_5)	
Total	0.0030***	−0.0021**	0.0180**	−0.0130**	6,053
	(7.02)	(−3.29)	(3.52)	(−2.27)	
Growth	0.0038***	−0.0026**	0.0134**	−0.0136**	5,867
	(7.81)	(−3.47)	(3.62)	(−3.73)	
Balance	0.0031***	−0.0030***	−0.0002	−0.0083**	5,867
	(5.59)	(−5.37)	(−0.05)	(−2.64)	
Value	0.0010**	−0.0003	0.0071**	−0.0131***	4,193
	(2.57)	(−0.76)	(2.54)	(−7.91)	

Note：This table reports the coefficient differences estimated from OLS Regression and AR(p)-GJR-GARCH (1,1). Two models are specified as equation (1) and (2). The columns marked 'β_1-Avg (β_2 to β_6)' reports the difference between β_1 and average of coefficients of $\beta2$ to $\beta6$ for full sample and style-based subsample. The columns marked 'β_6-Avg(β_1 to β_5)' reports the difference between β_6 and average of coefficients of β_1 to β_5 for full sample and style-based subsample. T-statistics are calculated with Newey and West (1987) adjusted standard error. ***，**，and * indicate statistical significance at the 1%，5%，and 10% levels.

We have already shown that the one-year DCA performance of the first 5-day interval outperforms average of the remaining days. To rule out the possibility that the other 5-day intervals also have similar higher returns than the 'remaining days', we replicate the above analysis testing the hypothesis $\beta_2 > (\beta_1 + \beta_3 + \beta_4 + \beta_5 + \beta_6)/5$ and so on for β_3, β_4, β_5, and results are presented in Table A1 in the Internet Appendix. As expected, the difference in the coefficients of the dummy variables is not significant across all other 5-day intervals for the regression models either with controls or not, indicating that the returns on DCA investment for other 5-day intervals are not significantly better or worse than the average of remaining days. Therefore, the extra findings reinforce the conclusion in table 5.

To summarize, the results from the sorting method and GJR regression are powerful in rejecting the null of market efficiency, and we draw the conclusion that seasonality effects exist to bring about returns starting from first five days of the month are higher than for others, while returns starting from final six days of the month relatively lower to the rest of the days. Moreover, these effects are more evident in growth funds than others. Analysing for the mechanisms of day-of-the-month effect for DCA will impart further clarity on the occurrence of this anomaly and its related characteristics.

Table 5 Potential explanations to the day-of-the-month effect for mutual funds DCA

Model #	Buying Pressure				Selling Pressure			
	1	2	3	4	1	2	3	4
Holiday	0.0201*				−0.0170***			
	(1.95)				(−8.21)			
Halloween		0.1283***				−0.1153***		
		(7.66)				(−4.47)		
Tournament			0.0593**				0.0330	
			(2.06)				(0.83)	
Anno				−0.0016				−0.0495***
				(−0.19)				(−7.36)

Note: Table 5 reports the relation between the hypothesis estimators and the return differences induced from calendar effect. As specified in Eq. (3), the independent variable is the difference in one-year term returns between the 1ˢᵗ Group (6ᵗʰ Group) and other groups to measure the calendar anomaly at the beginning (end) of month t, the dependent variables are dummies measure four effects. *Holiday* is the holiday dummy that takes a value of 1 if the months are February, May and October for buying pressure, and 0 otherwise; it takes a value of 1 if the months are January, April and September, and 0 otherwise for the selling pressure. *Halloween* is the May and June dummy that takes a value of 1 if the month is June, and 0 otherwise for buying pressure, and a value of 1 if the month is May, and 0 otherwise, for the selling pressure. *Tournament* is the fund tournament dummy that takes a value of 1 if the months are January, April, July and October for buying pressure, and 0 otherwise. For the selling pressure, *Tournament* takes a value of 1 if the months are March, June, September and December, and 0 otherwise. *Anno* is the earning announcement dummy that takes a value of 1 if months are February, May, September and November for buying pressure, and 0 otherwise. For the selling pressure, the dummy *Anno* takes a value of 1 if the months are January, March, July and December, and 0 otherwise. T-statistics are calculated with Newey and West (1987) adjusted standard error. ***, **, and * indicate statistical significance at the 1%, 5%, and 10% levels.

4 Potential explanations

After verifying that the start date of DCA investment greatly affects the final returns, and that the 1st to 5th of each month would be the best start date for DCA investment, we investigated the source of the high returns on these optimal days. We have four possible explanations based on the calendar anomaly literature: earnings announcement effect, holiday effect, fund tournament effect and Halloween effect. The earnings announcement hypothesis predicts that seasonality could be a reason for investor reaction, the timing of earnings news releases, and the evidence from the U. S. sample supports the hypothesis. Penman (1987) documents that the timing of earnings news published leads to market performance in first half-month during quarter two to four outperformed other times. Under the holiday effect hypothesis, seasonality is explained by risk avoidance for long holidays; investors sell shares at the end of the month before the holiday to avoid the risk induced by fluctuations of overseas markets during holidays, resulting in relatively low market returns at the end of the month before a long holiday. Pantzalis and Ucar (2014) test a U. S. sample to find that religious holidays would delay investors' information processing, thus causing a holiday-induced calendar anomaly. Under the fund tournament hypothesis, managers' performance ranking released at the end of a quarter would impose pressure on fund managers to adjust the holdings, thus generating buying power at the beginning of the first month of the upcoming quarter. Finally, the Halloween effect has been widely tested in the U. S. , and a similar anomaly, called the May and June effect, also exists in China. [①] Hence, our study considers the buying and selling pressures relevant to the Halloween effect.

We observe that the above explanations will only affect the return at the beginning and end of a specific month. To precisely capture the explanatory ability of the four hypotheses, we did a regression analysis, using the difference in the returns on one-year monthly DCA between the top (bottom) group and other groups for 12 months as the dependent variable and various hypothesis dummy variables as independent variables. The model equation is:

---

① May and June effect refers to the fact that market return of A shares are significantly lower during May and June. In the decade of 2010, the market return rate in May and June in the eight years is less than 0. Therefore, there is a proverb in the A-share market "Poor May and desperate June", which is similar as 'Sell in May and go away, but remember to come back in September' in U. S. market.

$$Adj\_R_t^{1st(6th)} - Adj\_R_t^{others} = \alpha_0 + \beta_i * Effect\_Dummy_i + \varepsilon_t \qquad (3)$$

where $Adj_R{}_{,t}^{1st(6th)} - Adj_R{}_{,t}^{others}$ is our dependent variable, the difference in returns of one year-term DCA between the 1st Group (6th Group) and other groups to measure the calendar anomaly at the beginning (end) of month t. $Effect\_Dummy_i$ is the main independent variable. *Holiday* is the holiday dummy that takes a value of 1 if the months are March, May and October for buying pressure, and 0 otherwise; it takes a value of 1 if the months are January, April, September and December, and 0 otherwise for the selling pressure. ①Halloween is the May and June dummy that takes a value of 1 if the month is June, and 0 otherwise for buying pressure, and again a value of 1 if the month is May, and 0 otherwise, for the selling pressure. ② *Tournaments* is the fund tournament dummy that takes a value of 1 if the months are January, April, July and October for buying pressure, and 0 otherwise. For the selling pressure, *Tournament* takes a value of 1 if the months are March, June, September and December, and 0 otherwise. ③ *Anno* is the earning announcement dummy that takes a value of 1 if the months are February, May, September and November for buying pressure, and 0 otherwise. For the selling pressure, the dummy *Anno* takes a value of 1 if the months are March, July and December, and 0 otherwise. ④

The results in Table 5 show the relation between the hypothesis

---

① For the first week of February, May and October of each year, China A-share market is closed for traditional holidays. Based on the holiday effect hypothesis, the selling pressure in the end of the prior month would depress the returns, and the purchasing power after the long holidays in February, May and October might drive price up.

② Based on the Halloween effect in A shares market, the May and June effect in China, investors tend to sell in the beginning of May and buy back at the end of June.

③ Under the fund tournament hypothesis, fund managers would increase net buying at the beginning of every quarter (January, April, July and October), thus driving returns up.

④ China publishes performance forecasts, annual reports and quarterly reports in January, April, August and October. To avoid risks of unexpected earnings surprises, investors will sell shares at the end of the corresponding month and buy them back at the beginning of the following month, resulting in a higher yield for DCA starting in the beginning of the months following publication, that is, February, May, September, and November.

estimators and the return differences induced by calendar effect, with the coefficients estimated from Eq. (3). For the holiday dummy variable *Holiday*, the calendar effects in stock returns of both sides are significant. Investors' trading exhibits a significant positive effect at the beginning of month after the long holiday and a significant negative effect at the end of the holiday month. Moreover, Halloween effect also plays a role in leading the calendar effect; the coefficients are significant for both sides, that is, in line with the Halloween effect, and investors sell more intensively when the market performance of first days of May is poor, and buy intensively when the market performance recovers at the end of June. Furthermore, for the tournament dummy variable *Tournament*, we observe a significant calendar effect induced by net buying after the ranking of each quarter, consistent with our insight that institutional trading displays a tournament effect. However, its impact on the selling pressure is insignificant, indicating that no obvious selling trades caused the stock price to fall at the end of each quarter. Finally, a significantly negative coefficient of *Anno* indicates net selling induced by avoiding earnings uncertainty, predicting poor performance at the end of the months just before earning news release, whereas an insignificant coefficient for the buying pressure shows that net buying at the beginning of subsequent months after the announcements does not generate profound positive returns.

In summary, our results show that return differences between the first five days (final six days) and the remaining days of each month are correlated with possible trading behaviour caused by different effects might lead to the calendar effects, as reflected in the literature. Therefore, this study provides evidence to support earnings announcement, holiday, fund tournament and Halloween effects explanations for the DCA calendar anomaly, the day-of-the-month effect.

Furthermore, we also tested whether there is a hierarchy among above four explanations which lead to the calendar effects. Specifically, we removed the data correlated to certain possible explanation one by one, and these results are reported in Table 6. Consistent with our findings in Table 5, the Halloween effect serves as a dominant factor in driving the calendar effect for both buying and selling pressure. After we remove the data in May and June which are relevant to the Halloween effect, the difference in the coefficients of the dummy variables between the 1st group and 2nd to 6th Groups is not significant for model with ARMA and even inverted for OLS regression model, indicating that the return of DCA investment starting from the first five days disappears when eliminating the Halloween effect. Moreover, the difference in the coefficients of the dummy variables between the 6th group and 1st to 5th Groups is insignificant for either model, which also reinforces the importance of the Halloween effect. Furthermore, Table 6 also provides the differences in the coefficients of the dummy variables when eliminating other effects that may lead to calendar effect. The results show that the superior performance of DCA investment starting from first five days remains significant after removing the influence of the Holiday effect, and poor performance of DCA investment starting from the last six days remains significant after removing the impacts of the Tournament effect. Finally, the differences in the coefficients of the dummy variables are insignificant or inverted for either test when eliminating the announcement effect, indicating that the announcement effect is as important as the Halloween effect. Therefore, our findings confirm that there is a hierarchy of causes inducing the calendar effects, that is, the Halloween effect and the announcement play a more important role than the other two effects in driving the calendar effects of DCA investment.

Table 6　A hierarchy analysis of factors driving the calendar effect for mutual funds DCA

	No AR-GJR-GARCH		With AR-GJR-GARCH	
	β_1-Avg(β_2 to β_6)	β_6-Avg(β_1 to β_5)	β_1-Avg(β_2 to β_6)	β_6-Avg(β_1 to β_5)
RMV Holiday	−0.0120**	−0.0120	0.0100**	0.0102*
	(−3.39)	(−1.15)	(1.99)	(1.90)
RMV Halloween	−0.0285***	0.0054	0.0034	−0.0011
	(−4.60)	(1.04)	(0.55)	(−0.35)
RMV Tournament	−0.0315***	−0.0440***	−0.0073*	−0.0072*
	(−4.23)	(−5.06)	(−1.90)	(−1.71)
RMV Anno	−0.0054	0.0152**	−0.0045	0.0026
	(−0.96)	(2.16)	(−1.36)	(0.57)

Note: This table reports the coefficient differences estimated from OLS Regression and AR(p)-GJR-GARCH (1,1) after removing the data relevant to certain effect. Two models are specified as in equations (1) and (2). The columns marked "0-Avg(β_2 to β_6)" report the difference between 0 and average of coefficients of $\beta2$ to $\beta6$ for sub sample that removing the data relevant to certain effect. The columns marked "0-Avg(β_1 to β_5)" report the difference between 0 and average of coefficients of $\beta1$ to $\beta5$ for sub sample that removing the data relevant to certain effect. T-statistics are calculated with Newey and West (1987) adjusted standard error. ```, ``, and ` indicate statistical significance at the 1%,5%, and 10% levels.

5   Robustness checks

To test whether the weekday effect wanders to a halt, first, we split the entire sample into two bull and bear cycles.① Table 7 presents the results. We find that our results remain strong in the first bull-bear cycle. However, the difference in returns in the second bull-bear cycle is not as significant as that in the first. The result confirms the wandering calendar effect documented in the literature. Investors will learn and adapt to market anomalies, and the anomalies will gradually disappear.

------

① China's A-share market has experienced two big bull and bear cycles from 2005 to 2020, and their representative events are the two notorious bubble-crash, the 2007-2008 crash and the 2014-2015 crash (Luo et al., 2022). Specifically, the Shanghai Composite Index rose from 998 points in June 2005 to 6124 points in October 2007, and then experienced a 72.8% crash to 1,664 points till October 2008. A cash crunch that hit the Chinese financial system on June 25, 2013, driving interbank rates to unprecedented highs and the Shanghai Composite Index to its lowest point since January 2009, 1849 points. Since then, the Shanghai Stock Exchange Index has never fallen below 1849, and risen all the way to 5178 in June 2015 and fell to 2,638 points in January 2016, The Research report (https://www.vzkoo. comread202211124aeb978e016070a7bdd3449c. html) report titled 'Summarizing the bull and bear cutting points in China's A-share market in the last 10 years' released by Pacific Securities in 2022 also took June 2013 as the starting point of the 2015 bubble. Therefore, June 2013 when Shanghai Composite Index hit 1849 points could be recognized as the cutting point of the two market cycles.

Table 7　The day of the month effect for mutual funds DCA: Bull-Bear cycle

Return difference of ith and jth five-day		(1) First Bull-Bear period	(2) Second Bull-Bear period
1st-jth	1 Minus 2	0.0042***	0.0004
		(6.26)	(0.07)
	1 Minus 3	0.0074***	−0.0011***
		(2.23)	(−4.96)
	1 Minus 4	0.0055***	0.0007***
		(6.85)	(5.78)
	1 Minus 5	0.0049***	0.0016***
		(5.16)	(2.92)
	1 Minus 6	0.0054***	0.0028
		(8.24)	(1.32)
6th-jth	6 Minus 1	−0.0054***	−0.0028
		(−8.24)	(−1.32)
	6 Minus 2	−0.0012**	−0.0023***
		(−2.69)	(−1.55)
	6 Minus 3	0.0020	−0.0039
		(1.35)	(−1.63)
	6 Minus 4	0.0001	−0.0021
		(0.08)	(−0.96)
	6 Minus 5	−0.0005	−0.0012
		(−0.32)	(−0.54)

Note: This table reports the benchmark-adjusted returns between the different groups of each month. We divide a total of 31 DCA investment days into 6 groups: dates 1−5 are in the 1st Group, 6−10 in the 2nd Group, and so on, ending with dates 26−31 in the 6th Group. Column (1) presents the results from first bull-bear cycle from 2004−2013. Column (2) presents the results from second bull-bear cycle from 2014−2020. In the first half of the table, we report the return difference between the 1st group and the other groups. In the second half of the table, we report the return difference between the 6th group and the other groups. T-statistics are calculated with Newey and West (1987) adjusted standard error. ***, **, and * indicate statistical significance at the 1%, 5%, and 10% levels.

We further investigated the explanations for calendar effect for two cycles separately in Table 8. The *Halloween* effect on calendar anomaly in each cycle is quite stable over time, while the other three measures on the differences in returns between the first five days (final six days) and the remaining days appear to vary over time in two cycles. In the first cycle, the holiday and earnings announcement effects significantly predict the negative returns difference for the selling pressure, and the tournament effect significantly generates the positive return difference for the buying pressure. For the second cycle, only the tournament and holiday effects significantly predict the positive returns difference for the buying pressure, while other coefficients are not significant. In short, in addition to the Halloween effect, the other three effects have weakened the explanatory power of the calendar anomaly in the second cycle.

Table 8 Potential Explanations to the day of the month effect for mutual funds DCA:

Bull-Bear cycle

Panel A: First Bull-Bear period

Model #	Buying Pressure				Selling Pressure			
	1	2	3	4	1	2	3	4
Holiday	0.0101				−0.0478***			
	(0.63)				(−3.52)			
Halloween		0.0852**				−0.2024***		
		(4.44)				(−7.03)		
Tournament			0.0703***				0.0221	
			(5.38)				(0.33)	
Anno				−0.0255				−0.0927**
				(−0.37)				(−2.09)

Panel B: Second Bull-Bear period

Model #	Buying Pressure				Selling Pressure			
	1	2	3	4	1	2	3	4
Holiday	0.0309***				0.0167			
	(4.68)				(1.10)			
Halloween		0.1722***				−0.0275		
		(9.76)				(−1.15)		
Tournament			0.0478***				0.0450	
			(2.58)				(0.85)	
Anno				0.0245				−0.0010
				(0.57)				(−0.16)

Note: Table 5 reports the relation between the hypothesis estimators and the return differences induced from calendar effect. As specified in Eq. (3), the independent variable is the difference in one-year term returns between the 1st Group (6th Group) and other groups to measure the calendar anomaly at the beginning (end) of different month t, and while the dependant variables are dummies to measure four effects. The definition of dummy variables is the same as that in Table 5. T-statistics are calculated with Newey and West (1987) adjusted standard error. ***, **, and * indicate statistical significance at the 1%, 5%, and 10% levels.

Second, we extended the DCA investment term to 36 months. Table 9 presents the results, and Column 1 reports the difference in fund returns on DCA investment starting between the 1st Group (first 5 days) and the 6th Group (Final 6 days) of each month. Our results provide supportive evidence for the persistence of the calendar anomaly. However, the effect tends to fade away as the number of fixed investment increases, because the essence of DCA is to smooth the impact of timing on investment through a sufficient time period. We find that the significance of the optimal day effect holds up to three years hence. Notably, we also show that the differences in returns become smaller as DCA terms increase, which is consistent with the intuitive prediction. The returns of the best five days and the worst five days of fixed investment vary from 0.48% of the one-year period to 0.41% of the three-year period, while the returns of the best 10 days and the worst 10 days of fixed investment vary from 0.32% of the one-year period to 0.26% of the three-year period.

Table 9   Day of the month effect persistence

Horizon	1st- 6th	Top 5 - Bottom 5	Top 10 - Bottom 10
1 year	0.0044***	0.0048***	0.0032***
1.5 years	0.0031***	0.0035***	0.0027*
2 years	0.0024***	0.0034***	0.0026***
2.5 years	0.0018***	0.0028***	0.0023***
3 years	0.0004	0.0041***	0.0026**

Note: This table reports day of the month effect persistence using different terms of DCA (1 year, 1.5 years, 2 years, 2.5years and 3 years) for the overall equity mutual funds. Column 1 reports the difference in fund returns on DCA investment starting between the 1st Group (first 5 days) and the 6th Group (Final 6 days) of each month. Column 2 reports the return differences between the best five days and the worst five days for various terms of DCA. Column 3 reports return differences between best 10 days and the worst 10 days for various terms DCA. *T*-statistics are calculated with Newey and West (1987) adjusted standard error. ***, **, and * denote significance at the 1%, 5%, and 10% level.

6 Conclusions

A number of studies have investigated DCA investments and the relevant behavioural framework. DCA investments have been widely welcomed by ordinary individual investors, because of their many advantages, as verified in the empirical and theoretical literature. However, to our knowledge, the calendar anomaly for mutual funds DCA investment has not been studied. Based on data from 2004 to 2020, we investigate which day is the optimal or worst day for monthly mutual fund DCA investment and what are the possible sources of abnormal returns on DCA starting on certain dates of the month.

Our findings are as follows. First, the results of our investigation into the Chinese mutual fund market for the optimal starting day of DCA mutual funds investment show that different start dates of DCA investment will lead to a huge difference in returns, which has not been discussed in the DCA investment literature. Therefore, based on our sample period estimation results, investors should choose the first five days of each month to start DCA investment, rather than randomly picking the starting date of each month. Second, the results also shed light on the source of DCA investment returns on different starting days; we find that the earnings announcement, holiday, fund tournament, and Halloween effects contribute to the DCA calendar anomaly. Finally, we investigate the heterogeneity and robustness of the optimal starting day of DCA, classify different funds according to investment styles, and extend the term of the DCA investment strategy, all of which verify that our findings are applicable to different types of funds and different periods.

References

Birru J, 2016. Day of the week and the cross-section of returns[J]. Journal of Financial Economics, 130(1): 182-214.
Bouman S, Jacobsen B, 2002. The halloween indicator, sell in May and go

away: Another puzzle[J]. American Economic Review, 92: 1618-1635.

Braselton J, Rafter J, Humphrey P, et al, 1999. Randomly walking through Wall Street: Comparing lump-sum versus dollar-cost average investment strategies[J]. Mathematics & Computers in Simulation, 49(4-5): 297-318.

Cao J, Chordia T, Zhan X, 2021. The calendar effects of the idiosyncratic volatility puzzle: A tale of two days? [J]. Management Science, 67(12): 7866-7887.

Constantinides G M, 1979. A note on the suboptimality of dollar-cost averaging as an investment policy[J]. Journal of Financial and Quantitative Analysis, 14(2): 443-450.

Douglas F F, Viswanathan S, 1990. A Theory of the interday variations in volume, variance, and trading costs in securities markets[J]. Review of Financial Studies, 4: 593-624.

Doyle J R, Chen C H, 2009. The wandering weekday effect in major stock markets[J]. Journal of Banking & Finance, 33(8):1388-1399.

Dubil R, 2005. Lifetime dollar-cost averaging: Forget cost savings, think risk reduction[J]. Journal of Financial Planning, 18(10):86-88,90.

Fong W M, 2017. Beating the market: Dollar-cost averaging with the profitable dividend yield strategy[J]. Journal of Wealth Management, 20(2): 54-66.

Glosten L R, Jagannathan R, Runkle D E, 1993. On the relation between the expected value and the volatility of the nominal excess return on stocks[J]. The Journal of Finance, 48: 1779-1801.

Grable J E, Chatterjee S, 2015. Another look at lump-sum versus dollar-cost averaging[J]. Journal of Financial Services Professionals, 69(5): 16-18.

Huang Y S, Chiu J, Lin C Y, et al, 2022. The effect of Chinese lunar calendar on individual investors' trading[J]. Pacific-Basin Finance Journal, 71:1-9.

Israelsen C L, 1999. Lump sums take their lumps[J]. Financial Planning, 29(1): 51-54.

Jacobsen B, Marquering W, 2008. Is it the weather? [J]. Journal of Banking & Finance, 32: 526-540.

Kang M，2010. Probability of information-based trading and the January effect [J]. Journal of Banking & Finance，34(12)：2985-2994.

Kapalczynski A，Lien D，2021. Effectiveness of augmented dollar-cost averaging[J]. The North American Journal of Economics and Finance，56(4)：101370.

Khouja M，Lamb R P，1999. An optimal schedule for dollar cost averaging under different transaction costs[J]. International Transactions in Operational Research，6(2)：245-261.

Kirkby J L，Mitra S，Nguyen D，2020. An analysis of dollar cost averaging and market timing investment strategies[J]. European Journal of Operational Research，286(3)：1168-1186.

Knight J，Mandell L，Review F S，et al，1992. Nobody gains from dollar cost averaging analytical，numerical and empirical results[J]. Financial Services Review，2(1)：51-61.

Lakonishok J，Maberly E，1990. The weekend effect：Trading patterns of individual and institutional investors[J]. Journal of Finance，45(1)：231-243.

Lei A Y C，Li H，2007. Automatic investment plans：Realized returns and shortfall probabilities[J]. Financial Services Review，16：183-195.

Levy T，Yagil J，2012. The week-of-the-year effect：Evidence from around the globe[J]. Journal of Banking & Finance，36(7)：1963-1974.

Liu W，2013. Lunar calendar effect：Evidence of the Chinese Farmer's Calendar on the equity markets in East Asia[J]. Journal of the Asia Pacific Economy，18(4)：560-593.

Luo D，Yao Z，Zhu Y，2022. Bubble-crash experience and investment styles of mutual fund managers[J]. Journal of Corporate Finance，76：1-12.

Luskin J M，2017. Dollar-cost averaging using the cape ratio：An identifiable trend influencing outperformance[J]. Journal of Financial Planning，30(1)：54-60.

Meir S，1995. A behavioral framework for dollar-cost averaging[J]. The Journal of Portfolio Management，22(1)：70-78.

Miller E M，1988. Why a weekend effect[J]. The Journal of Portfolio Management，14：43-48.

Newey W K, West K D, 1987. A simple, positive semi-definite, heteroskedasticity and autocorrelation consistent covariance matrix [J]. Econometrica, 55(3)：703-708.

Ogden J P, 2012. Turn—of—month evaluations of liquid profits and stock returns：A common explanation for the monthly and january effects[J]. Journal of Finance, 45(4)：1259-1272.

Pantzalis C, Ucar E, 2014. Religious holidays, investor distraction, and earnings announcement effects[J]. Journal of Banking & Finance, 47(oct.)：102-117.

Panyagometh K, Zhu K X, 2016. Dollar-cost averaging, asset allocation, and lump sum investing[J]. The Journal of Wealth Management, 18(4)：75-89.

Penman S H, 1987. The distribution of earnings news over time and seasonalities in aggregate stock returns[J]. Journal of Financial Economics, 18(2)：199-228.

Rubin H, Spaht C, 2018. Quality dollar cost averaging investing versus quality index investing [J]. Journal of Applied Economics and Business Research, 20(6)：137-152.

Sialm C, Kacperczyk M, Zheng L, 2008. Unobserved actions of mutual funds [J]. Review of Financial Studies, 21(6)：2379-2416.

Sias R, Starks L, 1995. The day-of-the-week anomaly：The role of institutional investors[J]. Financial Analysts Journal, 51(3)：58-67.

Tomlinson L E, 2012. Successful investing formulas[M]. Kingston：Barron's Publishing Company, 2012.

Trainor W J, 2005. Within-horizon exposure to loss for dollar cost averaging and lump sum investing[J]. Financial Services Review, 14(4)：319-330.

Ulku N, Rogers M, 2018. Who drives the Monday effect? [J]. Journal of Economic Behavior & Organization, 148(APR.)：46-65.

Urquhart A, Mcgroarty F, 2014. Calendar effects, market conditions and the Adaptive Market Hypothesis：Evidence from long-run U. S. data [J]. International Review of Financial Analysis, 35(oct.)：154-166.

Vora P P, Mcginnis J D, 2002. The asset allocation decision in retirement：lessons from dollar-cost averaging[J]. Financial Services Review, 9(1)：47-

63.

Wang K，Li Y，Erickson J，1997. A new look at the monday effect[J]. Journal of Finance，52：2171-2186。

Williams R E，Bacon P W，2004. Lump sum beats dollar-cost averaging[J]. Journal of Financial Planning，17(6)：92.

Yan X，Zhang Z，2009. Institutional investors and equity returns：Are short-term institutions better informed? [J]. Social Science Electronic Publishing，22(2)：893-924.

Table A1 The day of the month effect for mutual funds DCA: Coefficients differences from Regression

	No Control				With Control				Observations
	(β_2)	(β_3)	(β_4)	(β_5)	(β_2)	(β_3)	(β_4)	(β_5)	
Total	0.0011	-0.0002	-0.0010	-0.0009	0.0011	-0.0002	-0.0009	-0.0009	6,053
	(1.50)	(-0.24)	(-1.33)	(-1.23)	(1.50)	(-0.24)	(-1.33)	(-1.23)	
Growth	0.0009	-0.000007	-0.0012	-0.0008	0.0009	-0.00006	-0.0012	-0.0008	5,867
	(1.01)	(-0.08)	(-1.38)	(-0.93)	(1.00)	(-0.07)	(-1.37)	(-0.92)	
Balance	0.0009	-0.0004	-0.000007	-0.0004	0.0010	-0.0005	-0.00007	-0.0005	5,867
	(1.18)	(-0.52)	(-0.01)	(-0.56)	(1.23)	(-0.58)	(-0.08)	(-0.61)	
Value	0.0011**	0.0006	-0.0014***	-0.0010**	0.0011**	0.0006	-0.0014***	-0.0010**	4,193
	(2.97)	(1.46)	(-4.06)	(-2.59)	(2.97)	(1.38)	(-4.01)	(-2.58)	

Note: This table reports the coefficients differences which estimated from OLS Regressions. The columns marked "β_i" reports the difference between 0 and average of coefficients of other five betas for full sample. T-statistics are calculated with Newey and West (1987) adjusted standard error. ***, **, and * indicate statistical significance at the 1%, 5%, and 10% levels.

How Does the COVID-19 Pandemic Change the Disposition Effect in Fund Investors?[①]

Abstract This study investigates the influence of COVID-19 pandemic on the disposition effect of mutual fund investors in China. Utilizing account data from the Ant Group spanning January 2019 to April 2022, we find evidence of disposition-prone behavior across the entire sample and various investor groups. Moreover, our analysis suggests that the pandemic can attenuate the manifestation of the disposition effect. We propose three potential drivers for the observed decrease in behavioral bias: i) heightened risk aversion leading to a tendency to realize losses more than gains, driven by fear of a worsening situation; ii) forced sales due to cash shortages triggered by the pandemic; and iii) reduced self-image damage associated with selling at a loss when peer performance is relatively stronger. These findings shed light on the complex interplay between investor behavior and external shocks during pandemic periods.

Keywords Diposition effect; Mutual funds; Pandemic; Prospect theory; Credit Consumption

1 Introduction

While the existing literature has extensively examined the impact of the COVID-19 pandemic on capital markets and investor reactions, most of these

---

① Originally published in *Pacific-Basin Finance Journal*(vol. 5,2023) by Jin Xuejun, Li Hongze, Yu Bin and Zheng Yijing.

studies have focused on the overall market level. However, there remains a gap in understanding how individual investors' investment behavior may have changed during the pandemic, particularly concerning prominent behavioral biases like the disposition effect. This paper delves into an investigation of how the COVID-19 pandemic affects the disposition effect of fund investors in China. By utilizing a comprehensive dataset encompassing 33,040 equity mutual fund investors' holdings, corresponding characteristics, and consumption data spanning January 2019 to April 2022, this study identifies evidence of disposition-prone behavior among investors and reveals that the pandemic weakens this effect. Moreover, the research delves into prospect theory, mean-reversion theory, and psychological factors to shed light on the underlying reasons behind the weakened disposition effect during the pandemic. The study's findings demonstrate that the decrease in the disposition effect can be attributed to several factors, including increased risk aversion, forced sales due to cash shortage, and a reduction in the negative impact on self-image when selling at a loss.

The disposition effect, characterized by the tendency to sell winning investments and retain losing ones, has received extensive scrutiny from scholars. Empirical investigations have employed either laboratory experiments or investor account data to assess the prevalence of this effect across various market participants, including retail investors (Shefrin and Statman, 1985; Odean, 1998), fund managers (Frazzini, 2006; Singal & Xu, 2011; Andreu et al., 2020), and even sports wagers (Andrikogiannopoulou & Papakonstantinou, 2020).

Several studies have sought to identify the underlying drivers of the disposition effect. Firstly, prospect theory, introduced by Kahneman and Tversky (1979), posits that investors exhibit risk aversion towards gains and risk-seeking behavior towards losses, contributing to the disposition effect (Barberis & Xiong, 2009). However, prior studies lacked precise proxy variables to measure investors' degree of risk aversion, resulting in a lack of empirical evidence concerning the clear role of prospect theory in explaining the heterogeneity among risk-averse investors' dispositions. Notably, Dohmen et al. (2010) and Noussair et al. (2014) document that individuals with low risk aversion exhibit reduced credit card debt and engage in fewer high-risk financial activities. Therefore, the consumption information available in our dataset allows us to employ credit consumption as a mean to gauge investors' attitudes towards risk and explore how investors with different risk profiles behave during a pandemic.

Secondly, an irrational belief in mean reversion, wherein investors expect the price of a losing investment to revert to its original purchase price over time, can also induce the disposition effect (Weber & Camerer, 1998; Kaustia, 2010). On the one hand, during the pandemic, investors may encounter declining income or heightened unemployment risk, leading to cash shortages and time pressure, compelling them to sell portfolio securities. This urgent liquidity demand may force investors to sell losing assets, even if they anticipate price recovery to the purchase level. Empirical studies (Islam & Maitra, 2012) have also demonstrated that illness shocks prompt financially constrained individuals to sell assets for immediate consumption. On the other hand, some studies have revealed that time pressure induced by the pandemic could have a contrasting impact on the disposition effect (Dror et al., 1999; Cici, 2012). As these two streams of literature present opposing views, the COVID-19 pandemic provides an opportune empirical setting to examine how investors respond to liquidity needs and pressure.

Thirdly, psychological factors such as pride seeking and regret minimization may further contribute to the propensity to sell winning assets more frequently than losing assets (Chang et al., 2016; Pelster & Hofmann, 2018). This behavior is particularly evident in individuals who place significant emphasis on their reputation, as demonstrated by Pelster and Hofmann (2018). Moreover, damage to self-image stemming from poor investment decisions can be assessed from various perspectives. Many studies have examined the disposition effect at the individual stock level, and a broader perspective is provided by Brettschneider et al. (2021), who explore the disposition effect across the entire portfolio level. Furthermore, investors' trading behavior can also be influenced by the overall returns of their peers.

During the pandemic-induced downturn, investors may strive to preserve their self-image by realizing losses in specific stocks, convincing themselves that they can still outperform their peers, despite the unfavorable financial performance. As corroborated by Chang et al. (2016), investors might decrease the disposition effect when attempting to justify wrong investment decisions with excuses.

The data used in this study comprise monthly consumption and trading information during the COVID-19 pandemic, sourced from Ant Group. This dataset offers a unique opportunity to investigate the impact of the pandemic on the disposition-prone behavior of investors, considering their diverse characteristics. Firstly, we established the existence of a disposition effect among fund investors in China, a robust finding across different sub-periods and investor subgroups. However, our primary focus lies in understanding how the disposition effect evolves as the pandemic progresses. To examine this, we adopted the difference-in-differences (DID) method, analyzing variations in investor sub-groups before and after the COVID-19 outbreak. Our results reveal a notable weakening of the disposition effect when the pandemic commenced in January 2020. Specifically, the pandemic induces increased risk-averse behavior among investors in both the gain and loss domains, and the impact on disposition effects in the loss domain surpasses that in the gain domain. Furthermore, we find that the influence of heightened risk aversion on the disposition effect is considerably weaker in extreme risk-seeking and risk-averse sub-groups, proxied by high and low credit consumption, respectively. Moreover, the results demonstrate that investors with lower consumption levels exhibit reduced disposition-prone behavior compared to before the pandemic. This observation aligns with the fact that low consumption groups often coincide with those possessing less wealth, leading to liquidity problems and a heightened likelihood of selling loss funds due to time pressure during the pandemic.

How does a pandemic weaken the disposition effect? In our analysis, we explore three contributing factors: prospect theory, mean-reversion theory, and psychological influences. Prospect theory posits that investors demonstrate risk-averse behavior when prices are above the reference point, while they display risk-seeking tendencies when prices fall below the reference point. We empirically tested McQueen and Vorkink's (2004) preference-based equilibrium model and find that investors adjust their levels of risk aversion significantly when faced with unexpected losses due to pandemic shocks. Our empirical findings align with the application of prospect theory incorporating dynamic realization preferences, providing an explanation for the observed weaker disposition effect following the pandemic.

Moreover, we explored an alternative explanation in this study. Abnormal consumption is employed as a proxy to capture investors' liquidity needs during a pandemic. Interestingly, we observe that investors are more inclined to sell funds when their latest quarterly consumption falls below the yearly average. This suggests that investors might resort to selling assets to sustain their daily living, unable to wait for a rebound in fund prices to the purchasing level. These findings provide supportive evidence that liquidity needs during a pandemic contribute to weakening the disposition effect driven by mean-reversion beliefs.

Regarding self-regard, investors perceive profits as positive reinforcement and losses as negative signals for their self-image. We find that investors tend to sell a greater proportion of their losses when their relative performance ranking surpasses the median, even if it leads to a negative return compared to the original purchase price. This confirms that relative returns compared to their peers significantly influence the disposition effect, indicating that investors may not refrain from selling loss assets when justified by reasonable excuses. Hence, psychological factors appear to exert a decisive explanatory power on disposition-prone behavior.

Our findings contribute to literature in three-ways. Firstly, recent studies have extensively explored the effects of the COVID-19 pandemic on investor behavior. For instance, Aggarwal et al. (2021) found that both investor panic and the expectation of reduced economic growth due to lockdowns led to a decrease in expected capital market returns. Similar results have also been found in emerging markets (Al-Awadhi et al., 2020). Additionally, studies have explored investor performance in the mutual fund and bond markets. Pastor and Vorsatz (2020) found that actively managed funds in the U. S. performed worse than passive benchmark funds during the pandemic in 2020, and investors displayed a preference for funds with higher sustainability ratings. O'Hara and Zhou (2020) discovered that, before intervention by the Federal Reserve, investors favored company bonds with better liquidity. However, there has been a lack of examination of individual investor behavioral biases during the pandemic, with past studies mainly focusing on the disposition effect as a primary behavior bias and largely centered on investor characteristics and market changes. Our study bridges these two categories of literature by investigating the disposition effect of individual investors in the context of the pandemic, offering a novel perspective that, to the best of our knowledge, has not been explored previously.

Secondly, our work provides empirical evidence for three existing theories (prospect theory, mean-reversion theory, and psychological issues) on the disposition effect. Our study aligns with McQueen and Vorkink's (2004) preference-based equilibrium model, which theoretically demonstrates that investors' prior levels of risk aversion deepen when confronted with unexpected losses due to negative shocks. Through empirical evidence, we corroborate the dynamic form of prospect theory, strengthening the preference-based explanation of the disposition effect. Our findings also align with the works of Dror et al. (1999) and Cici (2012), indicating that time pressure could increase investors' propensity for the disposition effect. However, in contrast, our results indicate that time pressure resulting from liquidity needs could reduce belief-induced behavioral biases. Moreover, our findings on the influence of the relative benefits of peers in reducing the disposition effect are consistent with those of Chang et al. (2012), who find that fund investors mitigate damage to their self-image by attributing blame to fund managers. Both aspects offer valuable insights into psychology-driven behavioral biases.

Lastly, our sample encompasses investor trading data, personal characteristics, and consumption behavior, allowing for more precise measurements of investor risk levels and trading biases. For instance, previous studies have used questionnaire data to gauge the extent of risk aversion in investors (Ahn, 2021). Our study complements existing research by employing credit consumption data to assess investor risk attitudes, which exhibits a highly positive correlation to the extent of risk aversion (Dohmen et al., 2010; Noussair et al., 2014). Additionally, past research on the disposition effect has predominantly focused on individual stock investors or fund managers, with limited studies centered on individual mutual fund investors, particularly in emerging markets. Our sample from the rapidly growing and largest emerging mutual fund industry[①] addresses this gap in the literature, presenting unique insights into individual investor behavior during the COVID-19 pandemic.

The remainder of this paper is organised as follows. Section 2 describes the main dataset and variables. Section 3 reports the main empirical findings. In Section 4, we offer supplementary empirical evidence to explore potential explanations for the effects of the pandemic. Section 5 reports robustness check and Section 6 concludes the paper, summarizing our key findings and their implications.

2 Data and methodology

2.1 Data

Our samples are provided by the Ant Group which operates Alipay, the largest internet platform[②] in China, it combines three aspects of monthly data from January 2019 to April 2022, investor basic information, investor fund

---

① Based on the report released by Investment Company Institute (ICI), the total size of China's open-end mutual funds reached US $ 3.53 trillion, ranking first in Asia and fourth in the world by the end of 2021.

② Based on the survey report released by China Central Television (CCTV) Finance in 2021, nearly 60% of China's netizens purchase fund products through Alipay, and WeChat, Tiantian Fund and JD. com are also common purchasing channels.

investment and investor consumption data. ① Specifically, investor basic information includes gender and age. Investor fund investment data includes fund holding value, purchase frequency, purchase value, redemption frequency, redemption value, monthly return, month-end portfolio value. The above variables are for each fund held by each investor. The investor consumption data includes monthly consumption value, number of consumption times, credit card payment value, number of credit card payment times, internet credit payment, and number of Internet credit payment times.

We followed several steps in cleaning and preparing the data. Firstly, monetary funds and bond funds are excluded from the sample, our sample only includes equity mutual funds. ② Secondly, to ensure the accuracy of our analysis, we exclude fund investment data from January 2019 due to the lack of intra-month transaction details. This omission is necessary as we cannot ascertain whether the funds held in January 2019 were newly purchased within that month or before the sample period. Consequently, we would be unable to determine the purchase cost of the funds, making it impossible to calculate the disposition effect variable. Similarly, we remove data from other months where the purchase date of the funds held in the portfolio predates January 2019. Therefore, our sample comprises funds newly purchased by each investor from February 2019 onwards. Lastly, to mitigate the influence of outliers on our results, we apply winsorization to variables, including holding

---

① For the reason that the data provider protects the privacy of users of the data platform, this study was remotely conducted in the Ant Open Research Laboratory within an Ant Group Environment. The data was sampled and desensitized by the Ant Group Research Institute and stored on the Ant Open Research Laboratory. The laboratory is a sandbox environment where the authors can only remotely conduct empirical analysis and individual observations are not visible. The main regression variables include basic variables, investment variables, and consumption variables.

② In previous literature on the disposition effect in mutual funds, the focus has often been solely on equity funds. For instance, Fu and Wedge (2011) collected a dataset comprising a total of 1,406 funds, but their final research sample included only 913 active equity funds. Similarly, Singal and Xu (2011) excluded other fund types and index funds, focusing solely on active equity funds. To maintain consistency with past literature, we have chosen to exclude bond funds and money market funds from our sample.

value and consumption value, setting limits at the 1st and 99th return percentiles within each prior holding period.

Table 1 summarises the characteristics of mutual equity fund investors analysed in this study. Our sample includes 33,040 fund investors from February 2019 to April 2022.[①] The average number of funds held by individual investors is about six and the mean of holding value is 22181 yuan (or about 3169 USD). The *Purchase frequency* and *Purchase value* are 8.6 and 3371 yuan (or about 482 USD) per month, respectively; while the *Redemption frequency* and *Redemption value* are 0.61 and 1148 yuan (or about 164 USD) per month, respectively. This indicates that investors show a tendency to buy the same fund several times within a month and redeem it at the frequency of less than once a month; this helps determine with a degree of accuracy the return on each purchase in the absence of detailed transaction data within a month. The consumption of every investor is 4795 yuan (or about 685 USD) per month, and the sum of the *credit card payment* and *internet credit payment* is 2929 yuan (or about 430 USD), which accounts for 61.08% of total consumption. As for credit consumption, 69.68% is based on internet credit payments, which is consistent with the current situation of Chinese consumers.[②] Due to the extensive application of third-party electronic payment, most consumers choose online consumption and payment, and Ant Group, the data provider, is China's largest online credit consumption quota

---

① The initial sample comprises 812,007 variables, reflecting investor transactions such as redemptions and purchases, which narrows down to 517,260 variables directly related to investment behavior. To ensure precise DE calculations, data from January 2019 is excluded, and investors are required to have a minimum holding period of at least 6 months. Additionally, a 1% trimmed mean transformation is applied to each variable, while those lacking trading activity in a given month are assigned a value of 0. The final dataset consists of 718,725 fundamental variables. In the Difference-in-Differences (DID) empirical analysis, the sample size is approximately 660,000 observations due to missing observation of variables that measuring three mechanisms.

② Based on the report released by the China Internet Network Information Center (CNNIC), as of March 2020, the number of online shopping users in China reached 710 million, accounting for 78.6% of the total number of Internet users.

Table 1　Sample description

	Mean	S.D.	Median	Min	25th	75th	Max	Obs.
Panel A: Fund holdings & trading								
Holding_funds	5.69	12.98	3.00	1.00	1.00	6.00	996.00	718725
Holding_shares	14535.04	35141.56	1999.10	0.01	128.15	12381.03	1288662.00	718725
Holding_value	22181.29	53346.52	3158.31	0.01	207.79	19435.47	1603119.00	718725
Purchase frequency	8.6690	36.8572	1.00	0.00	2.00	5.00	4343.00	718725
Purchase value	3371.48	10987.30	20.00	0.00	0.00	150.00	565277.05	718725
Redemption frequency	0.6100	4.11	0.00	0.00	0.00	0.00	354.00	718725
Redemption value	1148.97	6318.67	0.00	0.00	0.00	0.00	371420.67	718725
Panel B: Investors consumptions								
Consumption	4795.02	6049.10	2648.83	32.00	1152.77	5905.86	70801.67	718725
Consumption(#)	50.09	98.54	40.00	1.00	21.00	68.00	54367.00	718725
Credit card payment	888.64	2547.85	0.00	0.00	0.00	289.91	22910.35	718725
Credit card payment(#)	6.59	23.45	0.00	0.00	0.00	3.00	6609.00	718725
Internet credit payment	2041.77	2976.74	983.30	0.00	191.30	2550.81	21509.85	718725
Internet credit payment(#)	30.61	41.08	21.00	0.00	5.00	45.00	13120.00	718725
Panel C: Basic characteristics								
Age	33.49	8.17	32.00	21.00	28.00	38.00	80.00	33040
Male	0.6126	0.4872	1.00	0.00	0.00	1.00	1.00	33040

This table reports mean, median, standard deviation, minimum, Q1, Q3 and maximum value statistics of the mutual fund investor' characteristics. Panel A presents the fund investors' holdings and trading characteristics: the average number, shares and value of funds held by each investor, the average of frequency and value of purchase and redemption for each investor of every month. Panel B presents fund investors' consumption characteristics: the average amount and frequency of total consumption, credit card payment and internet credit payment. Panel C presents fund investors' basic characteristics: gender and age. Parameters are calculated based on trade RMB Yuan.

provider. Finally, male investors are about 22.52% higher compared to their female counterparts in the sample. The investors are also relatively young, with an average age of 33.49 years, in line with the average[①] for the mutual market. [②]

2.2 Disposition effect measure

We followed Odean's (1998) approach to construct a measure for the disposition effect at a fund investor portfolio level and at a monthly frequency. As our study focuses on the disposition effect on fund investors and their corresponding characteristics, we first calculate realised gain (RG), realised loss (RL), paper gain (PG), and paper loss (PL) for each fund held by investors.

Specifically, we adopted a cost basis method to determine whether a fund's position represents a loss or a gain. Our data includes the monthly holding value, purchase value, and redemption value of each fund held by investors. We used transaction data to construct a holding sample containing an observation for each investor-fund-month. For example, we flagged the first purchase of the fund during the sample period if the transaction is sold within a few months, that is, the holding value became zero. We then compared the redemption and purchase values. If the redemption value is greater than the purchase value, then the transaction is recorded as a realised profit, otherwise it is a realised loss. For the months without trades before the sale, we compared the holding value with the purchase value. If the holding value is greater than the purchase value, it is regarded as a paper profit, and otherwise a paper loss.

In addition, the fund may also have been redeemed several times; hence, for each redemption, we summed the redemption and holding values, and then

---

① Based on the survey report on mutual fund investors (2020) released by the Asset Management Association of China in November 2021, among individual investors, 54.1% were male and 45.9% were female; Individual investors aged 30−45 accounted for 38.8%, the proportion of people under 30 and 45−60 years old was 27.7% and 25.8% respectively.

② A description of the investment data by year is presented in Appendix Table A1.

compare the sum with the purchase value. If the sum is greater than the purchase value, then it is considered a realised profit, otherwise it is a realised loss. If investors make additional purchases after the first one, we also sum the two purchase values, and compare it with the redemption value at the time of the full redemption or the sum of the redemption value and the holding value at the time of partial redemption, and then determine whether the transaction is profitable or not.

After obtaining the RG, RL, PG, and PL for each fund held by investors, we calculate the proportion of gains realised (PGR) funds and the proportion of loss realised (PLR) in the fund portfolio of each fund investor per month. The equations are as follows:

$$PGR_t^i = \frac{RG_t^i}{RG_t^i + PG_t^i} \tag{1}$$

$$PLR_t^i = \frac{RL_t^i}{RL_t^i + PL_t^i} \tag{2}$$

where RG_t^i is the number of realised gain funds of investor i in month t, PG_t^i is the number of paper gain funds of investor i in month t; RL_t^i is the number of realised loss funds of investor i in month t; and PL_t^i is number of paper loss funds of investor i in month t. The disposition effect (DE), is then calculated as the difference between PGR_t^i and PLR_t^i as follows:

$$DE_t^i = PGR_t^i - PLR_t^i$$

Specifically, the value of DE_t^i ranged from -1 to 1. A positive value of DE_t^i indicated that fund investors sold a greater proportion of winners than losers, in which case investor i exhibits the disposition effect.

As DE depends on portfolio size (Odean, 1998; Newton et al., 2016), we also use an alternative measure in the robustness check, namely the disposition ratio (DE_R), which we define as the ratio of PGR to PLR. A disposition ratio higher than 1 indicates the investor realises more winner funds than loser funds.

3 Empirical findings

3.1 Deposition effect of the full sample and the sub-groups

Table 2 summarises the disposition effects for the entire sample and different investor groups. Consistent with previous studies, mutual fund investors exhibit strong disposition-prone behaviour. For the whole sample, investors realize gains at a rate of 10.54% and losses at a rate of 6.05%. On average, mutual fund investors sell gains 74.22% (absolute value 4.49%) more often than losses when calculating the disposition effect measure at a frequency of one month. Compared to earlier studies, the extent of the disposition effect of fund investors in China is between stock investors (Odean, 1998; Leal et al., 2010) and fund managers (Frazzini, 2006; Cici, 2012).

Among the findings, we are mostly concerned with the effects of a pandemic on the disposition effect. Initially, in December 2019, the pandemic was limited to sporadic reports and did not garner significant attention from the financial markets and investors. It was only in mid-January 2020, when a surge in the number of cases was detected, that the pandemic began to have nationwide implications. Therefore, we defined the period up to and including December 2019 as the pre-pandemic period, and the period starting from January 2020 (inclusive) until the end of the sample in April 2022 as the pandemic period. Consistent with our prediction, the pandemic has a strong influence on fund investors' disposition behaviour. Investors are less subject to behavioural bias during the COVID-19 pandemic than in normal periods, even when they live in the same country and trade on the same market. Specifically, investors realize a higher proportion of winner funds in the gain domain, and realize a higher proportion of loser funds in the loss domain, indicating that investors are more risk-averse after the pandemic, regardless of profits or losses. Given this observation, we posit that a pandemic will increase the extent of risk aversion in both gain and loss, a finding that earlier studies have not investigated.

Table 2 Disposition effect for entire sample and clustering investors

	RG	PG	RL	PL	PGR	PLR	DE	t-Statistic
Disposition effect								
Entire sample	0.553	3.296	0.232	1.823	10.54%	6.05%	4.49%***	143.72
Disposition effect: Pandemic effect								
Pre-Pandemic	0.315	2.120	0.130	0.607	10.39%	5.75%	4.64%***	63.38
Pandemic	0.620	3.624	0.261	2.163	10.59%	6.14%	4.45%***	129.53
Difference(Pre-Pandemic-Pandemic)							0.11%**	2.52
Disposition effect: Age effect								
$21 \leqslant Age \leqslant 30$	0.574	3.068	0.275	1.891	12.20%	7.73%	4.47%***	82.51
$31 \leqslant Age \leqslant 40$	0.527	3.295	0.202	1.729	9.78%	5.21%	4.58%***	97.96
$41 \leqslant Age \leqslant 50$	0.544	3.657	0.198	1.783	8.70%	4.40%	4.30%***	58.66
$Age \geqslant 50$	0.633	4.038	0.231	2.165	9.06%	4.55%	4.50%***	36.29
Difference(Second Oldest-Youngest)							-0.17%*	-1.72
Disposition effect: Gender effect								
Male	0.581	3.287	0.254	1.789	11.14%	6.69%	4.45%***	106.73
Female	0.512	3.309	0.198	1.876	9.64%	5.08%	4.56%***	97.46
Difference(Male-Female)							-0.11%*	-1.78
Disposition effect: Consumption effect								
High-level	0.535	3.456	0.231	1.864	10.27%	6.00%	4.26%***	63.33
Mid-level	0.570	3.312	0.237	1.861	10.82%	6.21%	4.60%***	113.93
Low-level	0.531	3.065	0.221	1.649	10.22%	5.72%	4.50%***	60.33

continued

Difference(*High-Low*)							−0. 24%**	−2. 32
Disposition effect：Credit Consumption effect								
High-level	0. 541	3. 509	0. 222	1. 841	10. 05%	5. 67%	4. 38%***	68. 30
Mid-level	0. 579	3. 302	0. 243	1. 869	11. 05%	6. 38%	4. 67%***	112. 56
Low-level	0. 498	3. 036	0. 213	1. 656	9. 75%	5. 60%	4. 15%***	57. 61
Difference(*High-Low*)							0. 23%**	2. 42
Disposition effect：Trading effect								
Non-frequent trader	0. 365	2. 742	0. 174	1. 484	10. 92%	6. 38%	4. 54%***	117. 26
Frequent trader	2. 411	8. 680	0. 874	5. 450	19. 73%	10. 59%	9. 14%***	100. 81
Difference(*Non-frequent-Frequent*)							−4. 60%***	43. 52

This table reports the Realized Gain (*RG*), Realized Loss (*RL*), Paper Gain (*PG*), Paper Loss (*PL*), the proportion of gains realized (*PGR*) and the proportion of loss realized (*PLR*) funds in the fund portfolio of each fund investor per month. The overall disposition effect measure is calculated as the difference between *PGR* and *PLR*, all disposition effect variables have been multiplied by 100 in percentage form in this table. We considered the following effect on the disposition effect of investors: gender effect, pandemic effect, age effect, consumption effect, credit consumption effect, trading frequency effect. Specifically, investors' consumption and credit consumption are sorted into five quintiles for each month, the top quintile is classified as high sub-group, the middle three quintiles are classified as middle sub-group, and the bottom quintile is classified as low sub-group. The investors whose trading frequency ranked top 20% are classified as frequent traders and the rest are classified as non-frequent traders. T-statistics are reported to show the significance, and ***, **, and * denote significance at the 1%, 5%, and 10% level.

Disposition effects are observed across all groups, and some subgroups are more prone to this bias than others. Specifically, we observed a decreasing (although not strictly monotonic) pattern for PGR among investors of all ages. Younger investors (aged 21-30 years) are more likely to demonstrate loss aversion in the gain region; the second-oldest group (41-50 years) demonstrates the least loss aversion; and the oldest group (50 years above) demonstrates a slightly stronger loss aversion compared to second-eldest group. The pattern of oldest group could be attributed to the relatively lower education levels of older investors. As higher education was widely popularised at the end of the 20th century in China, proportionally fewer investors older than 50 years will have a bachelor's degree. This finding is consistent with Vaarmets et al. (2019)'s argument that education would help investors to overcome the disposition effect. From the PLR measure, the pattern is similar to PGR. The overall DE is almost the same for all ages, while the difference between the second-eldest and youngest groups are statistically significant.

Our results also indicate that female investors are disposed to selling more winners than losers compared to male investors. Interestingly, the difference in the disposition effect between men and women is the opposite in the gain and loss domains. In the gain domain, men are more inclined to sell profitable funds at a rate of 11.14%, while women only sell profitable funds at a rate of 9.64%; that is, men exhibit greater risk aversion than women. However, in the loss domain, men realize 1.61% higher proportion of loss funds than women: 6.69% (men) compared to 5.08% (women). These findings are consistent with Holger (2014), who find that women are more disposition prone, driven by their reluctance to realise capital losses.

By grouping investors according to their consumption, we observe a U-shaped pattern for the disposition effect. It is lower in the high-consumption group (top 20%) than the low-consumption group (bottom 20%), and reaches the maximum in the middle group (middle three quintiles). Noticeably, there is a similar U-shaped pattern across credit consumption subgroups, where the disposition effect in the high-credit consumption group (top 20%) is higher than in the low-credit consumption group (bottom 20%) at a 5% significance level, and reaches a maximum in the middle group (middle three quintiles).

Last, investors who trade frequently (top 20%) are more likely to be risk averse in the gain domain to sell winner assets and more risk seeking in the loss domain compared to other investors. This finding contradicts the evidence raised by Odean (1998), who finds that frequent traders are more immune to the disposition effect because they adjust reference points more quickly. However, frequent traders and overconfident investors might overlap. Trejos et al. (2019) find that overconfident investors are more prone to exhibit the disposition effect.

3.2 Multivariate tests for the deposition effect and fund investor characteristics

We further investigated investor characteristics and the disposition effect by adopting multivariate regressions. We regress DE on the various determinants discussed in the previous section while controlling for total fund holdings of investors and time effects. The baseline model is specified as follows:

$$DE_t^i = const + \beta_{CH} CHARC_t^i + \beta_1 Log(TNA)_t^i + \varepsilon_{i,t} \qquad (3)$$

where DE_t^i is the dependent variable disposition effect for investor i in month t, and $CHARC_t^i$ is various investor characteristics for investor i in month t. The characteristics include age, sex, consumption, credit consumption, and trading frequency. $Log(TNA)_t^i$ is the logarithm of total fund holdings for investor i in month t. Our regression includes fixed effects controls for time and fund styles.

Table 3 presents the results of the multivariate tests for the deposition effect and fund investor characteristics. Columns (1) — (5) show the regression results for the deposition effect measure on each characteristic, and columns (6) and (7) shows the results when combining non-collinear variables. First, in column (6), the results show that male investors sold

Table 3　Cross-sectional regression analysis for disposition effect: Measure DE

	(1)	(2)	(3)	(4)	(5)	(6)	(7)
Male	-0.1354**					-0.1679***	-0.1658***
	(-2.09)					(-2.59)	(-2.56)
Age_{31-40}		-0.0188				0.1854***	0.1827***
		(-0.26)				(2.60)	(2.57)
Age_{41-50}		-0.3627***				-0.2939***	-0.2691***
		(-3.71)				(-3.02)	(-2.77)
$Age_{above\ 50}$		-0.0795				-0.1820	-0.1006
		(-0.53)				(-1.21)	(-0.67)
High-Consumption			-0.4813***			-0.5233***	
			(-6.05)			(-6.59)	
Low-Consumption			0.1292			0.3659***	
			(1.48)			(4.17)	
High-Credit-Consumption				-0.5314***			-0.5612***
				(-6.73)			(-7.11)
Low-Credit-Consumption				-0.3932***			-0.2203**
				(-4.58)			(-2.57)
Ln(Frequency)					1.7079***	1.7141***	1.7096***
					(82.50)	(82.73)	(82.52)
Ln(Portholdings)	0.1887***	0.1938***	0.1962***	0.1967***	-0.4114***	-0.4050***	-0.4066***
	(16.90)	(17.22)	(17.52)	(17.59)	(-31.00)	(-30.15)	(-30.28)
Constant	3.3476***	3.2903***	3.2880***	3.3912***	2.2702***	2.3265***	2.4599***
	(32.04)	(33.43)	(33.35)	(35.12)	(23.95)	(20.79)	(22.23)
Time FE	Yes	Yes	Yes	Yes	Yes	Yes	Yes
Fund Style FE	Yes	Yes	Yes	Yes	Yes	Yes	Yes

	(1)	(2)	(3)	(4)	(5)	(6)	(7)
Adjusted R^2	0.004	0.0041	0.0044	0.0043	0.0349	0.0355	0.0350
Obs.				718725			

This table presents results about the effects of investor characteristics on disposition effect using panel data regressions controlling for time and fund style fixed effects, as shown in equation (3). Disposition effect, DE, is measured using disposition spread, which is calculated the proportion of gains realized (PGR) subtracting the proportion of loss realized (PLR) funds in the fund portfolio of every investor in each month. $Male$ is a dummy variable equals 1 for male, and 0 otherwise. Age_{31-40} is a dummy variable equals 1 for investors' age between 31 to 40, and 0 otherwise. Age_{41-50} is a dummy variable equals 1 for investors' age between 41 to 50, and 0 otherwise. $Age_{above\ 50}$ is a dummy variable that equals 1 for investors' age above 50, and 0 otherwise. $High\text{-}Consumption$ is a dummy variable equals 1 for investors' consumption ranked top quintile in month t, and 0 otherwise. $Low\text{-}Consumption$ is a dummy variable equals 1 for investors' consumption ranked bottom quintile in month t, and 0 otherwise. $High\text{-}Credit\text{-}Consumption$ is a dummy variable equals 1 for investors' credit consumption ranked top quintile in month t, and 0 otherwise. $Low\text{-}Credit\text{-}Consumption$ is a dummy variable equals 1 for investors' credit consumption ranked bottom quintile in month t, and 0 otherwise. Ln ($Frequency$) is the logarithm of number of trading times for investor in month t. Ln ($Port\ holdings$) is the logarithm of value of fund portfolio holdings for investor at the end month t. $*$, $**$, and $***$ denote significance at the 10%, 5%, and 1% levels, respectively.

disproportionately fewer winners than losers compared to female investors. Second, investors aged 31-40 years exhibit the most severe behaviour bias, while investors aged 41-50 years show mild behaviour bias. Third, high-consumption investors are significantly less disposition prone than the other investors, while low-consumption investors are significantly more disposition prone. Fourth, frequent trading generates more disposition bias behaviour. In column (7), we used credit consumption as a proxy for investors' risk aversion. These findings indicate investors with credit consumption ranked top 20%, as well as investors with credit consumption ranked in bottom 20%, exhibit relative weaker disposition effect than their peers. Assuming credit consumption is an appropriate measure for risk attitudes based on prior studies (Dohmen et al., 2010; Noussair et al., 2014), we infer that extreme risk seeking and risk averse investors are less susceptible to the disposition effect. Therefore, our multivariate regression results confirm the results obtained from the difference test method.

Earlier studies (e. g. Holger 2014) have shown that the reluctance to realise a loss might primarily contribute to the overall disposition effect of investors. The components of DE, PGR, and PLR, allow us to explore the different behaviours in the gain and loss domains. Therefore, we replace DE with PGR and PLR in the regressions. The corresponding results are presented in Appendix Tables A2 and A3.

3.3 Effects of the pandemic on the deposition effect

In addition to the relation between fund investor characteristics and the disposition effect, we further investigate the effects of the COVID-19 pandemic on disposition-prone behaviour. We considered the same multivariate regression specification as above, except that we added a pandemic dummy variable and its interaction term with investor characteristics to perform a DID test. The regression specification is as follows:

$$DE_t^i = const + \beta_{CH}CHARC_t^i + \beta_{pan}Pandemic_t + \beta_{CH*pan}CHARC_t^i$$
$$* Pandemic_t + \beta_1 Log(TNA)_t^i + \varepsilon_{i,t} \tag{4}$$

where DE_t^i is the dependent variable disposition effect for investor i in month t, and $CHARC_t^i$ is various investor characteristics for investor i in month t. These characteristics include age, sex, consumption, internet credit consumption, and trading frequency. We generated the dummy variable $Pandemic_t$ that takes the value of 1 if the sample periods are after January 2020, and 0 otherwise. $Log(TNA)_t^i$ is equal to the logarithm of total fund holdings for investor i in month t.

The results are reported in Table 4. The coefficients of the pandemic dummy variable across all models are significantly negative, indicating that the pandemic could weaken disposition-prone behaviour. Column (2) shows that investors older than 50 years will show an increased disposition effect during the pandemic. Column (3) shows that investors with low consumption (bottom 20%) will reduce their behaviour bias during the pandemic, as low consumption is a proxy for people with less wealth or disposable income. Hence, our finding indicates that poorer people will reduce the disposal effect. This may be because they are more likely to face a cash shortage, so they would need to sell assets to compensate. Another possible explanation is that poorer people are the least concerned about their self-image, so they ignore the psychology of minimising regret during the pandemic. Column (4) shows that the interaction term between the pandemic dummy and the credit consumption variables is significantly positive, indicating that the group with the lowest and highest credit consumption is least affected by the pandemic than other investors. As credit consumption is a variable that measures risk aversion, it indicates that the biased behaviour of the most risk-seeking and risk-averse investors is least corrected by the pandemic. Column (5) shows that the interaction term between the pandemic dummy and trading frequency is significantly positive, indicating that investors with the most frequent transactions are least affected by the pandemic. As frequent transactions may be a proxy variable for professional background or overconfidence, we infer that such investors reduce their disposal effect to a lesser extent than other investors during the pandemic. Last, we combine non-collinear variable together in columns 6 and 7. The results remain robust to separate regression models.

Table 4　Pandemic effects on disposition effect: Measure DE

	(1)	(2)	(3)	(4)	(5)	(6)	(7)
$Pandemic$	-0.3565^{***}	-0.3286^{***}	-0.2031^{**}	-0.3947^{***}	-0.1758	-0.3870^{*}	-0.5759^{***}
	(-2.90)	(-2.59)	(-2.07)	(-3.97)	(-1.06)	(-1.74)	(-2.59)
$Male$	-0.2357^{*}					-0.4461^{***}	-0.4651^{***}
	(-1.71)					(-3.24)	(-3.37)
$Male \times Pandemic$	0.1679					0.3845^{**}	0.4094^{***}
	(1.07)					(2.46)	(2.62)
Age_{31-40}		-0.0351				0.2047	0.1817
		(-0.23)				(1.33)	(1.18)
$Age_{31-40} \times Pandemic$		0.0393				0.0094	0.0317
		(0.23)				(0.05)	(0.18)
Age_{41-50}		-0.3244				-0.2081	-0.1840
		(-1.62)				(-1.04)	(-0.92)
$Age_{41-50} \times Pandemic$		-0.0235				-0.0839	-0.0862
		(-0.10)				(-0.37)	(-0.38)
$Age_{above\ 50}$		-0.7378^{**}				-0.8965^{***}	-0.7697^{***}
		(-2.48)				(-3.00)	(-2.58)
$Age_{above\ 50} \times Pandemic$		0.9247^{***}				0.9864^{***}	0.9287^{***}
		(2.68)				(2.86)	(2.69)
$High\text{-}Consumption$			-0.5002^{***}			-0.6438^{***}	
			(-2.99)			(-3.85)	
$HC \times Pandemic$			0.0361			0.1642	
			(0.19)			(0.86)	

continued

	(1)	(2)	(3)	(4)	(5)	(6)	(7)
Low-Consumption			0.3887**			0.6430***	
			(2.13)			(3.52)	
LC×Pandemic			-0.3682*			-0.3624*	
			(-1.77)			(-1.74)	
High-Credit-Consumption				-0.7370***			-0.7751***
				(-4.48)			(-4.70)
HCC×Pandemic				0.3120*			0.3027
				(1.67)			(1.61)
Low-Credit-Consumption				-0.6935***			-0.4221**
				(-3.80)			(-2.32)
LCC×Pandemic				0.3430*			0.2545
				(1.66)			(1.23)
ln(*Frequency*)					1.7191***	1.7393***	1.7293***
					(42.55)	(42.79)	(42.62)
ln(*Frequency*)× *Pandemic*					0.1488***	0.1329***	0.1396***
					(3.43)	(3.04)	(3.20)
Ln(*Port holdings*)	0.1720***	0.1761***	0.1787***	0.1794***	-0.4675***	-0.4619***	-0.4633***
	(15.39)	(15.63)	(15.94)	(16.03)	(-35.65)	(-34.79)	(-34.92)
Constant	3.7401***	3.6774***	3.5875***	3.8339***	2.4259***	2.6207***	2.9006***
	(27.27)	(27.06)	(29.97)	(32.42)	(15.08)	(12.64)	(14.11)

	(1)	(2)	(3)	(4)	(5)	(6)	(7)
Time *FE*	Yes	Yes	Yes	Yes	Yes	Yes	Yes
Fund Style *FE*	Yes	Yes	Yes	Yes	Yes	Yes	Yes
Adjusted R^2	0.0032	0.0034	0.0038	0.0037	0.0336	0.0343	0.0338
Obs.				718725			

This table presents results about the effects of pandemic on disposition effect using panel data regressions controlling for time and fund style fixed effects, as shown in equation (4). Disposition effect, *DE*, is measured using disposition spread, which is calculated the proportion of gains realized (*PGR*) subtracting the proportion of loss realized (*PLR*) funds in the fund portfolio of every investor in each month. *Pandemic* is a dummy variable that equals 1 for sample periods from Jan 2020 to Apr 2022, and 0 for sample periods from Jan 2019 to Dec 2020. The definitions of explanatory variables and control variables are the same as those in Table 4. *, **, and *** denote significance at the 10%, 5%, and 1% levels, respectively.

The components of *DE*，*PGR* and *PLR* allow us to display the magnitudes of the propensities to realise gains and losses affected by a pandemic. We replaced *DE* with *PGR* and *PLR* in the regressions，the results of which are summarized in Appendix Tables A4 and A5. There are several findings worth noting. First，the coefficients of *Pandemic* across all models in Appendix Tables A4 and A5 are significantly positive，indicating that pandemic increases risk aversion in investors in both situations，thus selling even more in the gain and the loss domains. As the latter's impact exceeds that of the former，thus the results present an overall weaker disposition effect (Table 4). Second，based on the interaction term between *Age above* 50 and *Pandemic* in column (2) of Appendix Tables A4 and A5，the propensity to realise a loss decreased significantly for investors older than 50 years during the pandemic，while the propensity to realise a gain did not vary significantly. Combining the reduction in the disposition effect for the oldest investors during the pandemic presented in Table 4，which shows that the overall stronger disposition effect of the oldest group is largely driven by a reduction in the propensity to realise a loss. Third，in column (3) of Appendix Tables A4 and A5，the pandemic makes investors whose consumption ranked in the bottom 20% decrease significantly to realise a loss and a gain，and the extent of the former exceeds the latter，which together have an observable overall negative impact on the disposition effect brought on by the pandemic which is described in column (3) of Table 4.

In short，it is important to investigate the pandemic's effect on the propensity to realise funds in the gain and loss domains separately. This allows us to clarify the extent of the change induced by the pandemic on tendencies to realise a gain and a loss conditioned on the various investors' characteristics，and how it contributes to heterogeneity in the disposition effect across different investor sub-groups.

4　Potential explanations

In this section，we attempt to shed light on the potential reasons for the effects of the pandemic on the deposition effect.

4.1 Explanation I: Prospect theory

In the prospect theory framework, the disposition effect has always been ascribed to investor preferences rather than beliefs (Odean 1998; Barberis & Xiong 2009). Specifically, investors are assumed to have a dual risk preference feature on both sides of the reference point introduced by Kahneman and Tversky (1979). However, the reference point is more difficult to capture when holding periods are longer or adjustments are updated quickly (Henderson, 2009; Ben-David & Hirshleifer, 2012; Meng & Weng, 2018). Therefore, recent studies consider a dynamic realisation preference that incorporates past returns. McQueen and Vorkink (2004) developed a preference-based equilibrium model, which documents that, when faced with unexpected past losses, investors' prior levels of risk aversion adjust, and investors become more risk averse. The negative shock of a pandemic on the capital market provides us with an empirical opportunity to examine this theoretical model. We consider the following empirical specification:

$$DE/PGR/PLR_t^i = const + \beta_{negret} NegRet_t^i + \beta_{pan} Pandemic_t$$
$$+ \beta_{int\ er} NegRet_t^i * Pandemic_t + \gamma' Z_t^i + \varepsilon_{i,t} \qquad (5)$$

where $NegRet_t^i$ equals 1 if the individuals' fund return is negative, otherwise 0. $Pandemic_t$ equals 1 if the sample is in the months of pandemic peak, otherwise 0. Specifically, in our sample, the pandemic peak months are Jan 2020 to Mar 2020 (original strain), Sep 2020 (Alpha strain), Jun 2021 to July 2021 (Delta strain) and Jan 2022 to April 2022 (Omicron strain). The peak of different strains of COVID-19 has brought a series of unpredictable external shocks, which provide a rare opportunity for model testing. ① $Z_{i,t}$ represents the characteristics of investor i in month t, including gender, age, total consumption, and trading frequency within a month and the value of portfolio holdings at the end of month.

Table 5 presents the results of the regression analysis concerning dynamic realization preferences and the impact of a pandemic on the disposition effect. In Specification 1 of Table 5, we use the disposition effect (DE) as the dependent variable. Our findings indicate that negative returns lead to a reduction in the disposition effect. Furthermore, during pandemic peak months, investors also exhibit a decreased disposition effect. It is noteworthy that the coefficient of the interaction term between $NegRet$ and $Pandemic$ is also significantly negative, suggesting that the pandemic period further decreases the disposition effect for investors experiencing negative investment returns. These results suggest that changes in investor behavior are not solely attributed to negative returns; the pandemic itself significantly influences the disposition effect.

Moreover, we proceeded to examine the different behavioral changes of investors when experiencing gains or losses. In Specification 2 of Table 5, we used the proportion of gains realized (PGR) as the dependent variable. Our findings reveal that investors tend to sell a greater proportion of gains when their overall performance is poor. In other words, negative returns increase the disposition effect for profit-taking. However, we observe that the coefficient of $Pandemic$ is significantly negative, indicating that the pandemic significantly reduces the disposition effect in the profit domain. Moreover, the

---

① The modifications made to the definition of "pandemic" do not result in inconsistencies between the preceding and subsequent sections. We used a consistent definition with the one stated in the first section for section four. and when we refined the "pandemic" variable to capture the outbreak period more accurately, the results remained unchanged. Thus, these adjustments can be regarded as robustness tests for the original "pandemic" variable. This allows us to precisely investigate the changes in investor behavior during these pandemic outbreaks, thereby differentiating the effects of the pandemic from other market changes. Due to space constraints, we only present the empirical findings related to the "pandemic" peak variable.

interaction term's coefficient is also significantly negative, implying that, under the impact of a series of pandemic shocks, the disposition effect in the profit domain is further diminished when investors' performance is poor.

Moving to Specification 3 of Table 5, we used the proportion of losses realized (PLR) as the dependent variable. Our findings indicate that both negative returns and pandemic peak months increase the likelihood of investors selling their losing assets, thereby reducing the disposition effect. A plausible explanation for this phenomenon lies in the negative influence brought on by the pandemic, which leads to unexpected bad news and lowers investors' reference point. Consequently, the kink separating the loss and gain regions moves leftward. Assets that were initially considered small losses might now be perceived as gains, prompting investors to sell them based on their original purchase prices. However, the negative coefficient of the interaction term suggests that the likelihood of selling losing assets decreases when both the pandemic peak and negative investment returns occur simultaneously.

In summary, the impact of the pandemic on selling gains exceeds that on losses, resulting in an overall weaker disposition effect for investors during challenging times induced by a series of pandemic shocks. Our empirical findings thus corroborate that prospect theory, combined with dynamic reference point adjustment, can effectively explain the disposition effect.

Table 5 Dynamic realization preference and the pandemic impacts on disposition effect

	(1)	(2)	(3)
	DE	PGR	PLR
Pandemic	−0.5351***	−0.1059*	0.4292***
	(−7.75)	(−1.70)	(10.06)
NegRet_value	−0.6154***	1.2111***	1.8264***
	(−9.82)	(21.42)	(47.19)
NegRet_value * Pandemic	−0.4316***	−0.9212***	−0.4897***
	(−3.57)	(−8.44)	(−6.55)
Male	−0.0757	0.3212***	0.3970***
	(−1.55)	(7.31)	(13.19)
Age	−0.0199***	−0.0699***	−0.0500***
	(−6.82)	(−26.59)	(−27.80)

continued

	(1)	(2)	(3)
	DE	*PGR*	*PLR*
Consumption	0.0177***	−0.0157***	−0.0334***
	(4.47)	(−4.39)	(−13.63)
Ln(Frequency)	2.3837***	4.3990***	2.0153***
	(122.21)	(249.85)	(167.19)
Ln(Port holdings)	−0.2725***	−0.4038***	−0.1313***
	(−29.71)	(−48.77)	(−23.16)
Constant	2.2183***	3.8278***	1.6095***
	(17.79)	(34.01)	(20.89)
Time *FE*	Yes	Yes	Yes
Fund Style *FE*	Yes	Yes	Yes
Adjusted R^2	0.026	0.098	0.008
Obs.		659626	

This table presents the dynamic realization preference explanation for pandemic impacts on disposition effect using panel data regressions controlling for time and fund style fixed effects, as shown in equation (5). Disposition effect, *DE*, is measured using disposition spread, which is calculated as the proportion of gains realized (*PGR*) subtracting the proportion of losses realized (*PLR*) funds in the fund portfolio of every investor in each month. *NegRet* equals 1 if the individuals' fund return is negative, otherwise 0. *Pandemic* equals 1 if the sample is in the months of the pandemic peak, otherwise 0. Specifically, in our sample, the pandemic peak months are Jan 2020 to Mar 2020 (original strain), Sep 2020 (Alpha strain), Jun 2021 to July 2021 (Delta strain) and Jan 2022 to April 2022 (Omicron strain). The control variables include male, age, consumption, trading frequency and portfolio holdings value. *, **, and *** denote significance at the 10%, 5%, and 1% levels.

4.2　Explanation II: Mean-reversion theory

Besides preference theory, prior studies also use beliefs to explain behavioural bias (Weber & Camerer 1998; Kaustia 2010). One of the prerequisites for the return of the mean-reversion is that investors have enough time to wait for the loss assets to return to their break-even point. However, during the COVID-19 pandemic, various countries have implemented social distancing measures, including lockdowns, to curb the spread of the virus. Dingel and Neiman

(2020) found that such social distancing measures forced many individuals to work from home. In the United States, 37% of jobs can be performed entirely from home, representing 46% of all wages. However, low-income economies have an even lower proportion of jobs that can be done from home. The pandemic has increased the probability of unemployment and decreased workers' income, while isolation measures have also altered people's consumption habits. One of the time pressures brought on by a pandemic could be a greater demand for cash for daily consumption. The combination of a pandemic, unemployment, and unstable income may make investors more susceptible to cash shortages to maintain their daily consumption. Zhang et al. (2020) find that external shocks have heterogeneous effects on household consumption. Additionally, Islam and Maitra (2012) demonstrate that illness shocks may compel financially constrained individuals to sell assets for consumption purposes. Therefore, we posit that investors might have to rely on selling assets to sustain their daily lives, which could weaken the disposition effect driven by mean-reversion beliefs.

To examine how investors react when they are under liquidity pressure, we use abnormal consumption to capture the liquidity needs of investors and perform the following regression model:

$$
\begin{aligned}
DE/PGR/PLR_t^i = const + \beta_{CR} Consumption\_Reduction_t^i + \beta_{pan} Pandemic_t \\
+ \beta_{CR \times pan} Consumption\_Reduction_t^i \times Pandemic_t + \gamma' Z_t^i \\
+ \varepsilon_{i,t}
\end{aligned}
\tag{6}
$$

where $Consumption\_Reduction_t^i$ is the consumption reduction and equals absolute value of difference between the average monthly consumption in the latest quarter and that of the entire year. $Consumption\_Reduction_t^i \times Pandemic_t$ is the interaction term. We expect the coefficient to be positive, as more sales will be triggered by daily consumption induced by liquidity demand. $Z_{i,t}$ represents the characteristics of investor i in month t, including sex, age, total consumption, and trading frequency within a month and the value of their portfolio holdings at the end of the month.

Table 6 presents a summary of the regression results regarding consumption reduction and the pandemic's impact on the disposition effect. In

Specification 1 of Table 6, the interaction terms exhibit negative significance, indicating that when daily consumption declines, investors' disposition effect becomes weaker. Specifically, for every 1% decrease in consumption, the disposition effect reduces by 6.7%. [①] Moving to Specification 2 of Table 6, the coefficients of the interaction terms are found to be statistically insignificant. This suggests that the weakening of investors' disposition effect during periods of consumption reduction is not attributable to a change in their habitual treatment of profitable assets. However, in Specification 3 of Table 6, the coefficient of the interaction term is positively and significantly related, indicating that investors tend to sell more assets in the loss domain when faced with cash shortages that affect their daily consumption. This phenomenon contributes to an overall weakening of the disposition effect among investors. The findings presented in Table 6 reinforce the conclusion that despite investors' strong belief in the eventual return of an investment to its average value, time constraints force them to act. As a result, they end up selling assets with losses earlier than initially planned. This suggests that the disposition effect can be partially explained by the mean-reversion theory.

Table 6　Consumption reduction and the pandemic impacts on disposition effect

	(1) DE	(2) PGR	(3) PLR
Pandemic	−0.5994***	−0.3786***	0.2208***
	(−9.61)	(−6.72)	(5.72)
Consumption-Reduction	−0.0106	−0.0080	0.0026
	(−1.62)	(−1.36)	(0.63)
Pandemic * Consumption-Reduction	−0.0326***	−0.0043	0.0283***
	(−2.47)	(−0.36)	(3.46)
Male	−0.0775	0.3215***	0.3990***
	(−1.59)	(7.31)	(13.23)
Age	−0.0172***	−0.0735***	−0.0563***
	(−5.93)	(−28.03)	(−31.30)

---

　　① 6.7% is calculated as 0.0326 (coefficient) times 2.069 (standard deviation of the independent variable).

continued

	(1)	(2)	(3)
	DE	*PGR*	*PLR*
Consumption	0.0191***	−0.0171	−0.0361***
	(4.81)	(−4.77)	(−14.72)
ln(*Frequency*)	2.3891***	4.3869***	1.9978***
	(122.54)	(249.21)	(165.51)
ln(*Port holdings*)	−0.2790***	−0.3941***	−0.1151***
	(−30.45)	(−47.65)	(−20.30)
Constant	1.9758***	4.2305***	2.2547***
	(16.07)	(38.11)	(29.62)
Adjusted R^2	0.059	0.098	0.047
Obs.	659626		

This table presents the liquidity needs induced by consumption reduction and pandemic impacts on disposition effect using panel data regressions controlling for time and fund style fixed effects, as shown in equation (6). Disposition effect, *DE*, is measured using disposition spread, which is calculated the proportion of gains realized (*PGR*) subtracting the proportion of losses realized (*PLR*) funds in the fund portfolio of every investor in each month. *Consumption_Reduction$_i$* equals absolute value of difference between the average monthly consumption in the latest quarter and that of the entire year. otherwise. *Pandemic* equals 1 if the sample is in the months of pandemic peak, otherwise 0. Specifically, in our sample, the pandemic peak months are Jan 2020 to Mar 2020 (original strain), Sep 2020 (Alpha strain), Jun 2021 to July 2021 (Delta strain) and Jan 2022 to April 2022 (Omicron strain). The control variables include gender, age, consumption, trading frequency and portfolio holdings value. *, **, and *** denote significance at the 10%, 5%, and 1% levels, respectively.

Moreover, given the possibility of changes in consumer behavior during lockdowns, we have decomposed consumption into durable consumption and non-durable consumption, and conducted separate tests to assess the effects of each type of consumption reduction on investor disposition effects. The results are presented in Appendix Tables A6. They show that the reduction of durable consumption does not significantly increase the probability of investors selling their assets, while a significant increase in the probability of asset selling is observed when non-durable consumption declines. This finding is reasonable as non-durable consumption is closely associated with daily living expenses. In order to meet basic living needs, they may choose to forgo mean-reversion-driven belief and sell assets, regardless of whether they are profitable or not. By distinguishing between the different consumption categories, the results in Table Appendix Tables A6 further support the findings presented in Table 6.

4.3 Explanation III: Psychology issues

Chang et al. (2016) show that in the United States, fund investors forgive their own investment mistakes and behave less disposition-prone when fund managers are thought to be scapegoats. This fact is consistent with the argument that the disposition effect is at least partially driven by psychological issues, such as regret minimisation and self-image protection. In other words, as long as an investment is not judged as a failure, there will not be irrational to hold on to loss assets. Brettschneider et al. (2021) find that investors not only calculate profit/loss in a narrow framing (single asset) but also in wide framing (portfolio level). A natural question is whether the performance of investors relative to their peers can also be used as a criterion to judge whether an investment has failed. The overall performance of the capital market during a pandemic is poorer, and the possibility of investors achieving positive investment return is reduced. Therefore, if the investment returns of peers are taken into account to measure the success of investors' own investment, the sale of loss assets will not be regarded as a regret when investors' rankings are relatively higher. Our sample collection platform displays each investor's performance ranking among all the users in the account interface; hence, investors can easily determine their relative performance ranking. We used the following model to check the relation between the relative performance of peers and the disposition effect during the pandemic:

$$DE/PGR/PLR_t^i = const + \beta_{PR} PeerRanking_t^i + \beta_{pan} Pandemic_t$$

$$+ \beta_{PR \times pan} PeerRanking_t^i \times Pandemic_t + \gamma' Z_t^i + \varepsilon_{i,t} \qquad (7)$$

where $PeerRanking_t^i$, the peer relative performance dummy, equals 1 if the return of investors is negative but above the median, and 0 otherwise. $PeerRanking_t^i \times Pandemic_t$ is the interaction term. Based on our prediction, to have higher returns than other investors during the pandemic is also an excuse to eliminate regret. We expect investors to sell more loss assets despite their negative performance. $Z_{i,t}$ represents the characteristics of investor i in month t, including sex, age, total consumption, and trading frequency within a month and the value of their portfolio holdings at the end of a month.

Table 7 summarises the regression results of the relative performance of peers and the pandemic's impact on the disposition effect. In specification 3, we use PLR as the independent variable. We find that the coefficient of the interaction term of the pandemic dummy and peer ranking is significantly positive, hence to have relatively better returns compared to peers reduces investors' tendency to hold onto funds trading below their purchase price, which is consistent with our argument that the disposition effect is psychologically driven. However, in Specification 1, the coefficients of the interaction terms are found to be statistically insignificant, indicating that these changes do not significantly reduce investors' overall disposition effect. Similarly, the coefficients of the interaction terms in Specification 2 are also found to be statistically insignificant, suggesting that peer ranking does not significantly influence investors' investment habits in the profit domain.

Overall, while psychological factors measured by peer ranking can significantly mitigate behavioral biases in the loss domain, they are insufficient to substantially reduce investors' disposition effect on the whole.

Table 7　Relative performance of peers and the pandemic impacts on disposition effect

	(1) DE	(2) PGR	(3) PLR
Pandemic	−0.5801*** (−9.21)	−0.3773*** (−6.63)	0.2028*** (5.20)
PeerRanking	0.0394 (0.15)	−0.2291 (−0.97)	−0.2685* (−1.66)
Pandemic×PeerRanking	0.0412 (0.10)	0.5304 (0.1695)	0.4893* (1.85)
Male	−0.0728 (−1.48)	0.3299*** (7.43)	0.4026*** (13.24)
Age	−0.0181*** (−6.17)	−0.0741*** (−27.96)	−0.0560*** (−30.87)

continued

	(1)	(2)	(3)
	DE	*PGR*	*PLR*
Consumption	0.0189***	−0.0171***	−0.0360***
	(4.74)	(−4.73)	(−14.567)
ln(*Frequency*)	2.4003***	4.3921***	1.9918***
	(122.14)	(247.29)	(163.85)
ln(*Port holdings*)	−0.2829***	−0.3978***	−0.1149***
	(−30.52)	(247.29)	(−20.05)
Constant	2.0297***	4.2799***	2.2502***
	(16.31)	(38.07)	(29.24)
Adjusted R^2	0.026	0.098	0.047
Obs.		647623	

This table reports the psychology explanation for pandemic impacts on disposition effect using panel data regressions controlling for time and fund style fixed effects, as shown in equation (7). Disposition effect, *DE*, is measured using disposition spread, which is calculated as the proportion of gains realized (*PGR*) subtracting the proportion of losses realized (*PLR*) funds in the fund portfolio of every investor in each month. *PeerRanking*$_t^j$, the peer relative performance dummy, equals 1 if the return of investors is negative but above the median, 0 otherwise. *Pandemic* equals 1 if the sample is in the months of pandemic peak, otherwise 0. Specifically, in our sample, the pandemic peak months are Jan 2020 to Mar 2020 (original strain), Sep 2020 (Alpha strain), Jun 2021 to July 2021 (Delta strain) and Jan 2022 to April 2022 (Omicron strain). The control variables include male, age, consumption, trading frequency and portfolio holdings value. *, **, and *** denote significance at the 10%, 5%, and 1% levels, respectively.

4.4 Test of the combined explanatory powers of three hypotheses

The following section presents the results of combining the variables to assess the influence of the pandemic on the disposition effect, drawing from prospect theory, mean-reversion, and psychological factors. The findings are reported in Table 8. In Specification 1 of Table 8, the disposition effect (*DE*) serves as the dependent variable. The results indicate a significant negative coefficient for the two interaction terms-prospect theory and mean-reversion, while the interaction term measuring psychological factors does not exhibit significance. These results suggest that prospect theory and mean-reversion theories have the potential to explain the weakened disposition effect. However, when controlling for the aforementioned explanations, the explanatory power of psychological factors becomes subsumed under the former two.

In Specifications 2 and 3 of Table 8, it is observed that the decrease in PGR primarily arises from prospect theory, whereas the increase in PLR mainly stems from the mean reversion theory. After accounting for these two theories, psychological factors do not significantly affect investors' behavioral biases. Consequently, we can deduce that prospect theory and mean-reversion theory both contribute to the changes in investor behavior during the pandemic period.

Table 8   The explanatory power of three hypotheses on impacts of pandemic on Disposition Effect

	(1) DE	(2) PGR	(3) PLR
Pandemic	-0.5131***	-0.0928	0.4203***
	(-7.38)	(-1.48)	(9.79)
NegRet_value	-0.6086***	1.2433***	1.8519***
	(-9.61)	(21.72)	(47.35)
NegRet_value×Pandemic	-0.4281***	-0.9271***	-0.4990***
	(-3.49)	(-8.38)	(-6.60)
Consumption-Reduction	-0.0094	-0.0102*	-0.0007
	(-1.43)	(-1.70)	(-0.18)
Consumption-Reduction×Pandemic	-0.0300**	-0.0090	0.0290***
	(-2.25)	(-0.08)	(3.54)
PeerRanking	-0.2878	-0.2082	0.0795
	(-1.143)	(-0.92)	(0.61)
PeerRanking×Pandemic	0.7057*	0.5730	-0.1327
	(1.68)	(1.51)	(-0.51)
Male	-0.0592	0.3371***	0.3963***
	(-1.20)	(7.59)	(13.06)
Age	-0.0201***	-0.0700***	-0.0499***
	(-6.85)	(-26.37)	(-27.50)
Consumption	0.0179***	-0.0157***	-0.0336***
	(4.48)	(-4.35)	(-13.62)

continued

	(1)	(2)	(3)
	DE	PGR	PLR
ln(*Frequency*)	2.3971***	4.4025***	2.0053***
	(121.88)	(247.75)	(165.15)
ln(*Port holdings*)	−0.2776***	−0.4083***	−0.1307***
	(−29.91)	(−48.68)	(−22.80)
Constant	2.2458***	3.8529***	1.6071***
	(17.80)	(33.80)	(20.63)
Adjusted R^2	0.027	0.099	0.051
Obs.		645762	

This table reports the explanatory power of three hypotheses on impacts of the pandemic on Disposition Effect using panel data regressions controlling for time and fund style fixed effects. Disposition effect, *DE*, is measured using disposition spread, which is calculated the proportion of gains realized (*PGR*) subtracting the proportion of losses realized (*PLR*) funds in the fund portfolio of every investor in each month. *NegRet* equals 1 if the individuals' fund return is negative, otherwise 0. *Consumption_Reduction*$_i$ equals absolute value of difference between the average monthly consumption in the latest quarter and that of the entire year. otherwise. *Peer Ranking*$_i$, the peer-relative performance dummy, equals 1 if the return of investors is negative but above the median, 0 otherwise. *Pandemic* equals 1 if the sample is in the months of pandemic peak, otherwise 0. Specifically, in our sample, the pandemic peak months are Jan 2020 to Mar 2020 (original strain), Sep 2020 (Alpha strain), Jun 2021 to July 2021 (Delta strain) and Jan 2022 to April 2022 (Omicron strain). The control variables include male, age, consumption, trading frequency and portfolio holdings value. *, **, and *** denote significance at the 10%, 5%, and 1% levels, respectively.

5 Robustness checks

In this section, we perform several tests to check for robustness. Detailed results are provided in the Internet Appendix Table A7 to Table A8.

Firstly, we used ratio variables to measure disposition effect. We use disposition ratio (*DE_R*), defined as the ratio of *PGR* to *PLR*. Appendix Table A7 shows that our results remain the same when ratio variables are used. The only difference is that male investors exhibit higher disposition-prone behavior than female investors, and the possible reason might be that male investors' portfolio values are higher than those of females'. Therefore, when the overall disposition effect is measured by the difference between PGR and PLR, men's disposition effect is milder, while when measured by the proportion of PGR and PLR, women's disposition effect is milder. Hence our findings are significant across different measure applied.

Secondly, we examined whether our findings remain the same using an alternative regression method. Appendix Table A8 reports regression results when we use Probit regression estimation method, and our results remain robust.

6 Conclusions

The disposition effect is a well-researched area in behavioural finance. Our study contributes to the literature by investigating the effects of the COVID-19 pandemic on the disposition effect to elaborate on the mechanism through which a pandemic influences the disposition effect based on prospect theory, mean-reversion theory, and psychological issues.

Using the unique monthly dataset of a Chinese online fund investment platform, we constructed a measure of the disposition effect for mutual fund investors. We find evidence that disposition-prone behaviour exists for the entire sample and different investor groups. Our results show that female investors, investors between the ages of 31 and 40 years, and frequent traders display more serious behavioural biases. By classifying investors by consumption data, we show that the disposition effect has a U-shaped feature, that is, investors' consumption in the middle three quintiles is more susceptible to the disposition effect. We also used investors' credit consumption data to measure the extent of investors' risk aversion and find that the most risk-seeking investors sell disproportionately more winning assets than losing assets compared to most risk-averse investors. Our primary findings are unaffected when using different disposition measures as dependent variables or applying different regression methods.

We then considered potential explanations for the impact of the pandemic on the disposition effect. First, we show that during the pandemic, investors become more risk-averse, thus selling more assets in the loss domain when experiencing negative fund performance induced by a series of pandemic shocks. From the perspective of prospect theory, this could be because the pandemic greatly reduced the expectations of the capital market, making investors dynamically adjust their reference points. Therefore, by incorporating expected changes brought about by the pandemic into the analysis of the disposition effect, we provide empirical support for prospect theory. We also find that during the pandemic, when an investor's consumption in the latest quarter is lower than their average consumption for a year, they sell more loss-making funds after the pandemic. Thus, only when investors find it difficult to maintain their basic consumption level will they sell assets at a loss; in other situations, they wait until the asset price rebounds to the breakeven point before selling, consistent with mean-reversion theory. Finally, we find that during the pandemic period, when investors' relative performance among their peers is ranked above the median, investors are more likely to sell assets at a loss despite their negative return. This is in line with minimising regrets in psychological issues, that is, an investor will discard disposition-prone behaviour when they can excuse their failed investment.

References

Aggarwal S, Nawn S, Dugar A, 2020. What caused global stock market meltdown during the covid pandemic—Lockdown stringency or investor panic? [J]. Finance Research Letters, 38(4): 1-6.

Ahn Y, 2021. The anatomy of the disposition effect: Which factors are most important? [J]. Finance Research Letters, 44: 1-6.

Al-Awadhi A M, Alsaifi K, Al-Awadhi A, et al, 2020. Death and contagious infectious diseases: Impact of the covid-19 virus on stock market returns[J]. Journal of Behavioral and Experimental Finance, 27: 1-8.

Andreu L, Ortiz C, Sarto J L, 2020. Disposition effect in fund managers. fund and stock-specific factors and the upshot for investors[J]. Journal of Economic Behavior & Organization, 176: 253-268.

Andrikogiannopoulou A, Papakonstantinou F, 2020. History-dependent risk preferences: Evidence from individual choices and implications for the disposition effect[J]. The Review of Financial Studies, 33: 3674-3718.

Barberis N, Xiong W, 2009. What drives the disposition effect? An analysis of a long-standing preference-based explanation[J]. Journal of Finance, 64 (2): 751-784.

Ben-David I, Hirshleifer D, 2012. Are investors really reluctant to realize their losses? Trading responses to past returns and the disposition effect[J]. The Review of Financial Studies, 25(8): 2485-2532.

Brettschneider J, Burro G, Henderson V, 2021. Wide framing disposition effect: An empirical study[J]. Journal of Economic Behavior & Organization, 185(1-3): 330-347.

Chang T, Solomon D H, Westerfield M M, 2016. Looking for someone to blame: Delegation, cognitive dissonance, and the disposition effect [J]. Journal of Finance, 71(1): 267-302.

Cici G, 2012. The prevalence of the disposition effect in mutual funds' trades [J]. Journal of Financial and Quantitative Analysis, 47(4): 795-820.

Dhar R, Zhu N, 2006. Up close and personal: Investor sophistication and the disposition effect[J]. Management Science, 52(5): 726-740.

Dierick N, Heyman D, Inghelbrecht K, et al, 2019. Financial attention and the disposition effect[J]. Journal of Economic Behavior & Organization, 163: 190-217.

Dingel J I, Neiman B, 2020. How many jobs can be done at home? [J]. Journal of Public Economics, 189:104235.

Dohmen T, Falk A, Huffman D, et al, 2010. Are risk aversion and impatience related to cognitive ability? [J]. American Economic Review, 100 (3): 1238-1260.

Dror I E, Busemeyer J R, Basola B, 1999. Decision making under time pressure: An independent test of sequential sampling models[J]. Memory and

Cognition, 27: 713-725.

Feng L, Seasholes M S, 2005. Do investor sophistication and trading experience eliminate behavioral biases in financial markets? [J]. Review of Finance, 9(3): 305-351.

Fischbacher U, Hoffmann G, Schudy S, 2017. The causal effect of stop-loss and take-gain orders on the disposition effect[J]. The Review of Financial Studies, 30(6): 2110-2129.

Frazzini A, 2006. The disposition effect and underreaction to news [J]. Journal of Finance, 61(4): 2017-2046.

Fu R, Wedge L, 2011. Managerial ownership and the disposition effect[J]. Journal of Banking & Finance, 2011, 35(9): 2407-2417.

Henderson V, 2009. Prospect theory, liquidation, and the disposition effect [J]. Management Science, 58(2): 445-460.

Holger A, 2014. The disposition effect and loss aversion: Do gender differences matter? [J]. Economics Letters, 123(1): 33-36.

Islam A, Maitra P, 2012. Health shocks and consumption smoothing in rural households: Does microcredit have a role to play? [J]. Journal of Development Economics, 97(2): 232-243.

Kahneman D, Tversky A, 1979. Prospect theory: An analysis of decision under risk[J]. Econometrica, 47(2): 263-291.

Kaustia M, 2010. Prospect theory and the disposition effect[J]. Journal of Financial and Quantitative Analysis, 45(3): 791-812.

Leal C, Armada M J, Duque J, 2010. Are all individual investors equally prone to the disposition effect all the time? New evidence from a small market [J]. Frontiers in Finance and Economics, 7: 38-68.

McQueen G, Vorkink K, 2004. Whence GARCH? A preference based explanation for conditional volatility[J]. The Review of Financial Studies, 17(4): 915-950.

Meng J, Weng X, 2018. Can prospect theory explain the disposition effect? A new perspective on reference points[J]. Management Science, 64(7): 3331-3351.

Newton D, Marco G, Cesar C, et al, 2013. The disposition effect and investor experience[J]. Journal of Banking and Finance, 37(5): 1669-1675.

Noussair C N, Trautmann S T, Kuilen G V D, 2014. Higher order risk attitudes, demographics, financial decisions[J]. The Review of Financial Studies, 81(1): 325-55.

Odean T, 1998. Are investors reluctant to realize their losses? [J]. Journal of Finance, 53(5): 1775-1798.

Pastor L, Vorsatz B, 2020. Mutual fund performance and flows during the COVID-19 crisis[J]. Review of Asset Pricing Studies, 10:791-833.

Pelster M, Hofmann A, 2018. About the fear of reputational loss: Social trading and the disposition effect[J]. Journal of Banking & Finance, 94(9): 75-88.

O'Ha M, Zhou X A, 2021. Anatomy of a liquidity crisis: Corporate bonds in the COVID-19 crisis[J]. Journal of Financial Economics, 142:46-68.

Rau H A, 2014. The disposition effect and loss aversion: Do gender differences matter? [J]. Economics Letters, 123(1): 33-36.

Roland G, Alex P, 2018. Does a scopic regime erode the disposition effect? Evidence from a social trading platform[J]. Journal of Economic Behavior & Organization, 154: 175-190.

Shefrin H, Statman M, 1985. The disposition to sell winners too early and ride losers too long: Theory and evidence[J]. Journal of Finance, 40(3): 777-790.

Singal V, Xu Z, 2011. Selling winners, holding losers: Effect on fund flows and survival of disposition-prone mutual funds[J]. Journal of Banking & Finance, 35(10): 2704-2718.

Trejos C, Deemen A V, Rodriguez Y E, et al, 2019. Overconfidence and disposition effect in the stock market: a micro world based setting[J]. Journal of Behavioral and Experimental Finance, 21: 61-69.

Vaarmets T, Liivamgi K, Talpsepp T, 2018. How does learning and education help to overcome the disposition effect? [J]. Review of Finance, 23 (4): 801-830.

Weber M, Camerer C F, 1998. The disposition effect in securities trading: An experimental analysis[J]. Journal of Economic Behavior & Organization, 33

（2）：167-184.

Zhang Y，Jia Q，Chen C，2020. Risk attitude，financial literacy and household consumption：Evidence from stock market crash in China［J］. Economic Modelling，94：995-1006.